Hardcover Print Edition [1.0] -1440 h. (2018 c.e.)

Copyright © 1440 H./2018 C.E.
Taalib al-Ilm Educational Resources

http://taalib.com
Learn Islaam, Live Islaam.^{SM}

All rights reserved, this publication may be not reproduced, stored in a retrieval system, or transmitted in any form or by any means, electronic, mechanical, photocopying, recording, scanning, or otherwise, except with the prior written permission of the Publisher.

Requests to the Publisher for permission should be addressed to the Permissions Department, Taalib al-Ilm Educational Resources by e-mail: **service@taalib.com**.

Taalib al-Ilm Education Resources products are made available through distributors worldwide. To view a list of current distributors in your region, or information about our distributor/referral program please visit our website. Discounts on bulk quantities of our products are available to community groups, religious institutions, and other not-for-profit entities, inshAllaah. For details and discount information, contact the special sales department by e-mail: **service@taalib.com**.

The publisher requests that any corrections regarding translations or knowledge based issues, be sent to us at: **service@taalib.com.** Readers should note that internet web sites offered as citations and/or sources for further information may have changed or no longer be available between the time this was written and when it is read.

We publish a variety of full text and free preview edition electronic ebook formats. Some content that appears in print may not be available in electronic book versions.

ISBN EAN-13:   978-1-938117-80-0   [Hardcover Print Edition]

From the Publisher

Golden Words Upon Golden Words…For Every Muslim.

"Imaam al-Barbahaaree, may Allaah have mercy upon him said:

May Allaah have mercy upon you! Examine carefully the speech of everyone you hear from in your time particularly. So do not act in haste and do not enter into anything from it until you ask and see: Did any of the Companions of the Prophet, may Allaah's praise and salutations be upon him, speak about it, or did any of the scholars? So if you find a narration from them about it, cling to it, do not go beyond it for anything and do not give precedence to anything over it and thus fall into the Fire.

Explanation by Sheikh Saaleh al-Fauzaan, may Allaah preserve him:

'Do not be hasty in accepting as correct what you may hear from the people, especially in these later times. As now there are many who speak about so many various matters, issuing rulings and ascribing to themselves both knowledge and the right to speak. This is especially the case after the emergence and spread of new modern day media technologies. Such that everyone now can speak and bring forth that which is, in truth, worthless; by this, meaning words of no true value - speaking about whatever they wish in the name of knowledge and in the name of the religion of Islaam. It has even reached the point that you find the people of misguidance and the members of the various groups of misguidance and deviance from the religion speaking as well. Such individuals have now become those who speak in the name of the religion of Islaam through means such as the various satellite television channels. Therefore be very cautious!

It is upon you, oh Muslim, and upon you, oh student of knowledge, individually, to verify matters and not rush to embrace everything and anything you may hear. It is upon you to verify the truth of what you hear, asking, 'Who else also makes this same statement or claim?', 'Where did this thought or concept originate or come from?', 'Who is its reference or source authority?' Asking what are the evidences which support it from within the Book and the Sunnah? And inquiring where has the individual who is putting this forth studied and taken his knowledge from? From who has he studied the knowledge of Islaam?

Each of these matters requires verification through inquiry and investigation, especially in the present age and time. It is not every speaker who should rightly be considered a source of knowledge, even if he is well spoken and eloquent and can manipulate words captivating his listeners. Do not be taken in and accept him until you are aware of the degree and scope of what he possesses of knowledge and understanding. Perhaps someone's words may be few, but possess true understanding, and perhaps another will have a great deal of speech yet he is actually ignorant to such a degree that he doesn't actually possess anything of true understanding. Rather he only has the ability to enchant with his speech so that the people are deceived. Yet he puts forth the perception that he is a scholar, that he is someone of true understanding and comprehension, that he is a capable thinker, and so forth. Through such means and ways he is able to deceive and beguile the people, taking them away from the way of truth.

Therefore, what is to be given true consideration is not the amount of the speech put forth or that one can extensively discuss a subject. Rather, the criterion that is to be given consideration is what that speech contains within it of sound authentic knowledge, what it contains of the established and transmitted principles of Islaam. Perhaps a short or brief statement which is connected to or has a foundation in the established principles can be of greater benefit than a great deal of speech which simply rambles on, and through hearing you don't actually receive very much benefit from.

This is the reality which is present in our time; one sees a tremendous amount of speech which only possesses within it a small amount of actual knowledge. We see the presence of many speakers, yet few people of true understanding and comprehension.' "

[The eminent major scholar Sheikh Saaleh al-Fauzaan, may Allaah preserve him- 'A Valued Gift for the Reader Of Comments Upon the Book Sharh as-Sunnah', page 102-103]

The Seeking Of Proof & Evidence Is From The Weapons Of The Believer

❧ *Is not He better than your so-called gods, He Who originates creation and shall then repeat it, and Who provides for you from heaven and earth? Is there any god with Allaah? Say: 'Bring forth your proofs, if you are truthful.'* ❧ -(Surah an-Naml: 64)

Explanation: ❧ *Say: "Bring forth your proofs..*❧ This is a command for the Prophet, may Allaah's praise and salutation be upon him, to rebuke them immediately after they had put forward their own rebuke. Meaning: '*Say to them: bring your proof, whether it is an intellectual proof or a proof from transmitted knowledge, that would stand as evidence that there is another with Allaah, the Most Glorified and the Most Exalted*'. Additionally, it has been said that it means: '*Bring your proof that there is anyone other than Allaah, the Most High, who is capable of doing that which has been mentioned from His actions, the Most Glorified and the Most Exalted.*' ❧...*if you are truthful.*❧ meaning, in this claim. From this it is derived that a claim is not accepted unless clearly indicated by evidences."

[Tafseer al-'Aloosee: vol. 15, page 14]

Sheikh Rabee'a Ibn Hadee Umair al-Madkhalee, may Allaah preserve him said,

'It is possible for someone to simply say, "*So and so said such and such.*" However we should say, "*Produce your proof.*" So why did you not ask them for their proof by saying to them: "*Where was this said?*" Ask them questions such as this, as from your weapons are such questions as: "*Where is this from? From which book? From which cassette?...*"'

[The Overwhelming Falsehoods of 'Abdul-Lateef Bashmeel' page 14]

The guiding scholar Imaam Sheikh 'Abdul-'Azeez Ibn Abdullah Ibn Baaz, may Allaah have mercy upon him, said,

'It is not proper that any intelligent individual be misled or deceived by the great numbers from among people from the various countries who engage in such a practice. As the truth is not determined by the numerous people who engage in a matter, rather the truth is known by the Sharee'ah evidences. Just as Allaah the Most High says in Surah al-Baqarah, ❧ *And they say, "None shall enter Paradise unless he be a Jew or a Christian." These are only their own desires. Say "Produce your proof if you are truthful."*❧-(Surah al-Baqarah: 111) And Allaah the Most High says ❧ *And if you obey most of those on the earth, they will mislead you far away from Allaah's path. They follow nothing but conjectures, and they do nothing but lie.*❧-(Surah al-'Ana'an: 116)'

[Collection of Rulings and Various Statements of Sheikh Ibn Baaz -Vol. 1 page 85]

Sheikh Muhammad Ibn 'Abdul-Wahaab, may Allaah have mercy upon him, said,

'Additionally, verify that knowledge held regarding your beliefs, distinguishing between what is correct and false within it, coming to understand the various areas of knowledge of faith in Allaah alone and the required disbelief in all other objects of worship. You will certainly see various different matters which are called towards and enjoined; so if you see that a matter is in fact one coming from Allaah and His Messenger, then this is what is intended and is desired that you possess. Otherwise, Allaah has certainly given you that which enables you to distinguish between truth and falsehood, if Allaah so wills.

Moreover, this writing of mine- do not conceal it from the author of that work; rather present it to him. He may repent and affirm its truthfulness and then return to the guidance of Allaah, or perhaps if he says that he has a proof for his claims, even if that is only a single statement, or if he claims that within my statements there is something unsupported, then request his evidence for that assertion. After this if there is something which continues to cause uncertainty or is a problem for you, then refer it back to me, so that then you are aware of both his statement and mine in that issue. We ask Allaah to guide us, you, and all the Muslims to that which He loves and is pleased with.'

[*Personal Letters of Sheikh Muhammad Ibn 'Abdul-Wahaab- Conclusion to Letter 20*]

Sheikh 'Abdullah Ibn 'Abdur-Rahman Abu Bateen, may Allaah have mercy upon him, said,

'And for an individual, if it becomes clear to him that something is the truth, he should not turn away from it and or be discouraged simply due to the few people who agree with him and the many who oppose him in that, especially in these latter days of this present age.

If the ignorant one says: "*If this was the truth so and so and so and so would have been aware of it!*" However this is the very claim of the disbelievers, in their statement found in the Qur'aan ﴾ **If it had truly been good, they would not have preceded us to it!**﴿-(Surah al-Ahqaaf: 11) and in their statement ﴾ **Is it these whom Allaah has favored from amongst us?**﴿-(Surah al-Ana'am: 53). Yet certainly, as Alee Ibn Abee Taalib, may Allaah be pleased with him, stated "*Know the truth and then you will know it' people.*" But for the one who generally stands upon confusion and uncertainty, then every doubt swirls around him. And if the majority of the people were in fact upon the truth today, then Islaam would not be considered strange, yet, by Allaah, it is today seen as the most strange of affairs!"

[*Durar As-Sanneeyyah -vol. 10, page 400*]

30 Days of Guidance: Learning Fundamental Principles of Islaam

A Short Journey Within the Work al-Ibaanah al-Sughrah With Sheikh 'Abdul-'Azeez Ibn 'Abdullah ar-Raajhee

[Self Study/Teachers Edition] -Hardcover

Compiled and Translated by:
Abu Sukhailah Khalil Ibn-Abelahyi

Student name:_____

Date started:_____

Date completed:_____

Online login:_____

Online pass:_____

A SHORT EXPLANATION OF THE TITLE OF THIS COURSE

Sheikh Muhammad Ibn Saaleh al-'Utheimeen, may Allaah have mercy upon him, said,

> "Allaah the Most High's Sharee'ah, is likely to be attacked, from the time that it emerged from Makkah until this very day. Indeed the Sharee'ah of Allaah is something which is regularly, or often, attacked.
> Just as Allaah, the Most High says, ❖ **Thus have We made for every Prophet an enemy among the disbelievers, polytheists, and criminals.** ❖ -(Surah Al-Furqaan: 31).

> Certainly every prophet had enemies, and everyone who followed one of the prophets who was sent, would likewise have enemies. This is something which is necessary, as it is the sunnah of Allaah, the Most Glorified and the Most Exalted. The true path is not a smooth path with no obstacles, surrounded by only flowers and blossoms. Rather the true path of Allaah is hard and difficult.

> It is necessary that Allaah, the Most Glorified and the Most Exalted, according to a wisdom that is with Him, places those who would oppose the truth in order that the truth be known, and in order that it become something which manifests as something clear and dominant over falsehood.

> Additionally, this is in order that Allaah would make clear who are those individuals who strive in His path, and those who proceed patiently upon His guidance."

(From his well-known series -Open Door Gatherings 3/66. may Allaah have abundant mercy upon him)

Table of Contents

Compiler's Introduction — 018

Day 01: The Importance Of Asking To Be Guided In What You Say & Do — 040
    Text from Introduction of al-Ibaanah al-Sughrah: — 040
    Explanation by Sheikh 'Abdul-'Azeez Ibn 'Abdullah ar-Raajhee — 041
    Points Of Benefit — 042
    LEVEL 1: Test Your Understanding: — 043
    LEVEL 2: Interactive Questions & Exercises — 043

Day 02: The Clear Guidance Of The Final Messenger Is For All Humanity — 044
    Narration from al-Ibaanah al-Sughrah: — 044
    Explanation by Sheikh 'Abdul-'Azeez Ibn 'Abdullah ar-Raajhee — 045
    Points Of Benefit — 047
    LEVEL 1: Test Your Understanding: — 048
    LEVEL 2: Interactive Questions & Exercises — 048

Day 03: There Is A Single Straight Path Surrounded By Other False Paths — 050
    Narration from al-Ibaanah al-Sughrah: — 050
    Explanation by Sheikh 'Abdul-'Azeez Ibn 'Abdullah ar-Raajhee — 051
    Points Of Benefit — 052
    LEVEL 1: Test Your Understanding: — 053
    LEVEL 2: Interactive Questions & Exercises — 053

Day 04: Every Ummah Divided But Those Upon The Truth Remain — 054
    Narration from al-Ibaanah al-Sughrah: — 054
    Explanation by Sheikh 'Abdul-'Azeez Ibn 'Abdullah ar-Raajhee — 055
    Points Of Benefit — 057
    LEVEL 1: Test Your Understanding: — 058
    LEVEL 2: Interactive Questions & Exercises — 058

Day 05: Allaah Is With Those Who Remained Upon Revealed Guidance — 060
    Narration from al-Ibaanah al-Sughrah: — 060
    Explanation by Sheikh 'Abdul-'Azeez Ibn 'Abdullah ar-Raajhee — 061
    Points Of Benefit — 062
    LEVEL 1: Test Your Understanding: — 063
    LEVEL 2: Interactive Questions & Exercises — 063

Day 06: Allaah Has Ordered Us To Stand United Upon The Truth & Not Divide

Narration from al-Ibaanah al-Sughrah: 064
Explanation by Sheikh 'Abdul-'Azeez Ibn 'Abdullah ar-Raajhee 065
Points Of Benefit 066
LEVEL 1: Test Your Understanding: 067
LEVEL 2: Interactive Questions & Exercises 067

Day 07: Every Name That Opposes The Guidance Of The Sunnah Is Rejected 068

Narration from al-Ibaanah al-Sughrah: 068
Explanation by Sheikh 'Abdul-'Azeez Ibn 'Abdullah ar-Raajhee 069
Points Of Benefit 071
LEVEL 1: Test Your Understanding: 072
LEVEL 2: Interactive Questions & Exercises 072

Day 08: The Strangeness Of Islaam Is Something Expected 074

Narration from al-Ibaanah al-Sughrah: 074
Explanation by Sheikh 'Abdul-'Azeez Ibn 'Abdullah ar-Raajhee 075
Points Of Benefit 078
LEVEL 1: Test Your Understanding: 079
LEVEL 2: Interactive Questions & Exercises 079

Day 09: That One Individual Whose Religion You Should Stand Upon 080

Narration from al-Ibaanah al-Sughrah: 080
Explanation by Sheikh 'Abdul-'Azeez Ibn 'Abdullah ar-Raajhee 081
Points Of Benefit 084
LEVEL 1: Test Your Understanding: 085
LEVEL 2: Interactive Questions & Exercises 085

Day 10: The Sunnah Is Revealed Knowledge From Allaah 086

Narration from al-Ibaanah al-Sughrah: 086
Explanation by Sheikh 'Abdul-'Azeez Ibn 'Abdullah ar-Raajhee 087
Points Of Benefit 090
LEVEL 1: Test Your Understanding: 091
LEVEL 2: Interactive Questions & Exercises 091

Day 11: Hold Firmly To The Sunnah As The Rope Of Allaah — 092
    Narration from al-Ibaanah al-Sughrah: — 092
    Explanation by Sheikh 'Abdul-'Azeez Ibn 'Abdullah ar-Raajhee — 093
    Points Of Benefit — 095
    LEVEL 1: Test Your Understanding: — 096
    LEVEL 2: Interactive Questions & Exercises — 096

Day 12: Success Is To The Degree You Adhere To The Sunnah — 098
    Narration from al-Ibaanah al-Sughrah: — 098
    Explanation by Sheikh 'Abdul-'Azeez Ibn 'Abdullah ar-Raajhee — 099
    Points Of Benefit — 101
    LEVEL 1: Test Your Understanding: — 102
    LEVEL 2: Interactive Questions & Exercises — 102

Day 13: The Incredible Reward For Firmly Holding To The Sunnah — 104
    Narration from al-Ibaanah al-Sughrah: — 104
    Explanation by Sheikh 'Abdul-'Azeez Ibn 'Abdullah ar-Raajhee — 105
    Points Of Benefit — 108
    LEVEL 1: Test Your Understanding: — 109
    LEVEL 2: Interactive Questions & Exercises — 109

Day 14: Follow The Prophet's Sunnah & That Of His Guided Successors — 110
    Narration from al-Ibaanah al-Sughrah: — 110
    Explanation by Sheikh 'Abdul-'Azeez Ibn 'Abdullah ar-Raajhee — 111
    Points Of Benefit — 115
    LEVEL 1: Test Your Understanding: — 116
    LEVEL 2: Interactive Questions & Exercises — 116

Day 15: Do Not Speak Against The Best Of Generations — 118
    Narration from al-Ibaanah al-Sughrah: — 118
    Explanation by Sheikh 'Abdul-'Azeez Ibn 'Abdullah ar-Raajhee — 119
    Points Of Benefit — 124
    LEVEL 1: Test Your Understanding: — 125
    LEVEL 2: Interactive Questions & Exercises — 125

Day 16: Know That Knowledge Is Received And Can Be Lost — 126
   Narration from al-Ibaanah al-Sughrah: — 126
   Explanation by Sheikh 'Abdul-'Azeez Ibn 'Abdullah ar-Raajhee — 127
   Points Of Benefit — 130
   LEVEL 1: Test Your Understanding: — 131
   LEVEL 2: Interactive Questions & Exercises — 131

Day 17: The Reality Of The People Of Misguidance & Their Deceptions — 132
   Narration from al-Ibaanah al-Sughrah: — 132
   Explanation by Sheikh 'Abdul-'Azeez Ibn 'Abdullah ar-Raajhee — 134
   Points Of Benefit — 137
   LEVEL 1: Test Your Understanding: — 138
   LEVEL 2: Interactive Questions & Exercises — 138

Day 18: The Believers Are Distinct Upon Revealed Guidance — 140
   Narration from al-Ibaanah al-Sughrah: — 140
   Explanation by Sheikh 'Abdul-'Azeez Ibn 'Abdullah ar-Raajhee — 141
   Points Of Benefit — 145
   LEVEL 1: Test Your Understanding: — 146
   LEVEL 2: Interactive Questions & Exercises — 146

Day 19: Advice of The Companions 'Uthman, 'Alee & Ibn 'Abbaas — 148
   Narration from al-Ibaanah al-Sughrah: — 148
   Explanation by Sheikh 'Abdul-'Azeez Ibn 'Abdullah ar-Raajhee — 149
   Narration from al-Ibaanah al-Sughrah: — 150
   Explanation by Sheikh 'Abdul-'Azeez Ibn 'Abdullah ar-Raajhee — 151
   Narration from al-Ibaanah al-Sughrah: — 152
   Explanation by Sheikh 'Abdul-'Azeez Ibn 'Abdullah ar-Raajhee — 153
   Points Of Benefit — 154
   LEVEL 1: Test Your Understanding: — 155
   LEVEL 2: Interactive Questions & Exercises — 155

Day 20: Those Astray Turned Away From The Guidance Brought To Them — 156
   Narration from al-Ibaanah al-Sughrah: — 156
   Explanation by Sheikh 'Abdul-'Azeez Ibn 'Abdullah ar-Raajhee — 157
   Points Of Benefit — 158
   LEVEL 1: Test Your Understanding: — 159
   LEVEL 2: Interactive Questions & Exercises — 159

Day 21: The People Of Misguidance Want You To Turn From Revealed Guidance   160
    Narration from al-Ibaanah al-Sughrah: 160
    Explanation by Sheikh 'Abdul-'Azeez Ibn 'Abdullah ar-Raajhee   161
    Narration from al-Ibaanah al-Sughrah: 162
    Explanation by Sheikh 'Abdul-'Azeez Ibn 'Abdullah ar-Raajhee   163
    Points Of Benefit   165
    LEVEL 1: Test Your Understanding: 167
    LEVEL 2: Interactive Questions & Exercises   167

Day 22: Those Who Debate Frequently Change Their Religion   168
    Narration from al-Ibaanah al-Sughrah: 168
    Explanation by Sheikh 'Abdul-'Azeez Ibn 'Abdullah ar-Raajhee   169
    Points Of Benefit   170
    LEVEL 1: Test Your Understanding: 171
    LEVEL 2: Interactive Questions & Exercises   171

Day 23: The Blessing of Learning the Sunnah When Young   172
    Narration from al-Ibaanah al-Sughrah: 172
    Explanation by Sheikh 'Abdul-'Azeez Ibn 'Abdullah ar-Raajhee   173
    Points Of Benefit   179
    LEVEL 1: Test Your Understanding: 181
    LEVEL 2: Interactive Questions & Exercises   181

Day 24: The Importance Of Both Loving & Hating For Allaah's Sake   182
    Narration from al-Ibaanah al-Sughrah: 182
    Explanation by Sheikh 'Abdul-'Azeez Ibn 'Abdullah ar-Raajhee   183
    Points Of Benefit   184
    LEVEL 1: Test Your Understanding: 185
    LEVEL 2: Interactive Questions & Exercises   185

Day 25: A Person Stands Upon The Religion Of His Close Companion   186
    Narration from al-Ibaanah al-Sughrah: 186
    Explanation by Sheikh 'Abdul-'Azeez Ibn 'Abdullah ar-Raajhee   187
    Points Of Benefit   190
    LEVEL 1: Test Your Understanding: 191
    LEVEL 2: Interactive Questions & Exercises   191

Day 26: Innovation That Is Disbelief Destroys All One's Good Deeds … 192
    Narration from al-Ibaanah al-Sughrah: … 192
    Explanation by Sheikh 'Abdul-'Azeez Ibn 'Abdullah ar-Raajhee … 193
    Points Of Benefit … 195
    LEVEL 1: Test Your Understanding: … 196
    LEVEL 2: Interactive Questions & Exercises … 196

Day 27: Innovations In Islaam May Mislead You To Leave Islaam … 198
    Narration from al-Ibaanah al-Sughrah: … 198
    Explanation by Sheikh 'Abdul-'Azeez Ibn 'Abdullah ar-Raajhee … 199
    Points Of Benefit … 200
    LEVEL 1: Test Your Understanding: … 201
    LEVEL 2: Interactive Questions & Exercises … 201

Day 28: The One Who Changes Islaam Is Cursed By Allaah & Creation … 202
    Narration from al-Ibaanah al-Sughrah: … 202
    Explanation by Sheikh 'Abdul-'Azeez Ibn 'Abdullah ar-Raajhee … 203
    Points Of Benefit … 205
    LEVEL 1: Test Your Understanding: … 206
    LEVEL 2: Interactive Questions & Exercises … 206

Day 29: Repentance from Innovation Must Be Clear & Apparent … 208
    Narration from al-Ibaanah al-Sughrah: … 208
    Explanation by Sheikh 'Abdul-'Azeez Ibn 'Abdullah ar-Raajhee … 209
    Points Of Benefit … 211
    LEVEL 1: Test Your Understanding: … 212
    LEVEL 2: Interactive Questions & Exercises … 212

Day 30: What Religion Will You Die Upon? … 214
    Narration from al-Ibaanah al-Sughrah: … 214
    Explanation by Sheikh 'Abdul-'Azeez Ibn 'Abdullah ar-Raajhee … 215
    Points Of Benefit … 217
    LEVEL 1: Test Your Understanding: … 218
    LEVEL 2: Interactive Questions & Exercises … 218

Answer Key … 220

Course Appendices — 281

Course Appendix 1:
Leaving The Straight Way Occurs In Two Ways — 282

Course Appendix 2:
Concise Descriptions Of Twenty Seven Modern & Historical Sects/Groups/Religions/Ideologies of Misguidance — 286

Course Appendix 3:
Warning Away From The One Upon Innovation Even If He Does Good Works — 290

Course Appendix 4:
99 Characteristics Of Various Misguided Groups — 296

Course Appendix 5:
It Is Not From The Way Of The First Three Generations To…" — 316

Course Appendix 6:
The Reality Of Secularism: "We Warn Against This Ideological Colonization…" — 324

The Nakhlah Educational Series: — 335

THE "30 DAYS OF GUIDANCE" SERIES

The goal of the "*30 Days of Guidance*" book series is to better enable us, as worshipers of Allaah, to embody and reflect in the various different areas of life for a Muslim, our connection and adherence to the believer's path of the first three believing generations. Many Muslims, due to lacking opportunities to study consistently and be cultivated at the feet of noble steadfast scholars, have an inconsistency they themselves recognize- an inconsistency between the clear path of Islaam of the first Muslims, which they have connected themselves to, and what they have actually been successful in making a daily reality in their practice of Islaam. Sheikh Saaleh Ibn al-Fauzaan, may Allaah preserve him, explained the importance of striving to rectify this,

"... For the one who proceeds upon the methodology of the best generations, even if that is during the very last days of the existence of earth, then he is safe, saved, and protected from entering the Hellfire. As Allaah, the Most Glorified and the Most Exalted, said, **And the first to embrace Islaam of the Muhaajiroon (those who migrated from Makkah to Al-Madinah) and the Ansaar (the citizens of Al-Madinah who helped and gave aid to the Muhaajiroon) and also those who followed them exactly (in faith). Allaah is well-pleased with them as they are well-pleased with Him. He has prepared for them Gardens under which rivers flow (Paradise), to dwell therein forever. That is the supreme success.**—(Surah Al-Tawbah:100)

So Allaah, the Most Exalted, the Most Magnificent, has included and described them as those who follow Muhaajiroon and the Ansaar, upon a condition, **"who followed them exactly (in faith)."** *Meaning truly followed them with precision and integrity, not merely putting forth a claim or outwardly attributing or attaching themselves to them without actually realizing their guidance. This is true whether that shortfall is caused by ignorance or by the following of desires. Not everyone who attributes himself to the first three generations is true in his assertion unless he follows them precisely and with integrity. This is in fact a condition, a condition placed by Allaah, the Most Glorified and the Most Exalted. The wording* **"exactly (in faith).** *meaning precisely, with integrity, as well as entirely.*

What is required in truly following them is that you study the methodology of the Salaf, that you understand it, and that you are firmly attached to it. But as for individuals who simply attribute themselves to them, while they do not really understand their methodology nor their way, then this does not really benefit them with anything, and does not actually help them in any way. Such people are not from those upon the way of the Salaf and should not be considered Salafees, because they are not following the first generations precisely with integrity, as indeed Allaah, the Most Glorified and the Most Exalted, has placed this as the condition for their following of them to be true.

....The one who proceeds upon the methodology of the Salaf must have two characteristics, as we have previously mentioned. Firstly, actually understanding the methodology of the first generations, and the second matter is adhering firmly to it, even when it causes him hardship and discomfort. As he will certainly encounter a great deal of that from those who oppose this path of guidance. He will encounter harassment. He will encounter stubbornness. He will encounter false accusations. He will face having directed towards him evil names and false labels. However, he must remain patient in the face of this, as he is convinced and satisfied with what he stands upon. He should be not shaken or troubled in the face of a whirlwind of difficulties. He should not be affected or changed by what he encounters of different trials, but remains patient when facing them until he meets his Lord.

Accordingly, one must firstly learn the methodology of the first three generations, and then follow it exactly with integrity, while being patient with what he encounters from the people due to this adherence. Yet this, in and of itself, is also not enough; it is additionally necessary to spread the methodology of the first generations. It is required to invite the people to Allaah and invite them to the way of the Salaf, to explain it to the people and spread this way among them. The one who does this is Salafee in reality and truth. But as for the one who claims Salafeeyah, yet he does not truly understand the methodology of the Salaf, or he does indeed understand it yet fails to truly follow it, but simply follows what the people are upon, or merely follows what happens to agree with his desires, this one is not Salafee, even if he calls and labels himself that.

This fact demands from us that we place great importance in fully comprehending the way of the first generations and studying their methodology in beliefs, character, and actions in every environment and situation. As the path and methodology of the first three generations is that methodology upon which the Messenger of Allaah, may the praise and salutations be upon him, was upon, and is that way which those who follow the best of generations and walk upon their path, will proceed upon until the Final Hour is established....

...As such, it is required that the one who claims this way, or connects himself to the Salaf make this descriptive name a reality and make his attachment to them something which truly reflects the way of the first generations in beliefs, and in statements, and in actions, and in general dealings so that he may be a true Salafee and that he may be a righteous example to others and someone who sincerely reflects the way of the righteous first generations of Islaam." [1]

We ask Allaah for success in each of our efforts to both learn and reflect the clear path of the first three generations, in every area of our individual lives, the lives of our spouses, and the lives of our children. And the success is from Allaah.

---

[1] From the lecture "Salafeeyah, Its Reality And Its Characteristics" http://www.alfawzan.af.org.sa/

COMPILER'S INTRODUCTION

All praise is due to Allaah alone, we praise Him, we seek His assistance and we ask for His forgiveness. We seek refuge in Him from the evils of our souls and the evils of our actions. Whoever Allaah guides, no one can lead him astray and whoever is caused to go astray, there is no one that can guide him. I bear witness that there is no deity worthy of worship except Allaah alone with no partners. And I bear witness that Muhammad is His worshipper and Messenger, peace and salutations be upon him, his household, his Companions, and all those who follow his guidance until the day of Judgment. To proceed:

One of the leading scholars living today, Sheikh Saaleh Fauzaan, may Allaah preserve him, was asked, **"How do our essential beliefs influence and affect the life of a Muslim and how he lives it?"** He replied, [1]

"Yes, the correct essential beliefs enable a Muslim to proceed upon clarity and understanding in the affairs of his religion. As these beliefs are the very head and core of the religion. Your actions and endeavors will not be truly correct until after your fundamental beliefs have been corrected and made sound. As one's endeavors must be based upon you having the correct beliefs, and those evidences found in the Book of Allaah and the Sunnah of the Messenger of Allaah, may Allaah's praise and salutations be upon him."

Sheikh Zayd Ibn Muhammad al-Madkhalee, may Allaah have mercy upon him, said, [2]

"The need of the people today in every village and remote valley to understand the fundamentals of their religion and have a clear explanation of its overall merits and beneficial characteristics is more significant today than in any previous age!!

How could this not be the case when they live in a time that has so many entertaining and enticing things which make attractive and beautify for human beings what is in fact evil and wrongdoing, doing so in an elaborate way. It is a time with many matters which call to the souls by tempting means, with a flood of overwhelming seductive invitations, inviting towards their destructive forms of misguidance.

Despite all of this, which reflects our dangerous condition, many of the people still get annoyed if the imaam lengthens his khutbah, or extends a lecture he is giving an extra fifteen minutes. Such that when the Jumu'ah prayer is finished or that lecture he lengthened has concluded, you hear them remarking about it, "You have made it too long for us! This is not the way those who speak in front of the people should do!!' Or similar statements.

---

[1] Audio from from alfawzan.af.org.sa
[2] From the work: "The Strong Reliable Methodology In Establishing a Foundation which Was Set Forth by the Noble Prophet, page 28-29

Yet they, may Allaah guide them and us to what is correct, they never get tired or bored of spending many long hours listening to flirtatious songs or watching corrupting soap operas and harmful dramatic television shows which do not bring about any good for anyone, and which the one listening to them does not even gain a single thing of benefit.

In this way the true realities of what should be valued have been reversed with this type of people. They cannot even come close to properly distinguishing between what is beneficial and helpful and that which is actually harmful and damaging, nor between a blessed good sitting companion, and an evil destructive offensive associate. Indeed there is no strength nor power to change except in Allaah."

This attention and concern for understanding our fundamental beliefs and concepts, which shape our outlook and perspective, is even more important when it comes to the young generation of Muslims. Sheikh Zayd Ibn Muhammad al-Madkhalee, may Allaah have mercy upon him, reminds us that,[3]

"...It is necessary to put forth concerted efforts, especially in relation to the young Muslims, in order that they gain Sharee'ah knowledge. This is in order that the younger Muslims take on the knowledge possessed by the older knowledgeable Muslims among them. Then when one of the older Muslims who had Sharee'ah knowledge dies and returns to his Lord, his knowledge remains with those living who still carry it, meaning his students, regardless of whether that be a few or many students."

We are all in need of either learning our fundamental beliefs comprehensively, or strengthening our understanding of the details and their proofs, so that we can remain steadfast as well as call and spread them among other Muslims, including our own families. Furthermore, discussing the the benefits to each of us personally, Sheikh Zayd Ibn Muhammad al-Madkhalee, may Allaah have mercy upon him, said,[4]

"We are all in urgent need of hearing reminders and of listening to issues and statements of knowledge in every chance and time possible. Through this our hearts are enlivened and a person is stimulated to undertake more acts of obedience and refrain from committing different acts of disobedience, and to move from an acceptable state to one which is even better. Whereas if this is neglected, what a person brings upon themselves is heedlessness, neglecting the knowledge they do have and falling short in acting according to it..."

Indeed, the guiding scholar Sheikh Ibn Baaz, may Allaah have mercy upon him, said,[5]

"A person is always in need of gaining knowledge until he reaches death."

And there is no doubt that if we understand matters correctly, we would not complain about the length of reminders or sermons, but instead, say what Sheikh Zayd Ibn Muhammad al-Madkhalee, may Allaah have mercy upon him, said,[6]

"A true life is only found in the shade of Sharee'ah knowledge."

---

[3] Nuzhat al-Qaaree fee Sharh Kitaab al-Ilm min Saheeh al-Bukhaaree
[4] Clarifying the Meaning In Explaining The Introduction of the Treatise of Abee Zayd al-Qayruwaanee, page 64
[5] Majmu' al-Fataawa: vol.6 pg.71
[6] Clarifying the Meaning In Explaining The Introduction of the Treatise of Abee Zayd al-Qayruwaanee, page 218

THE FALSE CLAIM THAT CORRECT BELIEFS ARE A SIMPLE QUICK MATTER

Sheikh Zayd Ibn Muhammad al-Madkhalee, may Allaah have mercy upon him, has addressed a common misconception among Muslims who neglect studying beleifs due to having priorities other that strengthening the essential foundation of authentic Sharee'ah knowledge among Muslims, authentic beliefs in particular, when he said,[7]

> *"There is no proof or no actual basis for the one who falsely claims,* **'If the people basically understand the beliefs of Islaam in a single gathering, or through a month or a year of study, then they no longer need to keep studying."**
>
> *Yet consider that the related texts, scholastic researches, writing, and authored works in this field of knowledge are tremendously vast and exemplary. Because of this, the person who wishes to explore and catalog the number of books written in the subject of beliefs, will find hundreds of different works, varying and ranging from longer writing to shorter summarized works, from original texts to commentaries upon texts, from books written in a question and answer format, to those written and organized in an poetic format and style. This is something that you all are generally aware of.*
>
> *So there is no basis for the one who claims that only a little time is enough to take care of understanding the beliefs of Islaam, and that after this there is no need to return back to it again or further study it nor to publish works about it. Whereas, in fact it is required that we truly understand this false claim, and reject such statements of those individuals who are so frustrated by our extensive attention to gaining firm understanding in the noble branch of knowledge. And Allaah know best."*

Rather we believe that studying the fundamental beliefs and the areas of knowledge related to it in Islaam are the means for the success, honor, and victory of the Muslims, and stands at the heart of the true methodology of Islaam which the Messenger of Allaah taught his Companions. Sheikh Muqbil Ibn Haadee, may Allaah have mercy upon him stated,[8]

> *"We believe that honor and high standing cannot be achieved nor will victory reach the Muslims until they return back to the guidance of the Book of Allaah and the Sunnah of His Messenger, may Allaah's praise and salutation be upon him and his family."*

This is especially true in this age in which many of the well known scholars who steadfastly guided the Muslims upon the Sunnah have died, may Allaah have mercy upon them all.

---

[7] al-Aqd al-Mundheed al-Jadeed Fee al-Ijaabat Alaa Masaa'il Fee Fiqh wal- Manaahij wa at-Tawheed vol. one pg 30

[8] The Da'wah Journey of Sheikh Muqbil ibn Haadee Al-Waadi'ee And Harvested Gems from His Statements and Rulings" by Abu Ramzee Naasir Ibn 'Alee Muhammad ad-Dab Al-Waadi'ee, pg. 110-117

INTRODUCTION

YOUR BELIEFS MUST BE THE BELIEFS OF THE FIRST GENERATIONS OF MUSLIMS

Sheikh Ibn Baadees, may Allaah have mercy upon him, said, [9]

"We come to know the level of intelligence of an individual by knowing which books he reads. Such that the one that we do not see having a focus upon the books of the Sunnah, then indeed we do not consider his knowledge reliable in terms of understanding the religion."

This course book strives to explain and convey some of the important principles held by the Salaf as-Saaleh, or the righteous first three generations of Muslims, whose merit was indicated by the Messenger of Allaah, may the praise and salutations of Allaah be upon him. It does not convey the misguided beliefs of the Ash'aree sect or any other later sets of beliefs which some have accepted long after the early generations who held firmly to what the Companions stood clearly upon. It conveys the Salafee beliefs, upon the methodology of Salafeeyah. The guiding scholar Muhammad 'Amaan Ibn 'Alee al-Jaamee stated in his work discussing the correct beliefs about Allaah's attributes why we must stand upon what those Muslims were upon,[10] -

"When we generally use the term 'as-Salaf', what we specifically mean by it in relation to terminology is: The Companions of the Messenger of Allaah, may Allaah's praise and salutations be upon him, who were present in his time, as they took both the fundamentals and the secondary aspects of Islaam, vibrant and strong, directly from him. Similarly what is included in the meaning of this term is the generations coming after the Companions- the Taaba'een, those to whom the Companions passed over their legacy of endeavors before many years had passed by.

This is since they are included in the merit which the Messenger of Allaah, may Allaah's praise and salutations be upon him, testified and bore witness to. He praised their generation when he described who were **{The best among people"** *Just as was found in the hadeeth narration* **"The best among people are of my generation, then those who come after them to them, then those who come after them to them. }** [11] *Likewise this term also included the Taaba'ee at-Taaba'een, the generation who came after the generation of Successors to the Companions. So it is a phrase also correctly used in relation to include this third generation of Muslims.*

The term as-Salaf began to be used increasingly when disputes and controversies erupted regarding the fundamental principles of the religion from those sects involved in rhetoric and misguiding intellectual speculation, such that all the various sects tried to generally claim that their own beliefs were those of the first generations.

They would announce that whatever belief and way they stood upon was the same as the righteous predecessors were upon! For this reason, it was required to make matters apparent, and that is our current situation today, making clear the established foundations, and clear affirmed distinguishing principles of the actual Salafee way. To prevent any confusion and uncertainty as to its reality by anyone who sincerely strives to connect themselves to this generation of the first Muslims, those struggling to follow and pattern themselves upon their way and model. It is possible to summarize those different principles of their way and methodology to the following:

---

[9] Athaar Sheikh Ibn Baadees, may Allaah have mercy upon him: vol.4 pg. 244
[10] as-Sifaat al-Ilaaheyaah, pg. 57-60
[11] Saheeh al-Bukhaaree vol. 5 page 285, Saheeh Muslim 2533, and within the Musnad of Imaam Ahmad Vol. 4 page 427,

The first principle: To give final authority and predominance to transmitted revealed knowledge over using speculative intellectually developed knowledge and conclusions and intellectual efforts. However, our affirmation of the predominance of transmitted knowledge over intellectual efforts and conclusions does not mean that it is proper that we understand from this that the first three generations absolutely condemned intellectual efforts and what is reached through properly using them of goodness, or condemn the contemplation and considering with wonder the creation of the heavens and the earth, and the other numerous physical examples of wonder in creation. Not at all. But what it meant is that we should not adopt a way of utilizing intellectual ability similar to that which was proceeded upon by the misguided scholars of philosophical rhetoric in deriving conclusions only through intellectual consideration when establishing the proof of Allaah's existence and divine ascendency over His creation...

...Rather, the first three generations of believers held as being part of their methodology that there was no true conflict between the two types of evidence, transmitted revealed knowledge and intellectual examination, when both are properly used and correctly understood. In fact they rejected this alleged conflict which the misguided scholars of philosophical rhetoric incorrectly assumed and adopted due to being affected by the concepts and methods of Greek philosophy. This is taking into account that fact that the path proceeded upon by the scholars of philosophical rhetoric is in reality the same methodology of the disbelieving philosophers from outside the people of Islaam upon the foundation that they do not recognize and affirm the truth of prophethood at all...

....In summary, the first three generations gave dominant authority to the body of evidences from transmitted revealed knowledge over any authority of intellectually derived conclusions and derived evidences. The had full faith in them, believing that Allaah sent to humanity messengers, and revealed books of guidance to these messengers, and made these messengers responsible for explaining and clarifying what the people needed to understand (as this was part of their purpose and affair). This principle means that whatever knowledge and guidance that was generally sent down in these revealed books and that these messengers spread among the various people and nations, is what is most fundamentally important. It is knowledge which is completely true, having no need of anything else to affirm its being true nor any need for anything to prove that it is sufficient as the foundation for the guidance of humanity. This specific point is the hidden root of the issue that makes everything clear.

For example it is not possible for those individuals and groups from the later generations to, in truth correctly follow the general way and methodology of the Salaf, except when they affirm that the way of the Salaf was not only safer, but that their way, meaning the Salaf's, was also wiser and more intelligent. As was said in poetry:

> ***Every form of goodness is found in***
> > ***following the first early generations,***
> ***and every form of misguidance and straying***
> > ***is found in the newly conceived matters of the later generations.***

How correct is what is found within these lines of poetry, despite the fact that the one who said it was himself someone upon the way of the later generations, not the early generations.

...From what has been discussed up until this point, it has been made clear that the significance and intent of the word Salafeeyah has come to be a well known term which means, "the path proceeded upon by the first generations, along with all those who also followed their path in taking and gaining knowledge, their method of properly understanding it, and well as also, naturally, the way of calling and inviting to it."

For this reason, it cannot accurately be restricted to a specific historical period or era in time. Rather it is, in fact, obligatory that it be a term understood to indicate a continuous realization of their way in the lives of the Muslims throughout history. Similarly, it is a necessary to confine those referred to as "the saved sect" from the scholars, to that scholar clearly upon the hadeeth narrations and upon the authentic Sunnah, as they are the people truly upon this methodology. And this saved sect will always continue to be present until the Day of Judgment.

This is as affirmed by the authentic statement, may Allaah's praise and salutations be upon him, **{A group of people from my Ummah will continue to obey Allaah's Command, and those who desert or oppose them shall not be able to do them any harm. They will be dominating the people until Allaah's Command is executed (Resurrection is established).}**

In this work Sheikh ar-Raajhee, may Allaah preserve him, mentioned in his classes explaining al-Ibaanah as-Sughrah, a warning about,

"Becoming distressed due to worldly affairs or making them your happiness

Yes, this is not something which it is proper for an individual to do, because this world is something which is passing and temporary in nature. It is not right that a person become distressed due to affairs of this world, nor that they become his reason for happiness and joy. Rather an individual's happiness or sadness should be connected to the state of his religion and connected to his religious life. It should come about due to the state of his way of life and religion.

He becomes pleased and happy with the blessing of Allaah upon him in his learning knowledge through the Qur'aan, and by his being granted success to put forth righteous deeds. Likewise becoming saddened by his sins and transgressing within his religion. And Allaah the Most High said: Say: ❦**In the Bounty of Allaah, and in His Mercy (i.e. Islaam and the Qur'aan); -therein let them rejoice." That is better than what (the wealth) they amass.**❦-*(Surah Yunus: 58)"*

The first key to accomplishing this is having sound and correct fundamental beliefs as Muslims. And the success in this is a blessing from Allaah alone.

INTRODUCTION

Overview Of This Specific "30 Day" Course

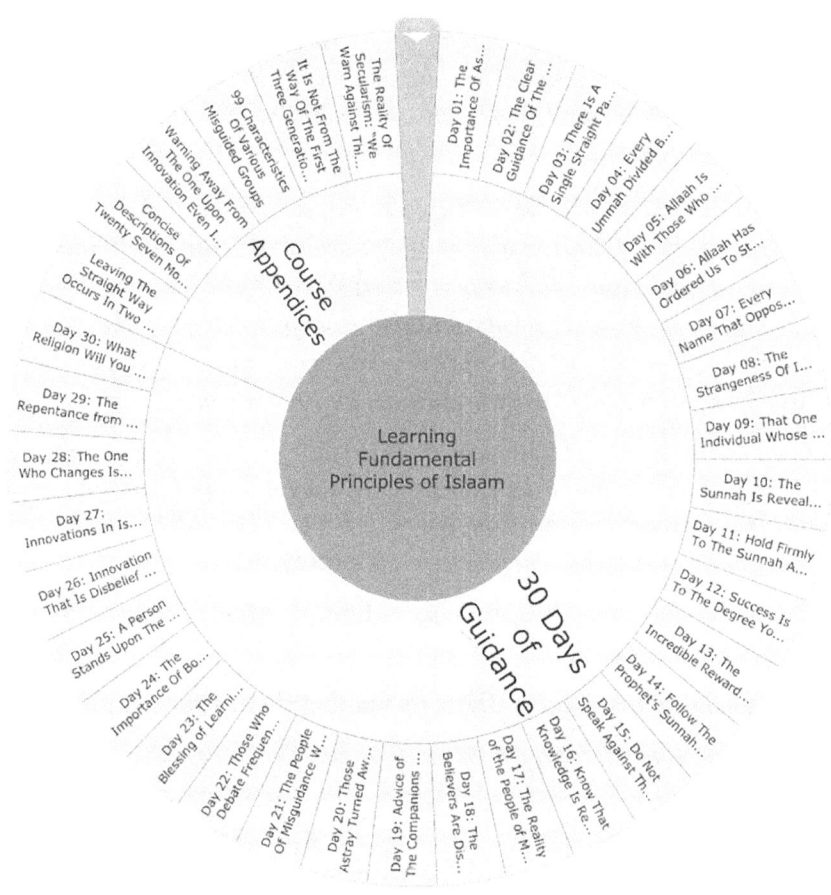

AL-IBAANAH AL-SUGHRAH

The work by the noble scholar Abu Abdullah 'Ubaydullah Ibn Muhammad Ibn Battah al-'Ukbaree al-Hanbalee, well-known as Ibn Battah, who was born at 'Ukbara in 304 H. It is well known by the name al-Ibaanah as-Sughrah.

The commentary is based upon a series of classes given by one of the noble scholars of our time Sheikh 'Abdul-'Azeez Ibn 'Abdullah ar-Raajhee, may Allaah preserve him, who is from those scholars upon the Sunnah known to have been a close associate and companion of the leading scholar Sheikh 'Abdul-'Azeez Ibn Abdullah Ibn Baaz, may Allaah have mercy upon him.

His commentary is based upon a scholastic hadeeth verification of the original work which indicated those narrations that are not authenticated or are unreliable in the original work. He further classifies and identifies those narrations and statements which are authentic in the chain and those statements which are only correct in their meaning, due to having support from other sources for what they convey. The references of all narrations are taken from his transcribed classes.

This work is part a new series of books whose aim was explained in the section found just before this introduction "The "30 Days of guidance" Series". By Allaah's mercy, seven years ago we were blessed to produce our first course book upon a specifically designed learning framework, as mentioned at that time,

> "The origin and basis for this format of study which we have developed is from the excellent book of the guiding scholar Sheikh Saaleh Ibn Fauzaan al-Fauzaan, may Allaah preserve him, in his book *"Mulkhis fee Sharh Kitaab at-Tawheed"*. In the introduction he states (page 5),
>
> *"This is an abridged commentary of the work "Kitaab at-Tawheed" of Sheikh al-Islaam Muhammad 'Abdul-Wahaab, may Allaah have mercy upon him, which I have composed upon a modern educational methodology, in order to make it easier to understand for the beginners in their studies. I hope that Allaah will bring benefit through it, and grants it a contributing role in the spreading of knowledge and the correction of the beliefs of the Muslims..."*
>
> His basic framework for the beginner's study of that essential book was initially the foundation for the (ongoing) development of an extended course on *"Kitaab at-Tawheed,"* as as well later being further adapted and modified for other knowledge based projects - including the present course –by incorporating some of those same beneficial characteristics." [12]

With this new series of books we take an additional step by using a format intended to facilitate consistent easy study by an individual or together with others, and by laying the groundwork for implementing two distinct online course paths based upon each book in the series.

1) The first is a full course testing regimen to assist with self-study, as a supplement to the purchased books.

2) The second is planned, periodic, full live ILT (instructor led training) classes based upon the series, also to be offered online.

This course and course book covers and discusses several correct principles and concepts of the religion, which are reflected in the understanding and practice of the guided Muslims who have always adhered to the pure Sunnah. Despite this, there is little doubt that many today do not have a firm handhold upon these principles either in their understanding, their practice, or in both. The selections in the work include authentic hadeeth narrations, statements of the Companions, as well as statements of guided scholars who came in the generations following the first three generations and diligently walked in their footsteps.

This course follows the established framework of utilizing three print publications:

[Self-Study/Teachers Edition] - all course materials, appendices, and answer key

[Directed Study Edition] - all course materials, appendices, without answer key for groups

[Exercise Workbook]- supplementary course workbook formatted to facilitate homework

---

[12] Publisher's Introduction to "Al-Waajibaat: the Obligatory Matters" First Edition 1430

This course book is structured in a simple way in order to:

1. Make it easy to read and understand the selected original authentic narrations and scholastic statements

2. Build upon that basic knowledge and understanding found in the original narration through the clarifying words of explanation and practical discussion from a well-known, distinguished scholar

3. Offer possible points of benefits from both the narration and scholarly commentary. [13]

4. Offer a basic level of relevant questions in order to enable review and testing the student's knowledge of what has been presented from these authentic narrations and their explanation

5. Offer the reader an additional level of interactive discussion through on site forums to help him consider his current situation as a Muslim and possible ways to best implement this guidance in the daily lives of himself and his family.

The overall goal is to enable each reader to understand and practice these principles in their lives, and be able to distinguish both the people who proceed upon the original methodology and call of the final messenger as well as identify those individual, groups, and sects who oppose and fight against these correct evidenced principles and beliefs. As today we find that there are many different types of misguidance and innovations in the different areas of Islaam. Sheikh 'Abdul-'Azeez Ibn 'Abdullah ar-Raajhee, may Allaah preserve him, was asked,[14]

> "Are there innovations in matters of belief as well there also being innovations related to worship ?
>
> *Answer: Yes, there are innovations related to one's beliefs, such as the innovations of Asha'rees, the Mu'tazilah, and the Jahmeeyah, and there also innovations connected to one's acts of worship such as the outward speaking of one's inner intention when performing an act. And innovations in the religion are in reality numerous and varied."*

We must remember that the spread of such innovations causes the Sunnah to leave the people as Hassan Ibn 'Ateeyah, may Allaah have mercy upon him, said, [15]

> *"There is no people who bring forth an innovation within their religion except that Allaah takes away from them a true practice of the Sunnah of the same type, and that practice of the Sunnah will never be returned to them until the Day of Judgment."*

---

[13] It should be noted that the points of benefit are general and connected directly to the context of the sections narrations. There may be other external discussion points which apparently contradict specific points, but usually these are actually within of a different specific area of knowledge, different context, or different intended meaning. However, any points that are not understood should be referred back to one of the scholars for the best understanding of the intended guidance in the original text as well as that of any external discussion.

[14] From His explanation of the work Kitaab as-Sunnah by Imaam al-Barbahaaree, Lecture no. 10

[15] Narrated by Imaam ad-Daaramee in as-Sunan no. 98 with a sound chain of narration.

Educational Elements of New "30 Day" Course Structure

Several course appendices on related subjects in same course book for reference

Derived possible points of benefit allows you to review conclusions from text

The explanation of a scholar which encompasses both meaning and practice

The general ruling of authenticity of the text being studied

One or more texts from al-Ibaanah al-Sughrah which are for each of the 30 days

Basic & simple questions to check correct understanding of both text & commentary

Completion exercises requiring understanding of specific terms used in course

Interactive discussion questions for effective group study in school or circle

Online version of testing & course forum for beneficial student discussion

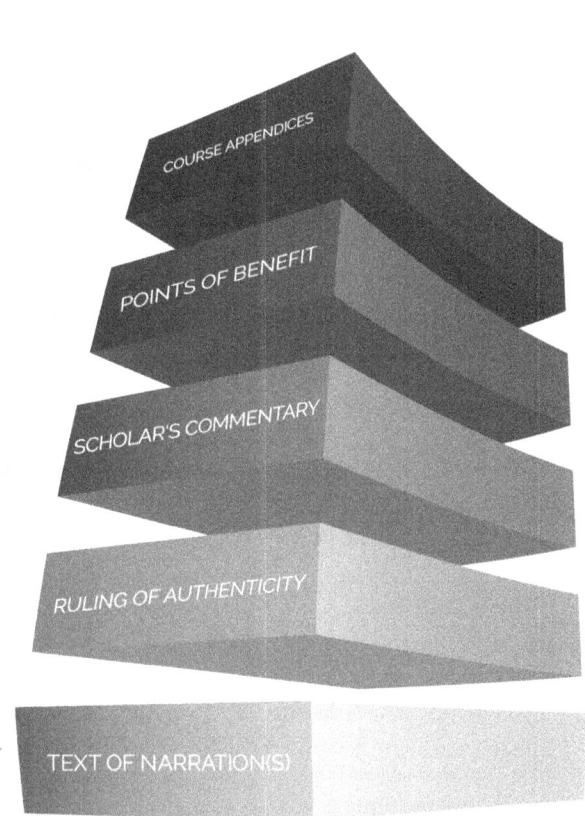
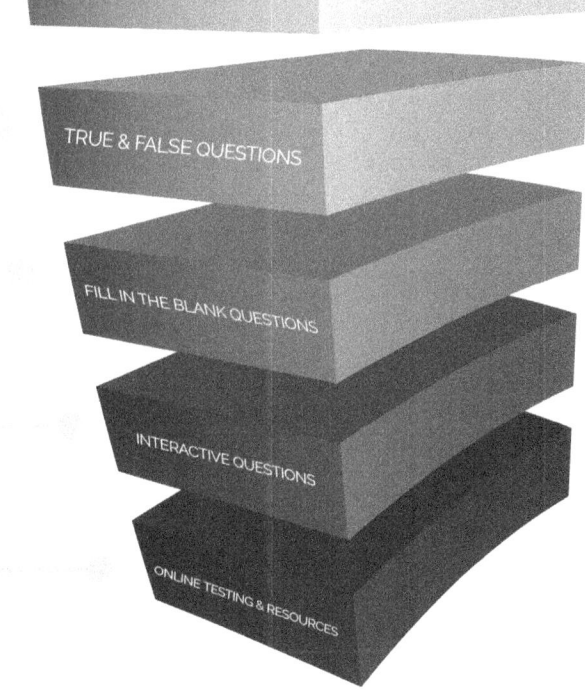

INTRODUCTION

THE SUBJECTS & AIM OF THE COURSE APPENDICES

Included along with the course, as part of the course book, there are six separate appendices:

Course Appendix 1:
Leaving The Straight Way Occurs In Two Ways

This short discussion from Sheikh 'Abdul-'Azeez Ibn 'Abdullah ar-Raajhee, may Allaah preserve him, helps us understand some detailed matters about those who fall into misguidance.

Course Appendix 2:
Concise Descriptions Of Twenty Seven Modern & Historical Sects/Groups/Religions/Ideologies of Misguidance

These concise definitions Sheikh Zayd Ibn Muhammad al-Madkhalee, may Allaah have mercy upon him, provide a good foundation for understanding some of the major groups of misguidance throughout the history of the Muslim Ummah.

Course Appendix 3:
Warning Away From The One Upon Innovation Even If He Does Good Works

This important clarification from Sheikh Muhammad Ibn Saaleh al-'Utheimeen, may Allaah have mercy upon him, removes a misconception common among many Muslims.

Course Appendix 4
99 Characteristics Of Various Misguided Groups

This collection of very detailed characteristics by Sheikh Abdullah Ibn Muhammad Ibn Saaleh al-Ma'taar enables the striving Muslim to better identify many misguided groups, sects, and new movements who are present among the Muslims today.

Course Appendix 5:
It Is Not From The Way Of The First Three Generations To...

This series by Sheikh Muhammad Baazmool, may Allaah preserve him, help a seeker in knowledge better understand detailed aspects of the beleifs and methodology of the Salaf.

Course Appendix 6:
The Reality Of Secularism: "We Warn Against This Ideological Colonization..."

These selections from various reliable scholars discuss the ideological characteristics and practical methods of propagation of this specific ideological aspect of modern Western thought, which the Muslims of this century have been confronted with.

INTRODUCTION

Many of the appendices deal with specific and detailed descriptions which assist a striving Muslim to better identify the many misguided ideas, concepts, and beliefs present today as well as and the numerous individuals sects, groups, and movements which call and propagate them. This is something important, despite the serious misconception held by some Muslims that discussing the differences between the Muslims in their beliefs and methodology only increases the Ummah in separation, and that it is better, at this time, to act as if these differences do not exist. The eminent guiding scholar Sheikh Saaleh Ibn Fauzaan al-Fauzaan, may Allaah preserve him, clarified and explained the falsehood of this misconception, in a response to the following question[16]

"May Allaah increase you in goodness. This questioner asks and is saying, there has appeared in recent days those who absolutely reject classifying people according to what they stand upon of opposing something in Islaam due to the need to unite the Muslims together. What is your view of this, esteemed sheikh? What are the guidelines regarding this?

Answer: This cannot be stated generally without restrictions, because the one who opposes what is correct can be a disbeliever and not a Muslim, or they could be someone severely astray, a wrongdoer, or an open sinner. The people differ greatly: among them there is the disbeliever, among them there is the hypocrite, among them is the wrongdoer, among them is the open sinner, and among them is the obedient steadfast believer.

So it is required that you place the people at their proper levels and in the proper places. Do not put the open sinner on the place or level of the obedient Muslim, nor put the obedient Muslim on the place or level of the open sinner. Allaah, the Most Exalted, the Most Magnificent, says, **Or do those who earn evil deeds think that We shall hold them equal with those who believe in the Oneness of Allaah and do righteous good deeds, in their present life and after their death? Worst is the Judgment that they make.** *-(Surah Al-Jaathiyah: 21)* **Shall We then treat the submitting Muslims like the mujrimoon (criminals, polytheists and disbelievers, etc.). What is the matter with you? How judge you?** *-(Surah Al-Qalam: 35-36) and* **Shall We treat those who believe (in the Oneness of Allaah Islamic monotheism) and do righteous good deeds, as mufsidoon (those who associate partners in worship with Allaah and commit crimes) on earth? Or shall We treat the muttaqoon, as the fujjaar (criminals, disbelievers, wicked, etc)?** *-(Surah Saad:28)*

Allaah is the one who differentiated between these people and individuals and these other people and individuals, according to the deeds that they did, and according to the beliefs that they hold. This is just as we have heard in the authentic narration that this Ummah will divide into seventy-three sects. Every sect has a specific methodology, has a specific path by which it differs and is distinguished by the path proceeded upon by other sects, excepts for that sect which remains steadfast upon the Book of Allaah and the Sunnah, as their path continues to be a single path, without separating between themselves. This is something which is clear and understood.

As for the one who says do not differentiate between the people, nor categorize the people according to their beliefs and actions, then this is the statement of error and of misguidance. As it is Allaah who has separated and differentiated between the people.

---

[16] Taken from an audio file in the voice of the Sheikh

> *Mentioned within the Book of Allaah and the Sunnah are the disbelievers, and mentioned within the both of them are the hypocrites, and mentioned within them are the believers, and mentioned within them are the wrongdoers and transgressors. As such, Allaah Himself has categorized the different types of people. So now will we contradict and turn away from that understanding which Allaah has sent down within His Book?!* ﴾**He it is Who created you, then some of you are disbelievers and some of you are believers. And Allaah is All-Seer of what you do.**﴿ *–(Surah Al-Taghaabun: 2)*
>
> *Should we be those who then still say "No no, there is no difference between the people." The one who says this is straying and deviating away from Allaah and His Messenger. Yes."*

Indeed from the scholars of our modern age had indicated importance of not only identifying those upon innovation generally, but also specifically in relation to the gatherings of those seeking knowledge. As the scholars have identified that it is from the practices of the people of innovation to put forth questions which cause confusion among the Muslims. Sheikh al-'Utheimeen, may Allaah have mercy upon him, clarified this important fact, regarding innovators that we come to know stand among the sitting of the scholars, saying,[17]

> *"…In this way, it is proper that the people of knowledge if they see within the ranks of the people innovators sitting among them, that they expel them from amongst the ranks. Because the innovator and his presence amongst the people the Sunnah is only an evil. As innovation is a sickness like cancer, which no one can hope to be free of except when Allaah wills it.*
>
> *His statement, meaning Imaam Maalik, "**I do not see you as anything else but an innovator (and then had him expelled)**" It cannot be understood to have any other meaning, than him being innovator due to this question of his, or to mean "You can only be from the people of innovation." Because the people of innovation are those who have the habit of specifically asking about the unclear verses for the purpose of causing confusion among the people.*
>
> *Yet regardless of which meaning is intended, what it indicates is that it is from the guidance of the Salaf to eject the innovators from among the ranks of those who are learning the religion. Moreover, it is indeed proper to remove them from within moving within the society as a whole, and to tighten the restrictions upon them such that they do not spread and propagate their innovation.*
>
> *As it should not be said, 'Every person is completely free to do whatever they like.' No, in fact what should be said is that everyone is free in our lands, within the guided limits of the Sharee'ah. But if they oppose the Sharee'ah then in his obligation is to confront them, and to clarify the truth to them. Such that if they return back to what is correct, then this is accepted. But if they do not then they should be dealt with in whatever way is suitable and required by the extent of their innovation, meaning whether it be from the haphazard declaration of Muslims as disbelievers, or something else which is wrongdoing and sin."*

---

[17] Sharh al-Aqeedah as-Safaareeneeyah, pg. 229

The Muslim Understanding of True progress and civilization

One of the common false slanders against Islaam in our time is that it is reactionary and does not seek to enable the progress of humanity. However the scholars have affirmed and clarified that the guidance and beliefs of Islaam are intended to bring about the welfare and overall success of humanity in both their religious and worldly affairs. Sheikh ar-Raajhee, may Allaah preserve him, mentioned in his classes explaining the work al-Ibaanah as-Sughrah,

"The hadeeth narration "Indeed Allaah, the Most High and the Most Exalted, has not commanded His worshippers with anything except those things which benefit them."

'Umar Ibn al-Khattab, may Allaah the Most High be pleased with him, said: {**Indeed Allaah, the Most High and the Most Exalted, has not commanded His worshippers with anything except those things which benefit them, and He has not made forbidden for them anything except those matters which will harm them.**}

The meaning of this statement is correct without any doubt. Allaah, the Most High, is wise in what He has legislated, and He created the creation for a tremendous wisdom- that being that they direct worship towards Him, single Him out in worship alone, and that they come to know Him by His lofty names and attributes.

He, how free from any imperfection is He, has not commanded them with anything except that which benefits them in both their religious and their worldly affairs. And He has not prohibited them from any matter except that it would harm them in both their religious and worldly affairs. Since this is the case, it has become even more necessary to act according to the Book of Allaah and the Sunnah of His Messenger, and similarly more necessary to warn against innovation and invented matters introduced into this religion. Yes."

It is the belief of the people of the Sunnah that the foundation of success in our worldly life must be based upon a foundation of revealed knowledge before anything else. Yet it is incorrect for anyone to assert that our fundamental beliefs prevent the material betterment and development for the Muslims or others. Sheikh Muhammad Baazmool, explains stating,[18]

"What is our position towards civilization and development? There is not any matter in the Sharee'ah that stands between a Muslim and between civilization and development, nor anything that prevents a Muslim from taking those steps which advance material progress. Certainly our religion does not prevent us from those matters which contain goodness and overall benefit. Additionally, wisdom is the objective of the believer that wherever he finds it he takes it.

However this has a condition, that these matters do not have within them that which opposes the religion or the guidelines of the Sharee'ah. We wish for civilization and we wish for development! One can work to bring this about, but he must be warned against opposing the guidelines and guidance of the Sharee'ah in any matters.

---

[18] From the Facebook page of Sheikh Muhammad Baazmool, Ramadhaan 21, 1437

We, as Muslims, do not oppose what is called civilization. The one who attempts to describe us with this false description is someone unjust and is a deceiver. How could this be the case when the scholars of the Muslims were those who were the leaders of new discoveries in every field of practical knowledge. As such, those who attempt to describe the Muslim or Islaam as reactionary or backwards, then they simply do not understand Islaam, and they're discussing something that they don't properly comprehend. Or it may be the case that they themselves only desire civilization and advancement and development which has been stripped free of the religion of Islaam.

So what is the position of the material progress among the priorities of a Muslim? The issue of material progress in the view and priorities of a Muslim is that it is a tool and means but not the goal or objective. Meaning by this that he doesn't work and strive for the sake of achieving it simply for its own sake. Rather he works towards developing the world for the goal of establishing the Sharee'ah of Allaah, and being successfully prepared for the Last Day. Since this worldly life is considered only similar to a tree in which you take shade under briefly while traveling and then you leave it behind!

Allaah, the Most Glorified and the Most Exalted, said: **But seek, with that wealth which Allaah has bestowed on you, the home of the Hereafter, and forget not your portion of legal enjoyment in this world, and do good as Allaah has been good to you, and seek not mischief in the land. Verily, Allaah likes not the mufsidoon (those who commit great crimes and sins, oppressors, tyrants, mischief-makers, corrupts).** *-(Surah Al-Qasas: 77). The meaning of this verse, through what Allaah has given you in the world, seek success in the next world. Always keeping in mind that when you are properly engaged in seeking the Hereafter, there is no fear of forgetting the acceptable blessings of the world. As Allaah says,* **...do not forget and forget not your portion of legal enjoyment in this world**

But as for when an individual lacks any other focus or has no priority other than for material development and advancement for its own sake, even if this is done according to the limits of the religion and the Sharee'ah, then this clearly opposes what a Muslim should correctly stand upon. We ask Allaah to grant us and you success in everything that He loves and is pleased with."

As Sheikh Ahmad an-Najmee, explains that Muslims only oppose those different intellectual trends that oppose the very idea that we need to follow revealed guidance in our lives.[19]

"**Question: There is present among the intellectual fields and discussions of Muslims various ideas, concepts, different approaches, and new ideological trends that focus on calling for "women's liberation", and separating Islaam from any role in governing the Muslims in collective state and civil affairs. What is the position of Islaam towards these concepts, approaches, and trends?**

Answer: "The position of Islaam towards them is the position of enmity, censure, and struggling against them. Because they, meaning these concepts and ideas, only have the purpose and aim of destroying Islaam, and subverting it first from its foundations. For these reasons it is an obligation upon the Muslim Ummah to oppose without any exception and fight against these concepts and ideas with every kind and form of possible opposition."

---

[19] Question 13 of Questions Asked to Sheikh Ahmad an-Najmee by Sheikh 'Abdullah Ibn Salfeeq al-Dhaferee dated 6-14-1428

STRIVE TO ESTABLISH BENEFICIAL BROTHERHOOD UPON THE CORRECT BELIEFS

Many scholars have mentioned the benefit of having other Muslims as associates to assist you in your efforts to learn Islaam. Sheikh Zayd Ibn Muhammad al-Madkhalee, may Allaah have mercy upon him, said,[20]

"One of the specific characteristics of the true student is the selection of righteous associates and successful companions. Certainly gaining these types as companions from among the people is part of being guided and blessed with Allaah's favor, and interacting with them is a precious bounty.

Their striving to review and study matters in the different areas of knowledge has many significant benefits. From these benefits is learning excellent manners from each other, and the changing to a state of goodness the one who had become confused and mixed up, and through holding close to the company of such people you come to dominate and control the path of your seeking of knowledge."

Sheikh Zayd Ibn Muhammad al-Madkhalee, may Allaah have mercy upon him, also said,[21]

"The one who is truly a good companion is the one who assists his Muslim brother as much as he is able, even if only with a beneficial word or statement of good, as well as helping him by offering him advice about himself, and if his brother forgets a matter he reminds him. This is how he establishes the rights of true companionship, especially in relation to the matters connected to Islaam, he certainly reminds and advises his brother, and advises him with what is good for him.

All of these matters are part of fulfilling what is required from Muslim brotherhood and companionship. As for the one when you forget to do something, he doesn't remind you, and when you require his help he does not help you, then this one has not fulfilled the rights of companionship. He stands as someone who doesn't fully understand the extent of good companionship and everything relating to fulfilling it for one's companion."

The sheikh, may Allaah have mercy upon him, emphasizes what true brotherhood in his saying,[22]

"…Additionally it is not appropriate for the Muslims that their interaction with their brothers is only nice words and smiles, while they actually differ with them in what is within their hearts and in their words and statements that they speak. Rather what is obligatory is that they truly be brothers inwardly and outwardly. A brother who was a believer should not hold grudges against his believing brothers.

If there occurs between them that which at times occurs of differences, due to personal matters, or worldly and financial issues, these things still do not entitle him to have or hold ill will and malice against some of his Muslim brothers, or feelings of hatred, or to generally have bad suspicions about them. Rather what is obligatory is that they be sincere in their brotherhood, truthfully establishing it, until the hearts are joined together, and they come to stand united upon the truth."

---

[20] Relevant Responses to Guided Questions, pg. 225
[21] From his commentary of al-Adab al-Mufrad, vol. 1 pg. 166
[22] Clarifying the Meaning In Explaining The Introduction of the Treatise of Abee Zayd al-Qayruwaanee

INTRODUCTION

Sheikh Ahmad Ibn Yahya An-Najmee, may Allaah have mercy upon him, explained the reality of loving your brother in Islaam and upon the Sunnah truly for Allaah's sake[23]

> "Strive to love a Muslim who is not related to you by blood, nor is from those neighbors that you cooperate with, those who work with you to achieve a shared goal which you both benefit from. But strive to love that Muslims who lives in a distant country from you, and who has no family connections to you, but what there is - is that it has reached you that his is someone who adheres to the Sunnah, and then love him for the sake of Allaah alone. If you can achieve this, then you will be a believer."

Sheikh Zayd al-Madkhalee, may Allaah have mercy upon him, has given us excellent advice on how to strive to benefit from good and true brotherhood without mistakenly choosing brotherhood with someone who may be misguided in some way and eventually pulls you towards his misguidance. He was asked,[24] **"Esteemed sheikh, is it for a Muslim to look into the affairs of his Muslim brother to determine whether or not he is someone upon the innovation of some biased group partisanship or some other similar matter of misguidance, beyond what is openly apparent from his outward affairs which would clearly indicate that he stands upon some innovation or biased partisanship to one of the modern misguided groups or movements?**

> "Answer: The fundamental case or position of a Muslim is being considered free from innovation until there clearly is seen from him what indicated that he is upon something of innovation in the religion, not to look into anything other than what is apparent from him. However, an individual is known by who his companions and associates are, just as the Prophet, may Allaah's praise and salutations be upon him, said, {**A person is upon the religion and way of his close friend. So each of you look carefully to whom you take as your close friend.**}

> Just as it was said by the early poet [25]

>> Do not ask about a person directly,

>>> but inquire as to his companions,

>> As every person has those associates he is guided by.

> So when you enter into the companionship of the people, do so with the best of them. Do not stand with the ruined one, so that you are also ruined through his faults. Know that in reference to newly invented matters in the religion which someone may be upon which they do not openly show at this time, then they will eventually come out and be shown at some later time, and if they conceal it to one individual they will show it to some others. And we seek refuge in Allaah from the character of the people of hypocrisy and innovation, from their astray behaviors and their aspects of misguidance."

---

[23] Fath al-Raheem al-Wadood pg. 59
[24] al-Aqd al-Mundheed al-Jadeed Fee al-Ijaabat Alaa Masaa'il Fee Fiqh wal- Manaahij wa at-Tawheed pg 44
[25] a reference to 'Adee Ibn Zayd as mentioned my Imaam at-Tabaree in his tafseer, and one of the manuscript verifiers of our age Ahmad Shaakir, may Allaah have mercy upon them both.

Strengthen Yourself with Two Important Matters: Dhikr & Supplications

Sheikh Rabee'a Ibn Haadee was asked the following question about becoming steadfast,[26]

"This question is based upon the fact that you are from our senior scholars in both knowledge and age. What are the most important causes that lead the student of knowledge who strives upon the methodology of the first three generations of believers to be steadfast upon this path? We ask you due to your experience in dealing with a number of students over the years, your working with those who have proceeded upon this methodology, and your having encountered both those who were steadfast as well as those who unfortunately deviated and went astray- those who no longer stand upon what our righteous predecessors stood upon.

So what are those important causes which assist the student of knowledge to become steadfast upon this path of the Salaf, and to remain so despite the many trials we face? What is your cherished advice in light of your extensive experience and that which you have observed in this issue, may Allaah bless you?

Sheikh Rabee'a replied: In the name of Allaah. From the most significant causes is that an individual be aware and realize that he is in significant and in constant need of Allaah. That he indeed stands in need of Him in every moment of his life. Therefore he should ask Allaah to make him steadfast, and supplicate to Allaah with that which the Messenger of Allaah, upon him be Allaah's praise and salutations, taught us: **{ Oh Turner of the Hearts, make my heart steadfast upon Your religion. }** *The Companions said to him, "Oh Messenger of Allaah, you make this supplication very often. Are you afraid for us?" He replied,* **{ Indeed, as the hearts of the people are between the two fingers from the fingers of the Most Merciful and He turns then as He wills.}** *As such the worshipper of Allaah must take notice of himself, and seek the protection of Allaah, the Blessed and the Most High. He should not be deluded and deceived by the knowledge that he possesses. As conceit and vanity due to one's knowledge and one's extensive study will push him into suffering and misfortune. And we seek refuge with Allaah, and ask that we be made far from every misfortune. This is what happened to La'am Ibn Babura' and befalls many from among the people.*

From such individuals in our age is "Al-Qaasemee". He possessed intelligence and knowledge, and had clear intellectual brilliance but he became infatuated and dazzled by himself. But this "Al-Qaasemee" eventually came to apostate from Islaam altogether! And we seek refuge in Allaah! He used to produce writings which perhaps surpassed those of Ibn Taymeeyah in their brilliance, along with his memorization and his comprehension. But his vanity and conceit would openly reveal themselves within the pages that he composed. Therefore it is required that the Muslim seek protection in Allaah, the Blessed and the Most High, to make him steadfast.

Take those affirmed causes for steadfastness, meaning this supplication we have mentioned, and the contemplation of the Book of Allaah and the Sunnah of the Messenger of Allaah, may Allaah's praise and salutations be upon him. Honor the early ones our, forefathers, and honor the scholars, proceeding upon everything similar to this, may Allaah bless you all. These will be from the causes of remaining steadfast, if Allaah so wills..."

---

[26] From a transcribe lecture 'Nothing Will Liberate Palestine Except that Which Liberated it The First Time' taken from Sahab.net

Similarly Sheikh Muqbil ibn Haadee, may Allaah have mercy upon him, was asked,[27]

> *Question: How can one seeking knowledge become someone who is not focused upon worldly material benefits and gains, someone who is made humble by his knowledge and not arrogant due to it, and with his heart becoming attached to Allaah, the Most High?*
>
> *Answer: It is necessary that the one seeking knowledge be aware of his actual condition, truly understanding his clear weakness, inability, and poverty in front of Allaah, the Most Perfect and the Most High. Additionally, he should read from the account of the life history of the Prophet, may the praise and salutation of Allaah be upon him and his household, and those examples of his humbleness. Once a Bedouin Arab came to him and grabbed his cloak until it pulled very tightly marking his side and said to him,* "**Oh Muhammad give something to me, as you have not given me anything from your wealth or the wealth of your father!**" *So the Prophet, may the praise and salutation of Allaah be upon him and his household, gave to him some wealth. Then he, may the praise and salutation of Allaah be upon him and his household, said,* **{No one humbles himself except that Allaah raises and elevates him.}**
>
> *Therefore reading the life history of the Prophet, may the praise and salutation of Allaah be upon him and his household, and the life histories of the Companions will help and assist you in developing humbleness. This is along with truly knowing your actual condition, and what you have of general weakness and inability without Allaah. Always being aware that you are susceptible to diseases as well as other kinds of afflictions. All of this will push you to turn and seek success in this from Allaah, the Most Perfect and the Most High.*"

For the one who gives importance to Tawheed in his life, and directs his worship to Allaah alone, both the remembrance of Allaah and supplication are essential ingredients to our successfully being able to learn beneficial knowledge and put forth righteous deeds upon that knowledge. Certainly it is something the guided Muslims have given importance and focus in every century. Ibn Rajab, may Allaah have mercy upon him, mentioned in that work of tafseer compiled from his explanation of verses of the Qur'aan that al-Hasan al-Basree, from the Salaf, said,[28]

> "*Frequently seek the forgiveness of Allaah in your homes, at your tables, upon your lanes and roads, and in your sittings and gatherings. As you do not know when the forgiveness from Allaah may descend upon you.*"

Similarly Ibn al-Qayyim, may Allaah have mercy upon him, said,[29]

> "*The heart is like the earth it becomes dry and hardens if it lacks the worship of Allaah alone, His love, understanding Him, and the lack of remembering Him, and supplicating to Him.*"

---

[27] Tuhfat al-Mujeeb Question 132
[28] Tafseer Ibn Rajab vol. 1 page 150
[29] al-Israar al-Salah, page 69

Likewise Sheikh Zayd Ibn Muhammad al-Madkhalee, may Allaah have mercy upon him, from our age, said,[30]

"It is recommended for you to maintain and always consistently perform the affirmed remembrances specific to the morning and evenings, whether you are sick or in good health. As within this is tremendous good. Firstly, this is because doing so is from the ways to gain closeness to Allaah as it is one of the valid practices of dhikr.

Secondly, perhaps through performing these remembrances Allaah may bless and benefit you, and upon that initial benefit further grant you an immediate healing and rectification that brings goodness and benefits any Muslim man or any Muslim woman."

Sheikh Saaleh al-Fauzaan, may Allaah preserve him, was asked, [31]

Question: It is the habit of some people, whenever they intend to do anything from their everyday matters they say: "Bismillah." Is this practice something which has a basis in Islaam or is it something blameworthy?

Answer: This is dhikr or the remembrance of Allaah, the Most Exalted, the Most Magnificent. Moreover, saying the phrase, "Bismillah." is only strengthening yourself through the remembrance of Allaah, the Most Perfect and the Most High. As such this is something supported by the Sharee'ah, except in the situation where a person in entering a place to use the bathroom to relieve themselves. In this case, do not mention Allaah's name until you have left that area. When there you only remember Him within your heart, without pronouncing it upon your tongue."

Closing advice

Sheikh Muhammad Ibn Haadee al-Madkhalee, may Allaah preserve him, "**Question: We would like advice for those who were upon the methodology of the Salaf.** He replied, [32]

"The advices to be given are many, but that which I advise the one who understands the methodology of the Salaf is that he praises Allaah first and foremost.

Since the one who has come to comprehend the truth, it is upon him to praise Allaah, the Most Exalted, the Most Magnificent, firstly. As Allaah mentions ❖**..and they will say: "All the praises and thanks be to Allaah, Who has guided us to this, never could we have found guidance, were it not that Allaah had guided us!**❖-(*Surah Al-A'raaf: 43). That understanding is guidance from Allaah, the Most Perfect and the Most High, and it is a tremendous blessing. Therefore is upon you to praise and thank Him for guiding you.*

Secondly, it is upon you to seek steadfastness upon the truth after you have come to understand it. So ask Allaah, the Most Exalted, the Most Magnificent, to make you steadfast upon it. Thirdly, that you seek out the specific means, to bring this about for you.

The first of which is that knowledge which will assist you in this.

---

[30] ash-Sharooq Alaa al-Farooq: page 329
[31] Taken from the sheikh's website http://www.alfawzan.af.org.sa/node/16277
[32] From the lecture: The fifth meeting from the series of meeting with Students of Knowledge with the esteemed Sheikh Muhammad Ibn Haadee al-Madkhalee held on the 11th of Rabee'a ath-Thaanee, 1435

The second of them is the companionship of the people of knowledge and the people of goodness and rectification, or upon the straight way, as you will be strengthened by them, by Allaah's permission, and you will increase in benefit through them."

Sheikh Saaleh Ibn Fauzaan, may Allaah preserve him also reminds us,[33]

"Do not be allured by the good efforts you have been able to put forth, rather it is for you to continue to produce good actions, and hope that Allaah makes you from among those who are ultimately successful."

In one of his well-known works Imaam al-Aajuree, may Allaah have mercy upon him, one of the notable scholars of the fourth century, in his book, "The Strangers", wrote:

"If the intelligent believer, the one whom Allaah, the Most High, Most Exalted, has given understanding of the religion and insight into his own weaknesses, has made clear to him what the general people are actually upon, has granted him the understanding to distinguish between the truth and falsehood, and between what is good and what is repulsive, and between the harmful and that which benefits, and given him the knowledge of which of these matters he is truly upon, if he aims for success, then he holds himself firm upon acting according to the truth in the midst of those who are ignorant of the truth.

As the majority of the people simply adhere to their desires. They do not show any concern for the shortcomings in their practice of the religion even if their evil deeds are openly presented to them. Because if they were to look closely at those who differ from them in their misguided ways, then this would in fact weigh heavily upon them, hating this, as it would surely trouble them severely, so they point out the others' shortcoming or weaknesses. Even one's family will become discontent with him, and his own brothers will put pressure on him. They will treat him in a way which no one wishes to be treated. This is because the people who adhere to their desires are not upon the proper way of dealing with someone with whom they differ.

He that believer thus becomes like a stranger among his contemporaries and companions due to the spread of corruption in one's companionship and association among the people; a stranger in all of his worldly affairs as well as those of the Hereafter."

So, I offer my brothers and sisters what I hope will be a strengthening reminder and encouragement to remain firm upon the beliefs and guidance of Sunnah even when around you the people upon the Sunnah are few. As this situation is not something new but was also the situation of many believers in the past.

The eminent scholar from the first generations, and Imaam of the people of ash-Shaam in his time, al-Awzaaa'ee, may Allaah have mercy upon him, said about Ataa' who was a well-known scholar from the generation of the Successors, [34]

"'Ataa' Ibn Abee Rabaah died, and on the day he died and he would be someone considered to be from the most pleasing of the people of the earth. Yet when one looked at the size of his gathering of knowledge there would only be eight or nine people."

---

[33] Sharh al-Manthumatul- Haa'eyah, pg. 57
[34] Siyaar 'Alaam an-Nubalaa', vol.5 page 75

He also, may Allaah have mercy upon him, said,[35]

"Hold firmly to the transmitted narrations of the Salaf, even if you are rejected by the people."

In closing, I again say, as our dear and noble sheikh the guiding scholar Sheikh Ahmad Ibn Yahya an-Najmee, may Allaah have mercy upon him, has stated in his introduction to the book *'Al-Fataawa al-Jaleeyah'* part 2,

"I do not free myself from committing mistakes in this work, as indeed no one is free of this. And I hope from the noble reader that if he encounters something that it is obligatory to warn about that they should draw my attention to that as someone whom indeed I would thank, and that they inform me of that mistake, clarifying to me what exactly is the mistake in what was stated and how it conflicts with Sharee'ah evidences. As the brother who advises me will find me as one who submits and yields to the truth, turning towards it.

That which I do request from the reader is that they offer supplications for me in my absence. As indeed I am in need of such supplications, that Allaah forgive my sins, and that He give me insight into my shortcomings, and that He bless me with steadfastness upon the truth until I meet him as one clinging even to the very edges of the Sunnah, having proceeded upon the straight methodology and way, and having placed my reliance upon the Most Gracious, the Most Merciful."

That which is correct from my efforts as a student is from the guidance of Allaah and only through His mercy, and that which is deficient is only from myself and Shaytaan, the accursed enemy of those who believe.

May the praise and salutations of Allaah be upon the Messenger of Allaah, his household, his Companions, and all those who follow his guidance until the Day of Judgement. All praise is due to Allaah alone, Lord of all the worlds.

Abu Sukhailah Khalil Ibn-Abelahyi
Taalib al-Ilm Educational Resources
the 1st of Jumaadi al-Awwal, 1438
(Corresponding to January 27th, 2017)

---

[35] Narrated by Imaam al-Ajuuree in ash-Sharee'ah with a sound chain of narration.

Day 01: The Importance Of Asking To Be Guided In What You Say & Do

TEXT FROM INTRODUCTION OF AL-IBAANAH AL-SUGHRAH:

Imaam Ibn Battah, may Allaah have mercy upon him, said,

"We ask Allaah to guide us to sound correct speech and righteous actions and deeds."

SOURCE OF THIS TEXT OR NARRATION:

This is a statement of the compiler of this work: Abu 'Abdullah Ubayd'Allaah Ibn Muhammad Ibn Muhammad Ibn Hamdan Ibn Battah al-Ukbaree, may Allaah have mercy upon him.

Explanation by Sheikh 'Abdul-'Azeez Ibn 'Abdullah ar-Raajhee

We ask Allaah for this, meaning we ask Him for success in this. We supplicate to Allaah to successfully guide us to what is corrective, from our statements and what is righteous in our actions. This supplication is stated after the author, may Allaah have mercy upon him, has praised and glorified Allaah, the Most Glorified and the Most Exalted, and after he supplicated for Allaah's praise and salutations to be upon His Prophet, may Allaah's praise and salutations be upon him. He asks Allaah, the Most Glorified and the Most Exalted, and he implores Him supplicating to Him for success. We ask for, and seek to be granted success, meaning we are asking Allaah to bless us with success. The one who desires success is asking to be granted that success. And in this we are asking for success in what matter? We are asking for success to be sound and correct in our statements and that we are able to put forward righteous deeds and actions. As both of these matters, the first and the second together, are the path and the way to being content and happy.

Meaning that the one whom Allaah grants such success in being correct in his statements and in putting forth righteous deeds, then this is the one who is happy and contented. His actions will be righteous, and righteous actions have a meaning. That they are righteous means that it is something done purely for the sake of Allaah's face alone, as well as in conformance to Allaah's Sharee'ah and His revealed religion. As such, if an action is done purely for Allaah sake, and it conforms with the Sharee'ah, then that is a righteous deed or endeavor which is accepted by Allaah. But as for that action which is not done sincerely for Allaah sake, then this means that within one's intention there is a portion of associating something other than Allaah in that action. In relation to these two essential elements of anything we do, if one's sincerity is deficient or lacking, then the associating others with Allaah in worship appears related to it. Similarly, if one's is adherence to the Sharee'ah is deficient or lacking then innovation in the religion appears related to it.

So we ask Allaah, we ask Allaah for success. We ask Allaah to make successful in putting forth correct sound speech and statements, so that our words are correct, and also that our deeds are righteous, as this is the path of contentment. The one who Allaah grants success in making correct statements and putting forth righteous deeds, is from those who have been granted success and those who have been guided to contentment. Yes, we ask Allaah for success in both having sound deeds and statements as well as putting forth righteous actions.

DAY - 01

POINTS OF BENEFIT

1. A person who is blessed with knowledge understands what matters or goals are truly worthy of striving for and which are not.

2. A person who is blessed with knowledge understands that objectives and goals must be worked towards through the specific causes of achieving them.

3. The Muslims should seek Allaah's assistance in having both inward sincerity of their heart and outward conformity to the guidance of Islaam in what their tongue and limbs say and do.

4. From the fundamental causes of being successful is turning to the guidance that Allaah has sent to us, and applying it inwardly and outwardly.

5. From the fundamental causes of being successful is supplicating and asking Allaah for the different aspects of success.

6. Success consists of two aspects, an internal aspect of understanding the truth and an external aspect of acting upon the truth.

7. The first foundation of true success in every matter is sincerity of intention for Allaah alone.

8. The second foundation of true success in every matter is that your actions conform to the guidance of the Sharee'ah.

9. If an individual undertakes an action in the proper way, but lacks sincerity and purity of intention, then the sin of associating others with Allaah causes it to be corrupted and not accepted by Allaah

10. If an individual engages in an action with sincerity of intention, but performs it in a new manner that conflicts with the guidance of the Sharee'ah, then the sin of innovation in the religion causes it to be corrupted, and not accepted by Allaah.

11. Those who have sincere and pure intentions, correct statements, and correct actions in whatever they do, will proceed upon the path of contentment and success in this world and the next.

LEVEL 1: TEST YOUR UNDERSTANDING:

TRUE & FALSE QUESTIONS

[Circle the correct letter for each individual sentence from today's content.]

01. The main thing to consider when doing something is to make sure you have a good intention. [T / F]

02. It is important to ask Allaah to guide us to every matter that will make us successful as a Muslim. [T / F]

03. It is permissible to do acts of worship in a unique and new way as long as you are sincere and doing so purely for Allaah's sake. [T / F]

FILL IN THE BLANK QUESTIONS

[Enter the correct individual words to complete the sentences from today's content.]

04. Outward success is found if we are _____ in our statements and we put forward _____ actions.

05. If our deeds are lacking in _____ then this is a type of associating others with _____.

06. If our deeds are lacking in adherence to the _____ and we follow a new method of worshiping, then this is a type of _____ in the religion.

LEVEL 2: INTERACTIVE QUESTIONS & EXERCISES

COMPREHENSIVE UNDERSTANDING QUESTIONS

[In a study group or circle of learning with other students, these questions can be answered fully or partially by one student from the lesson, with another student completing the answer to the same question, by giving a comparable but different which is also correct.]

07. Why is it important for someone to seek Allaah's assistance in both adhering to the Sunnah and having sincerity of intention for Allaah alone, and not just one?

08. Give examples of three invalid intentions which a person may intend in his heart when doing an outwardly good action.

09. Give examples of three acts of worship which are done by Muslims sincerely, but which go against the revealed guidance of the Sharee'ah.

Day 02: The Clear Guidance Of The Final Messenger Is For All Humanity

NARRATION FROM AL-IBAANAH AL-SUGHRAH:

He, the Prophet, may Allaah's praise and salutations be upon him, said, *{By Allaah, if Moosa and 'Isaa were alive today, their position would be to follow me in the guidance I've been given.}*

Likewise in the narration previously mentioned it says: *{Indeed I have come to you with a clear white way, and by Allaah if Moosa and 'Isaa were to hear of me, their only choice would be to follow me.}*

AUTHENTICITY & SOURCE OF THESE TEXTS OR NARRATIONS:

Authentic: This was narrated in the Musnad of Imaam Ahmad vol. 3: no. 387 Sunan ad-Daarimee : Introduction - no. 435

Explanation by Sheikh 'Abdul-'Azeez Ibn 'Abdullah ar-Raajhee

He, may Allaah's praise and salutations be upon him, said, *{ By Allaah, if Musaa and 'Isaa were alive today, their position would be to follow me in the guidance I've been given.}* Likewise in the narration previously mentioned it says: *{Indeed I have come to you with a clear white way, and by Allaah if Musaa and 'Isaa were to hear, they only choice would be to follow me.}* This narration is authentic. Allaah has taken a covenant from every prophet that if Muhammad is sent, when they are still alive as a prophet that they would follow him and the guidance given to him specifically. Every prophet stands under this covenant and agreement that if Muhammad. upon him be Allaah's praise and salutations, comes forth and that prophet is still alive that they would follow him and his revealed guidance.

﴾And remember when Allaah took a covenant from those who were given the Scripture (Jews and Christians) to make it (the news of the coming of Prophet Muhammad and the religious knowledge) known and clear to mankind, and not to hide it,﴿-(Surah Aal-Imraan: 187) Allaah, the Most High, says, *﴾And remember when Allaah took the Covenant of the Prophets, saying: "Take whatever I gave you from the Book and Hikmah (understanding of the Laws of Allaah, etc.), and afterwards there will come to you a Messenger (Muhammad) confirming what is with you; you must, then, believe in him and help him." Allaah said: "Do you agree to it and will you take up My Covenant which I conclude with you?" They said: "We agree." He said: "Then bear witness; and I am with you among the witnesses for this.". Then whoever turns away after this, they are the Faasiqoon (rebellious: those who turn away from Allaah's Obedience)﴿*-(Surah Aal-Imraan: 81-82)

Within this verse there is evidence that Allaah has taken a covenant from every prophet that they believe in Muhammad, may the praise and salutations of Allaah be upon him. For this reason the Prophet, may the praise and salutations of Allaah be upon him, said, *{By Allaah, if Musaa and 'Isaa were alive today, their position would be to follow me in the guidance I've been given.}* Moreover when 'Isaa, upon him be Allaah's praise and salutations, does descend at the end of our time here on earth, certainly he would be considered as an individual member of the Ummah of Muhammad, and will rule by its revealed Sharee'ah. There are specific rulings of the Sharee'ah that will and when he defends, such as the taking of jizyah from the Christians and Jews. Generally in the Sharee'ah the jizyah is something expected from them. But when 'Isaa descends the jizyah will no longer be accepted from them. At the time of his descent this token payment would no longer be accepted from them. At that time, their choices will be to either accept Islaam or continue to fight against the Muslims.

Those Christians and Jews who live in a nation or territories governed by the Sharee'ah, what are the options available to them at present? They have the choice is between embracing Islaam, paying jizyah, or continuing to fight against the Muslims. But at the time when 'Isaa descends, one of these options will no longer be valid; the option of jizyah, will not be offered by him. They will have the option of embracing Islaam or continuing to fight against the Muslims in those lands and territories. The period of taking jizyah would have ended, having ended by the decent and return of 'Isaa. This is the ruling of the Sharee'ah, the Sharee'ah of the Prophet, may the praise and salutations of Allaah be upon him.

So when 'Isaa descends and returns back to earth he will judge and rule by the Sharee'ah of Muhammad, may the praise and salutations of Allaah be upon him, and he will be an be considered an individual from the members of the Ummah of Muhammad. He will then be the best of the Ummah, and the one with the most merit among the Muslims, after its prophet. Meaning by this, if it was asked at that time, who is the best from the Ummah of Muhammad? Who is the one who is higher in rank and merit then Abu Bakr according to the consensus of the Muslims? Who is that person from amongst the Muslims? It will be 'Isaa, upon him be Allaah's praise and salutations, as he is higher in rank and merit then Abu Bakr according to the consensus of the Muslims. He will be an individual from the ranks of this Ummah. He is a prophet, but will be from this Ummah at that time.

In addition, it is said by some of the scholars, that he is also considered a Companion. This is because he met the Prophet, may Allaah's praise and salutations be upon him, on the night that the Prophet ascended alive to heaven. So, he is a Companion, he is a prophet, and he is an individual from among the members of the Muslim Ummah. Additionally he is considered higher in rank and merit than Abu Bakr according to the consensus of the Muslims. He is the best of the people from amongst the Muslim Ummah after its own Prophet. So if it is said or asked, who is better than Abu Bakr according to the consensus of the Muslims? The answer is that the individual from the Ummah of Muhammad who is better than Abu Bakr according to the consensus of the Muslims is: 'Isaa. Then Abu Bakr, second to him in distinguished merit according to the consensus of the Muslims. This is because 'Isaa is a prophet, and Abu Bakr is the best of the Muslims after the prophets. So yes, 'Isaa is a prophet, but he is also from this Ummah, as he will descend and be part of it as has been narrated.

POINTS OF BENEFIT

1. Allaah has completed the guidance He sent to humanity through the revelation that was sent down to the Prophet Muhammad, may the praise and salutations of Allaah be upon him.

2. Every prophet had a covenant with Allaah that if the Prophet Muhammad, may the praise and salutations of Allaah be upon him, was sent while they were living, they would follow him and the guidance sent to him.

3. The revealed guidance given to the Prophet Muhammad, may the praise and salutations of Allaah be upon him, confirms, abrogates, and completes the revealed guidance given to all the previous prophets and messengers.

4. The acceptance of jizyah by the Christian and Jewish citizens of those nations which are guided by Islaam, is an established aspect of the Sharee'ah, until the descent of the prophet 'Isaa.

5. When the prophet 'Isaa, upon him be Allaah's praise and salutations, descends in the later times, he will be a member of the Muslim Ummah.

6. When the prophet 'Isaa, upon him be Allaah's praise and salutations, descends in the later times, he will be considered the best of the Muslim Ummah, after its own prophet and messenger, Muhammad.

7. The prophets of Allaah have the highest rank and position among all of humanity

8. The best of the general Muslims in rank and merit from this Ummah is Abu Bakr as-Siddeeq, may Allaah be pleased with him.

DAY - 02

LEVEL 1: TEST YOUR UNDERSTANDING:

TRUE & FALSE QUESTIONS

[Circle the correct letter for each individual sentence from today's content.]

01. The previous prophets did not know about the coming of the Prophet Muhammad. [T / F]

02. All the previous revealed guidance of Allaah has been completed in the guidance given to the prophet Mohammed. [T / F]

03. The righteous Muslims, as worshipers of Allaah, are all equal in rank and merit. [T / F]

FILL IN THE BLANK QUESTIONS

[Enter the correct individual words to complete the sentences from today's content.]

04. Every previous prophet had a _____ with Allaah about the coming of the Prophet Muhammad.

05. The prophet _____ will descend in the later times and judge according to the _____ .

06. _____ was the best of those within the Muslim Ummah who was not a _____ .

LEVEL 2: INTERACTIVE QUESTIONS & EXERCISES

COMPREHENSIVE UNDERSTANDING QUESTIONS

[In a study group or circle of learning with other students, these questions can be answered fully or partially by one student from the lesson, with another student completing the answer to the same question, by giving a comparable but different which is also correct.]

07. What is a possible benefit of knowing the different ranks and positions of excellence of those who are part of the Muslim Ummah?

08. Why is it important to understand that Islaam completes and abrogates the guidance given to the previous prophets and messengers?

09. Mention any two matters that the Muslims have agreed upon by consensus.

Day 03: There Is A Single Straight Path Surrounded By Other False Paths

NARRATION FROM AL-IBAANAH AL-SUGHRAH:

Ibn Masood,[1] may Allaah's be pleased with him, said:

One day the Messenger of Allaah, may Allaah's praise and salutations be upon him, drew for us a line and said, *{ "This is the path of Allaah." Then he drew other lines to the left of that and to the right of it and said, "These are other paths. Upon each one of them there is a Shaytaan inviting and calling to it."*

Then he recited the verse, " And verily, this is my Straight Path, so follow it, and follow not other paths, for they will separate you away from His Path. –(Surah Al-An'am:153).} Meaning those lines which were to the right and left of the first line."

AUTHENTICITY & SOURCE OF THIS TEXT OR NARRATION:

Authentic: This was narrated by an-Nasaa'ee, ad-Daarimee, and in the Musnad of Imaam Ahmad, . It was also narrated by Muhammad Ibn Nasir al-Maroozee in his work as-Sunnah. This author also narrated it in his related book al-Ibaanah al-Kubraa from a number of different routes of transmission.

---

[1] A Companion of the Messenger of Allaah, may the praise and salutations of Allaah be upon him

Explanation by Sheikh 'Abdul-'Azeez Ibn 'Abdullah ar-Raajhee

Yes, this hadeeth narration is authentically transmitted on the authority of Ibn Mas'ood, may Allaah be pleased with him, where he said, *{One day the Messenger of Allaah, may Allaah's praise and salutations be upon him, drew for us a straight line" ..... and He said" This is the path of Allaah." Then he drew other lines to the left of that and to the right of it and said, "These are other paths. Upon each one of them there is a Shaytaan inviting and calling to it. Then he recited the verse, ❴And verily, this is my Straight Path, so follow it, and follow not other paths, for they will separate you away from His Path.❵-(Surah Al-An'am:153).}* [2]

This hadeeth narration contains an exhortation and urging to stick firmly to the straight path. And that is what comes from the Book of Allaah and the Sunnah of His Messenger, may Allaah's praise and salutations be upon him, that is the path of Allaah. And what is meant by the path of Allaah, is the rope of Allaah and his religion. It means what Allaah has commanded in His Book, or what his Messenger has commanded, may Allaah's praise and salutations be upon him, and it means to adhere to the Sunnah.

So it is an encouragement and urging to adhere to the Sunnah, and to be warned away from innovation in the religion and sins and transgressions. As those lines which diverted away on the left and right, these are the paths of the people of misguidance, the paths of the people of sins, and the people of innovation. Yes, this hadeeth contains a warning from innovation as well as sin, along with an encouragement to adhere to the Sunnah, and to stand steadfastly upon the Sharee'ah of Allaah and his religion.

---

[2] Saheeh al-Bukhaaree: 6417, at-Tirmidhee: 2454, Ibn Maajah: 4231, az-Zuhd: 4231, Ahmad, vol. 1/385, ad-Daaremee: 2729

POINTS OF BENEFIT

1. The straight path of Islaam is one single path, not multiple paths.
2. The paths of misguidance are numerous, and have a Shaytaan calling to that specific way of misguidance.
3. Any path other than the straight path of Islaam, is sinful or innovative misguidance.
4. Allaah has commanded the believers to follow and remain upon the single revealed way of Islaam.
5. Allaah has warned the believers that following the paths of misguidance will take them away from the path of Islaam.
6. It is not possible to both follow the straight path of Islaam, and follow other ways and paths.
7. It is important to understand the characteristics of the straight path, and the characteristics of the paths of misguidance.
8. It is important to work and struggle to recognize and follow the single straight path of Islaam.
9. It is important to work and struggle to recognize and distance yourself from the many paths of misguidance.
10. To follow the straight path of Islaam means to adhere to the commands of Allaah found within the Qur'aan and Sunnah.
11. Following the straight path of Islaam means to adhere to the Sunnah and to stay away from innovations.

LEVEL 1: TEST YOUR UNDERSTANDING:

TRUE & FALSE QUESTIONS

[Circle the correct letter for each individual sentence from today's content.]

01. It is permissible to follow any path or religion as long as your intention is to please Allaah. [T / F]
02. Just as there are many ways of misguidance, there are many paths upon the truth and guidance. [T / F]
03. Each path of misguidance has a Shaytaan inviting to it and making it appealing to people. [T / F]

FILL IN THE BLANK QUESTIONS

[Enter the correct individual words to complete the sentences from today's content.]

04. There is a single _____ path and many paths of _____ .
05. Every path of misguidance has a _____ upon it _____ people to it.
06. Both _____ and _____ are part of the paths of misguidance.

LEVEL 2: INTERACTIVE QUESTIONS & EXERCISES

COMPREHENSIVE UNDERSTANDING QUESTIONS

[In a study group or circle of learning with other students, these questions can be answered fully or partially by one student from the lesson, with another student completing the answer to the same question, by giving a comparable but different which is also correct.]

07. What command and what prohibition is found within the mentioned verse in Surah Al-An'am? Give a practical everyday example of how someone may properly follow the command, and properly adhere to the prohibition mentioned.
08. Name two paths of misguidance and briefly describe why some people might believe that they are good to follow.
09. What are two possible important means of helping a Muslim understand what the straight path is, and proceed steadfastly upon it.

Day 04: Every Ummah Divided But Those Upon The Truth Remain

NARRATION FROM al-IBAANAH al-SUGHRAH:

He, the Messenger, may Allaah's praise and salutations be upon him, said:

{The ummah of the Jews divided into seventy two different sects. And my Ummah will divide into seventy-three sects, and there is one sect that is saved, with seventy-two who will enter the Hellfire.}

AUTHENTICITY & SOURCE OF THIS TEXT OR NARRATION:

Authentic: Sheikh ar-Raajhee states, "Yes, this hadeeth narration, as was mentioned by the modern verifier of the narrations found within this work, is narrated by Abu Dawood, at-Tirmidhee, al-Haakim, and al-Aajuree in his work ash-Sharee'ah. Within its chain of narration is in narrator whose reliability has been criticized, Abdur-Rahman Ibn Ziyaad al-Afreeqee, But this narration has been transmitted through numerous chains of transmission. As such its collective chains of narration are of the strength that is acceptable."

Explanation by Sheikh 'Abdul-'Azeez Ibn 'Abdullah ar-Raajhee

This hadeeth narration has been relied upon by the people of knowledge and the leading scholars and then accepted. So as we mentioned the strength of its different supporting chains of narration are acceptable, and the scholars have accepted and relied upon it. They have stated regarding its meaning that: These seventy-three sects within the Ummah are sects which all have some form of innovation, and have deviated to different degrees, with the exception of one of them. That being the people who adhere to the Sunnah and remain with the Jamaa'ah of Muslims united upon the truth. For this reason the scholars say that the Jahmeeyah, the Raafidhah, the Qadareeyah, and the extremely deviant groups, are in fact considered outside of the boundaries of these seventy-two misguided sects, due to being placed outside these limits due to their major disbelief and extreme misguidance which takes them outside Islaam.

Whereas the other seventy-two sects are from the sects that have innovated within Islaam as Muslims, and sects that have deviated from guidance. But they are not considered disbelievers according to what is correct. It is for this reason that the scholars do not consider the sect of the Jahmeeyah from among the seventy-two misguided sects. They say: this sect are considered disbelievers due to their major disbelief. Similarly, they make the same assessment of the sect of the extreme Qadareeyah who deny aspects of Allaah's knowledge, as well as the sect of the Raafidhah. They state regarding them, they are not to be considered from the seventy-two misguided sects. This hadeeth narration explains that this Muslim Ummah would divide into sects, all together seventy-three sects. It indicates that all of them would be under the threat of punishment in Hellfire except for the single saved sect. That sect being those people who adhere to the Sunnah and remain with the Jamaa'ah of Muslims united upon the truth.

It is mentioned in another hadeeth narration that the Prophet, may Allaah's praise and salutations be upon him, was asked about who were the saved sect. To this he replied, {*...Those who are upon what I and my Companions are upon today.*} In the wording of one of those additional narrations it states that they, {*...are the Jamaa'ah*}. They are those Muslims who adhere to the Sunnah and remain with the Jamaa'ah of Muslims united upon the truth, from the noble Companions, the successors to the Companions, and the leading scholars who followed them in their way in steadfastness upon the religion of Allaah and his Sharee'ah. Those who followed them in acting according to the guidance of the Book of Allaah and His Messenger, may the praise and salutations of Allaah be upon him, and adhered to the believers way, they are those who are saved.

Whereas those who turned away from the path of truth, and deviated away from the clear way, they are the misguided sects of destruction. This hadeeth narration and those that are similar to it in meaning, guide us to two specific beneficial understandings. The first point of benefit: Is that the knowledge of what would come in the future which is contained with these narrations is a clear sign or indication of the truth of the prophethood of our Messenger. Meaning that fact that these different sects would eventually appear among the Muslims. That is exactly what occurred, and so is a sign from among the signs of the validity of the prophethood of our Messenger. It is sign of the truthfulness of our Prophet, may Allaah's praise and salutations be upon him, and that he is a messenger from Allaah, due to the fact that this future event occurred just as he informed us it would occur.

The second benefit to be taken from them is the importance of the warning against the sects and groups upon innovation in the religion, those innovating sects. That an individual be warned himself against these sects, and that he should hold firmly to the Sunnah and the Jamaa'ah of Muslims remaining upon the truth, so that he may be part of that saved sect which the prophet of Allaah spoke of and described. So this hadeeth narration, brings us these two points of beneficial understanding.

Again, the first benefit is that these misguided sects must eventually appear among the Muslims. This is from the signs which affirms the truthfulness of the Prophet, may Allaah's praise and salutations be upon him, indicating that he was indeed a Messenger of Allaah, and his informing us of what would occur is a sign from the signs of his prophethood.

The second benefit, is that a Muslim should be warned from these misguided sects, and stay far from the behaviors and methods of the innovated paths that they proceed upon, while holding to the behavior and methods of the believers way made clear in the first generations of Islaam. And that a person should struggle and be diligent to ensure that they are from the saved sect. Meaning those Muslims hold firmly to the Sunnah and the Jamaa'ah of Muslims remaining upon the truth, and those who hold firmly to the Book and the Sunnah, and proceed steadfastly upon the clear way, and do not deviate from the straight path. Certainly Allaah has said, ❄*And verily, this is my Straight Path, so follow it, and follow not other paths, for they will separate you away from His Path. This He has ordained for you that you may become from the pious.*❄-(Surah Al-An'am: 153)

POINTS OF BENEFIT

1. Allaah informed the Prophet Muhammad, may the praise and salutations of Allaah be upon him, of the events which would happen to the Muslim Ummah until the Day of Judgment.

2. The fact that the Muslim Ummah divided just as the Prophet himself informed us is a sign of the truthfulness of his prophethood.

3. The Muslim Ummah is composed of seventy-three sects, all of them will enter Hellfire except for one.

4. The seventy-two misguided sects all have some form of innovation, and have deviated from the Sunnah to different degrees.

5. The people from the seventy-two misguided sects stand under the threat of punishment in Hellfire due to their misguidance.

6. The seventy-two misguided sects are considered within the Muslim Ummah and are considered to be Muslims, despite their deviation in some matters of the religion.

7. There are other extreme sects who are considered outside the Muslim Ummah and not Muslims, due to their significant deviation reaching the level of major disbelief in Islaam.

8. From the extreme sects who were not considered Muslims are the Jahmeeyah, the Raafidhah, and the extreme Qadareeyah.

9. It is important to warn against those sects and groups who call the Muslims to accept and practice innovation in Islaam.

10. The single saved sect is composed of those who adhere to the Sunnah and remain with the Jamaa'ah of Muslims upon the original guidance of Islaam.

11. The single saved sect is composed of those who remain upon the original Islaam of the Prophet Muhammad and his Companions.

12. The single saved sect is found in every age and century from those Muslims who followed those who followed the Companions, just as the Companions followed the Messenger of Allaah, may the praise and salutations of Allaah be upon him.

13. The believers' way, which is mentioned in the Qur'aan, is that of the saved sect who are first and foremost the Companions of the messenger of Allaah.

14. The methodology and characteristics of the straight path which is the 'believers' way' was made clear by the first generations of Islaam.

DAY - 04

LEVEL 1: TEST YOUR UNDERSTANDING:

TRUE & FALSE QUESTIONS

[Circle the correct letter for each individual sentence from today's content.]

01. There are many sects found within the history of the Muslim [T / F] Ummah and they are all considered Muslims.

02. The scholars have identified and distinguished the various sects [T / F] among the Muslims.

03. The saved sect is everyone who says they are Muslim, and [T / F] claims their religion is Islaam.

FILL IN THE BLANK QUESTIONS

[Enter the correct individual words to complete the sentences from today's content.]

04. The seventy-two astray sects within the Ummah all have some form of _____.

05. Due to major disbelief the extremely deviant sects such as the _____ , are considered _____ of the boundaries of Islaam.

06. The saved sect remains upon what the _____ and the _____ were upon originally.

LEVEL 2: INTERACTIVE QUESTIONS & EXERCISES

COMPREHENSIVE UNDERSTANDING QUESTIONS

[In a study group or circle of learning with other students, these questions can be answered fully or partially by one student from the lesson, with another student completing the answer to the same question, by giving a comparable but different which is also correct.]

07. Name three sects or groups who are misguided and upon innovation but remain within the Muslim Ummah.

08. Name two sects or groups whose extreme misguidance takes them outside the boundaries of the Muslim Ummah.

09. What are two essential characteristics that distinguish Muslims from the saved sect as compared to the astray sects?

Day 05: Allaah Is With Those Who Remained Upon Revealed Guidance

NARRATION FROM AL-IBAANAH AL-SUGHRAH:

Mua'adh[1], may Allaah the Most High be pleased with him, said,

"*The Hand of Allaah is over the Jamaa'ah, the united body of Muslims upon the truth, and whoever deviates from them Allaah has no concern for their deviations from the truth.*"

AUTHENTICITY & SOURCE OF THIS TEXT OR NARRATION:

Authentic: This narration is authentic in meaning by supporting chains and has been authenticated by Sheikh al-Albaanee, may Allaah have mercy upon him in Saheeh at-Tirmidhee, no. 2167 without the additional section of the hadeeth "...and whoever deviates...".

---

[1] A Companion of the Messenger of Allaah, may the praise and salutations of Allaah be upon him

Explanation by Sheikh 'Abdul-'Azeez Ibn 'Abdullah ar-Raajhee

Yes, this statement from Mua'adh where he says *"The Hand of Allaah is over the Jamaa'ah."* meaning that the hand of Allaah is with the Jamaa'ah or the united body of Muslims upon the Sunnah. They are the Jamaa'ah, and they are the Companions of the Messenger of Allaah, and the Successors to the Companions. It is an obligation to adhere to their path and way, as the Companions of the Messenger of Allaah, and their Successors stood firmly upon the truth. Certainly they were the best of people and the most excellent people according to the testimony of very revelation which Allaah send it to us. So listen carefully to the statement of the Prophet, may the praise and salutations of Allaah be upon him, as indeed they were the best of the people and the most excellent of them.

There was no one previously better than them nor will anyone better than them come after them. As such, the Jamaa'ah means the Companions of the Messenger of Allaah, the Successors to the Companions, and those who come after them of the leading scholars and people of knowledge. Therefore it is a requirement and obligation to follow and adhere to their path, to adhere to the Book of Allaah and the Sunnah and what the Companions of the Messenger of Allaah, and the Successors to the Companions stood upon. As they are the Jamaa'ah, the people of truth, and the foundation of the saved sect.

So certainly whoever deviates and separates from them, Allaah has no concern for their deviations caused by their leaving the way of truth. As the truth is what is found the Book of Allaah and in adherence to the Sunnah, it is what is found in the Book of Allaah and Sunnah of His Messenger, may Allaah's praise and salutations be upon him, and what the Companions of the Messenger of Allaah, the Successors to the Companions proceeded upon. Whereas those that deviated and separated from that, their deviation will lead them to the Hellfire and Allaah has no concern for their deviations from the truth. This is a tremendous warning from deviations and innovating in the religion, the deviations of innovation as well as doubts and misconceptions, all of them are considered deviations. So contained within this is a warning against innovation and misconceptions, and a command to adhere to the Sunnah and to those Muslims holding steadfastly to the truth. Yes.

POINTS OF BENEFIT

1. Allaah supports the Muslims who remain upon the revealed guidance He sent to them through the Final Messenger.

2. Whoever deviates and moves away from the guidance of Allaah, Allaah has no concern for them.

3. The Qur'aan testifies and bears witness to the excellence and merit of the Companions of the Messenger of Allaah, may the praise and salutations of Allaah be upon them.

4. It is important to understand the affirmed statements of the Messenger of Allaah, which indicate the rank and position of his Noble Companions.

5. The Jamaa'ah mentioned by the Messenger of Allaah, are his Noble Companions, and then afterwards all those that adhered to their path and remained upon the truth.

6. The foundation of the saved sect mentioned by the Messenger of Allaah, are the Companions of the Messenger of Allaah, as they are the people of truth and they are the Jamaa'ah.

7. It is an obligation upon all Muslims to follow the Book of Allaah and the Sunnah in both knowledge and practice, as understood and practiced by the Companions of the Messenger of Allaah.

8. Deviations away from the guidance of Allaah found in the Qur'aan and Sunnah, lead people to Hellfire.

9. The reminder that the Hand of Allaah is over the Jamaa'ah is a warning against innovations and misconceptions brought into people's understanding and practice of Islaam.

LEVEL 1: TEST YOUR UNDERSTANDING:

TRUE & FALSE QUESTIONS

[Circle the correct letter for each individual sentence from today's content.]

01. Allaah supports and is pleased with anyone who calls themselves Muslim. [T / F]
02. The foundation of the saved sect are the Companions of the Messenger of Allaah. [T / F]
03. People's deviations away from guidance will not lead them to the Hellfire if they are sincere. [T / F]

FILL IN THE BLANK QUESTIONS

[Enter the correct individual words to complete the sentences from today's content.]

04. The truth is what is found the Book of _____ and in adherence to the _____ .
05. It is an _____ to adhere to the _____ of the Companions of the Messenger of Allaah.
06. _____ as well as doubts and _____ are all considered deviations away from the Sunnah.

LEVEL 2: INTERACTIVE QUESTIONS & EXERCISES

COMPREHENSIVE UNDERSTANDING QUESTIONS

[In a study group or circle of learning with other students, these questions can be answered fully or partially by one student from the lesson, with another student completing the answer to the same question, by giving a comparable but different which is also correct.]

07. Give an example of one sect or group who has separated from the Jamaa'ah and one belief they have innovated.
08. Give an separate example of another sect or group who has separated from the Jamaa'ah and one practice they have innovated.
09. Is it possible to be part of the Jamaa'ah united upon the truth, but not follow the way of the Companions? Explain your answer.

Day 06: Allaah Has Ordered Us To Stand United Upon The Truth & Not Divide

NARRATION FROM AL-IBAANAH AL-SUGHRAH:

The first matter that we begin with and mention from this subject is what Allaah, the Most Glorified and the Most Exalted, has mentioned and has commanded in His Book, of the obligation of sticking close to the Jamaa'ah of Muslims upon the truth, and the prohibition of separating from them, is the statement of Allaah, the Most Glorified and the Most Exalted, ❈ ***And hold fast, all of you together, to the Rope of Allaah, and be not divided among yourselves*** ❈ –(Surah Aal-Imraan:103)

SOURCE OF THIS TEXT OR NARRATION:

This is a statement of the compiler of this work: Abu 'Abdullah Ubayd'Allaah Ibn Muhammad Ibn Muhammad Ibn Hamdan Ibn Battah al-Ukbaree, may Allaah have mercy upon him.

Explanation by Sheikh 'Abdul-'Azeez Ibn 'Abdullah ar-Raajhee

Meaning that the first matter to begin with, the author states, *"The first matter that we begin with and mention from this subject is what Allaah, the Most Glorified and the Most Exalted, has mentioned and has commanded in His Book, of the obligation of sticking close to the Jamaa'ah of Muslims upon the truth, and the prohibition of separating from them..."* This is the first section of the work, since the author, may Allaah have mercy upon him, as we've previously mentioned, has divided his book into four different sections. The first section is: Those revealed source texts which contain the command to hold firmly to the Jamaa'ah of Muslims upon the truth, and which prohibit differing and separating into different groups and sects. These are source texts which the Companions of the Messenger of Allaah, may Allaah be pleased with them all, adopted and held firmly to, and which they were far away from separating themselves from them or opposing their guidance

The author mentions the first text which is the statement of Allaah, the Most Glorified and the Most Exalted, ⟪*And hold fast, all of you together, to the Rope of Allaah (i.e. this Qur'aan), and be not divided among yourselves,*⟫ this is a command from Allaah, the Most Glorified and the Most Exalted, to his servants and worshipers for them to hold firmly to His Rope. The Rope of Allaah is: His religion, how free from any imperfection is He. So the command to hold firmly to His Rope means to His religion. And His religion is what He sent down within His Book, and upon the tongue of His Messenger, may Allaah's praise and salutations be upon him. Allaah has said, ⟪*And hold fast, all of you together, to the Rope of Allaah...*⟫ meaning that the Muslims should act according to the Book of Allaah and the Sunnah of Allaah's Messenger, may Allaah's praise and salutations be upon him, all of them. They must gather together and unite upon that without differing and separating, and not divide by abandoning the way of acting upon the Book of Allaah and the Sunnah of His Messenger. Differing and separating here occurs by failing to act upon it, just as gathering and uniting is through acting upon, working in implementing the guidance of the Book and the Sunnah.

Here Allaah states, ⟪*And hold fast, all of you together, to the Rope of Allaah (i.e. this Qur'aan), and be not divided among yourselves,*⟫, meaning to hold firmly to the Rope of Allaah and adhere to His religion, acting according to Allaah's Book and the Sunnah of His Messenger, may Allaah's praise and salutations be upon him, and to gather and unite upon this. This is so that the Muslims hearts become united, such that they may be those who are like a single hand defending against her enemies. Yes, not separating, as dividing and differing among the Muslims is an evil.

POINTS OF BENEFIT

1. In studying Islaam different matters have different levels of importance and priority.
2. The guided scholars cultivate the Muslims upon the most important matters of Islaam first and foremost.
3. A Muslim must pay attention to both the commands and prohibitions mentioned by Allaah in His Book.
4. Allaah has commanded the Muslims to always remain with the Jamaa'ah of Muslims upon the truth.
5. Allaah has prohibited the Muslims from dividing amongst themselves and separating from the Jamaa'ah.
6. Those who separate from the Jamaa'ah among the Muslims, break themselves into different groups and sects.
7. The Rope of Allaah is the revealed religion of Islaam.
8. Allaah has indicated to us the specific means and ways for us to remain united upon the path of truth.
9. The command to hold firmly to the rope of Allaah means to adhere to the Book of Allaah and the Sunnah.
10. The command to remain united upon the truth is connected to the prohibition against differing and separating.
11. One way of differing is failing to act upon the revealed guidance.
12. One of the ways of gathering and uniting is acting upon and implementing revealed guidance.
13. The Muslims holding firmly to the rope of Allaah and acting according to the Book and the Sunnah enables them to defend themselves against their enemies.

LEVEL 1: TEST YOUR UNDERSTANDING:

TRUE & FALSE QUESTIONS

[Circle the correct letter for each individual sentence from today's content.]

01. It is not an obligation to hold fast onto the rope of Allaah. [T / F]
02. The issue of sticking close to the Jamaa'ah, involves both a command and the prohibition. [T / F]
03. We can hold fast to the Rope of Allaah, by simply following only the guidance of the Qur'aan. [T / F]

FILL IN THE BLANK QUESTIONS

[Enter the correct individual words to complete the sentences from today's content.]

04. The revealed source texts _____ separating into different groups and _____ .
05. Allaah's religion is what He sent down within His _____ , and upon the tongue of His _____ .
06. _____ and _____ can result from failing to act upon revealed guidance.

LEVEL 2: INTERACTIVE QUESTIONS & EXERCISES

COMPREHENSIVE UNDERSTANDING QUESTIONS

[In a study group or circle of learning with other students, these questions can be answered fully or partially by one student from the lesson, with another student completing the answer to the same question, by giving a comparable but different which is also correct.]

07. What are two of the characteristics of the Jamaa'ah of the Muslims upon the truth in any age?
08. Give a practical example of how holding on to the Rope of Allaah establishes unity among Muslims?
09. What is something that leads to the hearts of the Muslims being united? What is a specific benefit of this in regard to the position of the Muslim Ummah in the world?

Day 07: Every Name That Opposes The Guidance Of The Sunnah Is Rejected

NARRATION FROM AL-IBAANAH AL-SUGHRAH:

Ibn Battah, may Allaah have mercy upon him said,

"From the Sunnah and the completion and perfection of faith is: declaring yourself free from every name which contradicts the guidance of the Sunnah and differs from what the Ummah has come to stand in consensus upon.

Additionally, that you separate from the people upon that new name, distance yourself from their beliefs, and that you seek closeness to Allaah, the Most Glorified and the Most Exalted, by opposing this new name. An example of such names is: Raafidhah or Shee'ah."

SOURCE OF THIS TEXT OR NARRATION:

This is a statement of the compiler of this work: Abu 'Abdullah Ubayd'Allaah Ibn Muhammad Ibn Muhammad Ibn Hamdan Ibn Battah al-Ukbaree, may Allaah have mercy upon him.

Explanation by Sheikh 'Abdul-'Azeez Ibn 'Abdullah ar-Raajhee

Yes, the author states, *"From the Sunnah and the completion and perfection of faith is: declaring yourself free from every name which contradicts the guidance of the Sunnah and differs with what the Ummah has come to stand in consensus upon.."* Meaning, that it is from the guidance of the Sunnah, and from faith or emaan and what perfects and completes it, that a Muslim frees and separates himself from these newly invented names which oppose the guidance of the Sunnah, and which are outside the guidance that the Ummah has come to consensus upon. Also to separate from the sect upon that new name. Meaning to intentionally distance yourself and keep away from them, shunning and running away from their false beliefs. Moreover, that you seek closeness to Allaah, the Most Glorified and the Most Exalted, by opposing and differing from that sect. Such as who? Such as the sects of the Raafidhah and the Khawaarij.

All of these newly invented names you should distance yourself from, and declare yourself free from association with them, turn away from their false beliefs, separate yourself from the people involved with them, and seek closeness to Allaah, the Most Glorified and the Most Exalted, by opposing and differing from them. An example of this would be the names the Raafidhah and the Shee'ah.

The term Shee'ah is a general name for all those who considered themselves supporters for the blood family of the Messenger of Allaah, may the praise and salutations of Allaah be upon him, specifically supporters of 'Alee and his family and those who supported them. Those under this general term are of different levels. The scholars who have knowledge of the sects through the history of the Ummah have stated that there are over twenty-four different levels who are referred to as Shee'ah. The most severe of them and the most misguided of them are the Nusayrees, those who say that: Allaah embodied Himself in the form of 'Alee. Then just below them in misguidance are the "Declarers of the Mistake" those who falsely claim that the angel Jibreel made a mistake. The claim that Jibreel was sent to bring revelation to 'Alee and he mistakenly gave sit to Muhammad. By this these people disbelieved in Islaam. Then below these are the Raafidhah, the Refusers. They are the ones who refused or turned away from Zayd Ibn 'Alee Ibn Husain, because he spoken well of and supplicated for Allaah to have mercy upon Abu Bakr and 'Umar when they went and asked him about them. He said, *"They were the righteous Ministers of my great great grandfather, the Messenger of Allaah."* and so they rejected him for this position. He said in response, *"You all have rejected me! You all have rejected me!"* Therefore they came to be known historically as the Raafidhah.

Before this they were often known as al-Khashabeeyah, as they would not fight others except with wooden weapons, saying that they would not fight with regular swords until the return of the infallible Mahdee. Then they came to later be named Raafidhah. They are those who direct aspects of worship towards the members and relatives of the blood family of the Prophet of Allaah, through 'Alee and Fatimah, may Allaah be pleased with them both. They also curse and declare the noble Companions of the Messenger of Allaah generally as apostates. They also claim that the Qur'aan is not preserved, and that only a third of the original revelation remains from what was truly revealed.

Yes, so it is obligatory upon a Muslim to declare himself free from the likes of the Raafidhah, and from the Shee'ah generally.

POINTS OF BENEFIT

1. A Muslim should disassociate himself from every name which contradicts the guidance of the Sunnah.

2. A Muslim should disassociate himself from every name which differs with what the guided Muslims have come to stand upon.

3. A Muslim should separate himself from those people who connect themselves with newly developed names which oppose the Sunnah.

4. A Muslim should separate himself and turn away from the false beliefs of those people who connect themselves to any newly developed names and sects which oppose the Sunnah.

5. Separating oneself and declaring yourself free from every name which contradicts the Sunnah is from the perfection of faith or emaan.

6. Opposing any new names which conflict with the guidance of the Sunnah is a means of seeking closeness to Allaah.

7. From those new names which contradict the guidance of the Sunnah are: Raafidhah or Shee'ah.

8. Historically, those people who were known by the name Shee'ah were of twenty-four different levels and categories.

9. From those historically known as the Shee'ah, are different sects, some of which have gone outside the boundaries of Islaam, such as the Nusayrees.

10. From the misguided beliefs of some of those called Shee'ah is the claim that the Qur'aan is not preserved, and only a portion of the original revelation remains.

11. From the characteristics which identified those called Raafidhah is their hatred and cursing of the Companions of the Messenger of Allaah, and claiming most of them apostated after the death of the Messenger of Allaah.

12. The various sects have been given or have taken new names according to the circumstances surrounding them or their own actions.

13. Every misguided sect which develops new beliefs and practices, and so comes to be distinguished by a new name, should be opposed and every Muslim should declare himself free of them and their misguidance.

LEVEL 1: TEST YOUR UNDERSTANDING:

TRUE & FALSE QUESTIONS
[Circle the correct letter for each individual sentence from today's content.]

01. Those known as Shee'ah have several different levels of misguidance. [T / F]

02. A Muslim should declare himself free from every misguided sect. [T / F]

03. Some extreme Shee'ah believe that Allaah embodied Himself in the form of 'Alee. [T / F]

FILL IN THE BLANK QUESTIONS
[Enter the correct individual words to complete the sentences from today's content.]

04. Zayd Ibn 'Alee Ibn Husain spoke well of and _____ for Allaah to have mercy upon Abu _____ and '_____ .

05. Some Shee'ah believe that the angel Jibreel made a mistake bringing the revelation to the _____ _____ , as they falsely claim that Jibreel was sent to bring revelation to '_____ .

06. A Muslim should oppose the incorrect _____ and separate from the _____ upon any new name which opposes the guidance of the _____ .

LEVEL 2: INTERACTIVE QUESTIONS & EXERCISES

COMPREHENSIVE UNDERSTANDING QUESTIONS
[In a study group or circle of learning with other students, these questions can be answered fully or partially by one student from the lesson, with another student completing the answer to the same question, by giving a comparable but different which is also correct.]

07 Name two countries where many people adhere to the misguided sect of the Shee'ah.

08. Name someone who opposed the false beliefs of the Raafidhah? Also discuss one of their false beliefs held by some of them connected to the Book of Allaah, the Qur'aan.

09. Who initially opposed the false beliefs of the sect of the Khawaarij? Also mention one of their well known false beliefs.

Day 08: The Strangeness Of Islaam Is Something Expected

NARRATION FROM AL-IBAANAH AL-SUGHRAH:

The Messenger of Allaah, may Allaah's praise and salutations be upon him, said,

{Islaam began as something strange, and will return as something strange just as it began. So Tooba is for the strangers.}

The Companions said, "Oh Messenger of Allaah, who are the strangers?"

He said, **{They are those who rectify themselves and others when the people become corrupt.}** *And the narration collected by Imaam Muslim in his Saheeh is shorter ending after the phrase,* **{....So Tooba is for the strangers.}**

AUTHENTICITY & SOURCE OF THIS TEXT OR NARRATION:

Authentic: Narrated in at-Tirmidhee with a wording close to that of Imaam Muslim and says This hadeeth narration is "hasan saheeh". It is also relayed in the Musnad of Imaam Ahmad, and by Ibn Wadhaah in his work "Innovation And The Prohibition Regarding It." Ibn Maajah narrates this with the wording "... Who are the strangers?" He said, "They are the strangers who have separated from their families and tribes" as did ad-Daarimee in his Sunan. It is also been narrated by the author in al-Ibaanah al-Kubraa and Ibn Qutaybah in his work Ta'weel al-Hadeeth

Explanation by Sheikh 'Abdul-'Azeez Ibn 'Abdullah ar-Raajhee

Yes, this hadeeth narration is authentic, and it is narrated by Imaam Muslim in his collection *as-Saheeh*. That narration has the wording, *{Islaam began as something strange, and will return as something strange just as it began. So Tooba is for the strangers.}*[1] The meaning of this is that Islaam emerged as something strange to the people, such that there were only a few people who entered into Islaam. The Prophet, may Allaah's praise and salutations be upon him, was the first Muslim of this Ummah, then Abu Bakr as-Siddeeq embraced Islaam. Also Khadeejah the wife of the Prophet, may Allaah's praise and salutations be upon him, embraced Islaam, as did 'Alee, may Allaah be pleased with him, and with all of them.

So the Prophet, may Allaah's praise and salutations be upon him, was the first Muslim from this Ummah. For this reason, as is found in the Qur'aan, he said, *﴿He has no partner. And of this I have been commanded, and I am the first of the Muslims.﴾*-(Surah Al-An'am: 163) and *﴿And I am commanded this in order that I may be the first of those who submit themselves to Allaah in Islaam as Muslims﴾*-(Surah Az-Zumar: 12). Then the first of those who believed in him from the men who were free was Abu Bakr as-Siddeeq, and the first of those who believed in him from those who were slaves was Bilaal, and the first of those who believed in him from the young was 'Alee Ibn Abee Taalib, and the first of those who believed in him from the women was Khadeejah Bint Khuwaylid, may Allaah be pleased with her. Then Suhaib, 'Ammaar Ibn Yasser, and a group of others embraced Islaam.

Therefore Islaam began as something strange amongst the people, and it was only embraced by a few. Then afterwards Islaam began to spread and many entered into it. Then the Prophet, may Allaah's praise and salutations be upon him, migrated to Medinah. Then when Allaah blessed the Prophet, may Allaah's praise and salutations be upon him, with the opening and conquest of Mecca, after this people entered into the religion of Allaah in large numbers.

In the ninth year after the emigration to Medinah the delegations came to the Prophet, may Allaah's praise and salutations be upon him, to embrace Islaam, delegations coming from the majority of the tribes from the different regions of the Arab world. In this way the people began to enter the religion of Allaah in large numbers, and Islaam spread significantly. Then came the period of the rightly guided khalifas of the Messenger of Allaah. In the period of the rightly guided khalifas, may Allaah be pleased with all of them, Islaam continued to spread and expand further. Yet in the end of time, Islaam will return to being something strange just as it began, where people will have turned away from the religion of Allaah,

---

[1] Narrated in Saheeh Muslim: 145, Ibn Maajah:3986 and in the Musnad of Imaam Ahmad vol.2 389

and there will only remain a few individuals truly practicing it. *{Islaam began as something strange...}* strange means: that no one or very few are upon that matter or affair. So from this comes strangers. They are called strangers in a land or country, because they are alone among the other people in what they are upon. Such an individual is a stranger among their family members and children. *{...So Tooba is for the strangers.}* Tooba means: one of the names of Jannah, or name for a specific tree in Jannah. This is considered an encouragement to hold firmly to the Sunnah, and to hold firmly to the religion in that age in which it is strange. This holing on to the religion in the age in which it is strange is through the presence of the one who supports it, through the one who adheres to the truth, and firmly holds onto the Sunnah.

{Islaam began as something strange, and will return as something strange just as it began. So Tooba is for the strangers.} Honor and the rewards of Jannah are promised to the ones who are strangers upon Islaam, those who are holding firmly to the religion of Islaam, clinging to it with your molar teeth, hanging onto it. Those who adhere strongly to the Sunnah, who distance and make themselves far away from the people of innovation in the religion, as well as the people who engage in practices of associating others with Allaah in worship.

So the Companions said, *"Oh Messenger of Allaah, who are the strangers?"* (And this addition to the narration is not found in what is reported by Imaam Muslim.) They said, *"Oh Messenger of Allaah, who are the strangers?"* He replied, *{They are those who when the people become corrupt, rectify themselves.}*[2] And in the wording found within a related narration, *"Oh Messenger of Allaah, who are the strangers?"* He said, *{There are those rectify themselves, when the people become corrupt.}* This is the definition of who are the strangers, *{They are those rectify themselves, when the people become corrupt.}* And it is mentioned with a different wording in a related narration *{They are those who rectify others when the people have become corrupted.}* [3] And in the wording found within another related narration, *{They are those who have separated from their families and tribes.}*[4] And as found in the wording of another related narration, *{They are a few righteous people amongst many people practicing wrongdoing and disobedience.}*[5]

These are four distinct wordings of the narration and within them there is: the first wording They said, *"Oh Messenger of Allaah, who are the strangers?"* He said, *{They are those rectify themselves when the people become corrupt.}* By this meaning that they rectify themselves, they are those who rectify their lives upon guidance, or those who adhere to the truth, clinging to it with their molar teeth, and holding firmly to the Sunnah when the people choose wrongdoing and become corrupted.

---

[2] Musnad of Imaam Ahmad vol. 4, pg. 73
[3] Jaame'a at-Tirmidhee : 2630
[4] Ibn Maajah: 3988 and in the Musnad of Imaam Ahmad vol.1, pg. 398, ad-Daarimee in his Sunan: 2755
[5] Musnad of Imaam Ahmad vol.2, pg. 22

And in the wording of one of the narrations *{... those who rectify others when the people have become corrupted.}* Meaning callers for the people to rectify themselves. Meaning that the people strive to rectify themselves, and then struggled to rectify others. The person who calls others to rectification is unquestionably required to be a righteous person within himself, he is not called or considered someone who rectifies others except after he is first rectified himself.

And the wordings of these additional narrations bring additional meaning to what is found in the meaning of the first wording. The meaning of the first wording, *{... Those rectify themselves when the people become corrupt.}* meaning that they were righteous themselves as individuals. As for the second wording *{... Whose who rectify others when the people have become corrupted.}* This means callers to rectification, those who are rectifying what the people in general have corrupted. They are those who call to Allaah, and enjoin what is good, and forbid wrongdoing, and call people to the Sunnah, and warn people away from innovation in the religion.

And in the wording of one of the narrations *{...those who have separated from their families and tribes}* meaning that perhaps from every tribe there may be one or two individuals. Most of the tribe stands upon prcticing innovation in the religion, and wrongdoing, but one or two individuals have separated themselves from this, *{...those who have separated from their families and tribes}*

And in the fourth wording, *{They are a few righteous people amongst, many people practicing wrongdoing and disobedience.}* When it was asked, *{Who are the strangers?}* The Messenger of Allaah, may the praise and salutations of Allaah be upon him, said *{They are a few righteous people amongst many people practicing wrongdoing and disobedience.}* Meaning of a group of people who have rectified themselves, yet they are very small in number within a society that is upon many forms of corruption and wrongdoing.

POINTS OF BENEFIT

1. Islaam began as something strange.

2. The first Muslim from this Ummah was the Prophet Muhammad, may the praise and salutations of Allaah be upon him.

3. The first strangeness of Islaam was that in the beginning only a few people entered into it.

4. The first free adult man who believed in the Prophet Muhammad was Abu Bakr as-Siddeeq, may Allaah be pleased with him.

5. The first slave who believed in the Prophet Muhammad was Bilaal, may Allaah be pleased with him.

6. The first youth who believed in the Prophet Muhammad was 'Alee Ibn Abee Taalib, may Allaah be pleased with him.

7. The first woman who believed in the Prophet Muhammad was Khadeejah Bint Khuwaylid, may Allaah be pleased with her.

8. Later when knowledge of Islaam spread among the people, many entered into Islaam.

9. After the opening and conquest of Mecca, people entered into the religion of Allaah in large numbers.

10. Islaam continued to spread and expand further during the period of the rightly guided khalifas, may Allaah be pleased with all of them.

11. In later times after its initial growth and spread, Islaam will return again to being something strange.

12. The 'Strangers' upon Islaam mentioned by the Messenger of Allaah have praiseworthy characteristics.

13. The 'Strangers' upon Islaam mentioned by the Messenger of Allaah have a specific reward promised in Jannah.

14. A characteristic of the Strangers is that they stand alone in following Allaah's guidance among others who do not.

15. A characteristic of the Strangers is that they adhere to the truth and hold onto the Sunnah.

16. A characteristic of the Strangers is that they are far away from innovation and the people upon it.

17. A characteristic of the Strangers is that they are far away from associating others with Allaah and the people upon it.

18. A characteristic of the Strangers is that they rectify themselves when others are corrupt.

19. A characteristic of the Strangers is that they call others to rectification when people generally are corrupt.

20. A characteristic of the Strangers is that they are separated from their families and tribes upon misguidance by their choosing to follow guidance.

21. A characteristic of the Strangers is that they are a few upon guidance and obedience when many people are corrupt and disobedient.

LEVEL 1: TEST YOUR UNDERSTANDING:

TRUE & FALSE QUESTIONS

[Circle the correct letter for each individual sentence from today's content.]

01. The strangeness of Islaam is something negative. [T / F]
02. Islaam will never be strange again since it is all over the world. [T / F]
03. The Prophet praised the strangers who held firmly to revealed guidance. [T / F]

FILL IN THE BLANK QUESTIONS

[Enter the correct individual words to complete the sentences from today's content.]

04. Islaam _____ as something strange in the city of _____ .

05. Islaam spread significantly in the _____ year when the Arab tribes and _____ came to _____ .

06. _____ and the rewards of _____ are promised to the ones who are strangers upon _____ .

LEVEL 2: INTERACTIVE QUESTIONS & EXERCISES

COMPREHENSIVE UNDERSTANDING QUESTIONS

[In a study group or circle of learning with other students, these questions can be answered fully or partially by one student from the lesson, with another student completing the answer to the same question, by giving a comparable but different which is also correct.]

07. Describe three ways in which Islaam is considered strange in our time and age.

08. Explain two characteristics of the strangers by giving a possible practical example for each of those characteristics.

09. Can Islaam only be strange among non-Muslims or also possibly amongst the Muslims? Briefly explain your answer giving examples if necessary.

Day 09: That One Individual Whose Religion You Should Stand Upon

NARRATION FROM AL-IBAANAH AL-SUGHRAH:

Ibn 'Abbas[1] said that Mu'aweeyah, may Allaah have mercy upon them both, said to me, "*You stand on the way of 'Alee.*"

And I replied, "*No, nor do I stand upon the way of 'Uthmaan.*

Rather, I stand upon the way of the Messenger of Allaah, may Allaah's praise and salutations be upon him."

AUTHENTICITY & SOURCE OF THIS TEXT OR NARRATION:

Authentic: Narrated by 'Abdur-Razzaq in his work al-Musannaf with a sound chain of narration, and was also narrated by al-Laalakaa'ee in his work.

---

[1] A Companion of the Messenger of Allaah, may the praise and salutations of Allaah be upon him

Explanation by Sheikh 'Abdul-'Azeez Ibn 'Abdullah ar-Raajhee

Yes, this narration is transmitted by the author, may Allaah have mercy upon him, with the same chain of narration which he brings in his work al-Kubraa. He states, Abu al-Fadhl Shu'aib Ibn Raajyaan al-Kufee narrated to us, saying 'Alee Ibn Harb narrated to us, saying, Sufyaan Ibn 'Uyainah, informed us, on the authority of Ibn Taawoos from his father Taawoos Kaysaan al-Yamaanee the well-known and noble scholar from the generation of the Successors on the authority of Ibn 'Abbaas, may Allaah be pleased with him, that he narrated to me saying, that Mu'aweeyah, may Allaah have mercy upon him, meaning Mu'aweeyah Ibn Abee Sufyaan, said to me, *"You stand on the way of 'Alee."*

By this meaning that Ibn 'Abbaas had been from those who supported 'Alee, stood with him, and fought alongside him. This was at the time when there occurred a difference between the Companions of the Messenger of Allaah, between 'Alee and Mu'aweeyah, may Allaah be pleased with both of them and with those who were with them. When the difference occurred between them the majority of the Companions of the Messenger of Allaah stood with 'Alee, may Allaah be pleased with him, and held the view that he was the legitimate rightly guided Khalifah. They held that he was the one who was given the oath of allegiance by the majority of those leading Muslims of discernment, who determine and evaluate things among the Muslims, and so it was obligatory to hear and obey him acting upon the statement of Allaah, *And if two parties or groups among the believers fall to fighting, then make peace between them both, but if one of them rebels against the other, then fight you all against the one that which rebels till it complies with the Command of Allaah ...* -(Surah Al-Hujuraat: 9).

Therefore the majority of the Companions of the Messenger of Allaah stood with 'Alee and held the position that he was the one who was the legitimate rightly guided Khalifah, and that Mu'aweeyah and his supporters from the region of Shaam were those who incorrectly rebelled. This specific situation is just as the Prophet, may Allaah's praise and salutations be upon him, informed us as is found in the narration. *{May Allaah be Merciful to 'Ammar. He will be killed by a rebellious group....}* [2] This is what was correct and true, yet Mu'aweeyah and his supporters from the region of Shaam did not believe or know that they were those rebels due to what they were seeking of justice. They were those who independently came to a conclusion, however the conclusion that they reached was mistaken, so in this they received a single reward for their effort to reach the correct conclusion.

---

[2] Saheeh al-Bukhaaree: 447, Saheeh Muslim: 2915, and the Musnad of Imaam Ahmad: vol.3 no. 90

DAY - 09

Whereas 'Alee and those who stood with him also independently strived to reach the correct conclusion in the issue of the dispute, and they were correct in their conclusion. Therefore they received one reward for their effort to reach the correct conclusion, and a second reward due to being correct. And from among those individuals was Ibn 'Abbaas who had chosen to stand with 'Alee. So it is narrated that Mu'aweeyah said to Ibn 'Abbaas, *"You stand on the way of 'Alee."* Due to his choosing to stand with him during the dispute. But Ibn 'Abbaas, replied, *"No, nor do I stand upon the way of 'Uthmaan. Rather, I stand upon the way of the Messenger of Allaah, may Allaah's praise and salutations be upon him."*

By this it is as if he were saying, 'Both 'Alee and 'Uthmaan proceeded upon the path, however they were mistaken in some matters. They had some independently derived conclusions about issues, and so I do not absolutely follow them in every single conclusion. Rather I choose to stand upon the way of the Messenger of Allaah, may Allaah's praise and salutations be upon him. As for anyone other than the Messenger of Allaah, may Allaah's praise and salutations be upon him, in some of his statements or positions he is correct and in others he may be mistaken. Therefore I stand upon the way of the Messenger.' This is the way of truth, and this is the way of light, that an individual adhere to the Sunnah, that they adhere to the Sunnah and do not blindly follow different individuals.

As this religion, it is the religion of Allaah, and it is what is obligatory to follow absolutely. As for following different individuals, then they are those who make mistakes at times and are correct at times, even if they were from the Companions of the Messenger of Allaah. Whenever they came to a correctly independently derived conclusion they receive to rewards for this, and if they were incorrect in the conclusion that they came two then they still received a single reward. However, it undoubtedly remains an obligation to hold firmly to the Book of Allaah and the Sunnah.

Moreover individuals or men are known by the truth, and the truth is not known by individuals, the state of man is known by understanding the truth. The one whose position conforms with the truth we will know that he is correct in his position by the truth. But as for the truth it is not understood by simply looking at individuals who claim to be upon it. Such that someone might say, *"So and so makes such and such statement, therefore whatever is with him must be the truth"*, no. What is most important is the truth and understanding the truth, and those from amongst the people who conform to the truth are distinguished through our knowing the truth.

But as for distinguishing what is the truth by what men or individuals are upon, then this is not the case. We come to know and distinguish individuals by the truth, but do not know or distinguish the truth by individuals. For this reason Ibn 'Abbaas said, "... *I stand upon the way of the Messenger of Allaah, may Allaah's praise and salutations be upon him.*" He was not following the way of 'Alee nor the way of 'Uthmaan, despite the fact that they were both Companions and from the best of the Muslims, and that they both proceeded upon the way of the truth. However the foundation of the truth is the Sunnah, so what was said was, *"I stand upon the way of the Messenger of Allaah, may Allaah's praise and salutations be upon him"*. So whoever stands with me upon that way of guidance, then he is considered upon the truth. Yes.

POINTS OF BENEFIT

1. A Muslim should attach and attribute himself back to the guidance of the last Messenger of Allaah, may Allaah's praise and salutations be upon him.

2. The differences that occurred amongst the Companions of the Messenger of Allaah were in matters and issues in which the differing sides each strove to reach the correct conclusion based upon the source texts of Islaam in a matter requiring an independent judgment.

3. The khalifah of the Muslims should be given an oath of allegiance by the Muslims.

4. The khalifah of the Muslims must be listened to and obeyed in matters that are not disobedience to Allaah.

5. The Messenger of Allaah was given knowledge by Allaah of some of the trials that his Companions will encounter after his death.

6. The scholar who comes to an independently derived conclusion based upon the source texts which is in fact correct receives two rewards from Allaah.

7. The scholar who comes to an independently derived conclusion based upon the source texts which is actually incorrect receives a single reward from Allaah.

8. It is from the beneficial matters that whenever needed a Muslim declare himself free from appearing to have biased partisanship, or allegiance to anyone other than the Messenger of Allaah.

9. Having biased partisanship towards anyone is blameworthy, even the Companions of the Messenger of Allaah.

10. It is a blameworthy matter to blindly follow individuals rather than following the scholars who speak upon evidence from the source texts.

11. It is from the religion of Islaam that a Muslim accepts everything which the Messenger of Allaah brought to us.

12. The Messenger of Allaah, may the praise and salutations of Allaah be upon him, is infallible in every matter he conveyed regarding the religion of Islaam.

13. All other individuals other than the Messenger of Allaah may be correct in some matters and wrong in others.

14. Individuals or men are known by the truth, and the truth is not known by individuals.

15. The truth is not understood by simply looking at individuals who claim to be upon the truth.

LEVEL 1: TEST YOUR UNDERSTANDING:

TRUE & FALSE QUESTIONS
[Circle the correct letter for each individual sentence from today's content.]

3 min

01. The Companions of the Messenger of Allaah differed in some matters. [T / F]
02. It is wrong to blindly follow a scholar in every single thing they say. [T / F]
03. We can understand what is the truth simply by looking at someone who practices it. [T / F]

FILL IN THE BLANK QUESTIONS
[Enter the correct individual words to complete the sentences from today's content.]

6 min

04. In the dispute about the _____ the majority of the Companions of the Messenger of Allaah stood with _____ .
05. The scholars receive one _____ for their _____ to reach the correct conclusion, and a second _____ due to actually being _____ .
06. We always have an _____ to hold firmly to the _____ and the _____ .

LEVEL 2: INTERACTIVE QUESTIONS & EXERCISES

COMPREHENSIVE UNDERSTANDING QUESTIONS
[In a study group or circle of learning with other students, these questions can be answered fully or partially by one student from the lesson, with another student completing the answer to the same question, by giving a comparable but different which is also correct.]

21-36 min

07. Give an example of a matter of fiqh or implementation of the source texts in which you know some of our modern-day scholars differ with one another?
08. Give an example of a misunderstanding that some modern Muslims have regarding giving the oath of allegiance.
09. Try to explain one reason that the position of Ibn 'Abbaas in supporting 'Alee, was actually following the Messenger of Allaah, and not biased partisanship towards 'Alee.

Day 10: The Sunnah Is Revealed Knowledge From Allaah

NARRATION FROM AL-IBAANAH AL-SUGHRAH:

Hassaan Ibn Atiyyah said,

"The angel Jibreel would decend to the Messenger of Allaah, may Allaah's salutations be upon him, with the Sunnah just as he would descend to him with the Qur'aan.

And he taught him the Sunnah, just as he used to teach him the Qur'aan."

AUTHENTICITY & SOURCE OF THIS TEXT OR NARRATION:

Authentic: This was narrated by al-Maroodhee in his work as-Sunnah, by Imaam al-Laalakaa'ee, al-Harawee, ad-Daarimee in his Sunan, and by the author in the related work al-Ibaanah al-Kubraa.

Explanation by Sheikh 'Abdul-'Azeez Ibn 'Abdullah ar-Raajhee

This is an authentic statement, and it is the statement of Hassaan Ibn Atiyyah, where he said, *"Jibreel, upon him be Allaah's praise and His salutations, used to descend to the Messenger of Allaah, may Allaah's praise and salutations be upon him, to convey to him the Sunnah just as he descended to convey to him the Qur'aan. And he used to teach him the Sunnah just as he used to teach him the Qur'aan."*

And the meaning of this is that the Sunnah is the second source of revelation. The Sunnah is revelation from Allaah, not something simply coming from the Prophet, may Allaah's praise and salutations be upon him. This is something which the Qur'aan itself indicates, Allaah, the Most High, says in His magnificent Book, ❴*Nor does he speak of his own desire.*❵-(Surah An-Najm: 3) meaning the Messenger upon him be Allaah's praise and salutations. Allaah says, ❴*Nor does he speak of his own desire. It is only an Inspiration that is inspired. He has been taught this Qur'aan by one mighty in power Jibreel. Dhu Mirrah (free from any defect in body and mind), then he (Jibreel) rose and became stable.*❵-(Surah An-Najm: 3-6)

Moreover, the Messenger upon him be Allaah's praise and salutations, himself said, {*Indeed I've been given the Qur'aan and that which is like it.*}[1] Therefore the Sunnah is considered revelation, revealed knowledge from Allaah. However the Sunnah as a whole has two distinct categories. In one category both the specific wording and the meaning of those words are revelation from Allaah, this is the "hadeeth al-qudsee". Such as the hadeeth which Abu Dharr narrates from the Prophet, may Allaah's praise and salutations be upon him, regarding what had been narrated to the Prophet from his Lord were Allaah says, {*O My servants! I have forbidden oppression for Myself, and I have made it forbidden amongst you, so do not oppress one another....*}[2] Until the end of the hadeeth narration. {*...O My servants, all of you are hungry except those whom I have fed, so seek food from Me and I shall feed you. O My servants, all of you are naked except those whom I have clothed, so seek clothing from Me and I shall clothe you. O My servants, you commit sins by day and by night, and I forgive all sins, so seek forgiveness from Me and I shall forgive you. O My servants, you will not attain harming Me so as to harm Me, and you will not attain benefiting Me so as to benefit Me. O My servants, if the first of you and the last of you, and the humans of you and the jinn of you, were all as pious as the most pious heart of any individual amongst you, then this would not increase My Kingdom an iota...*} until the end of what this narration contains.

---

[1] Sunan Abu Dawood: 4604 and the Musnad of Imaam Ahmad vol.4 no. 130
[2] Saheeh Muslim: 2577, and the Musnad of Imaam Ahmad vol.5 no. 160

Similarly, what is contained in a narration of Abu Hurairah which is a "hadeeth al-qudsee", *{I will declare war against him who treats with hostility a pious worshipper of Mine....}*[3] This revelation is from Allaah in its exact wording and its meaning. Because the Prophet, may Allaah's praise and salutations be upon him, is transmitting this from His Lord. The Prophet, may Allaah's praise and salutations be upon him that Allaah, says in another "hadeeth al-qudsee", *{I am so self-sufficient that I am in no need of having an associate. Thus he who does an action for someone else's sake as well as Mine will have that action renounced by Me to him whom he associated with Me.}*[4]

This is another example where the exact wording and its meaning are from Allaah, similar to the Qur'aan, except that the rulings differ from those connected to the Qur'aan. Firstly, the recitation of the text of the Qur'aan is a form of worship, whereas the recitation of the text of a "hadeeth al-qudsee" is not a legislated form of worship. The Qur'aan should not be touched except for by the one who was in a state of purity, whereas the written text of a "hadeeth al-qudsee" can be touched by someone who is not in a state of purity. The words of the Qur'aan are considered miraculous, whereas the words found in the texts of the various "hadeeth al-qudsee" narrations are not considered miraculous.

So the rulings connected to these two sources of revelation differ. Yet everything from the Qur'aan and "hadeeth al-qudsee" narrations is from the speech of Allaah in its wording and meaning. However the remainder of the hadeeth narrations are not "al-qudsee", and do not transmit specific wording which comes from Allaah. Rather they are from Allaah in their meaning, and from the Messenger of Allaah, may Allaah's praise and salutations be upon him, in their specific wording. As the Messenger is the one who spoke and verbalized them, while the exact meaning itself is also from Allaah. The meaning is considered revelation from Allaah, while the Messenger is the one who has spoken that specific meaning. For this reason it is connected to the Prophet, may Allaah's praise and salutations be upon him, that he said, *{Actions are to be judged only by intentions and a man will have only what he intended...}*[5]

This narration conveys the words of the Messenger of Allaah, yet their meaning is from Allaah and is clear revelation. This is different from the "hadeeth al-qudsee" narrations, as they are from Allaah in both the exact wording and their meaning, but those narrations which are not "hadeeth al-qudsee" narrations, only their meaning is from Allaah, while their wording comes from the Messenger of Allaah, may Allaah's praise and salutations be upon him. So do not be misled or deceived by what may be found in some of the books of knowledge. Meaning some of the books that discussed the principles of explaining the Qur'aan, and related to the sciences of the Qur'aan, where they specifically transmit from as-Suyootee and

---

[3] Saheeh al-Bukhaaree: 6502
[4] Saheeh Muslim: 2985, Ibn Maajah: 4202, and the Musnad of Imaam Ahmad vol.2 no. 301
[5] Saheeh al-Bukhaaree: 1, Saheeh Muslim: 1907, and at-Tirmidhee: 1647, an-Nasaa'ee: 75, Sunan Abu Dawood: 2201, Ibn Maajah: 4227, and the Musnad of Imaam Ahmad vol.1 no. 25

other scholars that they held that, [The hadeeth al-qudsee narrations are from the words of the Messenger.] Because these scholars proceeded upon the methodology of the sect of the Ash'areeyah. The Ash'areeyah are among those who have denied that the Qur'aan itself is from the speech of Allaah in both wording and meaning. They reject that the Qur'aan is the speech of Allaah in both its exact wording and revealed meaning. They say, The speech of Allaah-generally, whether that be the speech of Allaah found in the Qur'aan or outside of the Qur'aan, then the meaning is established by itself, and has neither spoken letters nor spoken expression from Allaah.

For this reason they say, [Indeed the Qur'aan all of it, it's meaning, is meaning which exists in and of itself, and its exact wording is not from Allaah.] And this is a tremendous error claiming that the Qur'aan has neither letters nor voice. As the Qur'aan is the speech of Allaah in both its exact wording and the meaning of its letters and words, and its entire meaning is from Allaah. Related to this, the "hadeeth al-qudsee" narrations are that knowledge whose meaning and wording is from Allaah. While the authentic narrations that are not hadeeth al-qudsee narrations are from Allaah in their meaning, and from the Messenger of Allaah in the specific wording which he spoke, may Allaah's praise and salutations be upon him, yes.

POINTS OF BENEFIT

1. The Sunnah is a form of revelation which Jibreel brought down to the Prophet Muhammad, may the praise and salutations of Allaah be upon him.

2. Jibreel would teach the Messenger of Allaah the understanding of Sunnah, just as he taught him the understanding of the Qur'aan.

3. It is a misconception to claim that the Sunnah is something that came from the Prophet himself.

4. Allaah tells us in the Qur'aan that the Prophet Muhammad did not speak from his own desires, but from revelation.

5. The Sunnah has two distinct categories of its knowledge.

6. The first category of the Sunnah are those narrations in which both the meaning and the specific wording are from Allaah. This category of narration is known as "hadeeth al-qudsee".

7. The second category of the Sunnah are those narrations in which the meaning is from Allaah, but the specific wording is from the Prophet, may the praise and salutations of Allaah be upon him.

8. Both the Qur'aan and "hadeeth al-qudsee" narrations are from the speech of Allaah in their wording and meaning.

9. Despite the fact that the meaning and the specific wording of "hadeeth al-qudsee" narrations are also from Allaah, they differ from the text of the Qur'aan in several distinct ways.

10. The recitation of the text of the Qur'aan is a form of worship, this is not the case for ahadeeth al-qudsee.

11. The printed mushaf of the Qur'aan requires physical purity to be touched and held, this is not the case for ahadeeth al-qudsee.

12. The words of the Qur'aan are considered miraculous, this is not the case for ahadeeth al-qudsee.

13. Some of the misguided sects have false beliefs regarding the true nature of the Qur'aan and of hadeeth al-qudsee narrations.

14. The sect of the Asha'rees are among those who have denied that the Qur'aan is from the speech of Allaah in both wording and meaning.

15. The sect of the Asha'rees are upon a tremendous error in claiming that the Qur'aan has neither letters nor voice.

16. The sect of the Asha'rees are upon the incorrect belief that the hadeeth al-qudsee narrations are considered from the words of the Messenger, not from Allaah.

LEVEL 1: TEST YOUR UNDERSTANDING:

TRUE & FALSE QUESTIONS
[Circle the correct letter for each individual sentence from today's content.]

01. The angel Jibreel brought two types of revelation to the Messenger of Allaah. [T / F]
02. Some hadeeth narrations contain statements from Allaah. [T / F]
03. The Qur'aan is the only knowledge the Prophet of Allaah possessed. [T / F]

FILL IN THE BLANK QUESTIONS
[Enter the correct individual words to complete the sentences from today's content.]

04. _____ used to teach the prophet the _____ just as he used to teach him the Qur'aan.
05. The Prophet himself, said to us, {Indeed I've been _____ the _____ and that which is _____ it.}
06. Qur'aan itself is from the _____ of Allaah in both _____ and _____ .

LEVEL 2: INTERACTIVE QUESTIONS & EXERCISES

COMPREHENSIVE UNDERSTANDING QUESTIONS
[In a study group or circle of learning with other students, these questions can be answered fully or partially by one student from the lesson, with another student completing the answer to the same question, by giving a comparable but different which is also correct.]

07. Is it required that we accept all the knowledge which the Messenger of Allaah came with, or just the Qur'aan?
08. Describe one of the authentic ways the text of the Qur'aan is used in a form of worship.
09. What verse indicates to us that all religious statements of the Prophet are a form of revelation? How does it clarify the false claim that he made up parts of Islaam?

Day 11: Hold Firmly To The Sunnah As The Rope Of Allaah

NARRATION FROM AL-IBAANAH AL-SUGHRAH:

Abu Bakr as-Siddeeq[1], may Allaah the Most High be pleased with him, said,

"The Sunnah is the firm rope of Allaah, the person who turns away from it cuts his rope connecting him to Allaah."

AUTHENTICITY & SOURCE OF THIS TEXT OR NARRATION:

Authentic in meaning: narrated by the author in the original work.

---

[1] A Companion of the Messenger of Allaah, may the praise and salutations of Allaah be upon him

Explanation by Sheikh 'Abdul-'Azeez Ibn 'Abdullah ar-Raajhee

Yes, the meaning of this is correct. As there is no doubt that the Sunnah is the firm rope of Allaah. Because the Sunnah explains the Qur'aan and clarifies it, specifies its general meanings, and specifies that which is general, as well as bringing forth additional rulings not found within the texts of the Qur'aan. As such, the one who abandons the Sunnah has disbelieved in Islaam. The one who rejects the Sunnah, and chooses not to act upon the Sunnah, then this person disbelieves, because in regard to the Qur'aan, not every matter of Islaam is detailed in the Qur'aan. Rather the Sunnah brings forth the details of matters. The Qur'aan comes with the general command to perform the ritual prayer. However there is not found within the Qur'aan the fact that salaat adh-dhuhr is prayed in four raka'at, salaat al-'asr is prayed with four raka'at, salaat al-maghrib is prayed with three raka'at, salaat al-'ishaa' is prayed with four raka'at, and that salaat al-fajr is prayed with two raka'at. All of this is only found in the Sunnah.

For this reason the one who does not act upon the Sunnah disbelieves in Islaam. He is not able to properly pray, because within the general command found in the Qur'aan the number of raka'at is not specified. Similarly the command to give zakaat, the obligatory charity, is found in the Qur'aan. This is a command to give zakaat, that is an obligation. But there is not found in the Qur'aan the conditions of when that charity becomes obligatory, or about the period when that wealth was earned, or the minimum amount upon which zakaat is due. Similarly we find in the Qur'aan the command for the obligatory Hajj, but there is not found in the Qur'aan the specific details of how the rites of Hajj are performed. It does not indicate that it is obligatory on a person to make seven circuits around the house of Allaah, or they must proceed between as-Safa and al-Marwaa seven times, or that they must stay at Minaa, or that they rest at Arafat and Muzdalifah. All of these specific details are only found in the Sunnah. So the one who abandons, does not act upon the Sunnah, and rejects it, or generally does not act according to it, has in fact disbelieved in Islaam. So we ask Allaah for safety and well-being in our religion.

Additionally we have in the authentic hadeeth, that the Prophet, may the praise and salutations of Allaah be upon him, said *{Indeed I've been given the Qur'aan and that which is like it.}*[2] And that he said: *{I should not want to hear of a man, who while he is reclining on his couch, says: 'Between us and you is Allaah's Book. So whatever we find in it that is lawful, we consider lawful, and whatever we find in it that is unlawful, we consider it unlawful. And whatever we do not find within we will not act upon.}*. Again as he, may the praise and salutations of Allaah be upon him, said *{Indeed I've been given the Qur'aan and that which is like it.}*

---

[2] Sunan Abu Dawood: 4604 and the Musnad of Imaam Ahmad vol.4 no. 130

DAY - 11

Allaah, the Most High says, ❦*O you who believe! Obey Allaah and obey the Messenger (Muhammad), and those of you (Muslims) who are in authority. (And) if you differ in anything amongst yourselves, refer it to Allaah and His Messenger...*❦- (Surah An-Nisa': 59) As such the one who claims he is acting according to the Qur'aan and yet he turns away from the Sunnah, then he is denying this clear statement from Allaah, ❦*O you who believe! Obey Allaah and obey the Messenger (Muhammad)....* ❦-(Surah An-Nisa': 59)" " As well as Allaah's statement, ❦*And whatsoever the Messenger (Muhammad) gives you, take it, and whatsoever he forbids you, abstain (from it)* ❦-(Surah Al-Hashr: 7).

POINTS OF BENEFIT

1. The Sunnah can be correctly described as the firm rope of Allaah.
2. The Prophet of Allaah, may the praise and salutations of Allaah be upon him, explained that he was given the guidance of the Qur'aan and that which was like it, meaning the Sunnah.
3. The Prophet of Allaah, may the praise and salutations of Allaah be upon him, warned the Muslims against only referring to the verses of the Qur'aan and intentionally turning away from the guidance of the Sunnah.
4. Allaah commands the Muslims in the Qur'aan to obey Allaah, to obey His Messenger, and those Muslims who have authority over you.
5. Allaah orders the Muslims in the Qur'aan to accept those commands which the Messenger of Allaah gives them, and to accept those prohibitions which he brings to them.
6. Allaah commands the Muslims to refer back to the guidance of Allaah and His Messenger whenever a dispute arises among them.
7. The one who rejects the authority of the Sunnah in fact rejects the authority of the Qur'aan, which orders the Muslims to follow the Messenger of Allaah and his Sunnah.
8. A person is not able to properly fulfill the commands of the Qur'aan without referring to the Sunnah.
9. The Sunnah explains the Qur'aan and clarifies its guidance.
10. The Sunnah brings forth additional details for general rulings of Islaam found within the verses of the Qur'aan.
11. An example of a general command found in the Qur'aan where the specific details are found in the Sunnah is to perform the ritual prayer or salaat.
12. An example of a general command found in the Qur'aan where the specific details are found in the Sunnah is to make pilgrimage to the house of Allaah, or Hajj.
13. The Sunnah also brings forth additional valid rulings of Islaam, which are not found within the verses of the Qur'aan.
14. The one who rejects the Sunnah, and chooses to turn away from the Sunnah, disbelieves in Islaam and cuts off his connection to Allaah.

LEVEL 1: TEST YOUR UNDERSTANDING:

TRUE & FALSE QUESTIONS

[Circle the correct letter for each individual sentence from today's content.]

01. Many commands of the Qur'aan are general without specifics and details. [T / F]
02. The Sunnah clarifies the commands of the Qur'aan, but does not bring any new commands. [T / F]
03. A person can take what he wants from the Sunnah but must accept the entire Qur'aan. [T / F]

FILL IN THE BLANK QUESTIONS

[Enter the correct individual words to complete the sentences from today's content.]

04. The person who rejects and turns away from the Sunnah _____ off his _____ to Allaah.
05. Not every matter of _____ is detailed in the _____ .
06. The Messenger of Allaah was given the _____ and that which is like it, meaning the _____.

LEVEL 2: INTERACTIVE QUESTIONS & EXERCISES

COMPREHENSIVE UNDERSTANDING QUESTIONS

[In a study group or circle of learning with other students, these questions can be answered fully or partially by one student from the lesson, with another student completing the answer to the same question, by giving a comparable but different which is also correct.]

07. Give another example, other than those mentioned, of a command in Islaam in which the details are found in the Sunnah, not all in the Qur'aan.
08. Is it possible to follow the command in the Qur'aan to obey the Messenger while rejecting the Sunnah? Give an example to explain your answer.
09. Give authentic examples of one command, and one prohibition coming from the Messenger of Allaah, which are not found in the Qur'aan.

DAY - 11

Day 12: Success Is To The Degree You Adhere To The Sunnah

NARRATION FROM AL-IBAANAH AL-SUGHRAH:

Az-Zuhree said, *"Holding firmly to the Sunnah is success. Knowledge will be taken away suddenly.*

The reviving of knowledge makes both one's religion and worldly life steadfast and firm, and the departing of that knowledge occurs through the dying of the scholars."

AUTHENTICITY & SOURCE OF THIS TEXT OR NARRATION:

Authentic: This was narrated by ad-Daarimee and by the author in the related work al-Ibaanah al-Kubraa and al-Laalakaa'ee, and was mentioned by Qadhee 'Ayaadh in his work ash-Shifaa'a.

EXPLANATION BY SHEIKH 'ABDUL-'AZEEZ IBN 'ABDULLAH AR-RAAJHEE

This is a statement from az-Zuhree, who was one of the Successors of a lower rank of the Companions of the Messenger of Allaah, and he was a well-known scholar. His full name was Muhammad Ibn Muslim Ibn 'Ubaydullah Ibn Shihaab az-Zuhree. He was a leading scholar in the science of hadeeth whose renown and knowledge were significant. And this statement from az-Zuhree, may Allaah have mercy upon him, is a tremendous statement. He said, "*Holding firmly to the Sunnah is success.*" By this meaning saved and protected from trials and tribulation, saved from innovation in the religion, and regarding the life to come saved from entering Hellfire. So if an individual is saved from trials and tribulations, and from falling into innovation in the religion, and establishes himself firmly upon the Sharee'ah and the authentic Sunnah, then certainly he is from amongst those who are saved and successful.

Holding firmly to the Sunnah is to be successfully saved. The one who holds firmly to the revealed Sharee'ah of Allaah, and to His religion, and he distances himself from innovation in the religion, this is someone who has achieved salvation. This is the path of contentment and the path of peace.

Holding firmly to the Sunnah is to be successfully saved. Meaning to be saved from falling into trials and to be saved from engaging in that which has been innovated in the religion, and tribulations generally. Therefore the one who is steadfastly establishes himself upon the religion of Allaah, this is the one who is content and happy. Moreover, know that knowledge will be taken away suddenly. Yes, undoubtedly knowledge will being taken away suddenly just as was mentioned previously in the hadeeth narration: *{Verily, Allaah does not take away knowledge by snatching it from the people, but He takes it away by taking away the lives of the religious scholars till none of the scholars remains alive....}*[1] This is how knowledge will be taken away suddenly, through the death of the noble scholars one after the other. In this way knowledge is taken away and no one remains except for the ignorant ones. They then become the leaders of the people and they instruct them in rulings without sound knowledge, so they go astray and they will lead others astray.

---

[1] Saheeh al-Bukhaaree: 100, Saheeh Muslim: 2673, at-Tirmidhee: 2652, Ibn Maajah: 52, the Musnad of Imaam Ahmad: vol.2 no. 162, and ad-Darimee in the introduction to his Sunan: 239

Indeed knowledge will be taken away suddenly, while giving life to knowledge makes both one's religion and worldly life steadfast and firm. Meaning the presence of knowledge and its manifestation, the outward appearance of knowledge, and the spreading of knowledge among the people, this is something which brings steadfastness to the religion and success in one's worldly life. And whenever the presence of knowledge diminishes generally then ignorance spreads and overwhelms, then the people fall into ruin. And giving life to knowledge makes both one's religion and worldly life steadfast and firm. The giving life to knowledge is its manifestation, and its increasing presence, and its being spread among people. This leads to one's religious and worldly affairs becoming steadfast, just as the diminishing of knowledge leads to ruin. It leads to the ruin of both the affairs of the religion as well as those of the world. For this reason he said *{and the true disappearance of knowledge is through the dying of the scholars.}* This is the truth, may Allaah have mercy upon him.

Again he said, that holding firmly to the Sunnah is to be successfully saved and that knowledge will be taken away suddenly, and that steadfastness and the emergence of knowledge leads to steadfastness in one's religion and in one's worldly life. And that the disappearance of knowledge leads to ruin. And when does knowledge disappear? Knowledge is diminished and becomes near extinct, through the death of the knowledgeable scholars. This is why he stated that the true disappearance of knowledge is through the dying of the scholars. Within this is an encouragement to take knowledge from the scholars before they die, especially the scholars of the people of the Sunnah and the Jamaa'ah, the noble guiding scholars, the true scholars who endeavor to warn against innovation in the religion and against taking knowledge from the people of innovation.

POINTS OF BENEFIT

1. Success is generally defined through adherence to the Sunnah.
2. Success means to be saved by guidance from trials and tribulation and from falling into innovation in Islaam.
3. Beneficial knowledge directs a Muslim toward success in his worldly life and steadfastness in his religion.
4. The lack of sound knowledge leads to the ruin of both the affairs of the religion as well as those of the world.
5. The path to contentment and peace is to hold firmly to the revealed Sharee'ah of Allaah.
6. Muhammad Ibn Muslim Ibn 'Ubaydullah Ibn Shihaab az-Zuhree was from the well-known scholars upon the Sunnah in his age.
7. Knowledge is lost from among the people of this world through the dying of the scholars.
8. Knowledge will leave the Muslims suddenly through the deaths of their scholars, one after the other, who were the carriers and clarifiers of knowledge.
9. When the scholars pass away, some people wrongly turn to ignorant individuals to guide them in the matters of their religion.
10. The ignorant individuals who are turned to as leaders after the scholars die do not comprehend their ignorance. As they are misguided themselves, then they further speak from their lack of sound knowledge, and so misguide others, leading them astray.
11. Those harms which are received through the decrease of knowledge are prevented and pushed further away through giving life to and reviving of knowledge.
12. Whenever knowledge decreases, ignorance increases and spreads among the people.
13. The steadfast scholars warn against innovation in the religion and the people of innovation.
14. It is important to take knowledge from the steadfast scholars of the people of the Sunnah and the Jamaa'ah while they are alive.

LEVEL 1: TEST YOUR UNDERSTANDING:

TRUE & FALSE QUESTIONS

[Circle the correct letter for each individual sentence from today's content.]

01. Knowledge in Islaam is generally carried by the scholars. [T / F]
02. Those who are ignorant only cause harm to themselves and not others. [T / F]
03. Beneficial knowledge is something specific to the affairs of our religion. [T / F]

FILL IN THE BLANK QUESTIONS

[Enter the correct individual words to complete the sentences from today's content.]

04. The one who adheres firmly to the Sunnah is _____ in this world from entering into _____ and _____ , and in the life to come saved from entering _____ .
05. Giving life to knowledge makes both one's _____ and _____ life steadfast and firm.
06. The noble guiding scholars _____ against _____ in the religion and the people of _____ .

LEVEL 2: INTERACTIVE QUESTIONS & EXERCISES

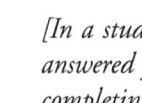

COMPREHENSIVE UNDERSTANDING QUESTIONS

[In a study group or circle of learning with other students, these questions can be answered fully or partially by one student from the lesson, with another student completing the answer to the same question, by giving a comparable but different which is also correct.]

07. Give examples of two guiding scholars who were upon the Sunnah who died in this age or modern period.
08. Give examples of two ignorant modern individuals who people wrongly consider scholars, and who misguide others.
09. Give two examples of incorrect rulings that you generally heard about coming from ignorant individuals which only increase the Muslims in misguidance and harm.

DAY - 12

Day 13: The Incredible Reward For Firmly Holding To The Sunnah

NARRATION FROM AL-IBAANAH AL-SUGHRAH:

The Messenger of Allaah, may Allaah's praise and salutations be upon him, said,

{The one who holds firmly to my Sunnah when corruption has spread among my Ummah has a reward of fifty [who died as martyrs, striving in the path of Allaah.]}

AUTHENTICITY & SOURCE OF THIS TEXT OR NARRATION:

Authentic: This was narrated by at-Tabaraanee in his work al-'Awsat, and Abu Nu'aim in his work al-Hilyah. It was declared weak by Sheikh al-Albaanee in his work Silsilatul-Ahaadeeth adh-Dha'eefah wal Mawdhoo'ah with the addition regarding martyrs, as well as in his verification of the hadeeth narrations in the collection Mishkaat al-Masaabeeh, but is strengthened by various chains of narration without that addition.

Explanation by Sheikh 'Abdul-'Azeez Ibn 'Abdullah ar-Raajhee

This hadeeth narration, *{The one who holds firmly to my Sunnah when corruption has spread among my Ummah has a reward of fifty martyrs}* is from those narrations well-known among the people of knowledge with the phrase *{has a reward of fifty}* without the additional specification of *{fifty martyrs.}* This hadeeth narration has several supporting narrations which strengthen it, and the stronger position regarding its reliability is that it is affirmed from the Messenger of Allaah. The guiding scholar Ibn al-Qayyim, may Allaah have mercy upon him, affirmed its reliability in his work 'al-Kaafeeyatu ash-Shaafeeyyah, bringing the narration *{The one who holds firmly to my Sunnah when corruption has spread among my Ummah has a reward of fifty .}*

Some of the narrations of this hadeeth contains an addition in which it says, *{The Companions said, ' Oh Messenger of Allaah, of fifty of us or from them?' He replied, 'Fifty of you.'}*[1] and in one wording of the narration it says, *{...the one who holds onto his religion will be like the one holding onto a burning ember. The one who holds firmly to my Sunnah has a reward of fifty. The Companions said 'Oh Messenger of Allaah, of fifty of us or from them?' He replied, "Fifty of you. As you have those who assist you upon what is good, but they will find none to assist them upon what is good.}*[2]

Yet this hadeeth narration does not indicate that the one who holds firmly to the Sunnah is better than the Companions of the Prophet! Rather what is intended is that they will receive the reward of fifty individuals, due to this aspect, and in this respect, and because of this specific matter. This matter being holding firmly to the Sunnah, and biting onto it, when there is tremendous wrongdoing and corruption around them. Moreover they will not find someone specific to assist them upon doing good. Such an individual receives the reward of fifty, however the meaning of this is not that due to this they are better than the Companions of the Prophet, no. As the Companions of the Messenger of Allaah have several distinctive merits. They have the merit of being from the Companions, a merit which no one will share with them after that generation until the Day of Judgment. They have the merit of being those who strove in jihaad in the path of Allaah along with the Messenger of Allaah, may the praise and salutations of Allaah be upon him. They have the merit of being those who carried and conveyed the Sharee'ah and the religion of Allaah. As such, the Companions have no comparison or equal to any others from those who come after.

---

[1] Narrated by at-Tirmidhee:3058
[2] Narrated by at-Tirmidhee:3058, Abu Dawood: 4341, Ibn Maajah: 4014

Here is an important principle: the possession of a specific merit or specific praiseworthy characteristic does not equate to having an overall or comprehensive merit. So understanding this principle means that the one who holds firmly to the Sunnah as mentioned from a later time, this is a specific merit, and that specific merit is not greater than the overall general merit of the Companions. So the one who holds firmly to the Sunnah during a time of general corruption spreading among the Muslim Ummah in the later ages, then he receives a reward from this equal to fifty of the Companions in this specific aspect and in relation to this particularly. This specific merit of adhering to the Sunnah in that condition, receives a reward of fifty.

Yet despite that, the Companions are still better than such a person, because the level of merit of the Companions generally cannot be equalled, nor compared to. Consider the merit of them striving in the path of Allaah. Therefore it must be understood that this specific merit of the reward of fifty is not equivalent to the general level of merit of the Companions. As the specific merit is not equivalent to a general, comprehensive, merit.

DAY - 13

Also related to understanding this principle is what is found in the authentic narration that the first one from mankind to be clothed on the Day of Resurrection will be Ibraheem, upon him be Allaah's praise and salutations. The people will be assembled on the Day of Resurrection barefoot, naked, and uncircumcised. The Prophet, upon him be Allaah's praise and salutations, said, *{The first man who will be dressed on the Day of Resurrection will be Ibraheem, upon him be Allaah's praise and salutations...}.*[3] This is a merit specifically for Ibraheem, upon him be Allaah's praise and salutations. Yet our Prophet, upon him be Allaah's praise and salutations, he is his grandson, who has greater merit then his grandfather Ibraheem. Ibraheem is near to him and his level, and this is why he stands back from interceding on the Day of Resurrection. Our Prophet, may Allaah's praise and salutations be upon him, is given precedence in the seeking of intercession by Allaah's permission. The distinctive merit of interceding is tremendous, something which both the early and later people would desire and envy, yet it is for our Prophet Muhammad, may Allaah's praise and salutations be upon him, while Ibraheem has his own unique specific merit, and that is that he will be the first one clothed on the Day of Resurrection.

Similarly, from the specific merits, is that which is held by Musaa, upon him be Allaah's praise and salutations. This is found in the hadeeth in which the Prophet, may Allaah's praise and salutations be upon him, said, *{The people will fall unconscious on the Day of Resurrection and I will be the first to gain consciousness, and behold! Musaa will be there holding the side of Allaah's Throne.}*[4]

---

[3] Saheeh al-Bukhaaree: 3349, Saheeh Muslim: 2860, and at-Tirmidhee:3167, an-Nasaa'ee: 2087, and the Musnad of Imaam Ahmad: vol.1 no. 253

[4] Saheeh al-Bukhaaree:6917 and the Musnad of Imaam Ahmad: vol.3 no. 40

In the wording of one narration *{...Musaa will be there holding the side of Allaah's Throne...}*[5] and in a similar narration *{I will wonder whether he has become conscious before me or he has been exempted, because of his unconsciousness at the Tur (mountain) which he received previously.}*[6] This is a trait of excellence and a distinct merit for Musaa, may Allaah's salutations be upon him, regardless of whether he was of those who were unconscious or he did not become unconscious. For if he did not become unconscious, that itself is a unique merit. If he did become unconscious and awoke before the Prophet Muhammad, may Allaah's praise and salutations be upon him, then that is also a unique merit. However it is a specific merit, since our Prophet, may Allaah's praise and salutations be upon him, possesses many other merits.

What is intended is that this hadeeth has an adequate chain of narration, which has additional chains of narration which support it. It was judged to be authentic by the guiding scholar Ibn al-Qayyim, may Allaah have mercy upon him, in his work al-Kaafeeyatu ash-Shaafeeyyah, as well as in other writings. Yet, it is important to note that the meaning of the narration is not that the one who holds firmly to the Sunnah is better than the Companions, rather as we have discussed, its meaning is clarifying the specific tremendous merit of holding firmly to the Sunnah.

Additionally, as mentioned, in the wording of one of the narrations it states, *{As you have those who assist you upon what is good, but they will find none to assist them upon what is good.}* As such, those who hold firmly to the Sunnah in the later ages will not find those to assist them, whereas the Companions had those who assisted them upon goodness. For this reason such individuals receive the reward of fifty Companions, and become those who have this specific merit.

Also within this narration is an encouragement to hold firmly to the Sunnah, and to cling to it when wrongdoing and innovation in the religion emerges. It also contains a warning against innovating in the religion, and this is the aspect which the author intended in transmitting this narration, may Allaah have mercy upon him, meaning the intention to warn against innovating in the religion. As the one who hold firmly to the Sunnah is far away from innovations and those upon them such as the sects of Jahmeeyah, the Mu'tazilah, the Khawaarij, and the Raafidhah. All of these sects are those who do not hold firmly to the Sunnah. Yet it is an obligation to hold firmly to the Sunnah and to warn against innovation and new matters which are brought forth within Islaam. Yes.

---

[5] Saheeh al-Bukhaaree:2411, Saheeh Muslim: 2373, Abu Dawood:4671
[6] Saheeh al-Bukhaaree:3398, and the Musnad of Imaam Ahmad: vol.3 no. 33

POINTS OF BENEFIT

1. The reward for an action or deed is directly related to the difficulty of fulfilling and achieving it.

2. There is a tremendous reward for the believer who holds firmly to the Sunnah during times of difficulty.

3. There will be periods for the Muslim Ummah in which corruption and wrongdoing is widespread.

4. There will be periods for the Muslim Ummah in which there will be few people to assist us in doing what is good.

5. The tremendous reward mentioned in this narration does not negate the many distinctive merits and exclusive high rank of the Companions generally.

6. There will never exist a generation that reaches the level of excellence reached by the generation of the Companions of the Messenger of Allaah, may Allaah be pleased with them all.

7. It is possible for someone to excel in a specific praiseworthy trait, and still not reach the overall rank of others, such as the rank of the Companions.

8. The Prophet Muhammad, may the praise and salutations of Allaah be upon him, has the highest position and merits among the prophets and messengers.

9. Various prophets and messengers have specific distinctive merits that are exclusive for them alone.

10. It is an obligation to hold firmly to the Sunnah in any age in which wrongdoing and innovations have spread.

11. It is a general obligation to warn against innovation and new matters which appear among the Muslims.

12. From those misguided sects who have separated from the authentic Sunnah are the Jahmeeyah, the Mu'tazilah, the Khawaarij, and the Raafidhah.

LEVEL 1: TEST YOUR UNDERSTANDING:

TRUE & FALSE QUESTIONS

[Circle the correct letter for each individual sentence from today's content.]

01. There is a greater reward for adhering to the truth during times of difficulty. [T / F]

02. The one who gains the reward of fifty of the Companions has excelled them in merit. [T / F]

03. None of the prophets and messengers have distinct merits. [T / F]

FILL IN THE BLANK QUESTIONS

[Enter the correct individual words to complete the sentences from today's content.]

04. The _____ of the Messenger of Allaah have several distinctive _____ .

05. Those who hold firmly to the _____ in the _____ ages will not find those to _____ them.

06. The Muslim who holds firmly to the _____ is far away from _____ .

LEVEL 2: INTERACTIVE QUESTIONS & EXERCISES

COMPREHENSIVE UNDERSTANDING QUESTIONS

[In a study group or circle of learning with other students, these questions can be answered fully or partially by one student from the lesson, with another student completing the answer to the same question, by giving a comparable but different which is also correct.]

07. Discuss two mentioned distinctive merits of the Companions, and explain why no one shares these merits with them.

08. Give two examples of matters which are difficult to do today, which may be part of adhering firmly to the Sunnah.

09. Give two possible examples of beneficial practices or deeds that might be considered from those in which it is hard to find other Muslims to assist them in doing.

Day 14: Follow The Prophet's Sunnah & That Of His Guided Successors

NARRATION FROM AL-IBAANAH AL-SUGHRAH:

The Messenger of Allaah, may Allaah's praise and salutations be upon him, said,

{*Adhere firmly to my Sunnah and the Sunnah of my rightly guided Successors who come after me. Hold firmly to them with your molar teeth.*}

AUTHENTICITY & SOURCE OF THIS TEXT OR NARRATION:

Authentic: This was narrated by at-Tirmidhee, Abu Dawood, Ibn Maajah, and the Musnad of Imaam Ahmad, ad-Daarimee in his Sunan, and al-Baghawee. Sheikh al-Albaanee authenticated it as narrated by adh-Dheeyaa' al-Maqdasee in his work al-Mukhtaarah. Sheikh al-Islaam Ibn Taymeeyah, may Allaah have mercy upon him, said, "adh-Dheeyaa' al-Maqdasee has a book entitled al-Mukhtaarah, and he authenticates this narration within it, in a stronger manner than the authentication of al-Haakim."

EXPLANATION BY SHEIKH 'ABDUL-'AZEEZ IBN 'ABDULLAH AR-RAAJHEE

As such, the hadeeth is authentic, and its chain of narration is acceptable. It is an evidence of the command to adhere closely to the Sunnah, and within it is an encouragement to adhere to the Sunnah of the Prophet, upon him be Allaah's praise and salutations, as well as the sunnah of his rightly guided khalifahs who came after him. It shows that we should hold firmly to the sunnah of his rightly guided khalifahs and they are: Abu Bakr, 'Umar, 'Uthmaan, and 'Alee. The rightly guided khalifahs are these four khalifahs: Abu Bakr, 'Umar, 'Uthmaan, and 'Alee, may Allaah be pleased with them all. We must hold firmly to their established sunnah whenever there is no related guidance from the Sunnah of the Prophet, may Allaah's praise and salutations be upon him, regarding an issue. If, regarding an issue, we do not have a relevant source text to guide us, then we take from the sunnah of these rightly guided khalifahs.

Whereas if there is a relevant source text regarding an issue, then in this case it is obligatory that we follow the guidance of that source text. Such that if there is evidence in a source text from the Book of Allaah and the Sunnah of His Messenger, may Allaah's praise and salutations be upon him, and there is a statement of one of the rightly guided khalifahs, where one of them makes a statement which contradicts or opposes a source text, then it is always obligatory to follow what that source text from Book of Allaah and Sunnah of His Messenger indicates. We consider that statement of one of the rightly guided khalifahs as a statement of independently derived rulings which was incorrect. We say that they attempted to independently derive the correct rulings lacking knowledge of the source text, and ask Allaah to be pleased with them.

From the examples of this is that three of the rightly guided khalifahs: Abu Bakr as-Siddeeq, and 'Umar, and 'Uthmaan, all stated rulings that the pilgrimage or Hajj should be performed by itself and not combined. This is what they stated in rulings they gave to the people after the death of the Prophet, may Allaah's praise and salutations be upon him, that they should perform the Hajj separately and not combined with the performance of 'Umrah. They made an independently derived ruling according to the evidence they possessed and would say to whoever asked them, *"Perform your Hajj separately and then later perform 'Umrah separately at another time."* Such that they would not go to the House of Allaah performing Hajj and then follow this directly with the performance of an 'Umrah.

Whereas the Prophet, may Allaah's praise and salutations be upon him, had commanded the people to combine them together or tamattu'. There are numerous hadeeth narrations from the Prophet, may Allaah's praise and salutations be upon him, where he commanded the Companions to do so during his final pilgrimage, and they would choose which to do when they had reached the point and place of commencing their pilgrimage. When they were close to Mecca he commanded them to enter ihraam and change their intention which was for Hajj alone or Hajj followed by 'Umrah to 'Umrah, so as to become those who were making tamattu' of both together. When they arrived in Mecca he told them to do this when they were at Marwah, such that they all did so except for those who had already brought their sacrificial animals with them.

For this reason, some of the scholars came to hold the view that tamattu' was obligatory. This is what has been narrated from Imaam Ahmad and was the view which was chosen as correct by Ibn al-Qayyim shown in his statement, "*I lean towards affirming the correctness of this statement from the statements of our sheikh, meaning Sheikh al-Islaam Ibn Taymeeyah.*" This was also the view which was held by Sheikh Muhammad Naasiruddeen al-Albaanee, may Allaah have mercy upon him, that tamattu' was obligatory. But what is soundest is what the majority of the scholars hold in that it was not actually an obligation.

Sheikh al-Islaam Ibn Taymeeyah held the view that tamattu' was obligatory upon the the Companions of the Messenger of Allaah so that a false belief held before the time of Islaam would be removed. This was because in the time of Jahiliyyah, before the coming of Islaam, tamattu' was something which was forbidden within the months of Hajj. They believed that tamattu' done in the months of Hajj was from the worst of acts that could be done. They used to say that there is no 'Umrah at the time of Hajj until the days of Hajj had finished. "*When Safar is over and when the sores on the backs of the camels have healed and their hair grown back.*" Meaning from the wounds which had occurred on the camels during Hajj' and they would say "*When signs of those wounds vanish then 'Umrah is permissible for the one who wishes to perform it.*"

So it is seen that the Prophet, may Allaah's praise and salutations be upon him, had stated what differs from their statement, since he commanded the Companions to enter ihraam with the intention of performing Hajj or Hajj along with Umrah, meaning as those doing tamattu'. This ruling was known and taken by Ibn 'Abbaas and 'Alee, may Allaah be pleased with both of them, as well as a group of other Companions. Since it is known that Abu Musaa al-Ash'aree had commanded the people with the ruling of making tamattu'. Yet when some of the people, saw Ibn 'Abbaas, may Allaah be pleased with both of them, commanding the people with this, they said to him, "*You are commanding the people with performing tamattu' in Hajj, but Abu Bakr and 'Umar had commanded the people to perform the Hajj by itself, so how can you oppose them?*"

Ibn 'Abbaas, may Allaah be pleased with them both, replied to them saying, *"I am conveying to you the ruling of the Sunnah, I have with my position the Sunnah, while you only have with your position the statement of Abu Bakr and 'Umar! Indeed, you are on the verge of having stones fall from the heavens upon you! I say to you the Messenger said such and such but you respond with Abu Bakr and 'Umar said?!"* So consider how could someone oppose the Sunnah with statements from Abu Bakr and 'Umar!? Such that if someone opposes the Sunnah with statements of Abu Bakr and 'Umar, it should be feared for them that stones might fall from the heavens upon them. As what else should we expect for someone who opposes the Sunnah with the statement of this person or that person?!?

What is intended in this is clarifying that the sunnah of the rightly guided khalifahs, is to be taken and adopted whenever there is no guidance within the Sunnah about a specific issue or matter. An example of this is: the utilization of an additional adhaan on the day of Jumu'ah. This was a practice which was established by the Commander of the Faithful 'Uthman. This is considered from the sunnah or practice of a rightly guided khalifah. Since in the time of the Prophet, may Allaah's praise and salutations be upon him, as well as that of Abu Bakr and 'Umar, there was only one adhaan on the day of Juma'ah, such that when the khateeb enters the masjid the adhaan would be given. This practice was established during the time when 'Uthman was the khalifah. Because when the number of people in the city of Medina increased, 'Uthmaan, may Allaah be pleased with him, commanded that an additional adhaan be given in the distant parts of the city to warn the people of the approach of Juma'ah. This practice was accepted and confirmed by the Companions at that time, and this is considered from the sunnah or practice of a rightly guided khalifah.

The Messenger of Allaah, may Allaah's praise and salutations be upon him, says in this narration *{...Adhere firmly to my Sunnah and the sunnah of my rightly guided Successors who come after me. Hold firmly to this with your molar teeth...}* and 'hold firmly' means to adhere closely to. And the nuwaajidh, is the plural of naajidh, and the naajidh is the second molar just before the final back molar. Everyone usually has four second molars in his mouth, they are found on every side before the back molars. There is one up here and here, and on the bottom there is one here and here, two on the upper jaw and two on the lower. The narrations says *{...Hold firmly to this with your molar teeth.}* This is said about something that you truly want to hold onto.

So that matter which is something that should be held strongly, it is said for this *{Hold firmly to this with your molar teeth.}* meaning do not be heedless or allow it to be lost so, *{Hold firmly to this with your molar teeth.}* Again, this means to grasp firmly onto, be concerned about maintaining that grasp, and be devoted to keeping that grasp firm. As once a person has devoted himself to something, he is committed to firmly holding onto it with his molar teeth without letting it go. He commits himself to keep a firm grip upon it with his molars, and not let go, yes. This is what the Prophet, may Allaah's praise and salutations be upon him, said.

From this narration the author, may Allaah have mercy upon him, desires to bring forth this warning about innovations related to the proper understanding of Allaah's names and attributes. As in this area there are misguiding innovations from the sects of the Jahmeeyah, the Mu'tazilah, the Ash'arees, and other sects. Therefore what is an obligation upon someone is that they hold firmly to the Sunnah with their molar teeth. That they adhere to the Sunnah of the Prophet, may Allaah's praise and salutations be upon him, as well as the sunnah of the rightly guided khalifahs, and stay far away from innovation and new matters brought forth within the religion of Islaam. This is what is needed regardless of whether the innovations are related to Allaah's names and attributes, or in acts of ritual worship, or in other deeds. Yes.

DAY - 14

POINTS OF BENEFIT

1. The Muslims have been commanded to adhere to the Sunnah of the Prophet, upon him be Allaah's praise and salutations.

2. The Muslims have also been commanded to adhere to the sunnah of his rightly guided khalifahs who came after him.

3. The rightly guided khalifahs are: Abu Bakr, 'Umar, 'Uthmaan, and 'Alee, may Allaah be pleased with them all.

4. The Muslim must hold firmly to the established sunnah of rightly guided khalifahs whenever no related guidance regarding an issue is found within the Sunnah of the Prophet.

5. If there is a contradiction between the statement of one of the rightly guided khalifahs and the authentic Sunnah of the Prophet, the authentic Sunnah of the Prophet is always what should be followed.

6. There were some minor matters in the Prophet's Sunnah which some companions had knowledge of while others did not.

7. The Prophet, may the praise and salutations of Allaah be upon him, commanded the Muslims to perform Hajj or 'Umrah in various ways. One of the affirmed ways was tamattu' where they are performed at the same time.

8. A valid example of the sunnah of the rightly guided khalifahs is the utilization of an additional adhaan on the day of Juma'ah when necessary. This practice was accepted and confirmed by the Companions at that time, and this is considered from the sunnah or practice of a rightly guided khalifah.

9. From the misguiding innovations of the sects of the Jahmeeyah, the Mu'tazilah, the Ash'arees, and others is a distorted understanding of Allaah's names and attributes, not taught by the Companions.

10. Adhering to the Sunnah also means to stay far away from innovation and new matters brought forth within the religion of Islaam.

LEVEL 1: TEST YOUR UNDERSTANDING:

TRUE & FALSE QUESTIONS

[Circle the correct letter for each individual sentence from today's content.]

01. The Hajj pilgrimage must only be performed completely [T / F] separately from 'Umrah.
02. It is only important that we adhere to the Qur'aan and Sunnah [T / F] the Prophet and nothing else.
03. A statement from one of the rightly guided khalifahs can be [T / F] followed instead of an authentic affirmed Sunnah.

FILL IN THE BLANK QUESTIONS

[Enter the correct individual words to complete the sentences from today's content.]

04. Before the coming of Islaam, tamattu' was something _____ within the months of _____ .
05. The sunnah of the rightly guided _____ is taken and _____ whenever there is no guidance within the _____ _____ about a specific issue or matter.
06. The additional _____ on the day of _____ , when necessary, is considered from the _____ of a rightly guided khalifah.

LEVEL 2: INTERACTIVE QUESTIONS & EXERCISES

COMPREHENSIVE UNDERSTANDING QUESTIONS

[In a study group or circle of learning with other students, these questions can be answered fully or partially by one student from the lesson, with another student completing the answer to the same question, by giving a comparable but different which is also correct.]

07. Give an example of a practice of the Sunnah that might be considered strange to some of the Muslims today.
08. Is it possible that a statement of one of the rightly guided khalifahs might be incorrect? Explain your answer.
09. Explain why Ibn 'Abbaas was upset with those Muslims who were following the position of some of the rightly guided khalifahs?

DAY - 14

Day 15: Do Not Speak Against The Best Of Generations

NARRATION FROM AL-IBAANAH AL-SUGHRAH:

The Messenger of Allaah, may Allaah's praise and salutations be upon him, said,

{Do not speak against or insult my Companions. As by the One who holds my soul in His Hand, if one of you were to give an amount of gold equal to the mountain of Uhud, it would not be comparable to a 'mudd' full of gold given by one of them or even half a 'mudd'.}

AUTHENTICITY & SOURCE OF THIS TEXT OR NARRATION:

Authentic: This was narrated by Imaam al-Bukhaaree, Imaam Muslim and at-Tirmidhee who said: This narration is "hasan saheeh" or authentic. It was also narrated by Imaam Ahmad in his work 'Fadhaa'il as-Sahabah', by Abu Dawood, and it was also narrated by Ibn Hibbaan in his work, Saheeh.

EXPLANATION BY SHEIKH 'ABDUL-'AZEEZ IBN 'ABDULLAH AR-RAAJHEE

Yes, this is a tremendous hadeeth narration, one which causes the believer to be amazed. The Prophet, may Allaah's praise and salutations be upon him, said, *{Do not speak against or insult my Companions...}*[1] This hadeeth narration has specific things which caused it. Firstly, this hadeeth is narrated by the two scholars, Imaam al-Bukhaaree and Imaam Muslim, may Allaah have mercy upon them both, in their well-known authentic hadeeth collections. Those two collections are considered the most authentic books in existence after the Book of Allaah, the Most Glorified and the Most Exalted.

The situation behind this hadeeth narration is that a verbal disagreement and a dispute occurred between two noble Companions. One of them was 'Abdur-Rahman Ibn 'Awf and the second was Khaalid Ibn al-Waleed. Between the two of them there had been some arguing, 'Abdur-Rahman Ibn 'Awf was one of the Muslims who embraced Islaam before the opening and victory of entering Mecca, and before the treaty of al-Hudaybeeyah, whereas Khaalid Ibn al-Waleed embraced Islaam after the treaty of al-Hudaybeeyah. It should be noted that the treaty of al-Hudaybeeyah is also called an opening and victory. This is because Allaah called it an opening and victory in his statement, ❖*Verily, We have given you (O Muhammad) a manifest victory.*❖-(Surah Al-Fath: 1) Why was it called a victory? Because after the Treaty of al-Hudaybeeyah, the general situation in the Arabian Peninsula became stable. A peace treaty had been established between the Prophet, may Allaah's praise and salutations be upon him, and those who associated others with Allaah from the leaders of Mecca, and their allies. The treaty caused the hostilities and military struggles between them to come to an end; it brought security to the people. Such that various people from those who associated others with Allaah came and interacted with the Muslims. They listened to the message of the Qur'aan, and a significant number of them embraced Islaam.

The Prophet, may Allaah's praise and salutations be upon him, had turned and focused upon the efforts for what would be the victory at Khaybar, and that battle of Khaybar was won. Thereafter, those who associated others with Allaah from the people of Mecca, or their allies, broke the treaty of al-Hudaybeeyah after two years. For this reason the Prophet, may Allaah's praise and salutations be upon him, reengaged them militarily and fought against them. Then Mecca was conquered. So Allaah, the Most High named the treaty of al-Hudaybeeyah a "manifest victory", because of all of the victories that came after it.

---

[1] Saheeh al-Bukhaaree: 3673, Saheeh Muslim: 2541, at-Tirmidhee: 3861, Abu Dawood: 4658, Ibn Maajah: 161 and the Musnad of Imaam Ahmad: vol.3 pg. 54

The conquest of Mecca was also a victory like that mentioned in His statement ❴*Verily, We have given you (O Muhammad) a manifest victory.*❵-(Surah Al-Fath: 1). Allaah called the opening of Mecca a victory in His statement, ❴*Not equal among you are those who spent and fought before the conquering (of Makkah) (with those among you who did so later). Such are higher in degree than those who spent and fought afterwards. But to all, Allaah has promised the best (reward). And Allaah is All-Aware of what you do.*❵-(Surah Al-Hadeed: 10) So they are not equal, meaning those who spent their wealth in the path of Allaah and struggled and fought in the path of Allaah before the Treaty of al-Hudaybeeyah, and those that did so afterwards, meaning after the treaty.

It is seen that the Treaty of al-Hudaybeeyah is what distinguishes between those who were designated as the "Saabiqoon al-Awwaloon" or the early Companions in the Qur'aan, those who were the first Muslims to embrace Islaam of the Muhaajiroon, who migrated from Mecca to Medinah, and those Muslims who embraced Islaam after the treaty of al-Hudaybeeyah. Those who embraced Islaam afterwards were not of this distinguished level, so this should be clear.

This is because the Companions of the Messenger of Allaah are of different levels. Among them are some of the Companions who embrace Islaam after the conquest of Mecca, they were called "those who had been released" or "those who had been liberated". Among this level of companions was Abu Sufyaan, and Mu'aweeyah, and his son Yazeed. So then how many levels are there among the Companions of the Messenger of Allaah? The "Saabiqoon al-Awwaloon" mentioned in the Qur'aan, those who were the first Muslims to embrace Islaam of the Muhaajiroon, who had embraced Islaam before the Treaty of al-Hudaybeeyah. Then coming after them in merit are those Companions who embraced Islaam after the Treaty of al-Hudaybeeyah but before the conquest of Mecca. Then coming after them in merit are those who embraced Islaam on the day that Mecca was conquered. These are three distinct levels. So from the "Saabiqoon al-Awwaloon" or the early Companions who had embraced Islaam before the Treaty of al-Hudaybeeyah was 'Abdur-Rahman Ibn 'Awf. He had embraced Islaam before the Treaty of al-Hudaybeeyah, and so was counted among the "Saabiqoon al-Awwaloon". Khaalid Ibn al-Waleed was from those Companions who embraced Islaam after the Treaty, and so was not considered from the highest rank of the "Saabiqoon al-Awwaloon" or the early Companions.

So when a misunderstanding occurred between 'Abdur-Rahman Ibn 'Awf and Khaalid Ibn al-Waleed, and Khaalid abused and spoke harshly to 'Abdur-Rahman Ibn 'Awf, the Prophet, may Allaah's praise and salutations be upon him, forbade Khaalid from speaking harshly to 'Abdur-Rahman. He, may Allaah's praise and salutations be upon him, said to Khaalid, {*Do not speak against or insult my Companions...*} Meaning by this those who had higher merit in precedence of being from the early Companions, even though Khaalid was also from his Companions.

The Prophet, may Allaah's praise and salutations be upon him, said, *{Do not speak against or insult my Companions. As by the One who holds my soul in His Hand, if one of you were to give an amount of gold equal to the mountain of Uhud, it would not be comparable to a mudd full of gold given by one of them or even half a mudd.}* So the Prophet, may Allaah's praise and salutations be upon him, forbade one who was from the later ranks of the Companions from abusing someone who was of the highest rank from among his Companions. He, may Allaah's praise and salutations be upon him, stated that if Khaalid Ibn al-Waleed was to give gold which equaled the weight of the sizable mountain of Uhud in the path of Allaah, and 'Abdur-Rahman Ibn 'Awf was to give gold equal to mudd or half this amount, the amount given by Khaalid would not be equal to that given by 'Abdur-Rahman, due to the difference in their two ranks as Companions.

But what exactly is a mudd in measurement? It is a volume measurement which was approximately the amount held in two average hands, and a specific container (which is around three quarters of a liter). It is comparable to the approximate amount of a double handful of an average man, not those hands which are large nor those which are small. This is what is designated as a mudd in measurement. The larger measurement of a Saa' is equal to four mudds in the mentioned volume combined or from those related containers known by this name. So if Khaalid Ibn al-Waleed was to give the amount of the mountain of 'Uhud in gold, and 'Abdur-Rahman was to give that in gold which was approximately a handful or half a mudd, 'Abdur-Rahman's given amount would have more value. Why is this the case? Because 'Abdur-Rahman was from the rank of the "Saabiqoon al-Awwaloon" or the early Companions, while Khaalid was from one of the later ranks of the Companions.

As such the Prophet, may Allaah's praise and salutations be upon him, spoke to Khaalid, saying what means do not abuse my early or first Companions, those whose precedence and companionship was established early. He spoke to one who had a lesser degree of Companionship, and said to him, *{Do not speak against or insult my Companions. As by the One who holds my soul in His Hand...}* So he said this to him through making an oath, and certainly the Prophet is the truthful one even if he had not made an oath. However to emphasize this distinction he said, *{As by the One who holds my soul in His Hand, if one of you were to give..}* Meaning those of you from the later Companions, *{..an amount of gold equal to the mountain of Uhud, it would not be comparable to a mudd full of gold given by one of them}* meaning the "Saabiqoon al-Awwaloon" or the early Companions *{...or even half a mudd.}*

If this distinction existed between and among the Companions of the Messenger of Allaah, may Allaah's praise and salutions be upon him, meaning between the "Saabiqoon al-Awwaloon", or the early Companions, and between those who embraced Islaam after the treaty of al-Hudaybeeyah, how significant is the difference between the one who embraced Islaam after the treaty of al-Hudaybeeyah, and someone who embraces Islaam on the day of the conquest of Mecca?? Moreover, how significant the difference would be between the Companions of the Messenger of Allaah generally, and those who came after them! The incredible degrees of this difference is something only known to Allaah.

When the Prophet, may Allaah's praise and salutations be upon him, addressed Khaalid and said *{Do not speak against or insult my Companions...}*, its meaning was, that it is not possible for you to reach the same rank and merit that they have reached. So how could this be possible for someone who comes after the generation of the Companions of the Messenger of Allaah, from the generation of the Successors, or from those who came after them? What about those that abuse and speak against the Companions?!? For this reason this indicates a tremendous issue, that the speaking against or cursing the Companions is a very significant and grave matter. That doing so is a very dangerous matter and is not something to be taken lightly.

DAY - 15

This narration also includes a warning against abusing the Companions, as well as that it is obligatory to: be pleased with them, be pleased with all of them, to always place them in their proper position and rank, to comprehend their merits and their precedence among the Muslims, to recognize their efforts of striving in the path of Allaah along with the Prophet, may Allaah's praise and salutations be upon him, and their efforts of conveying and spreading the religion of Allaah, the Most Glorified and the Most Exalted. It indicates that it is obligatory to have allegiance and support for them, to ask for mercy for them, and to believe that they are the best of the people, and the most virtuous of humanity.

Additionally, it informs us that the Companions are considered the best of humanity in merits, after the exclusive merit of the prophets of Allaah, that there was never a generation like them nor will there ever be, that it is not possible for anyone after them to reach their level and rank, and that whatever came from them of slips and misunderstandings is considered either an independently derived dconclusion they came to, in which they were correct and received two rewards, or an independently derived conclusion that they came to which was incorrect, leaving them with a single reward and a mistake which is forgiven by Allaah.

As for the numerous historical reports which are transmitted regarding disputes between the Companions, then they are as was mentioned by Sheikh al-Islaam Ibn Taymeeyah, may Allaah have mercy upon him, in his work al-'Aqeedah al-Waasiteeyah, that the majority of what has been transmitted regarding disputes between the Companions are fabrications, with no authentic basis to them. This is one category of these reports, those which are complete fabrications with no authentic basis. There is a second category of those that have a historical origin and basis, that have been corrupted through additions being added to them, or elements of the transmissions deleted and taken away. Moreover, there is the third category of that which is authentically related. Whatever is authentically related from them is considered the efforts of independently derived conclusions in which the one who was correct receives two rewards, and the one who was incorrect in his conclusion only receives a single reward.

Furthermore regarding whatever occurred of sins from the Companions, then it should be known that there are established reasons which ensured that their sins were forgiven generally. Additionally, due to their merit, one of them will be forgiven for something which another person, not from their generation, may not be forgiven for. Since if someone from the Muslims generally commits a sin, he may be forgiven by sincerely repenting from it, he may be forgiven by the intercession of the Prophet, may Allaah's praise and salutations be upon him, which will occur on the Day of Judgment, and he may be forgiven due to the many good deeds he has put forth. Yet the Companions are above this, since those sins which a Companion may have committed, indeed are forgiven simply due to their rank as Companions, due to their striving in the path of Allaah alongside the Prophet, may Allaah's praise and salutations be upon him, and due to their precedence in their being the first to embrace Islaam.

Likewise, they will be forgiven due to the intercession of the Prophet, may Allaah's praise and salutations be upon him, on the Day of Judgment of which they are the first people to receive it. They also have been blessed by Allaah to turn in repentance for their mistakes, their sins have been forgiven by their many good deeds which wipe away sins, or by the many trials they suffered. So how was it possible, after considering all of this, that some people would come in the later times, and abuse and speak against the Companions and even declare them disbelievers? Indeed we ask Allaah for safety and well-being. Yes.

POINTS OF BENEFIT

1. It is prohibited for any Muslim to insult or speak against the Companions of the Messenger of Allaah, may Allaah be pleased with all of them.

2. The Companions of the Messenger of Allaah sometimes disagreed and argued with each other.

3. The Companions of the Messenger of Allaah have different ranks and levels of merit among themselves in relation to when they embraced Islaam.

4. Those Companions who were of the highest rank and merit were those who embraced Islaam in Mecca and then emigrated to the city of Medina. These were the "Saabiqoon al-Awwaloon" mentioned in the Qur'aan,

5. Then there are those Companions who had embraced Islaam before the Treaty of al-Hudaybeeyah.

6. Then coming after them in merit are those Companions who embraced Islaam after the Treaty of al-Hudaybeeyah but before the conquest of Mecca.

7. Then coming after them in merit are those who embraced Islaam on the day that Mecca was conquered.

8. The treaty of al-Hudaybeeyah is considered an opening and victory for the Muslims.

9. The treaty of Hudaybeeyah enabled many to come and interact with the Muslims in peace and stability. As such many listened to the message of the Qur'aan, and significant numbers of them embraced Islaam.

10. Allaah, the Most High, named the treaty of al-Hudaybeeyah a "manifest victory", because of all of the victories that came after it.

11. The victory of the Muslims at Khaybar came after the treaty of al-Hudaybeeyah and before the conquest of Mecca.

12. The opening and victory of entering Mecca is considered an opening and victory for the Muslims.

13. A mudd is volume measurement which was approximately the amount held in two average hands, or a specific container.

14. A Saa' is a volume measurement equal to four mudds as described.

15. The Prophet was known to be truthful even if he had not made an oath, both before and after being given prophethood.

LEVEL 1: TEST YOUR UNDERSTANDING:

TRUE & FALSE QUESTIONS

[Circle the correct letter for each individual sentence from today's content.]

01. The Companions of the Messenger of Allaah all have the same rank. [T / F]

02. Some of the events during the life of the Prophet led to many people embracing Islaam. [T / F]

03. The treaty of al-Hudaybeeyah did not affect the spread of Islaam. [T / F]

FILL IN THE BLANK QUESTIONS

[Enter the correct individual words to complete the sentences from today's content.]

04. The first Muslims to embrace Islaam were the _____ , who migrated from _____ to _____

05. The treaty of al-Hudaybeeyah is called an _____ and _____ for Islaam, and the Muslims.

06. The people of Mecca, or their allies, _____ the treaty of al-Hudaybeeyah after _____ years.

LEVEL 2: INTERACTIVE QUESTIONS & EXERCISES

COMPREHENSIVE UNDERSTANDING QUESTIONS

[In a study group or circle of learning with other students, these questions can be answered fully or partially by one student from the lesson, with another student completing the answer to the same question, by giving a comparable but different which is also correct.]

07. Give examples of two difficulties which the Muhaajiroon faced that those who embraced Islaam later did not encounter.

08. How was the period right after the treaty of al-Hudaybeeyah different in terms of spreading Islaam to the people?

09. Name another well-known Companion from the Muhaajiroon, and describe one way that they helped support Islaam.

Day 16: Know That Knowledge Is Received And Can Be Lost

NARRATION FROM AL-IBAANAH AL-SUGHRAH:

The Messenger of Allaah, may Allaah's praise and salutations be upon him, said,

{Indeed Allaah will not withdraw knowledge by taking it out of the hearts of men, but it will be taken away through the death of the scholars with their knowledge. Such that when no scholars remain the people will take ignorant people as those to direct their affairs. When those people are asked, they will give people verdicts according to their opinions and, in so doing, they will misguide others and be misguided.}

AUTHENTICITY & SOURCE OF THIS TEXT OR NARRATION:

Authentic: This was narrated by at-Tirmidhee who said: This narration is "hasan saheeh" or authentic, by Ibn Maajah, and by Ibn Wadhaah in his work "Innovation & The Prohibition Regarding It" with an authentic chain of narration. It was also narrated by ash-Shihaab al-Qudhaa'ee in his Musnad, and al-Haythamee said about it in his work al-Majmu'a: it was narrated by at-Tabaraanee in al-Awsaat, al-Bazaar through chains of narration which have weakness, and it was narrated by 'Abdur-Razzaq in his Musannaf, as well as by Ibn al-Mubaarak in his work az-Zuhd.

Explanation by Sheikh 'Abdul-'Azeez Ibn 'Abdullah ar-Raajhee

Yes, the author, may Allaah have mercy upon him, has mentioned that this narration is narrated by at-Tirmidhee, ash-Shihaab, Ibn Maajah, and 'Abdur-Razzaq. However he failed to mention in the notes that this narration was one of those collected by the two well-known leading scholars of hadeeth: Imaam al-Bukhaaree and Imaam Muslim in their authentic collections. That citation from the two authentic well-known collections was also not mentioned by the verifier of this work. This hadeeth, which is narrated by both Imaam al-Bukhaaree and Imaam Muslim, is found in Saheeh al-Bukhaaree with the following wording: Ismaa'eel Ibn Abee 'Uwais narrated to us saying, Maalik narrated to me on the authority of Hishaam Ibn 'Urwaah from his father that 'Abdullah bin 'Amr bin Al-'As said:

I heard Allaah's Messenger, may Allaah's praise and salutations be upon him, saying, *{Allaah does not take away the knowledge by taking it away from the hearts of the people, but takes it away by the death of the religious learned men, till when none of the religious learned men with their knowledge remain, people will take as their leaders ignorant people, who, when consulted, will give their verdict without knowledge. So they will go astray and will lead the people astray.}*[1] al-Faraberee said, "'Abbaas narrated to us saying Qutaybah narrated to us saying Jareer narrated to us on the authority of Hishaam what is similar to this narration." Imaam Muslim narrated it similarly.

This was a slip and an error from the verifier, because the two authentic collections of Imaam al-Bukhaaree and Imaam Muslim are the stronger and more authentic sources of narrations. Therefore what would have been proper is that the verifier referred back to their source in the two Saheeh collections before the other citations. However perfection and completeness is for Allaah alone. The Prophet, may Allaah's praise and salutations be upon him, said, *{Allaah does not take away the knowledge by taking it away from the hearts of the people, but takes it away by the death of the religious learned men...}* This contains an encouragement towards acquiring knowledge, and taking knowledge directly from the mouths of the scholars before they are gone, before they die. It also contains an affirmation that the disappearance of knowledge is through the disappearance or leaving of the scholars, even if we have books remaining within our hands. The Qur'aan and the Sunnah are present with us, within our hands, however it is the scholars who are the ones who explain matters to the people. It is the scholars who clarify the meaning of the precious and noble Book of Allaah and the proper meanings of the narrations from the Sunnah. They are the ones who correctly reconcile between the different source texts, and suitably interpret them in a way which the evidences and principles indicate.

---

[1] Saheeh al-Bukhaaree: 100, Saheeh Muslim: 2673, at-Tirmidhee: 2652, Ibn Maajah: 52, ad-Daarimee in his Sunan: 239, and the Musnad of Imaam Ahmad: vol.2 pg.162

This is as opposed to the way of the people of innovation in the religion. As the people of innovation in the religion wrongly throw one source text against another so that they clash or conflict, interpreting them in a way which the evidences and principles do not indicate. And through doing so, they themselves are astray and they lead others astray, and indeed there is no strength nor power except through Allaah.

Within this narration is an encouragement towards seeking knowledge, giving importance to acquiring knowledge, and taking knowledge from the mouths of the scholars. It is not enough that a person just take knowledge from books and reading; this is not sufficient. There is no one who has properly learned and becomes a true grounded student of knowledge relying solely upon books, never. Rather knowledge is taken from the mouths of the scholars. If a person was to sit for the length of his entire life, and he had with him books, he would not reach the level of being a student of knowledge. That way is not sufficient to become a true student of knowledge. For this reason some of the scholars have said, *"The one whose scholar is his book, then his mistakes are greater than what he is correct in."* So this hadeeth narration is clear, the Prophet, may Allaah's praise and salutations be upon him, said, *{Allaah does not take away the knowledge by taking it away from the hearts of the people...}.* Knowledge is not removed by taking it out of people's hearts, but it is removed by what? By the deaths and the passing from this world of the scholars. The scholars die one after the other after the other, until knowledge disappears, and there is no strength nor power except in Allaah. Such that when no scholars remain, as is mentioned in one narration *{...till none of the scholars stays alive. Then the people will take ignorant ones as their leaders, who, when asked to deliver religious verdicts, will issue them without knowledge, the result being that they will go astray and will lead others astray.}* There is no strength nor power except in Allaah.

This, turning to ignorant people to act as scholars, occurs when the scholars die, then in relation to these societal positions, the scholars previous held, the ignorant take and occupy them. They wrongly take that general position of guiding the affairs of the people and explaining matters for them: issuing them rulings, judging between them, and teaching them the religion, and other similar matters which are required by the people. There must be those who fulfill these needs. Such that when the scholars die, those who are known as the people of insight or the people of knowledge, then who will explain and clarify matters to the general Muslims? Who will properly explain giving examples to follow from the sources of guidance? When the presence of the scholars comes to an end among the people, these affairs are taken up by those who are not from the people of knowledge.

Yet those who will be turned to in order to explain and clarify, it is inevitable that they will issue rulings, will judge in affairs, will teach the people, and convey to them knowledge. As within these institutions in society and in these positions, there will inevitably be someone considered a mufti who issues rulings, and someone considered a judge who issues judgments, and someone considered a teacher who instructs the people. But when such people in these positions do not possess clear Sharee'ah knowledge and insight, then they will issue rulings without sound knowledge, and they will teach the people while lacking sound knowledge, and they will issue judgments for the people in the absence of sound knowledge. Therefore, they themselves are misguided and call others to be misguided to fall into ruin. Certainly there is no strength nor power except in Allaah. Yes.

DAY - 16

POINTS OF BENEFIT

1. The two foremost collections of authentic hadeeth narrations are Saheeh al-Bukhaaree and Saheeh Muslim.

2. There is no book which is perfect other than the Qur'aan, as perfection is for Allaah alone.

3. A Muslim is encouraged to gain authentic knowledge whenever possible as there will be times in which sound knowledge is difficult to obtain.

4. Knowledge should first and foremost be taken directly from its carriers who are the scholars.

5. The disappearance of knowledge is caused by the dying of the scholars, and there being fewer people of knowledge among the people.

6. The source texts of the Qur'aan and Sunnah are preserved and present in every generation, however it is the scholars who properly explain the source texts.

7. The scholars of the Sunnah are the people who have the ability to properly interpret the evidences of the source texts and implement the principles and rulings found within them.

8. The scholars of the Sunnah are those who have the ability to understand the entire body of source texts, and reconcile their meanings in the way intended by Allaah.

9. The people of innovation are those whose misguided way is to wrongly interpret the source texts so that they conflict with one another, ignoring the sound principles of knowledge which the people of the Sunnah proceeded upon.

10. The people of innovation have deviated away from the Sunnah, and so became misguided, and then they further misguided others by spreading and calling to their innovations and misconceptions.

11. Studying only from books is only a means that should be turned to out of necessity, when our circumstances prevent us from taking knowledge from the scholars directly.

12. The individual whose only scholar is his book, then his mistakes are greater than what he is correct in.

13. When the reliable scholars die, the general people will wrongly turn for their knowledge to others who lack comprehensive sound knowledge and fail to understand the established principles within Islaam.

14. Those individuals who issue Islamic rulings without possessing the sound knowledge to do so are misguided, and so misguide others. They are deficient in their knowledge and understanding, and they pass that deficiency on to the people generally.

LEVEL 1: TEST YOUR UNDERSTANDING:

TRUE & FALSE QUESTIONS

[Circle the correct letter for each individual sentence from today's content.]

3 min

01. There is no difference in learning from books or from scholars directly. [T / F]
02. There will come a time in which knowledge will disappear and not be easily found among people. [T / F]
03. It is possible for anyone to issue correct rulings and judgments in Islaam. [T / F]

FILL IN THE BLANK QUESTIONS

[Enter the correct individual words to complete the sentences from today's content.]

6 min

04. Allaah does not take away the _____ by taking it away from the _____ of the people.
05. The _____ are needed to be those who _____ matters to the people and _____ the intended meanings of the Qur'aan and Sunnah.
06. The people of _____ wrongly throw one source text against another so that they clash or _____ .

DAY - 16

LEVEL 2: INTERACTIVE QUESTIONS & EXERCISES

COMPREHENSIVE UNDERSTANDING QUESTIONS

[In a study group or circle of learning with other students, these questions can be answered fully or partially by one student from the lesson, with another student completing the answer to the same question, by giving a comparable but different which is also correct.]

21-36 min

07. Explain misconceptions or ideas that people hold that cause them to refrain from learning from scholars.
08. Give the name of one well-known scholar of this age who has died, and mention one of the areas of knowledge which they were proficient in.
09. Discuss one shortcoming of studying only from books and not from the scholars themselves. Give a possible example to explain your answer.

Day 17: The Reality Of The People Of Misguidance & Their Deceptions

NARRATION FROM AL-IBAANAH AL-SUGHRAH:

Imaam Ibn Battah, may Allaah have mercy upon him, said, "*These different statements and various developed ways all have leaders and heads from among the people of misguidance, and forerunners in their advocating disbelief and putting forth misguided statements. They say about Allaah that which they have no basis for and no knowledge of. They find fault with the people of the truth in what they bring forth of truth, and criticize the reliable ones in what they transmit of guidance. Yet they fail to condemn their very own distorted interpretations found within their opinions.*

They have firmly planted the flags and banners of innovation among people, and set up marketplaces for the distribution of enticing trials and turmoil. They have opened the door of ordeals and afflictions, have fabricated falsehoods about Allaah, spoken about His Book upon lies, and have a hidden enmity to the truth. They proceed as the brothers to the Shaytaans among men and jinn, while standing as enemies of the believers, acting as a sheltering cave for the unjust wrongdoers, they serve as a refuge for those afflicted with jealousy.

They are of and from various people and tribes, and from different divisions and groupings of individuals. And I will mention a number of their names, and some of their characteristics, as they have writings which have circulated and statements that have appeared. Statements that will not easily be recognized as false by the unsophisticated people or the young person among the youth. Indeed, the majority of those who read it will not be able to recognize the errors within it.

Perhaps a young person will come across a book by one of the astray individuals who advocates these misguided statements, where that author begins with the praise of Allaah and glorifying Him, and then with the extensive sending of praise and salutations upon the Prophet, may Allaah's praise and salutations be upon him. Yet thereafter he brings forth his subtle and intricate forms of disbelief, and imperceptibly introduces his invented concepts and general evil.

So due to this a young person who does not possess a significant amount of knowledge, the non-Arabic speaking Muslim, and the unsophisticated general Muslim could wrongly come to believe that this author is a steadfast scholar from among the scholars, or is indeed a reliable scholar of the area of fiqh from among the scholars specializing in this area. Thereafter perhaps, through those misguided authors, he will then wrongly come to believe that these practices are correct, meaning what is seen among this Ummah of false practices related to worshiping idols, and he might eventually become someone who in fact fights against Allaah, standing as an associate to Shaytaan."

SOURCE OF THIS TEXT OR NARRATION:

This is a statement of the compiler of this work: Abu 'Abdullah Ubayd'Allaah Ibn Muhammad Ibn Muhammad Ibn Hamdan Ibn Battah al-Ukbaree, may Allaah have mercy upon him.

Explanation by Sheikh 'Abdul-'Azeez Ibn 'Abdullah ar-Raajhee

The author, may Allaah have mercy upon him, this is from his admonition and advice to the Muslims. The author, may Allaah have mercy upon him, says that as for these misguided statements and claims, these sects, these false methodologies of thought for which I will name their originators and leaders: meaning Jahm Ibn Safwaan is the originator of the sect of the Jahmeeyah, and the likes of 'Amr Ibn 'Ubayd and Waasil Ibn 'Ataa' are leaders of the the sect of the Mu'tazilah, and the likes of Ma'bad al-Juhanee, and Gheelaan ad-Damashqee, they are from the leaders of the sect of the Qadareeyah

He said: *"These different statements and various innovated ways all have leaders and heads from among the people of misguidance, and forerunners in their advocating disbelief and misguided statements..."* Then he continues to say, warning from them since they make statements of disbelief, *"...They say about Allaah that which they have no basis for and no knowledge of."* Meaning the various ways or methodologies of major disbelief whose adherents are disbelievers. As for those deviated ways whose deviation does not reach the level of major disbelief in Islaam, then they are not considered disbelievers.

What is intended here are the people who stand upon the various misguided ways and methodologies which are at the level of disbelief, about whom he says, *"...forerunners in their advocating disbelief and misguided statements..."* and *"They say about Allaah that which they have no basis for and no knowledge of. They find fault with the people of the truth in what they bring forth of truth and they criticize the reliable ones in what they transmit of guidance."* Due to this they will not accept those definitive source text from the authentic Sunnah, and *"they fail to condemn their very own distorted interpretations found within their opinions."*

"They have firmly planted the flags and banners of innovation among people, and established marketplaces for the distribution of enticing trials and turmoil." This is the general condition and way. *"They have opened the door of ordeals and afflictions,"* which they cause by establishing themselves upon innovation in the religion. *"...fabricated falsehoods about Allaah"*, this means they made false claims, by saying that they were upon the truth, and asserting that the people of the Sunnah are those who have gone astray. *"...spoken about His Book upon lies, and have a hidden enmity to the truth. They proceed as the brothers to the Shaytaans among men and jinn, while standing as enemies of the believers, acting as a sheltering cave for the unjust wrongdoers, they serve as a refuge for those afflicted with jealousy.*

They are of and from various people and tribes, and from different divisions and groupings of individuals."

Thereafter the author states, *"And I will mention a number of their names, and some of their characteristics. This is because they have writings which have circulated and statements that have appeared among the people,"* Meaning that I'm going to discuss a number of their characteristics so that a person will not be deceived. Because the inexperienced or unsophisticated person doesn't recognize them. An unsophisticated person who doesn't test and carefully weigh matters will be deceived by them, as he is someone who does not know the reality of their books, nor the misleading nature of their misguidance, and does not recognize what they have innovated.

"…or one of the youth." Because someone from the youth, meaning a young man or woman in their early years, and someone who has only begun seeking knowledge, will be deceived by their books. The meaning of the subtle misguidance in the books they have written will not be recognized by the majority of people who read them.

"Perhaps a young person" meaning someone who is still in the years of his youth *"will come across a book by one of the individuals who advocate these misguided statements,"* meaning misguided statements which are innovation. *"He begins with the praise of Allaah and glorifying Him, and with the extensive sending of praise and salutations upon the Prophet, may Allaah's praise and salutations be upon him. Yet after this he brings forth his subtle and intricate forms of disbelief."* This is in fact what is being seen. If you open up one of the books of the people of innovation, you'll find within it that first they praise Allaah, and then send salutations and praise upon the Messenger of Allaah, then they may bring an excellent description of the Prophet, may Allaah's praise and salutations be upon him. Therefore this deceives you, and you say, "This is a good book." For this reason the author is saying, do not be deceived by this! He continues, *"Yet after this he brings forth his subtle and intricate forms of disbelief, and imperceptibly introduces his invented concepts and general evil."* So again, don't be deceived by this, when you see that he begins the book by praising Allaah, and sending praise and salutations upon the Messenger of Allaah, because afterwards he follows this by presenting to you his subtle and intricate forms of disbelief, so you should be on your guard! He says, *"So the young person"* meaning the young person, beacause in his youth he does not have a good amount of knowledge.

"…or the non-Arabic speaking Muslim, or the unsophisticated general Muslim" as they are from those who often do not test and investigate matters coming from the people. Such people would wrongly assume that the one who authored a book which begins this way is a steadfast scholar from among the accepted scholars, or a knowledgeable scholar of fiqh from among the scholars specializing in this area of the Sharee'ah. What is such a person considered? Such a person is considered a beginner in understanding, and he will be deceived. What deceives them is that the author begins with the praising Allaah, and the sending of salutations and praise upon the Messenger of Allaah. When he sees the mention of salutations upon the

Prophet, may Allaah's praise and salutations be upon him, he says to himself *"This looks like a good book."* However, these beginning aspects of the book are in reality usually placed there both by a true scholar as well as usually being placed there by the misguided apostate upon extreme innovation!

Perhaps the one who authored such a misguiding book is actually one of the leaders of misguidance, from the forerunners advocating disbelief and misguided statements. One who wrongly believes and supports what may be seen from this Ummah of false practices related to worshiping idols, and wrongly believes that the people of the Sunnah and the Jamaa'ah are those who associate others with Allaah,. One who, in reality, fights against Allaah and unknowingly supports Shaytaan, yes.

DAY - 17

POINTS OF BENEFIT

1. The different paths of misguidance all have individuals and leaders that proceed upon them and call to them.

2. The people of misguidance speak about Allaah without having sound knowledge or evidence.

3. The people of misguidance interpret the Qur'aan with lies and misconceptions.

4. The people of misguidance criticize the people of the Sunnah, because what the people of the Sunnah transmit and call to contradicts them and their falsehoods.

5. The people of misguidance have based their distorted interpretations of the source texts upon their opinions and desires.

6. The people of misguidance actively invite to their innovation, pulling the people towards trials in several ways.

7. The people of misguidance are in fact enemies of the Sunnah and the people of the Sunnah.

8. The people of misguidance are varied in terms of their origin, types, and characteristics.

9. When their statements and writings have spread amongst the people, then identifying the people of misguidance by their specific names prevents harm coming to those who could not recognize their falsehood.

10. The people of misguidance disguise their misguidance under a misleading covering resembling the truth.

11. The people of misguidance may first bring general statements which are true and acceptable, and then after this bring specific statements of falsehood and innovation.

12. Some forms of misguidance will not be recognized by the common people, nor those who are young, nor by those Muslims who do not speak Arabic, but only by the discerning scholars.

13. Someone who fails to turn away from a work or book that has subtle forms of misguidance within it may eventually come to accept greater forms of misguidance and be misled away from the straight path of Islaam.

14. It is important to carefully consider the beliefs and methodology of the author of any book we choose to learn Islaam from.

LEVEL 1: TEST YOUR UNDERSTANDING:

TRUE & FALSE QUESTIONS

[Circle the correct letter for each individual sentence from today's content.]

01. The people of misguidance oppose the guidance of the Sunnah in several ways. [T / F]

02. It is not important to carefully select the books one reads, as long as they are from Muslims. [T / F]

03. People are often confused as to who are actually reliable scholars we should benefit from. [T / F]

FILL IN THE BLANK QUESTIONS

[Enter the correct individual words to complete the sentences from today's content.]

04. A _____ person who does not possess a significant amount of _____ can be misled by _____ .

05. Jahm Ibn Safwaan is the originator of the sect of the _____ .

06. The subtle _____ in the books of the people of falsehood may not be recognized by the _____ of people who read them.

LEVEL 2: INTERACTIVE QUESTIONS & EXERCISES

COMPREHENSIVE UNDERSTANDING QUESTIONS

[In a study group or circle of learning with other students, these questions can be answered fully or partially by one student from the lesson, with another student completing the answer to the same question, by giving a comparable but different which is also correct.]

07. Give one way the people are misled by those using modern technology, causing them to wrongly believe that someone is a reliable scholar.

08. Explain one way a general Muslim can be truly confident that a book they want to benefit from is sound and acceptable.

09. Name one of the leaders or ideological figureheads from any one of the misguided movements or groups present among the Muslims today.

DAY - 17

Day 18: The Believers Are Distinct Upon Revealed Guidance

NARRATION FROM AL-IBAANAH AL-SUGHRAH:

Imaam Ibn Battah, may Allaah have mercy upon him, said,

"Allaah the Most High's statement ﴾ *And it has already been revealed to you in the Book (this Qur'aan) that when you hear the Verses of Allaah being denied and mocked at, then sit not with them, until they engage in a talk other than that; (but if you stayed with them) certainly in that case you would be like them. Surely, Allaah will collect the hypocrites and disbelievers all together in Hell.* ﴿–(Surah an-Nisa' :140)

This is from what the believers have been commanded to do of separating from those who oppose their own sound beliefs, those who severed their attachment to it, those who speak against their clear religion, by this meaning a command to distance ourselves from them, refuse to sit with them or listen to their errors and their confusing statements."

SOURCE OF THIS TEXT OR NARRATION:

This is a statement of the compiler of this work: Abu 'Abdullah Ubayd'Allaah Ibn Muhammad Ibn Muhammad Ibn Hamdan Ibn Battah al-Ukbaree, may Allaah have mercy upon him.

Explanation by Sheikh 'Abdul-'Azeez Ibn 'Abdullah ar-Raajhee

Here the author speaks of their confusing mistakes and their misguided errors. Their errors meaning that a person makes slips and falls into errors, and their confusion, meaning confusion of the tongue, or slips and mistakes in what is said. These are what is meant by their confusing mistakes and their misguided errors.

This is connected to listening to their misguided errors and confused mistakes Allaah the Blessed and the Most High's, saying, *And it has already been revealed to you in the Book (this Qur'aan) that when you hear the Verses of Allaah being denied and mocked at, then sit not with them, until they engage in a talk other than that; (but if you stayed with them) certainly in that case you would be like them. Surely, Allaah will collect the hypocrites and disbelievers all together in Hell,* -(Surah An-Nisaa': 140).

Within this is what makes clear that Allaah, the Most Perfect and the Most High, has commanded the believers to separate from those who oppose what they hold, meaning those who differ with their sound beliefs. Therefore, the believers should separate from those who differ from their beliefs, such as the Jews, Christians, and the Pagans, all those whose beliefs differ and contradict the beliefs of a Muslim. It is required to separate from them, and distance yourself from them, and to not take any of them as close friends or intimate companions.

Allaah, the Most High, has commanded the believers to separate from those who oppose their sound beliefs, those who have severed their own attachment to the guided Muslims, and who speak against their clear religion. Allaah has commanded them to distance themselves from such people, meaning to stay away from them. That the believers are on one side and such people are left on the other side. That we abandon sitting with them and we do not take disbelievers as close friends, where you visit him and he visits you without there being a specific reason for that visit. If you happen to come to sit with them without choosing to do so then this is a different matter. But as for when you take them as your friend, such that you confide in them your personal matters, and consider them someone trustworthy to you, and that you visit them and they also visit you, then this is from the impermissible companionship and friendship. As such, it is required that you stay away from this. The exception is the situation in which you are specifically inviting him to Islaam, then in this case there is no harm if you were to visit them and speak about and invite them to Islaam. Just as the Prophet, may Allaah's praise and salutations be upon him, visited someone from the Jews, someone whom he was inviting to Islaam, and that person embraced Islaam. Also just as the Prophet visited his uncle Abu Taalib, and invited him to Islaam, but it was not within the decree of Allaah for his uncle to embrace Islaam.

It is upon a Muslim to separate from those who oppose their specific beliefs and their general worldview. They should distance themselves from them choosing not to sit with them nor to listen to their confusing mistakes and errors. This means not paying heed to their actions and deeds which are wrong and misguided, nor to their confusing statements, meaning the wrong or misguided things that they say. It is for this reason that Allaah, the Most High, says, *And whoever contradicts and opposes the Messenger (Muhammad) after the right path has been shown clearly to him, and follows other than the believers' way. We shall keep him in the path he has chosen, and burn him in Hell - what an evil destination.* -(Surah An-Nisaa': 115) Meaning the person who opposes the guidance of the Messenger of Allaah, and who chooses to follow some way other than the way and path of the believers, and what is meant by believers is firstly the Companions of the Messenger of Allaah, and then the Successors to the Companions, and then those scholars and leading people of knowledge who came after them. The one who chooses to follow a path other than the path of these people, and he opposes the guidance of the Messenger of Allaah then Allaah will keep him in whatever path of error he has chosen to be upon, leading to his final destination being Hellfire.

Allaah the Most Perfect said in this noble verse which the author quotes from Surah an-Nisaa', *And it has already been revealed to you in the Book (this Qur'aan) that when you hear the Verses of Allaah being denied and mocked at, then sit not with them, until they engage in a talk other than that; (but if you stayed with them) certainly in that case you would be like them. Surely, Allaah will collect the hypocrites and disbelievers all together in Hell,* -(Surah An-Nisa':140). So it must be understood that it is not permissible for a Muslim to sit in any gathering or sitting where the participants are sinning or transgressing against Allaah or the guidance of His Messenger in that sitting.

For if a person is in a sitting in which someone there mocks Allaah, or jokes about the Book of Allaah, or the Messenger of Allaah, it is an obligation that you speak up against this. If they stop doing so, then all praise is due to Allaah. But if they continue to speak in the same way, then it is an obligation upon you to separate from that gathering and to no longer sit with them. And if you continue to sit with them, then certainly you are like them.

The one who sits in a gathering in which the people are transgressing against Allaah's commands, where there are people stating that they disbelieve in Allaah, or that they disbelieve in His Book or in His Messenger, and that other person doesn't speak out against them and what they said of disbelieve, and who doesn't stand up and leave that gathering, then he falls under a ruling. In the Sharee'ah he the same ruling as those people, he may be considered a disbeliever as they are. Just as Allaah the Most Perfect said: ❴*And it has already been revealed to you in the Book (this Qur'aan) that when you hear the Verses of Allaah being denied and mocked at, then sit not with them, until they engage in a talk other than that; (but if you stayed with them) certainly in that case you would be like them. Surely, Allaah will collect the hypocrites and disbelievers all together in Hell,*❵-(Surah An-Nisa':140).

Similarly, if you are sitting in a gathering and among the people of that gathering there are those who are backbiting or spreading tales amongst the people to cause corruption, then it is upon you to advise them to stop. If they take heed of this and do so, then all praise is due to Allaah. But if they do not take heed of you advising them to stop, then you must stand up and leave. If you choose not to leave then you have taken upon yourself the same ruling that those people have, the ruling of those who choose to backbite, and the ruling of those who choose to carry tales between the people to cause corruption. Likewise, if you sit in a gathering in which some of the people are drinking intoxicants, it is an obligation that you speak up against those who are doing so. If they cease and stop drinking intoxicants or alcohol, then all praise is due to Allaah. But if they refuse to stop, then it is upon you to stand up and leave that gathering. If you choose not to stand up then you are a partner with them in what they're doing, and the ruling regarding you is the same ruling of the one who is drinking those intoxicant or alcohol.

The one who sits in a gathering where people are drinking alcohol has the same ruling that Islaam has for the one actually drinking alcohol. The one who sits in a gathering where the people are backbiting other people, he has the ruling of those who are backbiting. The one who sits in a gathering where the people are mocking the religion, and making statements which are considered disbelief in Allaah and His Messenger, his ruling and status is the same as those people. He may be considered a disbeliever like them, except if he speaks out to stop them from what they're doing, or if he stands up and leaves the gathering. But if he chooses to not speak out against them nor to stand up and leave that gathering, then the ruling regarding him is the same ruling and status that they have. Indeed we ask Allaah for safety and well-being.

DAY - 18

Yes, again if you see it in a gathering and are pleased with the statements of disbelief that are said, you are considered like one of those disbelievers. Similarly, if you are pleased with that sin and transgression that people are doing in a gathering you are considered like one of those sinners. If you sit in this gathering where people are mocking and joking about Allaah and His Messenger, you must speak up against this to stop it, and if they refuse to stop you should stand and leave that gathering. But if you choose not to stand, and instead remain there, then you are someone who is pleased with the disbelief in their statements, and so you becomes like a disbeliever. Likewise, if you were sitting in a gathering where someone is drinking alcohol, or smoking something, or backbiting people, or spreading tales which cause corruption between them, you must speak up and prevent them from doing these things. If they refuse to listen to you then stand and leave, but if you choose not to stand and leave, you become one that has the same ruling and status that they do. You become someone who is a sinner, someone upon transgression like they are. So we certainly ask Allaah for safety and well-being. Yes.

POINTS OF BENEFIT

1. There are specific commands in the Qur'aan related to gathering and interacting with people.
2. The Muslims have been commanded to separate and distance themselves from those who oppose their general beliefs and worldview.
3. The Muslims have been commanded to leave any gathering in which false or harmful speech is being spoken.
4. The Muslims have been commanded to not listen to the statements of those who mock, oppose, and speak against their religion.
5. The Muslims have been commanded to protect themselves from listening to those speeches containing misguided errors and confusing mistakes.
6. The Muslims have been commanded to not sit with, and to distance themselves generally, from those who reject Islaam, and not take them as close friends and intimate companions.
7. Regularly visiting and turning to non-Muslims and holding them as trustworthy friends to confide your personal affairs in is considered from the impermissible companionship and friendship.
8. Fulfilling the command to distance yourself from non-Muslims does not prevent interacting with them when there is a specific beneficial reason to do so.
9. From the exceptions to this command to distance ourselves from non-Muslims is taking part in sittings or gatherings with the purpose of inviting them to Islaam.
10. The command to distance ourselves from non-Muslims is part of the 'believers way' which Allaah mentions in Surah an-Nisaa'a, verse 115.
11. The 'believers' way' is what has been established by the Companions of the Messenger of Allaah, and then the Successors to the Companions.
12. It is an obligation for a Muslim to speak up against any speech within a gathering that mocks Allaah, or jokes about the Book of Allaah, or the Messenger of Allaah, and to leave if that speech continues.
13. A Muslim who sits in a gathering where people are stating that they disbelieve in Allaah, or in His Book, or in His Messenger and doesn't speak out against them or stand up and leave that gathering has the same ruling as those people.
14. A Muslim who sits in a gathering where people are backbiting or spreading tales amongst the people to cause corruption, and doesn't speak out against them or stand up and leave that gathering, then he has the same ruling as those people.
15. A Muslim who sits in a gathering where people are transgressing against Allaah's commands and some of the people are drinking intoxicants and he doesn't speak out against them or stand up and leave that gathering, then he has the same ruling as those people.

LEVEL 1: TEST YOUR UNDERSTANDING:

TRUE & FALSE QUESTIONS

[Circle the correct letter for each individual sentence from today's content.]

01. It acceptable to sit and listen to people mock Islaam, as long as you don't join in. [T / F]
02. The person who sits in a gathering of wrongdoing must speak up to stop them or leave. [T / F]
03. Muslims have been prohibited from taking non-Muslims as close friends. [T / F]

FILL IN THE BLANK QUESTIONS

[Enter the correct individual words to complete the sentences from today's content.]

04. The believers have been ordered to _____ from those who _____ against their clear religion.
05. It is allowed to _____ non-Muslims in order to _____ them to Islaam, just as the Prophet did.
06. If a Muslim is _____ with that sin and transgression that people are doing in a _____ where there is wrongdoing, he is considered like one of those _____ .

LEVEL 2: INTERACTIVE QUESTIONS & EXERCISES

COMPREHENSIVE UNDERSTANDING QUESTIONS

[In a study group or circle of learning with other students, these questions can be answered fully or partially by one student from the lesson, with another student completing the answer to the same question, by giving a comparable but different which is also correct.]

07. Give an example in which a Muslim might find themselves in one of the situations mentioned. What is a good way to implement the guidelines mentioned?
08. Briefly explain how speaking up when falsehood is mentioned benefits you.
09. What is one of the dangers of taking non-Muslims as close friends related to this discussion?

DAY - 18

Day 19: Advice of The Companions 'Uthman, 'Alee & Ibn 'Abbaas

NARRATION FROM AL-IBAANAH AL-SUGHRAH:

'Uthmaan[1], may Allaah the Most High be pleased with him, said,

"Falsehood is whatever agrees with what your desires themselves call to, even if you wrongly believe it is being done in obedience to Allaah, the Most Glorified and the Most Exalted."

AUTHENTICITY & SOURCE OF THIS TEXT OR NARRATION:

Authentic in meaning: narrated by the author in the original work.

---

[1] A Companion of the Messenger of Allaah, may the praise and salutations of Allaah be upon him

Explanation by Sheikh 'Abdul-'Azeez Ibn 'Abdullah ar-Raajhee

Yes, there is no doubt that this meaning is correct. Falsehood is what agrees with one's inner desires, and opposes the guidance of the source texts, even if you feel within yourself that this is an act of obedience to Allaah. Because this opinion is simply that, just one's opinion. As such, what is seen as falsehood is whatever agrees with one's inner desires, and opposes the source texts, even if an individual claims that the matter which his inner desires agree with should be seen as obedience to Allaah. This still remains falsehood, as the truth is whatever comes in the revealed source texts of the Book of Allaah and the Sunnah of His Messenger. Whereas falsehood is whatever agrees with your inner desires and contradicts the guidance of the source texts. Within this narration there is also found a warning against bringing new things and innovations into the religion, and a warning against the people of innovation and against listening to their doubts and claims about whatever they have innovated into Islaam. Yes.

NARRATION FROM AL-IBAANAH AL-SUGHRAH:

Alee[2], may Allaah the Most High be pleased with him, said,

"*Desires block the acceptance of the truth and acting upon it.*"

AUTHENTICITY & SOURCE OF THIS TEXT OR NARRATION:

Authentic in meaning: narrated by the author in the original work.

---

[2] A Companion of the Messenger of Allaah, may the praise and salutations of Allaah be upon him

Explanation by Sheikh 'Abdul-'Azeez Ibn 'Abdullah ar-Raajhee

Yes, this is correct, desires are something which act as a barrier towards the truth and cause someone to be blind to it. Such that you will be a person who acts according to his desires and whatever his inner desires direct him to even if it opposes the guidance of the revealed source texts. So there is no doubt that it is something which blocks, and is a barrier, to the truth and causes one's heart to be blinded. As such, it is obligatory to be warned against following one's desires, and one's opinions, as well as against innovation in the religion. Rather, an individual must act according to the Book of Allaah and the Sunnah, yes.

This is a statement of 'Alee, (as some say) may Allaah ennoble his face, This is a statement of 'Alee, (and we say) may Allaah be pleased with him. We say only this, after his name, because there is no matter related to mentioning him name, that is specified just for him and not others. For all of the Companions of the Messenger of Allaah, we say may Allaah be pleased with them all, and we say about them all may Allaah ennoble all of their faces, without restriction.

As specifying this just for 'Alee is one of the distinguishing practices of some of the people of innovation in Islaam, they say ['Alee, may Allaah ennoble his face.] or they say ['Alee, may Allaah's salutations be upon him.] But the Companions are all considered equally deserving in such matters. So these separate statements are something that was written by certain individuals from the generation of the Successors. They wrote this of their own accord, yes.

NARRATION FROM AL-IBAANAH AL-SUGHRAH:

'Uthmaan ibn Haadhir al-'Azdee said, I went and visited Ibn 'Abbaas[3] and said, "Advise me."

So he said to me, *"Hold firm to being steadfast in Islaam, follow what has been established of guidance and do not innovate new things into it."*

AUTHENTICITY & SOURCE OF THIS TEXT OR NARRATION:

Authentic: This was narrated by ad-Daarimee in his Sunan, by the author in the related work al-Ibaanah al-Kubraa, by Ibn Wadhaah, and by al-Haraawee in his work.

---
[3] A Companion of the Messenger of Allaah, may the praise and salutations of Allaah be upon him

Explanation by Sheikh 'Abdul-'Azeez Ibn 'Abdullah ar-Raajhee

Yes, this is a statement of 'Uthmaan Ibn Haadhir al-'Azdee, in which he narrates from Ibn 'Abbaas that when he visited him he said to Ibn 'Abbaas *"Advise me."* Ibn 'Abbaas told him, *"Hold firm to being steadfast in Islaam, follow what has been established of guidance and do not innovate new things into it."*. The statement *"Hold firm to being steadfast in Islaam..."* means be steadfast upon the Sunnah, and be steadfast upon the religion of Islaam follow and adhere to the Qur'aan and Sunnah.

Then he said, *"...follow what has been established of guidance and do not innovate new things into it."* So he warned him against innovation, and he commanded him to stay firmly upon being steadfast. Steadfastness means: being steadfast upon the religion of Islaam, and the religion means to hold firmly to the Book of Allaah and the Sunnah of the Messenger of Allaah. So after he had commanded him to be steadfast upon the religion generally as an overall advice, then he advised him specifically in detail saying to him, *"...follow what has been established of guidance and do not innovate new things into it."* Meaning follow what has come within the revealed source texts. Additionally he said *"...and do not innovate new things into it."*, meaning do not become one of the people of innovation. So this contains a warning and a caution away from innovating within the religion of Islaam. Yes.

POINTS OF BENEFIT

1. Falsehood is what agrees with one's inner desires and opposes guidance, even if you wrongly feel it is an act of obedience.

2. The truth is whatever comes in the revealed source texts of the Book of Allaah and the Sunnah of His Messenger.

3. Proclaiming the falsehood of inner desires is also a warning against innovation and the people of innovation. As the innovators are people who follow their false desires in understanding and practicing the religion.

4. Desires are something which act as a barrier to accepting the truth and cause someone's heart to be blinded to the truth.

5. The supplications which are made for the Companions of the Messenger of Allaah are general and not specific to any one of them.

6. The use of specific terms and phrases in reference to 'Alee is one of the practices which distinguish and identify some of the people of innovation.

7. There is tremendous benefit in asking one of the people of knowledge to advise you.

8. The Companions of the Messenger of Allaah generally advised the people to be steadfast upon Islaam by holding firmly to the Book of Allaah and the authentic Sunnah.

9. The Companions of the Messenger of Allaah specifically advised the people to proceed upon the established guidance found in the source texts and not begin to innovate and change Islaam

LEVEL 1: TEST YOUR UNDERSTANDING:

TRUE & FALSE QUESTIONS

[Circle the correct letter for each individual sentence from today's content.]

01. People's desires generally guide them to that which is good for them. [T / F]
02. It is important to follow the truth no matter what our desires call us to. [T / F]
03. What is considered obedience to Allaah is different for every person. [T / F]

FILL IN THE BLANK QUESTIONS

[Enter the correct individual words to complete the sentences from today's content.]

04. Our _____ are often something which _____ and are a _____ to accepting the truth.
05. Steadfastness means to hold _____ to the _____ and the _____ .
06. We should _____ what comes within the _____ source texts, not our _____ .

LEVEL 2: INTERACTIVE QUESTIONS & EXERCISES

COMPREHENSIVE UNDERSTANDING QUESTIONS

[In a study group or circle of learning with other students, these questions can be answered fully or partially by one student from the lesson, with another student completing the answer to the same question, by giving a comparable but different which is also correct.]

07. What might be one cause of someone wrongly believing that our desires are something pleasing to Allaah?
08. Give a practical example of how someone's desires might prevent them from accepting something required in Islaam. Write out their possible false excuse.
09. Give a practical example of an issue a Muslim might need to be steadfast in, specifically in our modern age and time.

Day 20: Those Astray Turned Away From The Guidance Brought To Them

NARRATION FROM AL-IBAANAH AL-SUGHRAH:

'Umar Ibn al-Khattab[1], may Allaah the Most High be pleased with him, said,

"The people who rely upon their own perceptions and opinions are enemies of the authentic practices from the Prophet. They are brought hadeeth narrations so they can memorize and act upon them, but instead they break free of the guidance of these narrations and run away without returning. They speak and proceed upon their perceptions and opinions, standing as misguided and misguiding others."

AUTHENTICITY & SOURCE OF THIS TEXT OR NARRATION:

Authentic: as narrated by al-Laalakaa'ee in his work 'Sharh Usul Itiqaad Ahlus-Sunnah', by al-Haraawee in his work 'Dham al-Kalaam', as-Suyootee mentioned it in the work 'Mafaateeh al-Jannah bil-Ihtijaaj bis Sunnah', and additionally Imaam Ibn Hajr, in his work 'Fath Al-Baaree', attributed it to one of the works of Imaam al-Bayhaqee.

---

[1] A Companion of the Messenger of Allaah, may the praise and salutations of Allaah be upon him

Explanation by Sheikh 'Abdul-'Azeez Ibn 'Abdullah ar-Raajhee

Yes, this narration is authentic transmitted from 'Umar Ibn al-Khattab, may Allaah be pleased with him, and he is the well-known Companion. Additionally, what it conveys is something that is generally witnessed from the people who rely upon their perceptions and opinions, that they stand as opponents and enemies of the authentic practices from the Prophet, meaning the people who rely solely upon their opinions. The people of opinions are people who are following their desires, and such people are enemies and opponents of the authentic practices of the Prophet. They reject and turn away from these practices, and choose to act upon their opinions, their desires, their wants, and inclinations.

For this reason he said, *"...They are brought hadeeth narrations so they can memorize and act upon them, but they break free of their guidance and run away from them without returning. They choose to speak and proceed upon their perceptions and opinions, and so stand as those who are misguided and misguiding others."* Because the hadeeth narrations restrict them and prevent them from acting according to their opinions, and their wants and inclinations. They are brought hadeeth narrations in order that they memorize and act upon them, but they run from them and turned back to their inner desires and wants. It is for this reason it is said that they act according to *"their opinions"* and have abandoned acting upon the established authentic practices from the Sunnah. This causes them to be misguided and to misguide others; they became misguided from themselves, and then became those who additionally misguided others.

Within this narration there is a warning against the following of opinions and desires, as well is innovation in the religion. It contains a command to adhere firmly to the Sunnah, and a warning against innovating in the religion. It includes a warning against listening to the people of innovation from the sects of the Jahmeeyah, the Mu'tazilah, the Raafidhah, the Khawaarij, the Murji'ah, as well as others, yes.

POINTS OF BENEFIT

1. There is a significant difference between following the guidance of authentic narrations and following your own opinions and perceptions.

2. The people who follow and rely upon their own perceptions and opinions oppose the guidance of the Sunnah.

3. One of the purposes of conveying beneficial knowledge is that it be memorized when possible and then acted upon.

4. Anyone who turns away from the guidance of the authentic Sunnah, and instead chooses his opinion, is someone misguided.

5. Anyone who has turned away from the guidance of the authentic Sunnah, and then speaks and calls others to his own opinions, is someone misguided who additionally misguides others.

6. The people of opinion and personal perceptions are people who are only following their desires.

7. The following of opinions and personal perceptions can lead someone to reject and become an enemy of the Sunnah.

8. There is a connection and relationship between following opinions and personal perceptions, and the spread of innovations among the Muslims.

9. Among those misguided sects who have chosen their opinions and perceptions over authentic transmitted knowledge are: the Jahmeeyah, the Mu'tazilah, the Raafidhah, the Khawaarij, the Murji'ah, and others.

LEVEL 1: TEST YOUR UNDERSTANDING:

TRUE & FALSE QUESTIONS

[Circle the correct letter for each individual sentence from today's content.]

3 min

01. It is acceptable for a Muslim to choose between his opinion and what is found in the Sunnah. [T / F]

02. Speaking from your opinions in relation to the religion is something blameworthy. [T / F]

03. The Muslims upon guidance place the knowledge of the Sunnah above their opinions and perceptions. [T / F]

FILL IN THE BLANK QUESTIONS

[Enter the correct individual words to complete the sentences from today's content.]

6 min

04. The people of opinions who follow their _____ , are _____ and opponents of the authentic _____ of the Prophet.

05. The people who are infatuated with their own perceptions and opinions, break free of the guidance of the _____ from the _____ .

06. Beneficial narrations are brought to us so we can understand, try to _____ , and _____ upon them.

LEVEL 2: INTERACTIVE QUESTIONS & EXERCISES

DAY - 20

COMPREHENSIVE UNDERSTANDING QUESTIONS

[In a study group or circle of learning with other students, these questions can be answered fully or partially by one student from the lesson, with another student completing the answer to the same question, by giving a comparable but different which is also correct.]

21-36 min

07. Give an example of a common opinion or perception found among non-Muslims that goes against the guidance of Islaam.

08. Give an example of a common opinion or perception found among Muslims today that goes against the guidance of Islaam.

09. Explain one false reason an ignorant Muslim might use to justify placing his opinion over and above the clear guidance of Islaam.

Day 21: The People Of Misguidance Want You To Turn From Revealed Guidance

NARRATION FROM AL-IBAANAH AL-SUGHRAH:

Ishaaq Ibn 'Isaa said, I heard Maalik Ibn Anas criticize and speak against arguing and debating within Islaam by saying,

"Whenever some man comes to us who is proficient in debating and arguing, do you imagine that we should listen and abandon that guidance which the angel Jibreel brought directly to the Prophet, may Allaah's praise and salutations be upon him?!?"

AUTHENTICITY & SOURCE OF THIS TEXT OR NARRATION:

Authentic: This was narrated by ad-Daarimee, and by the author in the related work al-Ibaanah al-Kubraa, and al-Laalakaa'ee, and al-Haraawee

Explanation by Sheikh 'Abdul-'Azeez Ibn 'Abdullah ar-Raajhee

Yes, this is also narrated with an acceptable chain of narration. Ishaaq Ibn 'Isaa said, *"I heard Maalik Ibn Anas criticize and speak against arguing and debating about matters of the religion..."* Maalik Ibn Anas, the well-known leading scholar, may Allaah have mercy upon him, who is considered the Imaam of Dar al-Hijrah, the city of Medinah, during his age, here criticized the practice of arguing and debating issues of the religion. He spoke about this, stating what he said, because arguing about matters of the religion is what produces controversies, and similar disputes and problems. He said this because arguing about the affairs of religion produces controversies, disputes, conflicts, and disunity. Moreover, innovations are born from matters which are close to and similar what is produced from arguments and disputes, and the results of arguing generally.

For this reason Maalik Ibn Anas criticized those who engaged in arguing and debating the issues within Islaam when he said: *"Whenever some man comes to us who is proficient in debating and arguing, do you imagine that we should abandon that guidance which the angel Jibreel brought directly to the Prophet, may Allaah's praise and salutations be upon him?!?"* Meaning by this, does someone imagine that whenever an individual who is a better debater, someone stronger than him in the ability to present, argue, and debate points, that due to this we should leave the clear guidance which Jibreel brought down to the Prophet, may Allaah's praise and salutations be upon him, in the form of the Book of Allaah and the form of the Sunnah, which is the second source of revelation.

Does someone imagine that it makes sense to turn from this and choose to adhere to whatever misguided views and opinions they brought?!? Imaam Maalik is asking this as a rhetorical question for the purpose of showing that doing so is a wrong position and criticizing it. He's indicating to us that it is not permissible for a person to take on the various misguided views and opinions which are just the results of debates and argumentation, and so abandon the guidance of the Book of Allaah and the Sunnah. Moreover, he is indicating that the practice of debating and argumentation is what produces harmful controversies, doubts, and innovations within Islaam. Yes

NARRATION FROM AL-IBAANAH AL-SUGHRAH:

Mus'ab said,

"Do not sit and spend time with someone who has been put to trial through misguidance, because he will only bring you harm in one of two ways. Either he will bring you harm by drawing you fully into the trial of his misguidance so that you come to follow him and that. Or he will bring to you some lesser matters of misguidance, which still end up harming you before you have left spending time sitting with him."

AUTHENTICITY & SOURCE OF THIS TEXT OR NARRATION:

Authentic: This was narrated by Ibn Wadhaah with a chain of narration on the authority of al-Hasan al-Basree that he said, "Do not sit with a person whose way is to follow his desires, as he may throw into your heart some matter which you end up following and so become ruined or even though you oppose him generally you still end up taking something of the sickness of misguidance into your heart.

Explanation by Sheikh 'Abdul-'Azeez Ibn 'Abdullah ar-Raajhee

Yes this narration from Mus'ab, may Allaah have mercy upon him, *"Do not sit and spend time with someone who is been put to trial through misguidance..."* Meaning an innovator, as an innovator is put to trial by following misguidance in his understanding and practice of the religion. So if you sit with the one who has been put to trial, then undoubtedly he will only bring you harm in one of two ways. Either he will bring you harm by drawing you fully into the trial of his misguidance so that you come to follow him upon the innovation that he has, or he will bring you some lesser misconceptions and matters of misguidance, which still end up harming you before you have left spending time sitting with him. So what happens is that in any case you are harmed and damaged because of him.

This refers to the evil or bad sitting companion that bad companion which was mentioned by the Prophet, may Allaah's praise and salutations be upon him, when he said, {*The similitude of good company and that of bad company is that of the owner of musk and of the blacksmith. The owner of musk would either offer you some free of charge, or you would buy it from him, or at least you get to smell its pleasant fragrance...*}[1] Either you are able to buy some musk from him, or he gives you some musk as a gift, or at the very least you gain the pleasant fragrance of his musk, therefore to some degree you benefit from his company, no matter what.

So it is understood that having good company encourages you toward what is good or turns you away from what is bad and harmful, such as innovations in the religion. But as for bad company and companions, then undoubtedly you are always brought harm through them in every situation, {*...And as for the blacksmith, he either burns your clothes or you smell a repugnant smell*}. This is the same case with bad companionship in relation to the religion. Either he will make his innovation and wrongdoing look good to you, or he will lead you to actually embrace it and fall into it. Certainly, when sitting with him he may make his misguidance something appealing and easy for you to accept within yourself. It is for this reason that it mentions and states in this narration, *"Do not sit and spend time with someone who has been put to trial through misguidance, because he will only bring you harm in one of two ways..."*. What this means is that, in most cases, you will not be safe from one of two situations of harm reaching you,

The first situation: that you are put to trial through his company and eventually follow him upon his misguidance, meaning that he influences you and presents his innovation to you in a way which is appealing. This causes doubts within you, until his influence leads you to agree with him and you come to adopt and follow that misguidance he is upon.

---

[1] Saheeh al-Bukhaaree: 5534, Saheeh Muslim: 2628, and the Musnad of Imaam Ahmad: vol.4 pg.404

The second situation: he will bring you some lesser matters of misguidance or misconceptions, which still end up harming you before you have left sitting or spending time sitting with him. He influences and harms you with what he says, by producing doubts about your understanding and causing misconceptions, which he will present to you until he has harmed you and kindled some bad feelings within you. Therefore, you will suffer due to this, if you had a heart that was alive upon guidance. As a heart which is alive through faith and guidance, is harmed by evils, sins, and innovations which are presented to it. For this reason this narration is a general warning against innovation in the religion, and a command to adhere firmly to the Sunnah and to the Jamaa'ah of the Muslims upon the truth. Yes.

DAY - 21

POINTS OF BENEFIT

1. Imaam Maalik clarified to us that what is correct is the truth due to its nature, not simply due to how well it's presented and beautified with arguments.

2. Imaam Maalik pointed out the weakness of various rhetorical or purely intellectual arguments when compared to the transmitted knowledge of revelation.

3. It is not permissible to leave the revealed guidance of the Book of Allaah and the Sunnah for any human opinion or personally expressed view, regardless of how appealing it may be made to seem.

4. The guiding scholars have always, and continually, warned the Muslims against the dangers of entering into debates and arguments about the matters in Islaam.

5. The scholars have warned the Muslims that one of the results of entering into debates and controversies about Islaam, is that innovations in the religion developed among the Muslims because of this.

6. The scholars have criticized the practice of arguing and debating issues in the religion, due to the personal harm that this produces in a believing individual.

7. The way to be safe and protect your practice of Islaam is to avoid interaction with those who may cause harm to you as a Muslim.

8. The general results which come from the practice of debating and argumentation over matters in the religion are harmful controversies, doubts, and innovations within Islaam.

9. An individual of misguidance is considered from the bad sitting companions whom the Messenger of Allaah, warned us would always cause some degree of harm.

10. Interacting with the people of misguidance may cause you to embrace their misguidance as a whole and so follow them.

11. Interacting with the people of misguidance may cause you to accept parts of their misguidance and falsehood, even if you do not adopt their path of misguidance as a whole.

12. Interacting with the people of misguidance and distance from the Sunnah can cause you as a Muslim to be separated from the straight path either in your belief, your practice, or both.

13. Interacting with the people of misguidance can place false seeds of doubt within a Muslim that continue to slowly influence him and later cause him to stray from the straight path.

14. The heart of the believer can be badly affected by false arguments and misconceptions and start to die and lose the light of guidance of Islaam.

15. The heart of the believer can be badly affected by exposing itself to various evils, sins, and innovations.

16. The Muslim who understands the ways in which a believer can fall into misguidance will struggle and strive to adhere to the Sunnah and to remain close to its people, due to the protection and goodness this brings.

17. The Muslim who understands the ways in which a believer can fall into misguidance will struggle and strive to distance himself from every innovation and to stay far away from the people of innovation, due to the harm and damage they cause.

LEVEL 1: TEST YOUR UNDERSTANDING:

TRUE & FALSE QUESTIONS

[Circle the correct letter for each individual sentence from today's content.]

01. If we are strong in our faith then there is no harm in debating people. [T / F]
02. There is more than one type of danger involved in sitting with the people of misguidance. [T / F]
03. The revealed guidance of Islaam is always superior to human arguments and concepts. [T / F]

FILL IN THE BLANK QUESTIONS

[Enter the correct individual words to complete the sentences from today's content.]

04. The Sunnah is the _____ source of _____ .
05. The practice of _____ and argumentation produces _____ controversies, doubts, and _____ within Islaam.
06. Good company _____ you toward what is good, or turns you away from what is bad and _____, such as _____ in the religion.

LEVEL 2: INTERACTIVE QUESTIONS & EXERCISES

COMPREHENSIVE UNDERSTANDING QUESTIONS

[In a study group or circle of learning with other students, these questions can be answered fully or partially by one student from the lesson, with another student completing the answer to the same question, by giving a comparable but different which is also correct.]

07. Give an example of a misconception, which the people who falsely claim to be engaged in Jihaad in our time, spread amongst the Muslims.
08. Give an example of a misconception, which the people who claim to be engaged in efforts of calling to Allaah or da'wah in our time, spread amongst the Muslims.
09. Give an example of a possible good response that a Muslim can give to someone who tries to get them to enter into an argument or debate.

Day 22: Those Who Debate Frequently Change Their Religion

Narration from al-Ibaanah al-Sughrah:

'Umar Ibn 'Abdul-'Azeez said,

"The one who makes his religion the target or object of debates and controversies will be unsteady, changing often in understanding and practice."

Authenticity & Source of This Text or Narration:

Authentic: This was narrated by ad-Daarimee in his Sunan, with ad-Daarimee saying in relation to this narration "Frequently changing from one position to another" meaning changing from one opinion to another opinion. It was also narrated by al-Aajuree in his work 'ash-Sharee'ah' from two different routes of narration, as well as by al-Laalakaa'ee and al-Baghawee in his work 'Sharh as-Sunnah'. It was also narrated by Ibn Qutaybah in his work 'Ta'weel Mukhtalif al-Hadeeth' and by Ibn al-Binaa'.

Explanation by Sheikh 'Abdul-'Azeez Ibn 'Abdullah ar-Raajhee

Yes, this statement is from 'Umar Ibn 'Abdul-'Azeez, who was a rightly guided khalifah, may Allaah have mercy upon him. He was someone whom some of the scholars count among rightly guided khalifahs, meaning that they consider him the fifth rightly guided khalifah. His piety and justice among the people are well-known in history. So, may Allaah have mercy upon him, and be pleased with him. Despite the short length of him being a khalifah, just two years, the rectification among the Muslims that he brought about during his time was tremendous. He was also the first of the Muslim rulers to command the scholars to compile collections of hadeeth narrations.

He, may Allaah have mercy upon him, said, *"The one who makes his religion the target or object of debates and controversies will be unsteady, changing often."* Meaning the one who makes his religion the object or a target of these, and he indicated like the target which the people make and then shoot and aim towards. By target, he means that this other person aims what they have at him, and that other person also aims what they have at him, such that he becomes a target in which the people aim at, like a goal, or target, which anyone can aim at.

Such that this person aims his arguments at him, and this other person also aims his argument at him. Due to this, it is said the one who makes his religion a target which everyone can aim at with their arguments and controversies will be someone unsteady, who changes positions often. Meaning he changes from one position to another position, he moves from one opinion to another opinion. He is not steadfast upon the guidance of the religion and the Sunnah. As such, this statement is a warning away from entering into controversies and debates, because they produce doubts and misconceptions, and those misconceptions produce innovations within the religion of Islaam.

Therefore it is said that the one who makes his religion the target or object of debates and controversies will be unsteady, changing often from one position to another position, such that they do not stand firm upon the religion, nor adhere closely to the Sunnah. As such, this contains a warning against involving yourself in controversies, as they produce misconceptions and innovations within your understanding of Islaam, because the one involved in controversies is unable to stand steadfastly upon the religion and the Sunnah. Yes.

POINTS OF BENEFIT

1. The correct understanding of Islaam is based upon clear revealed knowledge, not various human arguments and personal views.

2. Allaah has, at times, blessed the Muslims of this Ummah to have some Muslim rulers who were steadfast scholars upon knowledge.

3. 'Umar Ibn 'Abdul-'Azeez was a rightly guided khalifah and brought tremendous rectification in his age.

4. The Muslim rulers of the past played a role in the preservation of the various branches of knowledge in Islaam.

5. The Muslim who makes his understanding of his religion a target for the people of argumentation cannot be steadfast upon Islaam.

6. The person who accepts opinions and views as the criterion of truth in Islaam, will continually move from one position to another.

7. The fruits of entering into controversies and debates about the religion are doubts and misconceptions.

8. It is important for a Muslim to distinguish between the guidance of the source texts and beneficial explanations from the scholars, and opinions, views, and concepts that have no basis in revealed knowledge.

9. Remaining steadfast upon the guidance of the Qur'aan and Sunnah requires turning away from the way of debates and argumentation.

LEVEL 1: TEST YOUR UNDERSTANDING:

TRUE & FALSE QUESTIONS

[Circle the correct letter for each individual sentence from today's content.]

01. A Muslim should listen to every argument and then decide [T / F] what is correct.
02. True knowledge in Islaam is based upon the foundation of [T / F] revealed guidance.
03. The early scholars of Islaam did not see any harm in personal [T / F] views and opinions.

FILL IN THE BLANK QUESTIONS

[Enter the correct individual words to complete the sentences from today's content.]

04. Some scholars consider 'Umar Ibn 'Abdul-'Azeez, the _____ rightly guided _____ .
05. Someone who makes his _____ of Islaam the object of _____ and controversies will be _____ .
06. Controversies produce _____ and _____ within your understanding of _____ .

LEVEL 2: INTERACTIVE QUESTIONS & EXERCISES

COMPREHENSIVE UNDERSTANDING QUESTIONS

[In a study group or circle of learning with other students, these questions can be answered fully or partially by one student from the lesson, with another student completing the answer to the same question, by giving a comparable but different which is also correct.]

07. Give an example of a misconception related to the correct beliefs about Allaah which people often debate about.
08. Give an example of a misconception related to women's dress which people often debate about.
09. Give an example of a misconception about correcting mistakes which people often debate about.

Day 23: The Blessing of Learning the Sunnah When Young

NARRATION FROM AL-IBAANAH AL-SUGHRAH:

'Amr Ibn Qays al Malaa'ee[1] said:

"If you see a youth, when starting out, upon the way of the people of the Sunnah and adherence to the Jama'ah then have hope for his success.

But if you see him with the people of innovation in the religion then lose heart about him, for certainly the youth is generally established upon his first orientation."

AUTHENTICITY & SOURCE OF THIS TEXT OR NARRATION:

Authentic in meaning: narrated by the author in the original work.

---

[1] A scholar from the Salaf

EXPLANATION BY SHEIKH 'ABDUL-'AZEEZ IBN 'ABDULLAH AR-RAAJHEE

Yes, this is also a statement of 'Amr Ibn Qays al Malaa'ee, Abu 'Abdullah, which clarifies the severe danger of innovation the religion. It makes clear that innovation is worse than falling into major sins. He said, *"If you see a youth initially upon the way of the people of the Sunnah and adherence to the Jamaa'ah then have hope for him..."*, Meaning that you should hope for him, goodness and success. This is what is hoped for such a young person.

Continuing, he said, *"....but if you see him with the people of innovation in the religion, then lose heart about him, for certainly the youth is generally established upon his first orientation."* Meaning that if someone is raised up upon the beliefs of the people of the Sunnah and the Jamaa'ah he will continue upon that, just as if he is raised upon the various misguided beliefs of the people of innovation, he will continue upon that.

So this statement contains a warning from innovation in the religion generally. Additionally, it shows us that it is necessary upon the seeker of knowledge to be diligent in learning and adopting the beliefs of the people of the Sunnah and the Jamaa'ah, and then holding onto them firmly with your molar teeth. Moreover, that you should be thankful and praise Allaah for having blessed you to be raised upon the beliefs of the people of the Sunnah and the Jamaa'ah.

In light of this, it should be noted that there are renowned leading scholars of the past, that were not granted the success to have scholars to raise them firmly from their youth upon the beliefs of the people of the Sunnah and the Jamaa'ah, and they were leading scholars who served Islaam. There is the example of al-Haafidh Ibn Hajr, may Allaah have mercy upon him, who compiled the well-known commentary of Saheeh al-Bukhaaree. He was a significant scholar, highly proficient, who had extensive knowledge and works in the various branches of the sciences of hadeeth. Yet despite this, it is noted that he wrongly misinterprets the meaning of the attributes of Allaah, according to the misguided beliefs of the Asha'ree sect. This was because he was not blessed to be raised upon the beliefs of the people of the Sunnah and the Jamaa'ah as a youth.

So we hope that these mistakes of his, which he did not intend to do, will be forgiven and wiped away within the deep ocean of his many good efforts and works. As he was not blessed to have a scholar to correctly raising him upon the beliefs of the people of the Sunnah and the Jamaa'ah in the beginning. So what he was taught is what he wrongly believed was the correct way and the truth, and that his misinterpretation contained preserving Allaah from being compared to the creation.

For instance, he misinterpreted the attribute of Allaah's anger, to wrongly mean that Allaah would retaliate due to something and similarly misinterpreted the affirmed fact that Allaah is pleased with a matter to wrongly mean that He would give a reward or recompense for a matter.

Likewise, another example is Nawawee, Imaam Nawawee, may Allaah have mercy upon him, was an exceptional scholar who has written several tremendous works such as Riyadh as-Saaliheen. This is such a tremendous book that is very rare to find a masjid or home that does not have a copy of Riyaadh as-Saaliheen, and this is from the sincerity of his efforts for Allaah's sake. Yet despite this, it is noted that he also misinterpreted the attributes of Allaah according to the misguided beliefs of the Asha'ree sect. This was because he was not raised as a youth upon the beliefs of the people of the Sunnah and the Jamaa'ah. He was not blessed from the early time of his initial foundation upon knowledge with a scholar who would raise him firmly upon the beliefs of the people of the Sunnah and the Jamaa'ah.

As such, sometimes if you read in these commentaries, such as the explanation and commentary of Saheeh al-Bukhaaree entitled 'Fath al-Baaree' or other works, they misinterpret them when they discuss the attributes of Allaah. They say for instance about verses such as, ❴*Remember the Day when the Shin shall be laid bare (i.e. the Day of Resurrection) and they shall be called to prostrate (to Allaah), but they (hypocrites) shall not be able to do so,*❵-(Surah Al-Qalam: 42)[2], or discuss some of such verses by conveying to the reader many statements from well-known scholars who made the mistake of his interpreting the attributes of Allaah, those scholars who did not hold the correct position of the people of the Sunnah and the Jamaa'ah in this specific matter of belief.

We find that Imam Nawawee, may Allaah have mercy upon him, in his explanation of Saheeh Muslim, whenever an attribute is mentioned for example in relation to the verse, ❴*Allaah Well-Pleased with them, and they with Him...*❵-(Surah Al-Baiyyinah: 8) or the verse ❴*Oh you who believe! Take not as friends the people who incurred the anger of Allaah (i.e. the Jews). Surely, they have been in despair to receive any good in the Hereafter...*❵-(Surah Al-Mumtahanah: 13) or the verse,

---

[2] From compiler: In summary, it should be noted regarding this specific verse about the Shin mentioned in the verse of the Qur'aan that from the Salaf themselves there are different reports about the understanding of this verse based upon whether it was connected to being an affirmed attribute of Allaah or not, their difference is not based upon the corrupt principles of the 'Asha'ree sect that were developed in later centuries. Rather, as some of the scholars mention the narrations which some scholars consider authentically attributed to Ibn 'Abbaas, may Allaah be pleased with him, explain this verse in a manner which shows that he did not consider it affirmed as an attribute of Allaah and so explained it in a manner conforming to this. Whereas other authentic narrations from other Companions such as Ibn Mas'ood, and others, indicate that they did in fact consider it from Allaah's affirmed attributes, as some scholars mentioned is affirmed by the authentic hadeeth of Abu Sa'eed al-Khudree in Saheeh al-Bukhaaree: 4919 and by an additional narration from Abu Hurairah narrated by ad-Daarimee in his Sunan (vol. 2. page 237) with an authentic chain. As such they explained this verse in that manner conforming to the position of affirming it as an attribute of Allaah, and in a manner that befits Allaah's majesty and transcendence. This is the strongest position held by many leading scholars past and present, including those of our time such as Sheikh Ibn Baaz, Sheikh al-Albaanee, may Allaah have mercy upon them both and others reliable scholars. This is despite the fact that several well known scholars through the centuries mistakenly misinterpreted or negated many of the verses related to attributes of Allaah in a way the first Muslims had no knowledge of. So do not be deceived by those who say "But Ibn Abbass said..." failing to scholastically discuss the general evidences of the differences and the strongest position of the scholars of the Sunnah which those evidences support. Your understanding lies in turning to the scholars to clarify.

❴*The Most Beneficent (Allaah) Istawaa (rose over) the (Mighty) Throne (in a manner that suits His Majesty).*❵-(Surah Ta-Ha: 5) or the verse ❴*Remember the Day when the Shin shall be laid bare...*❵-(Surah Al-Qalam: 42). We find that, he claims that the people has two different ways in explaining these verses: The way of the early generations and the way of the later generations. The way of the early generation is to not explain the attributes of Allaah and to state that their true meaning is only with Allaah, the way of the later generations is to explain and interpret them."

Yet neither of these mentioned ways conform to the way of the people of the Sunnah in understanding Allaah's attributes, upon the actual way of the first generations of believers. Firstly, what he wrongly claimed was the way of the Salaf, which he himself named as the way of consigning, meaning that we completely consign the actual meaning of the attributes to Allaah, which means not affirming them upon their apparent meaning as the Companions did. Secondly, the incorrect way of the later generations of misinterpreting away from their apparent meanings. Neither of these two ways actually conformed to the beliefs of the people of the Sunnah and the Jamaa'ah. Neither of these ways that he stated in fact agree with the way of the people of the Sunnah and the Jamaa'ah, not the first or the second claimed ways. But what is the reason for the ways which they stated and believe to be true, while are they actually incorrect? The cause is that these people of knowledge were not blessed in their youth to have scholars who raised them fully upon the correct beliefs of the people of the Sunnah and the Jamaa'ah. Rather the scholars that they had, raised them upon this incorrect understanding, and so they themselves came to believe it to be what was correct, meaning that they wrongly believed that to misinterpret or negate Allaah's attributes was in fact to free Him, the Most Glorified and the Most Exalted, from being compared to His creation.

Due to this, we understand that looking at and understanding their situation supports the correctness of what the people of knowledge have mentioned that from the greatest of blessings of Allaah upon a worshiper is that they are raised from youth upon the beliefs of the people of the Sunnah and the Jamaa'ah. Since if we recognize that these renowned leading scholars wrongly misinterpreted some of Allaah's attributes, and that it was never actually conveyed to them the clear beliefs of the people of the Sunnah and the Jamaa'ah which the Companions of the Messenger of Allaah held, and the Successors held, and the four well-known scholars in the area of fiqh generally held, as well as that which was held and affirmed by the reliable scholars generally, then certainly a person must rightly fear misguidance for himself. Moreover, it should push us to strive to hold firmly to the beliefs of the people of the Sunnah and the Jamaa'ah. If these leading scholars made such a mistake then you have a significant responsibility to ensure you understand what is correct.

Understanding this leads the Muslim youth and the seeker of knowledge to be diligent in gaining understanding of the beliefs of the people of the Sunnah and the Jamaa'ah, holding firmly onto those beliefs with their molar teeth, and praising Allaah for granting them success to be raised upon the correct beliefs of the people of the Sunnah and the Jamaa'ah.

Sheikh al-Islaam Ibn Taymeeyah, may Allaah have mercy upon him, as well as the guiding leading scholar Ibn al-Qayyim, spread the way of the people of the Sunnah and the Jamaa'ah after it had become obscure among the Muslims. There are tremendous books which were authored by Abu al-'Abbaas Sheikh al-Islaam Ibn Taymeeyah, may Allaah have mercy upon him, such as al-Aqeedat al-Waasiteeyah. It is a incredible work explaining beliefs which should be written in gold ink, and it is a work which is worthy of a student of knowledge memorizing.

It is a treatise composed of a concise number of words which he wrote in a single sitting after salatul-asr, writing in response to a question which he received from a land called Waasitah in Iraq, and so it was called al-Waasitteyah. As a work, it is a tremendous and focused explanation of beliefs, written to not be extensively long yet still suitably explain the beliefs of the people of the Sunnah and the Jamaa'ah regarding the attributes of Allaah, as well as His names, important rulings, and the correct position towards the Companions of the Messenger of Allaah. Indeed, it should be written in ink made from gold. But in fact it is more precious than simply something written in ink made from gold, as ink made from gold is not nearly as valuable as this work of knowledge is.

Similarly he has also written a work called al-Hamaweeyah, which is a tremendous writing, explaining the beliefs about Allaah and His transcendence, which he wrote in response to a question from the land or region of Hamaa. He also has authored at-Tadmureeyah, which was written to respond to a question from the region of Tadmur, which is also an incredible work. Additionally, in the area of correct beliefs there is also the work al-Aqeedah at-Tahaweeyah by different scholar, Abu Ja'far Ahmad at-Tahawee, may Allaah have mercy upon him, which generally explains the fundamentals of the religion. It should be noted that Sheikh al-Islaam Ibn Taymeeyah, has many other writings related to the correct belief, which have been collected in Majmou' al-Fataawa as well as separately, as does Ibn al-Qayyim.

Moreover, the leading scholars of the call of the reviver Imaam Sheikh Muhammad Ibn Abdul-Wahhab, may Allaah have mercy upon him, and the other scholars who supported his efforts, all of them spread the correct beliefs of the people of the Sunnah and the Jamaa'ah. They explain those beliefs in their writings, treatises, and classes such that their centers of learning became extensions of the efforts of teaching the correct beliefs which were put forward by Sheikh al-Islaam Ibn Taymeeyah and Ibn al-Qayyim, may Allaah have mercy upon them both.

This is a tremendous blessing which Allaah has granted us in the later ages, that in this age the way of the people of the Sunnah and the Jamaa'ah would be spread extensively. That these beliefs would be successfully spread during the time of Imaam Muhammad Ibn 'Abdul-Wahaab, and the leader Muhammad Ibn Sa'ud may Allaah have mercy upon them both, in the twelfth and thirteenth century after the Hijra. Such that these ages of theirs became those which joined back to the time of the Companions, and the Successors in the strength of their holding firmly to the truth, their enjoining what is good and forbidding what is wrong doing and evil, in the strength of their zeal and enthusiasm for Allaah's religion, and in their efforts to spread the beliefs of the people of the Sunnah and the Jamaa'ah.

We continue to be shaded under their protection of this clarity and manifestation of the true beliefs. We continue to stand in the shade of this revived Salafee call which Allaah blessed the Imaam Sheikh Muhammad Ibn 'Abdul-Wahaab, may Allaah have mercy upon him, to spread to the Eastern and Western corners of the earth. All praise is due to Allaah for this tremendous blessing which hss reached us in this later age.

This is a tremendous blessing from Allaah upon you, which if Allaah has not blessed us with having it, if Allaah has not blessed someone to be raised upon these beliefs of the people of the Sunnah and the Jamaa'ah, then he becomes someone on other beliefs. He may become someone following the beliefs of the sect of the Jahmeeyah, or the sect of the Asha'rees, or the sect of the Mu'tazilah, or the sect of the Raafidhah, or from those apostates who belief in the unity of the creation with the Creator. So we ask Allaah for safety and well-being, as all of these sects were present in the past and they are present today.

If you go to any land from the Muslim countries you will find within it Sufee groups. You'll find that land may be filled with different Sufee groups upon various Sufee paths. Within each Sufee path having a specific Sufee sheikh inviting them towards Hellfire, and we seek refuge in Allaah from their misguidance. Certainly you will find these Sufees in the Muslim lands, you will also find those who have apostated from Islaam, and you will find those who affirm the disbelief of the believing in the unity of the Creator and the creation. You will find people from the sect of the Jahmeeyah, the sect of the Ash'arees, the sect of the Mu'tazilah, the sect of the Raafidhah, the sect of the Murji'ah, and you will also find those from the sect of the Khawaarij.

Yet despite this, Allaah has blessed us in this land to stand upon the beliefs of the people of the Sunnah and the Jamaa'ah, and Allaah has blessed those who he wishes from the other lands and regions of the earth to also stand and proceed upon the beliefs of the people of the Sunnah and the Jamaa'ah, and to act according to in the Book of Allaah and the Sunnah of His Messenger, may Allaah's praise and salutations be upon him. All praise is due to Allaah for this tremendous blessing and favor.

Yes, 'Amr Ibn Qays al Malaa'ee, may Allaah have mercy upon him, said: "*If you see a youth initially upon the way of the people of the Sunnah and adherence to the Jamaa'ah, then have hope for him...*" Meaning hope for him to be upon good in general, and hope the best for him. But if you see him with the people of innovation in the religion then lose heart about him, as undoubtedly a youth is generally established upon his first orientation. This is generally known to be the case. As this is what most often happens in this situation, except when Allaah grant success for a person who used to be from among the people of innovation, to come to stand upon the beliefs of the people of the Sunnah and the Jamaa'ah. But generally in most cases, what this narration states is correct and true.

Certainly in most cases when a young Muslim is raised upon the beliefs of the people of the Sunnah and the Jamaa'ah, then he is someone whom we hope good for, that he continue to remain steadfast upon that. Likewise if a young Muslim is raised among the people of innovation, then generally what is seen is that he continues proceeding upon that innovation he was cultivated within. So we ask Allaah for safety and well-being, yes.

DAY - 23

POINTS OF BENEFIT

1. True success in this life and the next comes from gaining beneficial knowledge and preceding upon it.
2. The people of the Sunnah consider innovations in the religion to be more harmful than falling into major sins.
3. There is tremendous benefit in being raised upon authentic knowledge from an early age.
4. There is a significant danger in being raised upon misconceptions and false practices from an early age.
5. The results of someone's cultivation and education as a youth is that they usually remain upon that original way and do not change.
6. There are exceptions to this general occurrence, in which an individual changes from their initial orientation and upbringing.
7. It is very important for the Muslim who is seeking knowledge to ensure that he is learning the correct beliefs of the people of the Sunnah and the Jamaa'ah, and not the beliefs of the people of innovation.
8. A Muslim should hold firmly to the correct beliefs of the people of the Sunnah and the Jamaa'ah with their molar teeth, once they understand them.
9. A Muslim should be thankful and praise Allaah for the blessing of being guided to understand and then practice the Sunnah.
10. Some of the renowned scholars of the past, despite their extensive knowledge, misunderstood some aspects of Islaam.
11. Those well-known scholars who misunderstood some aspects of Islaam, did so upon sincerity and the belief that their error was correct.
12. Some of the renowned scholars of the past wrongly adopted the misguided beliefs of the Asha'ree sect because some of their scholars taught this to them.
13. Those well-known scholars who supported the Sunnah but misunderstood some aspects of Islaam will be forgiven and have their errors wiped away within the deep ocean of their many good efforts and works.
14. It is very important for a Muslim to strive to ensure he adopts the beliefs of Islaam that agree with original beliefs that the Messenger of Allaah taught his Companions, may Allaah be pleased with them all.
15. The scholars of the Sunnah throughout the centuries have continually written works which clarified the original beliefs that the Messenger of Allaah taught his Companions.

16. The various writings of the scholars of the Sunnah throughout the centuries reflect the same beliefs and each confirm the sound beliefs held by the guided Muslims who came before them.

17. The correct way to understand the affirmed names and attributes of Allaah is upon the apparent transmitted meaning, while understanding them in a way which benefits His transcendence and uniqueness from His creation.

18. There are various beliefs of falsehood and misguidance which are widespread within the different Muslim countries of the world.

19. From the misguided sects that are present today in Muslim countries are the sect of the Jahmeeyah, the sect of the Ash'arees, the sect of the Mu'tazilah, the sect of the Raafidhah, the sect of the Murji'ah, the sect of the Khawaarij, and others.

20. It is from the blessings of Allaah upon the Muslim Ummah in this age that the original beliefs which the Messenger of Allaah taught his Companions, and the works which explain them throughout the centuries, have become widespread and accepted.

21. It is important that a Muslim continually supplicate to Allaah for safety and well-being in his understanding and practice of Islaam.

DAY - 23

LEVEL 1: TEST YOUR UNDERSTANDING:

TRUE & FALSE QUESTIONS

[Circle the correct letter for each individual sentence from today's content.]

01. How someone starts out as a Muslim will not affect their practice. [T / F]
02. Muslims should strive to gain a foundation of sound knowledge while they are young. [T / F]
03. There have always been books which conveyed the correct beliefs of Islaam since the first three generations of Muslims. [T / F]

FILL IN THE BLANK QUESTIONS

[Enter the correct individual words to complete the sentences from today's content.]

04. If a Muslim is _____ upon the _____ of the people of the Sunnah and the Jamaa'ah he will generally _____ upon that.
05. The people of the Sunnah understand Allaah's _____ , upon the _____ of the first generations of _____ .
06. Allaah blessed Sheikh _____ Ibn 'Abdul-Wahaab, to _____ this revived _____ call.

LEVEL 2: INTERACTIVE QUESTIONS & EXERCISES

COMPREHENSIVE UNDERSTANDING QUESTIONS

[In a study group or circle of learning with other students, these questions can be answered fully or partially by one student from the lesson, with another student completing the answer to the same question, by giving a comparable but different which is also correct.]

07. Give an example of something we can do to try to ensure that young Muslims today gain a sound understanding of Islaam when they are young.
08. What should a Muslim do if he encounters a conflict between the beliefs of a well-known scholar and the beliefs of the Companions?
09. Describe one of the books of the beliefs of the people of the Sunnah which you have in your library, and write which scholar authored it.

Day 24: The Importance Of Both Loving & Hating For Allaah's Sake

NARRATION FROM AL-IBAANAH AL-SUGHRAH:

Imaam Ibn Battah, may Allaah have mercy upon him, said, "*Understanding Love For Allaah's Sake And Hate For Allaah's Sake.*

You should be one who loves for Allaah's sake the one who obeys Him, even if it is someone who lives far away from you, and differs with you in your worldly goals or affairs. Just as you should hate for the sake of Allaah the one who disobeys Him, and who supports the enemies of Allaah, even if he is someone close, being from your own land, or even if he is one who aids you in your worldly affairs.

So connect yourself to the first one, and distance yourself from the second. Moreover, do not make your discussions between yourselves about perceptions and opinions, nor listen to those who generally speak from these. As opinions and perceptions can be wrong and in error or they can possibly be correct."

SOURCE OF THIS TEXT OR NARRATION:

This is a statement of the compiler of this work: Abu 'Abdullah Ubayd'Allaah Ibn Muhammad Ibn Muhammad Ibn Hamdan Ibn Battah al-Ukbaree, may Allaah have mercy upon him.

Explanation by Sheikh 'Abdul-'Azeez Ibn 'Abdullah ar-Raajhee

Yes, loving for the sake of Allaah and hating for the sake of Allaah is a fundamental from the fundamentals of faith or emaan. It is from the strongest of bonds of emaan. Moreover, loving for Allaah and hating for Allaah means: That you love whomever Allaah loves from people and individuals, whatever Allaah loves from actions, rulings, and commands, and likewise that you hate whatever Allaah hates from people and individuals, and whatever Allaah hates from actions and rulings.

It means that you love an individual not because he is someone personally close to you, nor because between the two of you there is cooperation in some worldly endeavor or shared interest in something. Rather that you love him because he is someone steadfast in obeying Allaah, the Most Glorified and the Most Exalted. This should be true even if he is someone who a foreign Muslim who lives far from you, even if you live in a country in the east while he lives in the west, or the opposite of this. Similarly that you hate the one who commits sins and disobeys Allaah, that you hate him even if he is someone close to you. This means even if he is your blood brother from the same father and mother, you have hatred for him for Allaah's sake. As hatred for a worldly reason because of your experiences when working with him or due to some harmful dealings you had with him, is a different kind of hatred.

This is the belief of the people of the Sunnah and the Jamaa'ah. This is the meaning of loving for the sake of Allaah. For this reason it is said, "you should love for the sake of Allaah the one who obeys Him, even if it is a person who lives far away from you, and opposes you in some matter of your worldly efforts. Just as you should hate for the sake of Allaah the one who disobeys Him and supports Allaah's enemies, even if he is someone from your land, and works with you in some matter related to your worldly efforts.

Which means that you should connect yourself to the first type of person, and separate yourself from the second type. Additionally he also mentioned the importance of not speaking from your opinions and perceptions, nor listening to those who generally speak from their own opinions and perceptions. Do not adopt the way of speaking from your opinions in matters of the religion, as everyone's opinions may be either correct or may be wrong.

POINTS OF BENEFIT

1. Loving for the sake of Allaah is a fundamental aspect of our faith or emaan as Muslims.

2. Hating for the sake of Allaah is a fundamental aspect of our faith or emaan as Muslims.

3. Loving and hating for the sake of Allaah is from the strongest of bonds of faith in Allaah.

4. Loving someone for the sake of Allaah means doing so for His sake and for specific matters which are pleasing and important to Allaah, not for our own sakes or personal reasons.

5. Hating someone for the sake of Allaah means doing so for His sake and for specific matters which are displeasing and hated by Allaah, not for our own sakes or personal reasons.

6. A Muslim should have love for the one who obeys Allaah, even if they live far away.

7. A Muslim should have hatred for the one who disobeys Allaah, even if they live right next to him.

8. Our worldly interests and endeavors should not influence our loving and hating for Allaah's sake.

9. Personal opinions and perceptions concerning matters related to Islaam may be correct or incorrect, depending on whether they agree with the guidance of revelation.

10. A Muslim should be warned against making their own statements and discussions about personal perceptions and opinions.

11. A Muslim should be warned against listening to and being influenced by those people whose way is to generally speak from their personal perceptions and opinions.

DAY - 24

LEVEL 1: TEST YOUR UNDERSTANDING:

TRUE & FALSE QUESTIONS

[Circle the correct letter for each individual sentence from today's content.]

01. We should have a strong love for our relatives, even when we see them disobeying Allaah. [T / F]

02. Our love for individuals does not have any connection to our love for Allaah and His Messenger. [T / F]

03. Loving someone for the sake of Allaah is different than loving them for a worldly reason. [T / F]

FILL IN THE BLANK QUESTIONS

[Enter the correct individual words to complete the sentences from today's content.]

04. A Muslim should love someone who _____ Allaah, even if they _____ with him in his _____ affairs.

05. You hate the one who commits _____ and _____ Allaah, even if he is someone _____ to you personally.

06. The scholars have warned us from _____ to those who generally speak from their own _____ and perceptions.

LEVEL 2: INTERACTIVE QUESTIONS & EXERCISES

COMPREHENSIVE UNDERSTANDING QUESTIONS

[In a study group or circle of learning with other students, these questions can be answered fully or partially by one student from the lesson, with another student completing the answer to the same question, by giving a comparable but different which is also correct.]

07. Give a possible practical example of someone that we hear about, but don't know personally, whom we should strive to love for Allaah's sake.

08. Give a possible practical example of someone that we hear about, but don't know personally, whom we should have hatred towards for Allaah's sake.

09. Discuss one possible negative effect of getting iton the habit of generally speaking about religious matters from our opinions and perceptions.

Day 25: A Person Stands Upon The Religion Of His Close Companion

NARRATION FROM AL-IBAANAH AL-SUGHRAH:

The Prophet, may Allaah's praise and salutations be upon him, said,

{A person is upon the religion of his close associate, so look closely at who you take as a close friend.}

Sulaymaan Ibn Dawood, said, "*Do not conclude that someone is upon a specific matter or way until you look sufficiently at who his associates are.*"

AUTHENTICITY & SOURCE OF THIS TEXT OR NARRATION:

Authentic: Narrated in Abu Dawood: 4833, at-Tirmidhee: 2378, al-Qadhaa'aee on the authority of Abu Hurairah, Ibn Jawzee who is overly lenient in his authentication of narrations, mentioned it within the text of his work al-Mawdhua'at, with az-Zamaksharee declaring him mistaken, yet his ruling was mention in ad-Durur. Hafidh Ibn Hajr stated in his work al-Laalee' "He said what at-Tirmidhee stated: meaning the narration is authentic. It was also narrated by the author Ibn Battah in his work al-Kubraa with five different routes of transmission, and Ibn Wadhaah narrates it in "Innovation & The Prohibition Regarding It.". Shihaab al-Qadhaa'aee narrated in his Musnad on the authority of Abu Hurairah from the Prophet, and al-'Ajaloonee indicated this in his work Kashf al-Khafaa.

Explanation by Sheikh 'Abdul-'Azeez Ibn 'Abdullah ar-Raajhee

Yes, this hadeeth narration conveys that indeed, a person is upon the religion of his close friend. A person's religion and way of life is the religion and way of life of his close associate, meaning his friend or comrade. As such, everyone should look carefully to whom they take as their close associate. If a person has for his close friend, and the one he spends time with, a person who is upon the Sunnah, then he is considered from the Sunnah. But if his close friend, and the one he spends time with, is a person upon innovation in the religion, then he is likewise connected to the people of innovation. If his friend is someone involved in wrong doing and sins, then he is likewise a person involved in sins. It is for this reason that the poet says:

About a person do not ask - but ask about his associates.

Since every person with friends is guided by, and like, his close associate.

Within this narration is a clear warning against having companionship with the people of innovation or the people involved in sins and transgressions, because they will lead you towards what they are upon. If someone spends time with those people involved in associating others with Allaah in worship, they lead him towards that sin of shirk. Similarly, if one's companion is someone from the people of innovation, that companion leads him toward that innovation he is upon. If one's companion is from the people involved in transgressions and sins, he leads you toward the same transgressions and sins. Just as was mentioned in the previous hadeeth narration about companionship, *{The similitude of good company and that of bad company is that of the owner of musk and of the blacksmith. The owner of musk would either offer you some free of charge, or you would buy it from him, or at least you get to smell its pleasant fragrance. As for the blacksmith, he either burns your clothes or you smell a repugnant smell}.* [1]

Similar to this is the statement of Sulaymaan Ibn Dawood, who said, "*Do not conclude that someone is upon a specific matter or way until you look sufficiently at who his associates are.*" By this meaning, do not assess or determine the state or condition of the individual, until you look at his associates, his companions, his friends, and those whom he spends time with. As certainly, you will find that he will be similar to them. If his companion is someone who associates others with Allaah in worship, generally you will find that he agrees with him in that act of shirk. If his friend, is someone upon some innovation in the religion, he likewise is generally an innovator. If his friend, is someone involved in sins and wrongdoing, likewise he is usually also someone involved in that sin.

---

[1] Saheeh al-Bukhaaree: 5534, Saheeh Muslim: 2628, and the Musnad of Imaam Ahmad: vol. 4 pg.404

Similarly, if is close associate is someone who strives to obey Allaah from the people of the Sunnah, then generally he will also be someone strives to obey Allaah and from among the people of the Sunnah. Yes. We ask Allaah to grant us all success in being led to obeying him, and that Allaah grant us all beneficial knowledge, and righteous deeds. May the praise and salutations of Allaah be upon our prophet Muhammad, his household, and all his Companions.

Question:[2] May Allaah increase you in goodness, this questioner says, "Esteemed sheikh, very often when we hear these narrations we suppose that they are something only specific to the previous ages, and that such people of innovation do not presently exist in our age and time. Is this idea, or belief, correct?

Answer: This is not correct. In fact, innovation was present in the previous ages and it is present in our current age. The Jahmeeyah are present generally everywhere, and they are those that say Allaah exists in every place, in the heavens and beneath the earth. We seek refuge in Allaah from this falsehood, which they are saying.

The Mu'tazilah are present, the Asha'rees are present, the Raafidhah are present, the Khawaarij are present, the Murji'ah are present, and the Qadareeyah are present. In fact, there are even present those who falsely claim that the Creator and the creation are one! They assert that the Lord is the same as the worshiper, and the worshiper is the same as the Lord. This misguidance is all present, existing today.

Additionally their books are being printed, their old historical books are being verified and reprinted, and reprinted upon high quality thick paper. This last group of people, those who falsely claim that the Creator and the creation are one, have recently published a book inviting to this belief, called 'ad-Durrah' which is currently available in Egypt, Syria, Sudan, Pakistan, and every nation. In every country, such people upon disbelief can be found, meaning the extreme Sufees and the others of misguidance, those who falsely assert unity between the Creator and his creation.

Moreover, the Sufees have numerous tareeqahs or groups upon their different innovated paths. Within one country you might find twenty, fifty, or one hundred such different Sufee groups and paths. Each Sufee group has a sheikh as its leader, leading them towards Hellfire. Among these Sufee groups are those who have general innovations and among them are people who have, in fact, reached the level of disbelief due to their extreme innovation. Such people are present today in our age, yes.

---

[2] This question was asked during these series of classes on al-Ibaanah as-Sugrah

This means that these different innovations, they are all present. Every form of innovation which existed previously is alive and present today in our age. Moreover, there are in addition to these, other new innovations now, and other new deviated beliefs now, and new affiliations and allegiances upon misguidance, all of which are in addition to what existed previously.

So that this age has become one which has even more innovation than previous ages, because it also has, in addition to the innovations of the previous centuries, those new innovations that have been brought forth recently. Yes.

DAY - 25

POINTS OF BENEFIT

1. There is a direct connection between the way you live your life and the people you spend time with.

2. Every individual is influenced by the people around them.

3. Our close friends and associates have more influence upon us than other people.

4. To accurately understand someone's orientation, priorities, and focus, one must look at his associates and companions.

5. Generally, a person will stand upon the same way of life or religion as his close friends.

6. A Muslim should consider carefully whom he takes as his close friends, since this will affect his practice of Islaam.

7. The one who spends time with someone upon innovation in Islaam is connected to the people of innovation.

8. The one who spends time with someone upon sins and wrongdoing is connected to the people of wrongdoing.

9. The significant danger in spending time with someone of misguidance or wrongdoing is that they will lead you towards that misguidance or wrongdoing.

10. The Messenger of Allaah clarified that there are varying degrees of good or harm in the companionship we have with other people.

11. The various people of innovation mentioned by the scholars in their works are not only found in past historical periods, but also found in our modern times.

12. The various misconceptions and forms of falsehood mentioned by the scholars are not only found in the past historical periods, but also found in our modern times.

13. The Mu'tazilah, the Asha'rees, the Raafidhah, the Khawaarij, the Murji'ah, and the Qadareeyah are all from the misguided sects from the previous ages, which are also present among Muslims today.

14. There are many different variations of the innovations and misguidance of Sufees found within Muslim countries today.

15. Among the Sufees present today, there are those who are upon innovation who are Muslims, as well as extreme Sufees, whose extreme innovation has reached the level of major disbelief and are not considered Muslims

16. Our present age is one which has even more innovation than previous ages, due to having both older innovations as well as new developed innovations.

LEVEL 1: TEST YOUR UNDERSTANDING:

TRUE & FALSE QUESTIONS

[Circle the correct letter for each individual sentence from today's content.]

01. The people we spend time with do not have any significant effect upon us. [T / F]
02. There are no new religious innovations, only those which came about in the past. [T / F]
03. The previous misguided sects found throughout Muslim history still exist today. [T / F]

FILL IN THE BLANK QUESTIONS

[Enter the correct individual words to complete the sentences from today's content.]

04. Every form of _____ which existed previously is alive and _____ today in our age.
05. In addition to old forms of _____ , there are other _____ forms of innovations and deviated beliefs today.

06. Success is being led by Allaah to _____ Him, and being blessed with _____ knowledge, and to do _____ deeds.

LEVEL 2: INTERACTIVE QUESTIONS & EXERCISES

COMPREHENSIVE UNDERSTANDING QUESTIONS

[In a study group or circle of learning with other students, these questions can be answered fully or partially by one student from the lesson, with another student completing the answer to the same question, by giving a comparable but different which is also correct.]

07. Give a practical example of one way that good companionship may influence a Muslim toward what is good and beneficial to him.
08. Give a practical example of one way in which bad companionship may influence a Muslim toward what is bad and harmful to him.
09. Write down two misguided sects or groups which are found in the Muslim world today, and mention a Muslim country where that group or sect can be found.

Day 26: Innovation That Is Disbelief Destroys All One's Good Deeds

NARRATION FROM AL-IBAANAH AL-SUGHRAH:

al-Hasan said, "*Allaah does not accept from an extreme innovator in the religion those deeds done seeking closeness to him. Not his ritual prayers, nor his fasting, nor his obligatory zakaat, nor his performance of Hajj, nor his physical jihaad, nor his performance of 'Umrah, nor his generally giving in charity*", until he had mentioned many different types of good deeds.

The example of one of these innovating people is the example of a man who wishes to travel to a specific place. Yet as he travels towards where he intends to reach, it just keeps getting further and further away, in front of his very eyes.

Just like this, an innovator doesn't increase in his striving to put forth many actions seeking closeness to Allaah, the Most Glorified and the Most Exalted, except that it actually only increases his distance from Allaah because of his significant disbelieving innovation he is upon."

AUTHENTICITY & SOURCE OF THIS TEXT OR NARRATION:

Authentic in meaning: narrated by the author in the original work.

Explanation by Sheikh 'Abdul-'Azeez Ibn 'Abdullah ar-Raajhee

This narration is from al-Hasan al-Basree, may Allaah have mercy upon him, in which he said, *"Allaah does not accept from an extreme innovator in the religion those deeds done seeking closeness to him. Not his ritual prayers, nor his fasting, nor his obligatory zakaat, nor his performance of Hajj, nor his physical jihaad, nor his performance of 'Umrah, nor his generally giving in charity..."* This is to be generally understood to apply to that innovator whose innovation in the religion is extreme and takes them outside of the boundaries of Islaam. The extreme innovator, whose innovation reaches the level of major disbelief, certainly Allaah does not accept from him his deeds, nor his ritual prayers, nor his fasting, nor his obligatory zakaat, until he repents from that matter of major disbelief and significant misguidance that he fell into. Because when a person stands upon major disbelief, his good deeds are not accepted by Allaah, due to the presence of that disbelief.

Allaah, the Most High, says ❰*And indeed it has been revealed to you (O Muhammad), as it was to those (Allaah's Messengers) before you: "If you join others in worship with Allaah, then surely all your deeds will be in vain, and you will certainly be among the losers.*❱–(Surah Az-Zumar: 1).

And Allaah the Most Perfect said: ❰*But if they had joined in worship others with Allaah, all that they used to do would have been of no benefit to them"*❱–(Surah Al-An'am: 88) And Allaah the Most Perfect said: ❰*..And whosoever disbelieves in the Oneness of Allaah and in all the other Articles of Faith, then fruitless is his work, and in the Hereafter he will be among the losers*❱–(Surah Al-Ma'idah: 5) And Allaah the Most High said, ❰*And We shall turn to whatever deeds they (disbelievers, polytheists, sinners, etc.) did, and We shall make such deeds as scattered floating particles of dust.*❱–(Surah Al-Furqaan: 23). As such, it should be understood that for the individual who is innovating in the religion, whose innovation reaches the level of major disbelief in Islaam, then Allaah will never accept from him and his works or deeds done seeking closeness to Allaah.

Allaah will not accept his ritual prayers, nor his fasting, nor his obligatory zakaat, nor his pilgrimage, nor his efforts to strive in the path of Allaah, nor will he accept any of his charity. All of the works and deeds of such an individual are nullified and not accepted, and we seek refuge in Allaah from that. al-Hasan al-Basree, may Allaah have mercy upon him, then continued saying, *"The example of one of these people"* meaning that innovator whose innovation the religion has reached the level of disbelief, *"... is the example of a man who wishes to travel to a specific place. Yet as he travels towards where he intends to reach, it just becomes further and further away..."* In the same way, the extreme innovator in his efforts to come and move closer to

DAY - 26

Allaah, and through his actions seeking closeness to Allaah, the Most Glorified and the Most Exalted, only accomplishes increasing his distance away from Allaah. This is because the actions and efforts of any disbeliever are not accepted by Allaah.

But as for that innovator, who is upon innovation that doesn't reach the degree or level of major disbelief, then he is considered a believer but someone with week emaan or faith, and is considered someone who is committing a major sin and transgressions due to his innovation, even though he remains within Islaam and upon its truth generally. Additionally, both major sins and innovation in the religion are considered matters which may lead a person towards major disbelief. Yet if the misguidance they stand upon is a form of innovation that does not reach the level or degree of major disbelief, then his deeds and actions may be accepted by Allaah. What is correct to say is that such an innovator is someone who is weak in his faith, and someone who is committing a major transgression through his innovation, this is the sound position about him. But as for that extreme innovator, whose innovation reaches the level of major disbelief, then he is considered from those people who none of their deeds will be accepted. This was the understanding that al-Hasan al-Basree, may Allaah have mercy upon him, intended to convey, yes.

DAY - 26

POINTS OF BENEFIT

1. It is a general condition for the acceptance of good deeds by Allaah that someone be a Muslim.
2. Innovation in Islaam is of two different types in relation to belief and disbelief.
3. One category of innovation in Islaam is considered sin and wrongdoing, but not major disbelief in Islaam.
4. A second category of extreme innovation in Islaam, is considered sin and wrongdoing, as well as reaching the level of major disbelief which takes someone outside the boundaries of Islaam.
5. The person who is an extreme innovator destroys their own good deeds by proceeding upon that disbelieving innovation.
6. Gaining closeness to Allaah is only accomplished through deeds based upon both purity of intention and full conformance and compliance with the guidance of Islaam.
7. Sincerity and purity of intention in one's deeds is an absolute condition for their acceptance by Allaah.
8. From the matters which cause Allaah to reject good deeds is joining others with him in performing them as worship.
9. Those who associate others with Allaah in worship will ultimately be losers in the life of the Hereafter.
10. Some people put forth actions seeking Allaah's pleasure, yet this only increases them in distance from Allaah, due to either how or why they perform those actions.
11. The Muslim upon an innovation which is not major disbelief, is considered a believer who has weak emaan, and who is committing a major sin due to his innovation.

LEVEL 1: TEST YOUR UNDERSTANDING:

TRUE & FALSE QUESTIONS

[Circle the correct letter for each individual sentence from today's content.]

01. Allaah accepts all of our actions, as long as we are sincere in doing them for Him. [T / F]

02. From the dangers of innovation is the destruction of the rewards of our good deeds. [T / F]

03. There are conditions for the acceptance of our deeds by Allaah. [T / F]

FILL IN THE BLANK QUESTIONS

[Enter the correct individual words to complete the sentences from today's content.]

04. Both _____ sins and _____ in the religion may _____ a person towards major disbelief.

05. Allaah says that He will make the _____ of the _____ like scattered floating particles of dust.

06. The _____ innovator, whose innovation reaches the level of major _____ , is someone who none of their deeds will be _____ .

LEVEL 2: INTERACTIVE QUESTIONS & EXERCISES

COMPREHENSIVE UNDERSTANDING QUESTIONS

[In a study group or circle of learning with other students, these questions can be answered fully or partially by one student from the lesson, with another student completing the answer to the same question, by giving a comparable but different which is also correct.]

07 Give a specific example of any sect or group whose innovation reaches the level of major disbelief, and so have been declared by the people of knowledge to be disbelievers.

08. Give a specific example of any sect or group whose innovation is below the level of major disbelief, and so are Muslims.

09. Give a practical example of how someone might associate others with Allaah in their worship, and so have their deeds nullified and rejected.

Day 27: Innovations In Islaam May Mislead You To Leave Islaam

NARRATION FROM AL-IBAANAH AL-SUGHRAH:

Imaam Ibn Battah, may Allaah have mercy upon him, said,

"Every innovated statement, newly developed view, and false desire which is followed, all of these- as well as whatever has the same general characteristics and whatever is further derived from these or whatever is similar to them- all of these are evil corrupt sayings and newly conceived evil ways, which take the people who proceed upon them outside of the religion of Islaam, taking those who wrongly believe them outside of the body of the Muslim Ummah."

SOURCE OF THIS TEXT OR NARRATION:

This is a statement of the compiler of this work: Abu 'Abdullah Ubayd'Allaah Ibn Muhammad Ibn Muhammad Ibn Hamdan Ibn Battah al-Ukbaree, may Allaah have mercy upon him.

Explanation by Sheikh 'Abdul-'Azeez Ibn 'Abdullah ar-Raajhee

As was stated, it is obligatory upon you to free yourself from any connection to such innovators, and to free yourself from every statement of innovation. Every statement or claim which does not have a basis in the Sharee'ah, you should free yourself from it. Every newly developed opinion or view which does not have a basis within the Sharee'ah, you should free yourself from connection to it. Every followed desire which a person chooses to follow, distance yourself and turn away from it.

Then he said, *"...all of these- as well as whatever has the same general characteristics..."* Meaning in relation to all of these sects which he has discussed, *"...what is further derived from these or similar to them- all of these are evil corrupt sayings, and newly conceived evil ways, which take the people who proceed upon them outside of the religion of Islaam."* This must be understood to have a more detailed meaning and explanation.

What is correct to say is that some of these innovating matters cause those involved in them to leave the religion, whereas other lesser matters, which are innovation, do not cause those involved in them to leave the boundaries of Islaam. Not every innovation is one which causes someone to leave Islaam. Some innovations cause someone to leave Islaam, such as the beliefs of the Jahmeeyah, and the beliefs of the extreme Qadareeyah. The scholars of Islaam had stated that such sects have gone outside the boundaries of the seventy-two misguided sects within Islaam. But as for other misguided sects, such as the Zaydeeyah their misguidance does not cause them to leave Islaam. So for the matters of innovation in the religion, not all of them cause the individual upon them to leave Islaam.

As such, the statement of the author here is not perfect and complete in its precision and detail. His statement, *"... and take those who believe them outside of the body of the Muslim Ummah."* In fact regarding this statement, it must be understood with a more detailed meaning and explanation. That being that some of these innovations cause someone to leave the religion, meaning those whose innovation is in fact a form of major disbelief, and reaches the level of major disbelief. Whereas other individuals are considered from the people of innovation, yet still Muslims. Yes.

POINTS OF BENEFIT

1. A Muslim should free himself from any false desire that is followed.
2. A Muslim should free himself from any connection to a statement of innovation.
3. A Muslim should free himself from any connection to those preceding upon innovation.
4. A Muslim should free himself from any connection to every statement or claim which does not have a basis in the Sharee'ah.
5. A Muslim should free himself from any connection to every newly developed opinion or view which lacks a basis within the Sharee'ah
6. The matters of innovation in the religion are of varying degrees of severity which are assessed by the scholars.
7. Some major matters of innovation lead those who are involved in them to disbelieve in Islaam and leave the religion.
8. Some lesser matters which are innovation do not cause those involved in them to leave the boundaries of Islaam, but they stand upon misguidance and sin as Muslims.
9. The beliefs of the sect of the Jahmeeyah, and the beliefs of the extreme Qadareeyah are misguidance, which is major disbelief.
10. The beliefs of the sect of the Zaydeeyah is clear misguidance, but does not cause them to leave Islaam.
11. Those sects whom the scholars assess are extreme innovators stand outside the boundaries of the seventy-two misguided sects within Islaam.

LEVEL 1: TEST YOUR UNDERSTANDING:

TRUE & FALSE QUESTIONS

[Circle the correct letter for each individual sentence from today's content.]

01. Even though innovations are misguidance, they are not disbelief. [T / F]
02. A Muslim should free himself from any connection to every form of misguidance. [T / F]
03. Some of the astray sects have beliefs and practices that have taken them outside of Islaam. [T / F]

FILL IN THE BLANK QUESTIONS

[Enter the correct individual words to complete the sentences from today's content.]

04. A knowledgeable Muslim should free himself from _____ statement of _____ around him.
05. _____ yourself and turn away from every misguiding _____ which some people choose to follow.
06. Some matters of _____ innovation in the religion, cause an individual to _____ Islaam.

LEVEL 2: INTERACTIVE QUESTIONS & EXERCISES

COMPREHENSIVE UNDERSTANDING QUESTIONS

[In a study group or circle of learning with other students, these questions can be answered fully or partially by one student from the lesson, with another student completing the answer to the same question, by giving a comparable but different which is also correct.]

07. Give an example of one of the astray sects whose beliefs reach the level of major disbelief in Islaam. Describe that specific belief.
08. Give an example of one of the misguided sects or groups who proceeds on innovation, which the scholars do not view as major disbelief. Describe that specific innovation they proceed upon.
09. Give a specific example of any newly developed view or opinion some Muslims accept, which was unknown among the Companions of the Messenger of Allaah.

Day 28: The One Who Changes Islaam Is Cursed By Allaah & Creation

NARRATION FROM AL-IBAANAH AL-SUGHRAH:

The Messenger of Allaah, may Allaah's praise and salutations be upon him, said,

{If anyone introduces a new matter or gives shelter to a man who introduces a new matter in the religion, that person is cursed all those who curse the wrongdoers, meaning the angels and by all the righteous people. And Allaah will not accept from him repentance nor a ransom for this on the Day of Judgement.}

It was asked of al-Hasan al-Basree, "*What is the meaning of introduced new matters?*" He replied saying,

"*The people of trials among the Muslims, all of them are those who introduce these new matters wrongly brought into Islaam, as well as the people who adhere to their desires, all of them are those who are introducing new matters wrongly brought in Islaam.*"

AUTHENTICITY & SOURCE OF THIS TEXT OR NARRATION:

Authentic: This was narrated by Imaam al-Bukhaaree who mentioned it with the beginning of the narration saying {Medina is a sacred territory from 'Ayr to Thaur (it is most probably Uhud). He who innovates an act or practice...}. It was also was mentioned by at-Tirmidhee in his Sunan in the chapter "What Has Been Related About The Prohibition From Selling The Walaa' And (From) Conferring It"

Explanation by Sheikh 'Abdul-'Azeez Ibn 'Abdullah ar-Raajhee

This hadeeth narration is affirmed to be authentic, where the Prophet, may Allaah's praise and salutations be upon him, said, *{Medina is a sacred territory from 'Ayr to Thaur (it is most probably Uhud). He who innovates (an act or practice) or gives protection to an innovator, there is a curse of Allaah and that of His angels and that of the whole humanity upon him...}* What is most well-known from the wording of the hadeeth are the narrations which state, *{...that of His angels and that of the whole humanity upon him.}* But there also is found in some of the narrations the wording *{...curse of those who curse.}* However this narration states, *{...that of His angels and that of the whole humanity upon him.}* Within this is found a clear indication of the prohibition of bringing forth new religious matters in Islaam. What is intended by new religious matters are innovations and transgressions. The Messenger, upon him be Allaah's praise and salutations, said, *{He who innovates (an act or practice)...}* meaning an innovator, as such it warns against innovation generally, and accommodating those who innovate in Islaam. The one who brings forth a new religious matter, or innovates a new matter, is someone who has committed a major transgression, and committed a major sin. It is for this reason that the Prophet, upon him be Allaah's praise and salutations, said, *{....(then) there is a curse of Allaah and that of His angels and that of the whole humanity upon him...}* [1]

As for the meaning of what is considered a major sin, as we've previously discussed, the strongest and most correct regarding its definition is that a major sin is that matter which is mentioned in the source texts of the Sharee'ah as:

- being connected to a judicial punishment which handed out in this world for the person who commits it,
- the person who commits it is threatened with a punishment in the Hereafter,
- when it is mentioned for the person who commits it is cursed,
- or the person who commits it is threatened with being cursed,
- that matter or act is generally connected to the threat of punishment in the Hellfire,
- or that matter or act which is generally connected to earning Allaah's anger.

When act is connected to any of these matters in the texts of the Sharee'ah, then it is considered a major sin.

DAY - 28

---

[1] Saheeh al-Bukhaaree: 6755, Saheeh Muslim: 1370, at-Tirmidhee: 2127, an-Nasaa'ee: 4734, Abu Dawood: 2034, and the Musnad of Imaam Ahmad: vol.1 pg.151

As for the meaning of the section of the hadeeth which states {*....And Allaah will not accept from him repentance nor other deeds as a ransom for this sin on the Day of Judgment.*}[2] then what has been stated about this is that it refers to repentance, that Allaah will not accept that person's repentance. What is also said is that the word "as-sarf" means those obligatory actions which he had performed and that the word 'al-'adl' meaning those extra non-obligatory actions that he has performed. So {*....And Allaah will not accept from him repentance nor other deeds as a ransom for this sin on the Day of Judgment.*}[3] It has also been said that the word 'al-'adl' means a ransom as Allaah the Most High said, ❮*And leave alone those who take their religion as play and amusement, and are deceived by the life of this world. But remind them with it (the Qur'aan) lest a person be given up to destruction for that which he has earned, when he will find for himself no protector or intercessor besides Allaah, and even if he offers every ransom, it will not be accepted from him....*❯–(Surah Al-An'am: 70) meaning that they will not be able to ransom themselves out of the punishment of Allaah with anything.

It was said to al-Hasan "*What are these introduced innovations?*", meaning he was asked to explain what are meant by innovations that are brought forth by people. He responded to this saying. "*The people of trials among the Muslims, all of them are those who introduce these new matters wrongly brought into Islaam...*" He mentions both innovation and desires, meaning by this the people of innovation and desires are all people who bring new matters into the religion of Islaam. So what is meant or intended by this hadeeth narration is both innovation and sinful transgressions, yet innovation is worse and more significant. Therefore the narration has a warning against innovation, as well as accommodating the people of innovation. Therefore know that the Jahmeeyah are the people of innovation, the Raafidhah are the people of innovation, as well as the sects of the Mu'tazilah, the Khawaarij, and the Murji'ah. All of these are those who have brought innovations among the Muslims. Yes.

---

[2] Saheeh al-Bukhaaree: 1870, Saheeh Muslim: 1370, at-Tirmidhee: 2127, an-Nasaa'ee: 4734, Abu Dawood: 2034, and the Musnad of Imaam Ahmad: vol.1 pg.119

[3] Saheeh al-Bukhaaree: 7300, Saheeh Muslim: 1370, at-Tirmidhee: 2127, an-Nasaa'ee: 4734, Abu Dawood: 2034, and the Musnad of Imaam Ahmad: vol.1 pg.81

POINTS OF BENEFIT

1. It is prohibited to bring forth new religious matters in Islaam
2. Innovation in the religion is considered worse and more significant than engaging in major sins.
3. The people who follow and adhere to their desires try to introduce new things into Islaam.
4. It is a major sin to offer protection to someone changing and distorting any aspect of Islaam.
5. There is a significant danger in the sin of accommodating the people of innovation.
6. The righteous from creation curse those people who bring new religious matters into Islaam.
7. The one who brings forth a new religious matter, or innovates a new matter, is someone who has committed a major sin in Islaam.
8. There are several factors the scholars use to distinguish what is considered a major sin in the source texts.
9. A major sin is connected to a judicial punishment in this world which is given by legitimate Muslim governmental authorities.
10. A major sin is known by the one who commits it being cursed, or threatened with being cursed by Allaah and the creation.
11. A major sin is that matter which is connected to earning Allaah's anger.
12. A major sin is connected to a specific punishment in the Hereafter for the person who commits it.
13. A major sin is connected to general punishment in the Hellfire.
14. The explanation of this hadeeth narration i9ndicates the danger of committing innovation or sheltering an innovator, and is a warning that innovation leads only to punishment as well as possibly causing Allaah to accept neither their deeds nor their repentance on the Day of Judgment.
15. From the misguided sects whom the scholars state have wrongly innovated new matters into Islaam are the sects of the Jahmeeyah, the Raafidhah, the Mu'tazilah, the Khawaarij, the Murji'ah, as well as others.

LEVEL 1: TEST YOUR UNDERSTANDING:

TRUE & FALSE QUESTIONS

[Circle the correct letter for each individual sentence from today's content.]

01. It is acceptable to accommodate or support an innovator as [T / F] long as you don't innovate yourself.
02. Innovating something new is blameworthy but not as bad as [T / F] the many major sins people commit.
03. There is no clear way to tell what is considered a major sin by [T / F] Allaah.

FILL IN THE BLANK QUESTIONS

[Enter the correct individual words to complete the sentences from today's content.]

04. In this discussion what is intended by new _____ matters is: _____ .
05. The one who innovates a _____ matter in Islaam, has committed a major _____ .
06. The people of _____ and _____ are all those who bring new matters into the religion of Islaam.

LEVEL 2: INTERACTIVE QUESTIONS & EXERCISES

COMPREHENSIVE UNDERSTANDING QUESTIONS

[In a study group or circle of learning with other students, these questions can be answered fully or partially by one student from the lesson, with another student completing the answer to the same question, by giving a comparable but different which is also correct.]

07. Give a specific example of something new related to giving da'wah that some people have innovated into Islaam.
08. Give a specific example of the mistake of protecting or accommodating an innovator in Islaam which a Muslim might fall into.
09. Explain a specific reason why some people might wrongly believe that making new matters in Islaam is something good.

DAY - 28

Day 29: Repentance from Innovation Must Be Clear & Apparent

NARRATION FROM AL-IBAANAH AL-SUGHRAH:

Al-Hasan Ibn Shaqeeq said, "*I was with Ibn al-Mubaarak when a man came to him.*"

Ibn al-Mubaarak said to the man, "*You are that Jahmee.*"

The man replied, "*Yes, I was.*"

So Ibn al-Mubaarak said to the man, "*Then leave me, and do not come back near me.*"

But the man said to him, "*But I have repented from that!*"

Yet Ibn al-Mubaarak said, "*No, not until you make well known your repentance just as you previously had made well known that you proceeded upon that innovation.*"

AUTHENTICITY & SOURCE OF THIS TEXT OR NARRATION:

Authentic in meaning: narrated by the author in the original work.

EXPLANATION BY SHEIKH 'ABDUL-'AZEEZ IBN 'ABDULLAH AR-RAAJHEE

Yes, this is the statement of al-Hasan Ibn Shaqeeq Ibn 'Umar Ibn Shaqeeq al-Harmee narrating from 'Abdullah Ibn al-Mubaarak a well-known person of knowledge, who was a scholar who was known for his abstinence from worldly affairs. al-Hasan Ibn Shaqeeq narrates from him that a man came to him whom initially he didn't know, but then when he recognized him, he said to the man, *"You are that Jahmee."* meaning one who was speaking and putting forth the statements that conformed to the way of the Jahmeeyah. They are a sect that completely denies the meanings and reality of Allaah's names and attributes, and claim that Allaah is everywhere and in every place. So that man replied, *"Yes, I was."* Ibn al-Mubaarak then said to the man, *"Then leave me, and do not come back near me."*

This is an indication of him abandoning this man, due to his disbelief and misguidance, and it indicates the obligation of abandoning the people of innovation and the requirement of distancing ourselves from them. It is an obligation upon an individual that he abandon them, and distances himself from their settings and gatherings and spending time sitting with them. But the man said to him, *"But I have repented from that!"* As certainly that age was one in which the practices and the beliefs of the Sunnah were apparent and clear, while innovation was much less among the Muslims. The people of the Sunnah, the leading scholars and people of knowledge had a strong position, and influence in society, while the people of innovation had been turned away from. Due to this, the man, meaning that innovator, said to 'Abdullah Ibn al-Mubaarak *"...I have repented from that!"* Yet Ibn al-Mubaarak said, *"No..."* meaning that it will not be accepted by the people of the Sunnah, until you make your repentance as prominent and clearly apparent as you previously had made your proceeding upon that innovation prominent and clearly apparent. Meaning make your position upon the Sunnah well-known in those same places and areas in which you previously were well-known to stand upon innovation, such that it be a clear indication of your repentance from that. But as for the mere claim made with the tongue, then this will not be accepted from you.

This is an indication of the obligation of abandoning interacting with the people of innovation, such as the sects of the Jahmeeyah, the Mu'tazilah, the Raafidhah, and the Khawaarij. It is required and an obligation upon an individual, to abandon them and to not speak with them nor sit with them, and to expel and throw them out of your sittings and gathering until they make very clear their repentance from the innovation they were upon.

It is for this reason that 'Abdullah Ibn al-Mubaarak did not accept from him his claim, or his statement, until he also made readily apparent his repentance by actions. A statement of tongue indicating repentance is not enough until the person also makes apparent in their actions a clear repentance from innovation, just as they previously made clear their position and proceeded upon innovation. Yes.

POINTS OF BENEFIT

1. The Muslims judge an individual according to his outward statements and actions.
2. There are ages or times in which the practices and the beliefs of the Sunnah were apparent and clear, and innovation is much less among the Muslims.
3. There are ages or times in which the practices of innovation and misguidance are predominant and common, and the beliefs of the Sunnah are uncommon among the Muslims.
4. The people of the Sunnah are generally known among the Muslims for standing upon the Sunnah.
5. The people of innovation are generally known among the Muslims for being upon innovation.
6. There is a significant benefit in specifically identifying the sects and groups upon innovation, in order that the Muslims generally can be warned against interacting and being influenced by them.
7. The Jahmeeyah are a sect that completely denies the meanings and reality of Allaah's names and attributes.
8. The Jahmeeyah are a sect that claim that Allaah is everywhere and in every place.
9. It is a general obligation to abandon interacting with the people of innovation. An exception to this is specific interactions by people with knowledge for the purpose of guiding them towards true repentance from their misguidance.
10. The people of the Sunnah have conditions for repentance from an innovation which was called to openly in a specific region.
11. The individual who repents from innovation in the religion should make his repentance clear and distinct.
12. A statement of the tongue alone indicating repentance is not enough until the person also makes their repentance apparent in their actions and deeds.

LEVEL 1: TEST YOUR UNDERSTANDING:

TRUE & FALSE QUESTIONS

[Circle the correct letter for each individual sentence from today's content.]

01. The sin of innovation must be repented from like other sins [T / F] and transgressions.
02. Repentance from sin and transgression is only something in [T / F] the heart.
03. The Muslims judge other people according to their claims, not [T / F] their actions.

FILL IN THE BLANK QUESTIONS

[Enter the correct individual words to complete the sentences from today's content.]

04. Ibn al-Mubaarak abandoned this man mentioned, due to his failure to _____ make clear his _____ from previous misguidance upon the way of the _____ .
05. The Jahmeeyah wrongly _____ the meanings and the reality of Allaah's _____ and _____ .
06. It is a general obligation upon us to _____ the people of innovation, and not to _____ with them or _____ with them.

LEVEL 2: INTERACTIVE QUESTIONS & EXERCISES

COMPREHENSIVE UNDERSTANDING QUESTIONS

[In a study group or circle of learning with other students, these questions can be answered fully or partially by one student from the lesson, with another student completing the answer to the same question, by giving a comparable but different which is also correct.]

07. Give a specific example of one way that a Muslim can make clear his repentance from innovation in our modern age.
08. Name two possible things a Muslim must change, once he repents from some innovation which he previously accepted.
09. Name two possible things a Muslim must change, once he repents from some innovation which he previously accepted.

Day 30: What Religion Will You Die Upon?

NARRATION FROM AL-IBAANAH AL-SUGHRAH:

Maalik ibn Anas said to a man who was at the point of death, "*Upon which religion will you die?*"

He replied, "*Upon the religion of Abu 'Amaarah.*" This was a man who had been dominated and influenced by some of the people of desires. Then Maalik ibn Anas said,

"*He claimed the religion of Abul' Qaasem, (the Prophet Muhammad) yet he died upon the religion of Abu 'Amaarah.*"

AUTHENTICITY & SOURCE OF THIS TEXT OR NARRATION:

Authentic in meaning: narrated by the author in the original work.

Explanation by Sheikh 'Abdul-'Azeez Ibn 'Abdullah ar-Raajhee

Yes, this was from the statements of Maalik Ibn Anas, may Allaah have mercy upon him, the well-known leading scholar, and leading scholar of Dar al-Hijrah, the city of Medina. He said, *"It was said to a man who was at the point of death, "Upon which religion will you die?"* This is by a man who was present with him when he was close to death. The man who was close to death replied, *"Upon the religion of Abu 'Amaarah."* This was because he was an innovator. As Abu 'Amaarah was an innovator from amongst the people who have innovated in the religion.

This indicated that for this man that innovation had become settled and rooted within him. Again, *"It was said to a man who was at the point of death, "Upon which religion will you die?"* He replied, *"Upon the religion of Abu 'Amaarah."* So when he was asked about his religion he replied that of Abu 'Amaarah, who was from the people of innovation in his time. This man who was dying had this allegiance towards him, and he was connected to him, he supported him and agreed with him in his distorted path of Islaam. So the man who responded was someone who was connected to some of the people who were following their desires, meaning the people who had innovated in the religion.

Therefore Maalik ibn Anas said, blaming and censuring him *"He claimed to follow the religion of Abul' Qaasem"*, by this meaning the Prophet Muhammad, may Allaah's praise and salutations be upon him, and his religion the path of Islaam. *"... Yet he died upon the religion of Abu 'Amaarah."* So look closely at this man, someone who had turned away from practicing the religion of the Prophet, may Allaah's praise and salutations be upon him, and he chose to die upon the religion of Abu 'Amaarah, an innovated distorted understanding of the religion.

Within this narration there is a warning from innovations in the religion. As innovation, and we seek refuge in Allaah from it, comes to capture and take over the one engaged in it, such that even at the time of death he continues to proceed upon that innovation, and we seek refuge in Allaah from that. Just as was seen from this man, who at the very point of death was asked about his religion and what he would die upon, replied, *"Upon the religion of Abu 'Amaarah,"* meaning upon innovation in Islaam. He did not say, *"I die upon the religion of Islaam"*.

So we ask Allaah for protection and well-being. Since a person, if he is raised and cultivated when young upon a matter, then generally he continues upon this. If he was cultivated upon a manner when young, then most likely this is what he will die upon. Therefore, we ask Allaah protection and well-being.

If someone throughout his life is associated and connected strongly to the people of innovation and desires, and attached to the people of innovation, then generally he proceeds upon that, continues his life upon that, and dies upon that- except for the one that Allaah protects from this. We ask Allaah for protection and well-being by being warned away from innovation, yes.

POINTS OF BENEFIT

1. There is a difference between claiming something and making that claim a reality.

2. The people of innovation claim to adhere to the religion of the Prophet Muhammad, but in reality they follow the innovations of their misguided leaders and evil scholars.

3. The people of innovation generally turn towards their misguided leaders to understand the religion of Islaam, rather than turning to the statements and narrations of the Messenger of Allaah, may the praise and salutations of Allaah be upon him.

4. The people of innovation generally have a stronger connection to their misguided leaders and evil scholars than their connection to the Messenger of Allaah.

5. The one who proceeds upon innovation in his life is in danger of dying upon that innovation before true repentance.

6. The misguidance of innovation becomes settled and rooted within those who proceed upon it for an extended period of time.

7. The people who are upon innovation in the religion are those who follow their false desires.

8. Innovations in the religion often capture, dominate and take over the person who engages in them, until they die upon that innovation.

9. A Muslims should seek Allaah's protection from the trial of falling into innovation in his practice of Islaam.

10. A person generally remains upon that understanding and practice which they were cultivated upon and lived their life upon.

11. The exception is the person who was raised upon or lived upon innovation, yet Allaah guided them to abandon innovation and to proceed upon the straight path of the Book and the Sunnah , as understood by the Companions.

LEVEL 1: TEST YOUR UNDERSTANDING:

TRUE & FALSE QUESTIONS

[Circle the correct letter for each individual sentence from today's content.]

01. Maalik Ibn Anas, may Allaah have mercy upon him, was a well-known leading scholar in the city of Mecca. [T / F]

02. It is not possible to leave innovation that you fall into. [T / F]

03. The people of innovation have leaders who they take their understanding and practice from. [T / F]

FILL IN THE BLANK QUESTIONS

[Enter the correct individual words to complete the sentences from today's content.]

04. Abu 'Amaarah, was from the people of _____ in his time and a follower of his _____ .

05. Whatever we are cultivated upon when _____ , then most likely this is what we will _____ upon, except for those whom Allaah, in His mercy, guides.

06. The man who was _____ had this _____ towards Abu 'Amaarah, rather than being _____ to the Prophet Muhammad.

LEVEL 2: INTERACTIVE QUESTIONS & EXERCISES

COMPREHENSIVE UNDERSTANDING QUESTIONS

[In a study group or circle of learning with other students, these questions can be answered fully or partially by one student from the lesson, with another student completing the answer to the same question, by giving a comparable but different which is also correct.]

07. Give an example of something that someone might say that indicates that their love of and connection to their leader is stronger than their love and connection to the Messenger of Allaah.

08. Give a possible reason or cause that might make it difficult for people of innovation to realize that they are not actually upon the religion of the Prophet as they claim.

09. Give an example of a sect, group, or movement among the Muslims which people have a biased allegiance towards, which is greater than their attachment and allegiance to the Messenger of Allaah.

DAY - 30

ANSWER KEY

DAY 01: THE IMPORTANCE OF ASKING TO BE GUIDED IN WHAT YOU SAY & DO

TEST YOUR UNDERSTANDING:

TRUE & FALSE QUESTIONS
[Circle the correct letter for each individual sentence from today's content.]

01. The main thing to consider when doing something is to make sure you have a good intention. [T / **F**]

    This is incorrect. It is also a condition that they must fully conform to the guidance of Islaam. As the Sheikh mentioned *"…His actions will be righteous, and righteous actions have a meaning. That they are righteous means that it is something done purely for the sake of Allaah's face alone, as well as in conformance to Allaah's Sharee'ah and his revealed religion."*

02. It is important to ask Allaah to guide us to every matter that will make us successful as a Muslim. [**T** / F]

    This is correct. As the Sheikh mentioned *"…The one who Allaah grant success in making correct statements and putting forth righteous deeds, is from those who have been granted success and those who have been guided to contentment."*

03. It is permissible to do acts of worship in a unique and new way as long as you are sincere and doing so purely for Allaah's sake. [T / F]

    This is incorrect. As the Sheikh mentioned *"…As such, if an action is done purely for Allaah sake, and it conforms with the Sharee'ah, then that is a righteous deeds or endeavor which is accepted by Allaah… Similarly, if one is adherence to the Sharee'ah is deficient or lacking then innovation in the religion appears related to it."*

FILL IN THE BLANK QUESTIONS
[Enter the correct individual words to complete the sentences from today's content.]

04. Outward success is found if we are **correct** in our statements and we put forward **righteous** actions.
05. If our deeds are lacking in **sincerity** then this is a type of associating others with **Allaah**.
06. If our deeds are lacking in adherence to the Sunnah and we follow a new method of worshiping, then this is a type of **innovation** in the religion.

INTERACTIVE QUESTIONS & EXERCISES

COMPREHENSIVE UNDERSTANDING QUESTIONS
[In a study group or circle of learning with other students, these questions can be answered fully or partially by one student from the lesson, with another student completing the answer to the same question, by giving a comparable but different which is also correct.]

07. Why is it important for someone to seek Allaah's assistance in both adhering to the Sunnah and having sincerity of intention for Allaah alone, and not just one?

    Answers will vary per student, and should be discussed from any authentic source or sound perspective. This is important because if our efforts and deeds are lacking from either direction then, they are not accepted by Allaah.

08. Give examples of three invalid intentions which a person may intend in his heart when doing an outwardly good action.

    Answers will vary per student, and should be discussed from any authentic source or sound perspective. One example would be doing something so that people will notice you and praise you for them.

09. Give examples of three acts of worship which are done by Muslims sincerely, but which go against the revealed guidance of the Sharee'ah.

    Answers will vary per student, and should be discussed from any authentic source or sound perspective. An example would be supplicating to the Messenger of Allaah at his grave, instead of supplicating to Allaah alone. Another example would be collective performance of dhikr loudly.

DAY 02: THE CLEAR GUIDANCE OF THE FINAL MESSENGER IS FOR ALL HUMANITY

TEST YOUR UNDERSTANDING:

TRUE & FALSE QUESTIONS
[Circle the correct letter for each individual sentence from today's content.]

01. The previous prophets did not know about the coming of the Prophet Muhammad. [T / **F**]

   This is incorrect. As the Sheikh mentioned the verse"... ⸨*And remember when Allaah took the Covenant of the Prophets, saying: "Take whatever I gave you from the Book and Hikmah (understanding of the Laws of Allaah, etc.), and afterwards there will come to you a Messenger (Muhammad) confirming what is with you; you must, then, believe in him and help him...*⸩-(Surah Aal-Imraan: 81)

02. All the previous revealed guidance of Allaah has been completed in the guidance given to the Prophet Mohammed. [**T** / F]

   This is correct, since all other prophets would have to follow his final guidance. As the Sheikh mentioned from the authentic narration, *{Indeed I have come to you with a clear white way, and by Allaah if Musaa and 'Isaa were to hear, they only choice would be to follow me.}*

03. The righteous Muslims, as worshipers of Allaah, are all equal in rank and merit. [T / **F**]

   This is incorrect, as shown in the discussion about Abu Bakr and 'Isaa. As the Sheikh mentioned "...*Additionally he is considered higher in rank and merits then Abu Bakr according to the consensus of the Muslims. He is the best of the people from amongst the Muslim Ummah after its own Prophet. So if it is said or asked, who is better than Abu Bakr according to the consensus of the Muslims.*"

ANSWER KEY

FILL IN THE BLANK QUESTIONS

[Enter the correct individual words to complete the sentences from today's content.]

04. Every previous prophet had a **covenant** with Allaah about the coming of the prophet Muhammad.

05. The prophet **'Isaa** will descend in the later times and judge according to the **Sharee'ah**.

06. **Abu Bakr** was the best of those within the Muslim Ummah who was not a **prophet**.

INTERACTIVE QUESTIONS & EXERCISES

COMPREHENSIVE UNDERSTANDING QUESTIONS

[In a study group or circle of learning with other students, these questions can be answered fully or partially by one student from the lesson, with another student completing the answer to the same question, by giving a comparable but different which is also correct.]

07. What is a possible benefit of knowing the different ranks and positions of excellence of those who are part of the Muslim Ummah?

    Answers will vary per student, and should be discussed from any authentic source or sound perspective. An example would be understanding that there is a tremendous benefit in knowing the best righteous believers so that they can serve as examples and models for us in worshiping Allaah.

08. Why is it important to understand that Islaam completes and abrogates the guidance given to the previous prophets and messengers?

    Answers will vary per student, and should be discussed from any authentic source or sound perspective. An example would be the obligatory understanding of affirming that the Prophet Muhammad was sent to them, as this is something every person will be asked about in their grave. This is not true of the earlier prophets who were not sent to all humanity.

09. Mention any two matters that the Muslims have agreed upon by consensus.

    Answers will vary per student, and should be discussed from any authentic source or sound perspective. An example would be the most excellent of the people after the prophets is Abu Bakr. A second matter would be the consensus regarding the preservation of the Qur'aan from corruption.

DAY 03: THERE IS A SINGLE STRAIGHT PATH SURROUNDED BY OTHER FALSE PATHS

TEST YOUR UNDERSTANDING:

TRUE & FALSE QUESTIONS
[Circle the correct letter for each individual sentence from today's content.]

01. It is permissible to follow any path or religion as long as your intention is to please Allaah. [T / **F**]

    This is incorrect. Rather Allaah has stated clearly that only one way and one religion is acceptable to Him. As the Sheikh mentioned the verse ❴***And verily, this is my Straight Path, so follow it, and follow not other paths, for they will separate you away from His Path.***❵ –(Surah Al-An'am:153).}

02. Just as there are many ways of misguidance, there are many paths upon the truth and guidance. [T / **F**]

    This is incorrect. As the Sheikh mentioned within the hadeeth where the Messenger of Allaah, may Allaah's praise and salutations be upon him, draw one single line and said, { ***"This is the path of Allaah...***} Then he drew other multiple lines to the left of that and to the right of it, as misguided paths.

03. Each path of misguidance has a Shaytaan inviting to it and making it appealing to people. [**T** / F]

    This is correct. As the Sheikh mentioned from the authentic hadeeth narration that the Messenger of Allaah, may Allaah's praise and salutations be upon him, drew other lines to the left of that and to the right of it and said, {...***These are other paths. Upon each one of them there is a Shaytaan inviting and calling to it.***}

ANSWER KEY

FILL IN THE BLANK QUESTIONS

[Enter the correct individual words to complete the sentences from today's content.]

04. There is a single **straight** path and many paths of **misguidance**.
05. Every path of misguidance has a **Shaytaan** upon it **inviting** people to it.
06. Both **innovations** and **sins** are part of the paths of misguidance.

INTERACTIVE QUESTIONS & EXERCISES

COMPREHENSIVE UNDERSTANDING QUESTIONS

[In a study group or circle of learning with other students, these questions can be answered fully or partially by one student from the lesson, with another student completing the answer to the same question, by giving a comparable but different which is also correct.]

07. What command and what prohibition is found within the mentioned verse in Surah Al-An'am? Give a practical everyday example of how someone may properly follow the command, and properly adhere to the prohibition mentioned.

    Within that verse (153) there is both a command to follow the straight path of Islaam, and a prohibition against following other paths. Practical answers will vary per student, and should be discussed from any authentic source or sound perspective. An example would be a Muslim establishing his daily prayer according to the Sunnah, and turning away from any newly invented way of performing this essential act of worship that is presented to him.

08. Name two paths of misguidance and briefly describe why some people might believe that they are good to follow.

    Answers will vary per student, and should be discussed from any authentic source or sound perspective. An example would be a Sufee path which makes permissible matters forbidden, and a second example would be a Muslim claiming that the rules of marriage and divorce found in the Sunnah are no longer needed, wrongly saying we live in "modern" times.

09. What are two possible important means of helping a Muslim understand what the straight path is, and proceed steadfastly upon it.

    Answers will vary per student, and should be discussed from any authentic source or sound perspective. Two possible examples are consistently studying with trustworthy students or scholars, and a second example would be striving to live among the people who do their best to adhere to the Sunnah.

Day 04: Every Ummah Divided But Those Upon The Truth Remain

TEST YOUR UNDERSTANDING:

TRUE & FALSE QUESTIONS
[Circle the correct letter for each individual sentence from today's content.]

01. There are many sects found within the history of the Muslim Ummah and they are all considered Muslims. [T / **F**]

    This is incorrect some of the sects were upon major disbelief. As the Sheikh mentioned "...*Whereas the other seventy-two sects are from the sects that have innovated within Islaam as Muslims, and sects that have deviated from guidance. But they are not considered disbelievers according to what is correct. It is for this reason that the scholars do not consider the sect of the Jahmeeyah from among the seventy-two misguided sects. They say: this sect are considered disbelievers due to their major disbelief.*"

02. The scholars have identified and distinguished the various sects among the Muslims. [**T** / F]

    This is correct, this is an aspect of them safeguarding Islaam. As the Sheikh mentioned "...*Similarly, they make the same assessment of the sect of the extreme Qadareeyah who deny aspects of Allaah's knowledge, as well as the sect of the Raafidhah. They state regarding them, they are not to be considered from the seventy-two misguided sects.*"

03. The saved sect is everyone who says they are Muslim, and claims their religion is Islaam. [T / **F**]

    This is incorrect. As the Sheikh mentioned describing what distinguishes the saved sect"... *They are those Muslims who adhere to the Sunnah and remain with the Jamaa'ah of Muslims united upon the truth, from the noble Companions, the successors to the Companions, and the leading scholars who followed them in their way in steadfastness upon the religion of Allaah and his Sharee'ah. Those who followed them in acting according to the guidance of the Book of Allaah and His Messenger, may the praise and salutations of Allaah be upon him, adhered to the believers' way, they are those who are saved.*"

FILL IN THE BLANK QUESTIONS

[Enter the correct individual words to complete the sentences from today's content.]

04. The seventy-two astray sects within the Ummah all have some form of **innovation**.

05. Due to major disbelief the extremely deviant sects such as the **Jahmeeyah**, are considered **outside** of the boundaries of Islaam.

06. The saved sect remains upon what the **Prophet** and the **Companions** were upon originally.

INTERACTIVE QUESTIONS & EXERCISES

COMPREHENSIVE UNDERSTANDING QUESTIONS

[In a study group or circle of learning with other students, these questions can be answered fully or partially by one student from the lesson, with another student completing the answer to the same question, by giving a comparable but different which is also correct.]

07. Name three sects or groups who are misguided and upon innovation but remain within the Muslim Ummah.

    Answers will vary per student, and should be discussed from any authentic source or sound perspective. Example would be the Zaydeeyah, some of the general Shee'ah, as well as the Sufees from Naqshabadee Sufee way.

08. Name two sects or groups whose extreme misguidance takes them outside the boundaries of the Muslim Ummah.

    Answers will vary per student, and should be discussed from any authentic source or sound perspective. An example would be the Jahmeeyah and the Raafidhah, who actually deny the full preservation of the Qur'aan.

09. What are two essential characteristics that distinguish Muslims from the saved sect as compared to the astray sects?

    Answers will vary per student, and should be discussed from any authentic source or sound perspective. Two of their essential characteristics are adhering firmly to the authentic Sunnah, and remaining in the Jamaa'ah by understanding and practicing the Qur'aan and Sunnah the way the Prophet's Companions did.

DAY 05: ALLAAH IS WITH THOSE WHO REMAINED UPON REVEALED GUIDANCE

TEST YOUR UNDERSTANDING:

TRUE & FALSE QUESTIONS
[Circle the correct letter for each individual sentence from today's content.]

01. Allaah supports and is pleased with anyone who calls themselves Muslim. [T / **F**]

   This is incorrect, rather the companions understood that Allaah was pleased only with those Muslims who adhered to the Jamaa'ah and did not deviate. As the Sheikh mentioned the statement of Mua'adh *"The Hand of Allaah is over the Jamaa'ah, the united body of Muslims upon the truth, and whoever deviates..."*

02. The foundation of the saved sect are the Companions of the Messenger of Allaah. [**T** / F]

   This is correct. As the Sheikh mentioned *"... meaning that the hand of Allaah is with the Jamaa'ah or the united body of Muslims upon the Sunnah. They are the Jamaa'ah, and they are the Companions of the Messenger of Allaah, and the Successors to the Companions...."*

03. People's deviations away from guidance will not lead them to the Hellfire if they are sincere. [T / **F**]

   This is incorrect. As the Sheikh mentioned *"...Whereas those that deviated and separated from that, their deviation will lead them to the Hellfire and Allaah has no concern for their deviations from the truth. This is a tremendous warning from deviations and innovating in the religion, the deviations of innovation as well as doubts and misconceptions, all of them are considered deviations."*

FILL IN THE BLANK QUESTIONS

[Enter the correct individual words to complete the sentences from today's content.]

04. The truth is what is found the Book of **Allaah** and in adherence to the **Sunnah**.

05. It is an **obligation** to adhere to the **path** of the Companions of the Messenger of Allaah.

06. **Innovations** as well as doubts and **misconceptions** are all considered deviations away from the Sunnah.

INTERACTIVE QUESTIONS & EXERCISES

COMPREHENSIVE UNDERSTANDING QUESTIONS

[In a study group or circle of learning with other students, these questions can be answered fully or partially by one student from the lesson, with another student completing the answer to the same question, by giving a comparable but different which is also correct.]

07. Give an example of one sect or group who has separated from the Jamaa'ah and one belief they have innovated.

    Answers will vary per student, and should be discussed from any authentic source or sound perspective. An example would be the Khawaarij, and their innovated belief that the one who committed a major sin would remain in Hellfire permanently.

08. Give an separate example of another sect or group who has separated from the Jamaa'ah and one practice they have innovated.

    Answers will vary per student, and should be discussed from any authentic source or sound perspective. An example would be the Shee'ah, and their innovated belief that only the family of 'Alee should be the Muslim rulers.

09. Is it possible to be part of the Jamaa'ah united upon the truth, but not follow the way of the Companions? Explain your answer.

    No this is not possible because the Messenger of Allaah placed his Companions along with himself in describing the way of the saved sect, which is described in other narrations as the Jamaa'ah.

Day 06: Allaah Has Ordered Us To Stand United Upon The Truth & Not Divide

---

TEST YOUR UNDERSTANDING:

TRUE & FALSE QUESTIONS
[Circle the correct letter for each individual sentence from today's content.]

01. It is not an obligation to hold fast onto the rope of Allaah. [T / **F**]

    This is incorrect, rather it is an obligation upon every Muslim. As the Sheikh mentioned is found in the verse, ❧ ***And hold fast, all of you together, to the Rope of Allaah, and be not divided among yourselves*** ❧–(Surah Aal-Imraan:103)

02. The issue of sticking close to the Jamaa'ah, involves both a command and the prohibition. [**T** / F]

    This is correct, as is found in the verse of the Qur'aan which the Sheikh mentioned "❧***And hold fast, all of you together, to the Rope of Allaah (i.e. this Qur'aan), and be not divided among yourselves,***❧…"

03. We can hold fast to the Rope of Allaah, by simply following only the guidance of the Qur'aan. [T / **F**]

    This is incorrect, because His Rope means Allaah's religion. As the Sheikh mentioned this includes both the Qur'aan and the Sunnah "… *Allaah has said,* ❧*And hold fast, all of you together, to the Rope of Allaah…*❧ *meaning that the Muslims should act according to the Book of Allaah and the Sunnah of Allaah's Messenger, may Allaah's praise and salutations be upon him, all of them. They must gather together and unite upon that without differing and separating, and not divide by abandoning the way of acting upon the Book of Allaah and the Sunnah of His Messenger.*"

ANSWER KEY

FILL IN THE BLANK QUESTIONS

[Enter the correct individual words to complete the sentences from today's content.]

04. The revealed source texts **prohibit** separating into different groups and **sects**.

05. Allaah's religion is what He sent down within His **Book**, and upon the tongue of His **Messenger**.

06. **Differing** and **separating** can result from failing to act upon revealed guidance.

INTERACTIVE QUESTIONS & EXERCISES

COMPREHENSIVE UNDERSTANDING QUESTIONS

[In a study group or circle of learning with other students, these questions can be answered fully or partially by one student from the lesson, with another student completing the answer to the same question, by giving a comparable but different which is also correct.]

07. What are two of the characteristics of the Jamaa'ah of the Muslims upon the truth in any age?

    Answers will vary per student, and should be discussed from any authentic source or sound perspective. An example would be that the primary sources and references they refer to are the Qur'aan and the Sunnah. A second characteristic would be their staying far away from splitting from the Jamaa'ah into sects and groups.

08. Give a practical example of how holding on to the Rope of Allaah establishes unity among Muslims?

    Answers will vary per student, and should be discussed from any authentic source or sound perspective. A practical example would be the Muslims in a community agreeing upon of teaching establishing the prayer according to the Sunnah. This is something which helps bring about true unity.

09. What is something that leads to the hearts of the Muslims being united? What is a specific benefit of this in regard to the position of the Muslim Ummah in the world?

    One of the most important means towards establishing unity is uniting upon the correct authentic beliefs of Islaam. One benefit is then they are like a single hand defending against their enemies attacks.

DAY 07: EVERY NAME THAT OPPOSES THE GUIDANCE OF THE SUNNAH IS REJECTED

TEST YOUR UNDERSTANDING:

TRUE & FALSE QUESTIONS
[Circle the correct letter for each individual sentence from today's content.]

01. Those known as Shee'ah have several different levels of misguidance. [T / F]

    This is correct. As the Sheikh mentioned "... *Those under this general term are of different levels. The scholars who have knowledge of the sects through the history of the Ummah has stated that they are over twenty-four different levels who are referred to as Shee'ah.*"

02. A Muslim should declare himself free from every misguided sect. [T / F]

    This is correct. As the Sheikh mentioned "... *That is from the guidance of the Sunnah, and from faith or emaan and what perfects and completes it, that a Muslim frees and separates himself from these newly invented names which oppose the guidance of the Sunnah, which are outside the guidance what the Ummah has come to consensus upon.*"

03. Some extreme Shee'ah believe that Allaah embodied Himself in the form of 'Alee. [T / F]

    This is correct. As the Sheikh mentioned "... *The scholars who have knowledge of the sects through the history of the Ummah has stated that they are over twenty-four different levels who are referred to as Shee'ah. The most severe of them and the most misguided of them are the Nusayrees, those who say that: Allaah embodied Himself in the form of 'Alee.*"

ANSWER KEY

FILL IN THE BLANK QUESTIONS

[Enter the correct individual words to complete the sentences from today's content.]

04. Zayd Ibn 'Alee Ibn Husain spoke well of and **supplicated** for Allaah to have mercy upon Abu **Bakr** and **'Umar**.

05. Some Shee'ah believe that the angel Jibreel made a mistake bringing the revelation to the **Prophet Muhammad**, as they falsely claim that Jibreel was sent to bring revelation to **'Alee**.

06. A Muslim should oppose the incorrect **beliefs** and separate from the **people** upon any new name which opposes the guidance of the **Sunnah**.

INTERACTIVE QUESTIONS & EXERCISES

COMPREHENSIVE UNDERSTANDING QUESTIONS

[In a study group or circle of learning with other students, these questions can be answered fully or partially by one student from the lesson, with another student completing the answer to the same question, by giving a comparable but different which is also correct.]

07. Name two countries where many people adhere to the misguided sect of the Shee'ah.

    Two countries in which many people are Shee'ah are Iran and Iraq.

08. Name someone who opposed the false beliefs of the Raafidhah? Also discuss one of their false beliefs held by some of them connected to the Book of Allaah, the Qur'aan.

    One person from the family of 'Alee rejected their beliefs was Zayd Ibn 'Alee Ibn Husain. One of the grave errors of the Raafidhah is that they claim that the Qur'aan has been corrupted and altered, and only a portion of the original revelation remains.

09. Who initially opposed the false beliefs of the sect of the Khawaarij? Also mention one of their well known false beliefs.

    The Companions of the Messenger of Allaah, opposed the Khawaarij and refuted their falsehood. One of their false beliefs was that they understood the meaning of the verses of the Qur'aan better than the Companions of the Messenger of Allaah. Answers will vary per student, and should be discussed from any authentic source or sound perspective.

DAY 08: THE STRANGENESS OF ISLAAM IS NOT SOMETHING NEW

TEST YOUR UNDERSTANDING:

TRUE & FALSE QUESTIONS
[Circle the correct letter for each individual sentence from today's content.]

01. The strangeness of Islaam is something negative. [T / **F**]

    This is incorrect as it is description of those upon the truth. As the Sheikh mentioned "... *Therefore Islaam began is something strange amongst the people, and it was only embraced by a few. Then afterwards Islaam began to spread and many entered into it. Then the Prophet, may Allaah's praise and salutations be upon him, and emigrated to Medinah. Then when Allaah blessed the Prophet, may Allaah's praise and salutations be upon him, with the opening and conquest of Mecca, after this people entered into the religion of Allaah in large numbers.*"

02. Islaam will never be strange again since it is all over the world. [T / **F**]

    This is incorrect. As the Sheikh mentioned "... *Yet in the end of time, Islaam will return to being something strange just as it began, where people will have turned away the religion of Allaah, and there will only remain a few individuals truly practicing it. {Islaam began as something strange...} strange means: that no one or very few are upon that matter or affair. So from this comes strangers.*"

03. The Prophet praised the strangers who held firmly to revealed guidance. [**T** / F]

    This is correct. As the Sheikh mentioned "...*Meaning callers for the people to rectify themselves. Meaning that the people strive to rectify themselves, and then struggled to rectify others. As the person who calls others to rectification it is unquestionably required that he be a righteous person within himself, he is not called or considered someone who rectifies except after he is first rectified himself...*

    ...They are those who call to Allaah, and enjoin what is good, and forbid wrongdoing, and call people to the Sunnah, and warn people away from innovation in the religion."

ANSWER KEY

FILL IN THE BLANK QUESTIONS

[Enter the correct individual words to complete the sentences from today's content.]

04. Islaam **began** as something strange in the city of **Mecca**.
05. Islaam spread significantly in the **ninth** year when the Arab tribes and **delegations** came to **Medina**.
06. **Honor** and the rewards of **Jannah** are promised to the ones who are strangers upon **Islaam**.

INTERACTIVE QUESTIONS & EXERCISES

COMPREHENSIVE UNDERSTANDING QUESTIONS

[In a study group or circle of learning with other students, these questions can be answered fully or partially by one student from the lesson, with another student completing the answer to the same question, by giving a comparable but different which is also correct.]

07. Describe three ways in which Islaam is considered strange in our time and age.
    Answers will vary per student, and should be discussed from any authentic source or sound perspective. An example would be that many people have as their focus gaining material wealth and pleasures, whereas the focus of the life of a striving Muslim is worshiping Allaah properly, while not neglecting the permissible blessing in this life.

08. Explain two characteristics of the strangers by giving a possible practical example for each of those characteristics.
    Answers will vary per student, and should be discussed from any authentic source or sound perspective. An example would be a Muslim women striving to be modest in behavior and dress when others want to be outrageous in both.

09. Can Islaam only be strange among non-Muslims or also possibly amongst the Muslims? Briefly explain your answer giving examples if necessary.
    In fact the explanation of the scholars is general and includes strangeness among Muslims. This is especially true in an age in which knowledge of the Sunnah is not widespread among Muslims, and many innovations are present.

DAY 09: THAT ONE INDIVIDUAL WHOSE RELIGION YOU SHOULD STAND UPON

TEST YOUR UNDERSTANDING:

TRUE & FALSE QUESTIONS
[Circle the correct letter for each individual sentence from today's content.]

01. The Companions of the Messenger of Allaah differed in some matters. [**T** / F]

    This is correct. As the Sheikh mentioned "… *This was at the time when there occurred a difference between the Companions of the Messenger of Allaah, between 'Alee and Mu'aweeyah, may Allaah be please with both of them and with those who were with them. When the difference occurred between them the majority of the Companions of the Messenger of Allaah stood with 'Alee, may Allaah be please with him, and held the view that he was the legitimate rightly guided Khalifah.*"

02. It is wrong to blindly follow a scholar in every single thing they say. [**T** / F]

    This is correct. As the Sheikh mentioned "…*As for anyone other than the Messenger of Allaah, may Allaah's praise and salutations be upon him, in some of his statements or positions he is correct and in others he may be mistaken. Therefore I stand upon the way of the Messenger.' This is the way truth, and this is the way of light, that an individual adhere to the Sunnah, that they adhere to the Sunnah and do not blindly follow different individuals.*"

03. We can understand what is the truth simply by looking at someone who practices it. [T / **F**]

    This is incorrect. As the Sheikh mentioned "…*Moreover individuals or men are known by the truth, and the truth is not known by individuals, the state of man is known by understanding the truth. The one whose position conforms with the truth we will know that he is correct in his position by the truth. But as for the truth it is not understood by simply looking at individuals who claim to be upon it.*"

FILL IN THE BLANK QUESTIONS
[Enter the correct individual words to complete the sentences from today's content.]

04. In the dispute about the **khalifah** the majority of the Companions of the Messenger of Allaah stood with **'Alee**.

05. The scholars receive one **reward** for their **effort** to reach the correct conclusion, and a second **reward** due to actually being **correct**.

06. We always have an **obligation** to hold firmly to the **Qur'aan** and the **Sunnah**.

INTERACTIVE QUESTIONS & EXERCISES

COMPREHENSIVE UNDERSTANDING QUESTIONS
[In a study group or circle of learning with other students, these questions can be answered fully or partially by one student from the lesson, with another student completing the answer to the same question, by giving a comparable but different which is also correct.]

07. Give an example of a matter of fiqh or implementation of the source texts in which you know some of our modern-day scholars differ with one another?

    Answers will vary per student, and should be discussed from any authentic source or sound perspective. A well known example would be the ruling regarding veiling or covering the face as part of Hijaab. The differing scholars each have evidence to support their rulings concerning it.

08. Give an example of a misunderstanding that some modern Muslims have regarding giving the oath of allegiance.

    Answers will vary per student, and should be discussed from any authentic source or sound perspective. An example would be that it should be given to the leader of an Islamic movement or organization.

09. Try to explain one reason that the position of Ibn Abbaas in supporting 'Alee, was actually following the Messenger of Allaah, and not biased partisanship towards 'Alee

    One example reason would be that Ibn 'Abbaas was following the command to maintain unity among the Muslims. So he was supporting the legitimate khalifah whom the people of knowledge supported and had given the oath of allegiance to, not simply supporting 'Alee because any bias or partisanship. Answers will vary per student, and should be discussed from any authentic source or sound perspective.

DAY 10: THE SUNNAH IS REVEALED KNOWLEDGE FROM ALLAAH

TEST YOUR UNDERSTANDING:

TRUE & FALSE QUESTIONS
[Circle the correct letter for each individual sentence from today's content.]

01. The angel Jibreel brought two types of revelation to the Messenger of Allaah. [**T** / F]

    This is correct. As the Sheikh mentioned is supported in authentic narration *{Indeed I've been given the Qur'aan and that which is like it.}*

02. Some hadeeth narrations contain statements from Allaah. [**T** / F]

    This is correct. As the Sheikh mentioned "...*Therefore the Sunnah is considered revelation, revealed knowledge from Allaah. However the Sunnah as a whole has two distinct categories. In one category both the specific wording and the meaning of those words are revelation from Allaah, this is the "al-hadeeth al-qudsee".*"

03. The Qur'aan is the only knowledge the Prophet of Allaah possessed. [T / **F**]

    This is incorrect. As the Sheikh mentioned that the Qur'aan indicates that whatever he said regarding Islaam he spoke from revelation "...Allaah says, *"Nor does he speak of his own desire. It is only an Inspiration that is inspired. He has been taught this Qur'aan by one mighty in power Jibreel. Dhu Mirrah (free from any defect in body and mind), then he (Jibreel) rose and became stable.*"–(Surah An-Najm: 3-6)"

FILL IN THE BLANK QUESTIONS

[Enter the correct individual words to complete the sentences from today's content.]

04. <u>Jibreel</u> used to teach the prophet the <u>Sunnah</u> just as he used to teach him the Qur'aan.

05. The Prophet himself, said to us, {Indeed I've been <u>given</u> the <u>Qur'aan</u> and that which is <u>like</u> it.}

06. Qur'aan itself is from the <u>speech</u> of Allaah in both <u>wording</u> and <u>meaning</u>.

INTERACTIVE QUESTIONS & EXERCISES

COMPREHENSIVE UNDERSTANDING QUESTIONS

[In a study group or circle of learning with other students, these questions can be answered fully or partially by one student from the lesson, with another student completing the answer to the same question, by giving a comparable but different which is also correct.]

07. Is it required that we accept all the knowledge which the Messenger of Allaah came with, or just the Qur'aan?

    Yes it is required, this is shown by the evidence, as well as the narration indicating that Jibreel, who is an angel who only obeys Allaah's commands, was sent down to teach the Sunnah in addition to the Qur'aan. Answers will vary per student, and should be discussed from any authentic source or sound perspective.

08. Describe one of the authentic ways the text of the Qur'aan is used in a form of worship.

    Answers will vary per student, and should be discussed from any authentic source or sound perspective. An example would be that when the Qur'aan is recited it is a form of worship for which a Muslim receives a tremendous reward for every letter that they recite, according to authentic narrations.

09. What verse indicates to us that all religious statements of the Prophet are a form of revelation? How does it clarify the false claim that he made up parts of Islaam?

    The verse in Surah An-Najm: ❴*Nor does he speak of his own desire. It is only an Inspiration that is inspired....*❵ This is a refutation of that false claim, because it refers generally to the Prophet's statements as being that which was sent down as revelation through the angel Jibreel. Along with this are many other verses ordering us to take whatever the Prophet gives us.

DAY 11: HOLD FIRMLY TO THE SUNNAH AS THE ROPE OF ALLAAH

TEST YOUR UNDERSTANDING:

TRUE & FALSE QUESTIONS
[Circle the correct letter for each individual sentence from today's content.]

01. Many commands of the Qur'aan are general without specifics and details. **[T / F]**

    This is correct. As the Sheikh mentioned "… *The Qur'aan comes with the general command to perform the ritual prayer. However, there is not found within the Qur'aan the fact that salaat adh-dhuhr is prayed in four raka'at, salaat al"asr is prayed with four raka'at, salaat al-maghrib is prayed with three raka'at, salaat al-'ishaa' is prayed with four raka'at, and that salaat al-fajr is prayed with two raka'at. All of this is only found in the Sunnah.*"

02. The Sunnah clarifies the commands of the Qur'aan, but does not bring any new commands. **[T / F]**

    This is incorrect. As the Sheikh mentioned "…*Because the Sunnah explains the Qur'aan and clarifies it, specifies its general meanings, and specifies that which is general, as well as bringing forth additional rulings not found within the texts of the Qur'aan*"

03. A person can take what he wants from the Sunnah but must accept the entire Qur'aan. **[T / F]**

    This is incorrect. As the Sheikh mentioned "…*All of these specific details are only found in the Sunnah. So the one who abandons, does not act upon the Sunnah, and rejects it, or generally does not act according to it, has in fact disbelieved in Islaam.*"

ANSWER KEY

FILL IN THE BLANK QUESTIONS

[Enter the correct individual words to complete the sentences from today's content.]

04. The person who rejects and turns away from the Sunnah **cuts** off his **connection** to Allaah.

05. Not every matter of **Islaam** is detailed in the **Qur'aan**.

06. The Messenger of Allaah was given the **Qur'aan** and that which is like it, meaning the **Sunnah**.

INTERACTIVE QUESTIONS & EXERCISES

COMPREHENSIVE UNDERSTANDING QUESTIONS

[In a study group or circle of learning with other students, these questions can be answered fully or partially by one student from the lesson, with another student completing the answer to the same question, by giving a comparable but different which is also correct.]

07. Give another example, other than those mentioned, of a command in Islaam in which the details are found in the Sunnah, not all in the Qur'aan.

    Answers will vary per student, and should be discussed from any authentic source or sound perspective. An example would be the detailed rulings and guidelines for the obligatory fast of the month of Ramadhaan.

08. Is it possible to follow the command in the Qur'aan to obey the Messenger while rejecting the Sunnah? Give an example to explain your answer.

    This would not be possible, as in obeying the Messenger in the details of Islaam, a Muslim is following and accepting the Sunnah. An excellent example is the ritual prayer, the salaah, in which we pray exactly as the Messenger of Allaah, prayed and taught the companions to pray. In praying as he prayed, you are following his Sunnah in many specific matters where there are no details specifying them in the Qur'aan.

09. Give authentic examples of one command, and one prohibition coming from the Messenger of Allaah, which are not found in the Qur'aan.

    Answers will vary per student, and should be discussed from any authentic source or sound perspective. An example also related to the ritual prayer, is the commands of how to pray the witr salaah or to stand at night to pray. Likewise an example of prohibition is that against lengthening the prayer in jamaa'ah in the masjid, due to many different people praying together, including the weak and so forth.

DAY 12: SUCCESS IS TO THE DEGREE YOU ADHERE TO THE SUNNAH

TEST YOUR UNDERSTANDING:

TRUE & FALSE QUESTIONS
[Circle the correct letter for each individual sentence from today's content.]

01. Knowledge in Islaam is generally carried by the scholars. [**T** / F]

This is correct. As the Sheikh mentioned due to what is indicated within the in the authentic hadeeth narration: *{**Verily, Allaah does not take away knowledge by snatching it from the people, but He takes it away by taking away the lives of the religious scholars till none of the scholars stays alive....**}*

02. Those who are ignorant only cause harm to themselves and not others. [T / **F**]

This is incorrect. As the Sheikh mentioned *"...In this way knowledge is taken away and no one remains except for the ignorant ones. They then become the leaders of the people and they instruct them in rulings without sound knowledge, so they go astray and they will lead others astray."*

03. Beneficial knowledge is something specific to the affairs of our religion. [T / **F**]

This is incorrect. As the Sheikh mentioned *"... While giving life to knowledge makes both one's religion and worldly life steadfast and firm. Meaning the presence of knowledge and its manifestation, the outward appearance of knowledge, and the spreading of knowledge among the people, this is something which brings steadfastness to the religion and success in one's worldly life."*

FILL IN THE BLANK QUESTIONS

[Enter the correct individual words to complete the sentences from today's content.]

04. The one who adheres firmly to the Sunnah is **saved** in this world from entering into **trials** and **innovations**, and in the life to come saved from entering **Hellfire**.

05. Giving life to knowledge makes both one's **religious** and **worldly** life steadfast and firm.

06. The noble guiding scholars **warn** against **innovation** in the religion and the people of **innovation**.

INTERACTIVE QUESTIONS & EXERCISES

COMPREHENSIVE UNDERSTANDING QUESTIONS

[In a study group or circle of learning with other students, these questions can be answered fully or partially by one student from the lesson, with another student completing the answer to the same question, by giving a comparable but different which is also correct.]

07. Give examples of two guiding scholars who were upon the Sunnah who died in this age or modern period.

    Answers will vary per student, and should be discussed from any authentic source or sound perspective. Two examples would be Sheikh Ibn Baaz, and Sheikh al-'Utheimeen, may Allaah have mercy upon them both.

08. Give examples of two ignorant modern individuals who people wrongly consider scholars, and who misguide others.

    Answers will vary per student, and should be discussed from any authentic source or sound perspective. An example would be 'Amr Khaled and Tariq as-Swaydaan, who are both popular speakers not grounded in knowledge.

09. Give two examples of incorrect rulings that you generally heard about coming from ignorant individuals which only increase the Muslims in misguidance and harm.

    Answers will vary per student, and should be discussed from any authentic source or sound perspective. An example would be those who legitimize the visiting of graves to seek blessings and those who permit supplicating to the righteous dead Muslims to intercede for needs and problems.

DAY 13: THE INCREDIBLE REWARD FOR FIRMLY HOLDING TO THE SUNNAH

TEST YOUR UNDERSTANDING:

TRUE & FALSE QUESTIONS
[Circle the correct letter for each individual sentence from today's content.]

01. There is a greater reward for adhering to the truth during times of difficulty. [**T** / F]

This is correct. As the Sheikh mentioned is found in the authentic narration *{**The one who holds firmly to my Sunnah when corruption has spread among my Ummah has a reward of fifty**.}*

02. The one who gains the reward of fifty of the Companions has excelled them in merit. [T / **F**]

This is incorrect. As the Sheikh mentioned *"… Yet this hadeeth narration does not indicate that the one who holds firmly to the Sunnah is better than the companions of the Prophet! Rather what is intended is that they will receive the reward of fifty individuals, due to this aspect, and in this respect, and because of this matter."*

03. None of the prophets and messengers have distinct merits. [T / **F**]

This is incorrect. As the Sheikh mentioned *"… While Ibraheem has its own unique specific merit, and that is that he will be the first one clothed on the Day of Resurrection.*

Similarly from the specific merits is that which is held by Musaa upon him be Allaah's praise and salutations."

ANSWER KEY

FILL IN THE BLANK QUESTIONS
[Enter the correct individual words to complete the sentences from today's content.]

04. The **Companions** of the Messenger of Allaah have several distinctive **merits**.

05. Those who hold firmly to the **Sunnah** in the **later** ages will not find those to **assist** them.

06. The Muslim who holds firmly to the **Sunnah** is far away from **innovations**.

INTERACTIVE QUESTIONS & EXERCISES

COMPREHENSIVE UNDERSTANDING QUESTIONS
[In a study group or circle of learning with other students, these questions can be answered fully or partially by one student from the lesson, with another student completing the answer to the same question, by giving a comparable but different which is also correct.]

07. Discuss two mentioned distinctive merits of the Companions, and explain why no one shares these merits with them.

    Answers will vary per student, and should be discussed from any authentic source or sound perspective. An example would be firstly, they left everything and emigrated from Mecca to Medina, they stood firm and defended Islaam during the battle of Badr, when the disbelievers intended to extinguish the light of Islaam completely. These merits are specific to that time and place.

08. Give two examples of matters which are difficult to do today, which may be part of adhering firmly to the Sunnah.

    Answers will vary per student, and should be discussed from any authentic source or sound perspective. An example would be following the guidance regarding restricting free mixing in the workplace for Muslims living in Western countries. An additional example would be those punishments for transgressions that harm Muslim society, which some people do not implement in Muslim lands, despite the benefit they bring society.

09. Give two possible examples of beneficial practices or deeds that might be considered from those in which it is hard to find other Muslims to assist them in doing.

    Answers will vary per student, and should be discussed from any authentic source or sound perspective. An example would be and effort to build those Muslims schools to educate Muslim children upon the Sunnah. Another example might be regular consistent efforts to call non-Muslims to the worship of Allaah alone, and spread understanding of Islaam.

DAY 14: FOLLOW THE PROPHET'S SUNNAH & THAT OF HIS GUIDED SUCCESSORS

TEST YOUR UNDERSTANDING:

TRUE & FALSE QUESTIONS
[Circle the correct letter for each individual sentence from today's content.]

01. The Hajj pilgrimage must only be performed completely separately from 'Umrah. [T / **F**]

   This is incorrect. As the Sheikh mentioned "...*Whereas the Prophet, may Allaah's praise and salutations be upon him, had commanded the people to combine them together or tamattu'. There are numerous hadeeth narrations from the Prophet, may Allaah's praise and salutations be upon him, where he commanded the Companions to do so during his final pilgrimage....*"

02. It is only important that we adhere to the Qur'aan and Sunnah the Prophet and nothing else. [T / **F**]

   This is incorrect. As the Sheikh mentioned there is the authentic narration where The Messenger of Allaah, may Allaah's praise and salutations be upon him, says *{...Adhere firmly to my Sunnah and the Sunnah of my rightly guided Successors who come after me. Hold firmly to this with your molar teeth...}*

03. A statement from one of the rightly guided khalifahs can be followed instead of an authentic affirmed Sunnah. [T / **F**]

   This is incorrect. As the Sheikh mentioned "...*Such that if someone opposes the Sunnah with statements of Abu Bakr and 'Umar, it should be feared for them that stones might fall from the heavens upon them. As what else should we expect for someone who opposes the Sunnah, with the statement of this person or that person?!?*"

ANSWER KEY

FILL IN THE BLANK QUESTIONS

[Enter the correct individual words to complete the sentences from today's content.]

04. Before the coming of Islaam, tamattu' was something **forbidden** within the months of **Hajj**.

05. The sunnah of the rightly guided **khalifahs** is taken and **adopted** whenever there is no guidance within the **Prophet's** **Sunnah** about a specific issue or matter.

06. The additional **adhaan** on the day of **Juma'ah**, when necessary, is considered from the **sunnah** of a rightly guided khalifah.

INTERACTIVE QUESTIONS & EXERCISES

COMPREHENSIVE UNDERSTANDING QUESTIONS

[In a study group or circle of learning with other students, these questions can be answered fully or partially by one student from the lesson, with another student completing the answer to the same question, by giving a comparable but different which is also correct.]

07. Give an example of a practice of the Sunnah that might be considered strange to some of the Muslims today.

    Answers will vary per student, and should be discussed from any authentic source or sound perspective. An example would be the command in the Sunnah for the Muslim men to let their beards grow but trim the mustache.

08. Is it possible that a statement of one of the rightly guided khalifahs might be incorrect? Explain your answer.

    Yes it is possible, as is shown regarding the issue of the different types of Hajj. The belief of the people the Sunnah is that no one is infallible other than the Messenger of Allaah, who spoke from revelation.

09. Explain why Ibn 'Abbaas was upset with those Muslims who were following the position of some of the rightly guided khalifahs?

    Ibn 'Abbaas was upset with those Muslims who were following that position because doing so had caused them to turn away from an authentic affirmed Sunnah and command of their Prophet, who is the one they had been commanded to follow in every matter of Islaam.

DAY 15: DO NOT SPEAK AGAINST THE BEST OF GENERATIONS

TEST YOUR UNDERSTANDING:

TRUE & FALSE QUESTIONS
[Circle the correct letter for each individual sentence from today's content.]

01. The Companions of the Messenger of Allaah all have the same rank. [T / **F**]

   This is incorrect. As the Sheikh mentioned about their levels "...*Then coming after them in merit are those Companions who embraced Islaam after the Treaty of al-Hudaybeeyah but before the conquest of Mecca. Then coming after them in merit are those who embraced Islaam on the day that Mecca was conquered. This is three distinct levels.*"

02. Some of the events during the life of the Prophet led to many people embracing Islaam. [**T** / F]

   This is correct. As the Sheikh mentioned "...*A peace treaty had been established between the Prophet, may Allaah's praise and salutations be upon him, and those who associated others with Allaah from the leaders of Mecca, and their allies. The treaty caused the hostilities and military struggles between them to come to an end, it brought security to the people. Such that what happened was various people from those who associated others with Allaah, came and interacted with the Muslims, they listen to the message of the Qur'aan, and significant numbers of them embraced Islaam.*"

03. The treaty of al-Hudaybeeyah did not affect the spread of Islaam. [T / **F**]

   This is incorrect. As the Sheikh mentioned "...*So Allaah, the Most High named the treaty of al-Hudaybeeyah a "manifest victory", because all of the victories that came after it.*"

ANSWER KEY

FILL IN THE BLANK QUESTIONS

[Enter the correct individual words to complete the sentences from today's content.]

04. The first Muslims to embrace Islaam were the **Muhaajiroon**, who migrated from **Mecca** to **Medinah**.

05. The treaty of al-Hudaybeeyah is called an **opening** and **victory** for Islaam, and the Muslims.

06. The people of Mecca, or their allies, **broke** the treaty of al-Hudaybeeyah after **two** years.

INTERACTIVE QUESTIONS & EXERCISES

COMPREHENSIVE UNDERSTANDING QUESTIONS

[In a study group or circle of learning with other students, these questions can be answered fully or partially by one student from the lesson, with another student completing the answer to the same question, by giving a comparable but different which is also correct.]

07. Give examples of two difficulties which the Muhaajiroon faced that those who embraced Islaam later did not encounter.
    Answers will vary per student, and should be discussed from any authentic source or sound perspective. An example would be that many of them were forced to flee to Abyssinia twice to protect themselves from being killed in Mecca. Additionally, when they emigrated to Medinah they left their homes and much wealth behind them in Mecca.

08. How was the period right after the treaty of al-Hudaybeeyah different in terms of spreading Islaam to the people?
    Answers will vary per student, and should be discussed from any authentic source or sound perspective. An example would be that it enabled people to actually hear, talk, and spend time with Muslims to see what they actually believed and how they treated others who did not oppress them.

09. Name another well-known Companion from the Muhaajiroon, and describe one way that they helped support Islaam.
    Answers will vary per student, and should be discussed from any authentic source or sound perspective. An example would be Abu Bakr as-Siddeeq who helped Islaam in many many ways including advising the Prophet which tribes should be approached first to call them to embrace and support Islaam.

DAY 16: KNOW THAT KNOWLEDGE IS RECEIVED AND CAN BE LOST

TEST YOUR UNDERSTANDING:

TRUE & FALSE QUESTIONS
[Circle the correct letter for each individual sentence from today's content.]

01. There is no difference in learning from books or from scholars directly. [T / **F**]

    This is incorrect. As the Sheikh mentioned "…*Within this narration is an encouragement towards seeking knowledge, giving importance to acquiring knowledge, and taking knowledge from the mouths of the scholars. It is not enough that a person just take knowledge from books and reading; this is not sufficient. There is no one who has properly learned and becomes a true grounded student of knowledge relying solely upon books, never. Rather knowledge is taken from the mouths of the scholars.*"

02. There will come a time in which knowledge will disappear and not be easily found among people. [**T** / F]

    This is correct. As the Sheikh indicated the authentic narration informs us about what will occur "…*{…till none of the scholars stays alive. Then the people will take ignorant ones as their leaders, who, when asked to deliver religious verdicts, will issue them without knowledge, the result being that they will go astray and will lead others astray.}*"

03. It is possible for anyone to issue correct rulings and judgments in Islaam. [T / **F**]

    This is incorrect. As the Sheikh mentioned when anyone and everyone speak without knowledge the people are ruined "…*As within these institutions in society and in these positions, there will inevitably be someone considered a mufti who issues rulings, and someone considered a judge who issues judgments, and someone considered a teacher who instructs the people. But when such people in these positions do not possess clear Sharee'ah knowledge and insight, then they will issue rulings without sound knowledge, and they will teach the people while lacking sound knowledge, and they will issue judgments for the people in the absence of sound knowledge. Therefore, they themselves are misguided and call others to be misguided to fall into ruin.*"

ANSWER KEY

FILL IN THE BLANK QUESTIONS

[Enter the correct individual words to complete the sentences from today's content.]

04. Allaah does not take away the **knowledge** by taking it away from the **hearts** of the people.

05. The **scholars** are needed to be those who **explain** matters to the people and **clarify** the intended meanings of the Qur'aan and Sunnah.

06. The people of **innovation** wrongly throw one source text against another so that they clash or **conflict.**

INTERACTIVE QUESTIONS & EXERCISES

COMPREHENSIVE UNDERSTANDING QUESTIONS

[In a study group or circle of learning with other students, these questions can be answered fully or partially by one student from the lesson, with another student completing the answer to the same question, by giving a comparable but different which is also correct.]

07. Explain misconceptions or ideas that people hold that cause them to refrain from learning from scholars.

    Answers will vary per student, and should be discussed from any authentic source or sound perspective. An example would be that people wrongly believe that they can understand the knowledge in the source texts without outside help.

08. Give the name of one well-known scholar of this age who has died, and mention one of the areas of knowledge which they were proficient in.

    Answers will vary per student, and should be discussed from any authentic source or sound perspective. An example would be Sheikh Muhammad Ibn Saaleh al-'Utheimeen, who was proficient in many areas of Sharee'ah knowledge including fiqh or how to implement that guidance of texts.

09. Discuss one shortcoming of studying only from books and not from the scholars themselves. Give a possible example to explain your answer.

    Answers will vary per student, and should be discussed from any authentic source or sound perspective. An example would be that books generally cannot cultivate the right way to implement knowledge and spread it among people in the best way.

DAY 17: THE REALITY OF THE PEOPLE OF MISGUIDANCE & THEIR DECEPTIONS

TEST YOUR UNDERSTANDING:

TRUE & FALSE QUESTIONS
[Circle the correct letter for each individual sentence from today's content.]

01. The people of misguidance oppose the guidance of the Sunnah in several ways. [T / F]

    This is correct. As the Sheikh mentioned from Ibn Battah about the people of misguidance *"...They say about Allaah that which they have no basis for and no knowledge of. They find fault with the people of the truth in what they bring forth of truth, and criticize the reliable ones in what they transmit of guidance. Yet they fail to condemn their very own distorted interpretations found within their opinions."*

02. It is not important to carefully select the books one reads, as long as they are from Muslims. [T / **F**]

    This is incorrect. As the Sheikh mentioned *"...Perhaps a young person will come across a book by one of the individuals who advocate these misguided statements, where he begins with the praise of Allaah and glorifying Him, and with the extensive sending of praise and salutations upon the Prophet, may Allaah's praise and salutations be upon him. Yet after this he brings forth his subtle and intricate forms of disbelief, and imperceptibly introduces his invented concepts and general evil."*

03. People are often confused as to who are actually reliable scholars we should benefit from. [T / F]

    This is correct. As the Sheikh mentioned *"...So the young person who does not possess a significant amount of knowledge, or the non-Arabic speaking Muslim, or the unsophisticated general Muslim would wrongly come to assume that this author is a steadfast scholar from among the accepted scholars, or is indeed a reliable scholar of fiqh from among the scholars specializing in how we should implement the source texts."*

ANSWER KEY

FILL IN THE BLANK QUESTIONS

[Enter the correct individual words to complete the sentences from today's content.]

04. A **young** person who does not possess a significant amount of **knowledge** can be misled by **appearances**.

05. Jahm Ibn Safwaan is the originator of the sect of the **Jahmeeyah**.

06. The subtle **misguidance** in the books of the people of falsehood may not be recognized by the **majority** of people who read them.

INTERACTIVE QUESTIONS & EXERCISES

COMPREHENSIVE UNDERSTANDING QUESTIONS

[In a study group or circle of learning with other students, these questions can be answered fully or partially by one student from the lesson, with another student completing the answer to the same question, by giving a comparable but different which is also correct.]

07. Give one way the people are misled by those using modern technology, causing them to wrongly believe that someone is a reliable scholar.

    Answers will vary per student, and should be discussed from any authentic source or sound perspective. An example would be that some people believe that people who have many lectures or videos on Youtube which people are watching must have good knowledge of Islaam.

08. Explain one way a general Muslim can be truly confident that a book they want to benefit from is sound and acceptable.

    Answers will vary per student, and should be discussed from any authentic source or sound perspective. An example would be to ask a student of knowledge about good books in their own language to learn from.

09. Name one of the leaders or ideological figureheads from any one of the misguided movements or groups present among the Muslims today.

    Answers will vary per student, and should be discussed from any authentic source or sound perspective. An example would be Sayyed Qutb, who was a writer with enthusiasm for Islaam but not a scholar who learned sound knowledge from the scholars of his age. From the greatest misguidance found in his books is his evil speech about both some of the prophets of Allaah, as well as evil statements and positions against the Companions of the Messenger of Allaah, may Allaah be pleased with them all

DAY 18: THE BELIEVERS ARE DISTINCT UPON REVEALED GUIDANCE

TEST YOUR UNDERSTANDING:

TRUE & FALSE QUESTIONS
[Circle the correct letter for each individual sentence from today's content.]

01. It acceptable to sit and listen to people mock Islaam, as long as you don't join in. [T / **F**]

    This is incorrect. As the Sheikh mentioned from the verse ❋***And it has already been revealed to you in the Book (this Qur'aan) that when you hear the Verses of Allaah being denied and mocked at, then sit not with them...*** ❋

02. The person who sits in a gathering of wrongdoing must speak up to stop them or leave. [**T** / F]

    This is correct. As the Sheikh mentioned *"...As if a person is in a sitting in which someone there mocks Allaah, or jokes about the Book of Allaah, or the Messenger of Allaah, it is an obligation that you speak up against this. If they stop doing so. then all praise is due to Allaah."*

03. Muslims have been prohibited from taking non-Muslims as close friends. [**T** / F]

    This is correct. As the Sheikh mentioned *"...That we abandon sitting with them, and we do not take disbelievers as close friends where you visit him and he visits you, without there being a specific reason for that. If you happen to come to sit with them without choosing to do so then this is a different matter.*

    But as for when you take them as your friend, such that you confide in them your personal matters, and consider then someone trustworthy to you, and that you visit them and they also visit you. Then this is from the impermissible companionship and friendship. As such it is required that you stay away from this."

ANSWER KEY

FILL IN THE BLANK QUESTIONS

[Enter the correct individual words to complete the sentences from today's content.]

04. The believers have been ordered to **separate** from those who **speak** against their clear religion.

05. It is allowed to **visit** non-Muslims in order to **invite** them to Islaam, just as the Prophet did.

06. If a Muslim is **pleased** with that sin and transgression that people are doing in a **gathering** where there is wrongdoing, he is considered like one of those **sinners**.

INTERACTIVE QUESTIONS & EXERCISES

COMPREHENSIVE UNDERSTANDING QUESTIONS

[In a study group or circle of learning with other students, these questions can be answered fully or partially by one student from the lesson, with another student completing the answer to the same question, by giving a comparable but different which is also correct.]

07. Give an example in which a Muslim might find themselves in one of the situations mentioned. What is a good way to implement the guidelines mentioned?

    Answers will vary per student, and should be discussed from any authentic source or sound perspective. An example would be that a Muslim speaks up and says what is being said is not true and offensive to them. They could also offer, in a good way, to explain Islaam to help them understand.

08. Briefly explain how speaking up when falsehood is mentioned benefits you.

    Answers will vary per student, and should be discussed from any authentic source or sound perspective. An example would be that you are removed from the sin and wrong that they are doing. Secondly, you help stop the spreading of the falsehood that was found within their speech.

09. What is one of the dangers of taking non-Muslims as close friends related to this discussion?

    Answers will vary per student, and should be discussed from any authentic source or sound perspective. An example would be that we must remember that the Prophet told us that a person is on the religion or way of life of his close friend, and you often discuss beliefs, priorities, and ideas with someone who does not believe in Islaam.

DAY 19: ADVICE OF THE COMPANIONS 'UTHMAAN, 'ALEE & IBN 'ABBAAS

TEST YOUR UNDERSTANDING:

TRUE & FALSE QUESTIONS
[Circle the correct letter for each individual sentence from today's content.]

01. People's desires generally guide them to that which is good for them. [T / **F**]

    This is incorrect. As the Sheikh mentioned "...*Falsehood is what agrees with one's inner desires, and which opposes the guidance of the source texts, even if you feel within yourself that this is an act of obedience to Allaah.*"

02. It is important to follow the truth no matter what our desires call us to. [**T** / F]

    This is correct. As the Sheikh mentioned "...*desires are something which act as a barrier towards the truth and cause someone to be blind to it. ... Rather, an individual must act according to the Book of Allaah and the Sunnah, yes.*"

03. What is considered obedience to Allaah is different for every person. [T / **F**]

    This is incorrect, because we understand obedience not from our desires, but from the same two revealed sources. As the Sheikh mentioned "...*The statement "Hold firm to being steadfast in Islaam..." Means be steadfast upon the Sunnah, and be steadfast upon the religion of Islaam, follow and adhere to the Qur'aan and Sunnah.*"

ANSWER KEY

FILL IN THE BLANK QUESTIONS

[Enter the correct individual words to complete the sentences from today's content.]

04. Our **desires** are often something which **block** and are a **barrier** to accepting the truth.

05. Steadfastness means to hold **firmly** to the **Qur'aan** and the **Sunnah**.

06. We should **follow** what comes within the **revealed** source texts, not our **desires**.

INTERACTIVE QUESTIONS & EXERCISES

COMPREHENSIVE UNDERSTANDING QUESTIONS

[In a study group or circle of learning with other students, these questions can be answered fully or partially by one student from the lesson, with another student completing the answer to the same question, by giving a comparable but different which is also correct.]

07. What might be one cause of someone wrongly believing that our desires are something pleasing to Allaah?

    Answers will vary per student, and should be discussed from any authentic source or sound perspective. An example would be that this is caused due to a misconception someone has or this might be caused by the whisperings of Shaytaan to an individual.

08. Give a practical example of how someone's desires might prevent them from accepting something required in Islaam. Write out their possible false excuse.

    Answers will vary per student, and should be discussed from any authentic source or sound perspective. An example would be where someone doesn't want to stop spending time with friends who drink alcohol. Their excuse is that they are not harmed and are not drinking alcohol themselves.

09. Give a practical example of an issue a Muslim might need to be steadfast in, specifically in our modern age and time.

    Answers will vary per student, and should be discussed from any authentic source or sound perspective. An example would be the need to be steadfast in staying away from forms of entertainment which are either forbidden or contain mostly matters which are forbidden in Islaam. This is because these impermissible forms of entertainment are all around us today.

Day 20: The People Who Are Astray Turned Away From The Guidance Brought To Them

TEST YOUR UNDERSTANDING:

TRUE & FALSE QUESTIONS
[Circle the correct letter for each individual sentence from today's content.]

01. It is acceptable for a Muslim to choose between his opinion and what is found in the Sunnah. [T / **F**]

    This is incorrect. As the Sheikh mentioned "...*It is for this reason it is said that they act according to "their opinions" and have abandoned acting upon the established authentic practices from the Sunnah.*"

02. Speaking from your opinions in relation to the religion is something blameworthy. [**T** / F]

    This is correct, because it means turning away from revealed guidance. As the Sheikh mentioned "...*Additionally, what it conveys is something that is generally witnessed from the people who rely upon their perceptions and opinions, that they stand as opponents and enemies of the authentic practices from the Prophet, meaning the people who rely solely upon their opinions.*"

03. The Muslims upon guidance place the knowledge of the Sunnah above their opinions and perceptions. [**T** / F]

    This is correct, the statement of 'Umar shows that this is the way of the people of the Sunnah as opposed to others who have turned away from adhering to the Messenger's guidance in all matters. As the Sheikh mentioned "...*They are brought hadeeth narrations in order that they memorize and act upon them, but they run from them and turned back to their inner desires and wants.... It contains a command to adhere firmly to the Sunnah, and a warning against innovating in the religion.*"

ANSWER KEY

FILL IN THE BLANK QUESTIONS

[Enter the correct individual words to complete the sentences from today's content.]

04. The people of opinions who follow their **desires**, are **enemies** and opponents of the authentic **practices** of the Prophet.

05. The people who are infatuated with their own perceptions and opinions, break free of the guidance of the **narrations** from the **Sunnah**.

06. Beneficial narrations are brought to us so we can understand, try to **memorize,** and **act** upon them.

INTERACTIVE QUESTIONS & EXERCISES

COMPREHENSIVE UNDERSTANDING QUESTIONS

[In a study group or circle of learning with other students, these questions can be answered fully or partially by one student from the lesson, with another student completing the answer to the same question, by giving a comparable but different which is also correct.]

07. Give an example of a common opinion or perception found among non-Muslims that goes against the guidance of Islaam.
Answers will vary per student, and should be discussed from any authentic source or sound perspective. An example would be the misconception that Muslims are ordered to kill anyone who does not embrace Islaam when called.

08. Give an example of a common opinion or perception found among Muslims today that goes against the guidance of Islaam.
Answers will vary per student, and should be discussed from any authentic source or sound perspective. An example would be that it is acceptable to take rulings in Islaam from our customs or statements of people which have no connection to the source texts of the Qur'aan and Sunnah.

09. Explain one false reason an ignorant Muslim might use to justify placing his opinion over and above the clear guidance of Islaam.
Answers will vary per student, and should be discussed from any authentic source or sound perspective. An example would be that they say, "This is how all the Muslims in my country or land have always done this, so it must be correct and agree with the Sunnah!"

Day 21: The People Of Misguidance Want You To Turn From Revealed Guidance

TEST YOUR UNDERSTANDING:

TRUE & FALSE QUESTIONS
[Circle the correct letter for each individual sentence from today's content.]

01. If we are strong in our faith then there is no harm in debating people. [T / **F**]

    This is incorrect. As the Sheikh mentioned we may choose misguidance because of how well it is presented "...*Meaning by this does someone imagine that whenever an individual who is a better debater, someone stronger than him in the ability to present, argue, and debate points, that due to this we should leave the clear guidance which Jibreel brought down to the Prophet?*"

02. There is more than one type of danger involved in sitting with the people of misguidance. [T / F]

    This is correct. Above and beyond that danger of someone personally falling into misguidance, their sittings produce disunity and conflicts which often spread to others in society. As the Sheikh mentioned "...*He said this because arguing about the affairs of religion produces controversies, disputes, conflicts, and disunity. Moreover innovations are born from matters which are close to and similar to what is produced from arguments and disputes, and the results of arguing generally.*"

03. The revealed guidance of Islaam is always superior to human arguments and concepts. [T / F]

    This is correct. As the Sheikh mentioned this is why the scholars mention that subjecting revealed guidance to the scale of personal arguments is unreasonable and misguided "...*He's indicating to us that it is not permissible for a person to take on the various misguided views and opinions which are just the results of debates and argumentation, and so abandon the guidance of the Book of Allaah and the Sunnah.*"

FILL IN THE BLANK QUESTIONS

[Enter the correct individual words to complete the sentences from today's content.]

04. The Sunnah is the **second** source of **revelation**.

05. The practice of **debating** and argumentation produces **harmful** controversies, doubts, and **innovations** within Islaam.

06. Good company **encourages** you toward what is good, or turns you away from what is bad and **harmful**, such as **innovations** in the religion.

INTERACTIVE QUESTIONS & EXERCISES

COMPREHENSIVE UNDERSTANDING QUESTIONS

[In a study group or circle of learning with other students, these questions can be answered fully or partially by one student from the lesson, with another student completing the answer to the same question, by giving a comparable but different which is also correct.]

07. Give an example of a misconception, which the people who falsely claim to be engaged in Jihaad in our time, spread amongst the Muslims.

    Answers will vary per student, and should be discussed from any authentic source or sound perspective. An example would be that the efforts of fighting against the active enemies of Islaam is more important than teaching the people the essential foundation of worshiping Allaah alone, and the five pillars of Islaam.

08. Give an example of a misconception, which the people who claim to be engaged in efforts of calling to Allaah or da'wah in our time, spread amongst the Muslims.

    Answers will vary per student, and should be discussed from any authentic source or sound perspective. An example would be the belief that da'wah or calling should be focused on achieving a general overall unity among Muslims and not spreading the authentic fundamental beliefs of Islaam.

09. Give an example of a possible good response that a Muslim can give to someone who tries to get them to enter into an argument or debate.

    Answers will vary per student, and should be discussed from any authentic source or sound perspective. An example would be to say Islaam is based upon clear text and guidance, not your opinion or mine. And the explanations of the scholars of the Qur'aan and Sunnah clarify these issues which you are confused about.

DAY 22: THOSE WHO FREQUENTLY DEBATE ARBITRARILY CHANGE THEIR RELIGION

TEST YOUR UNDERSTANDING:

TRUE & FALSE QUESTIONS
[Circle the correct letter for each individual sentence from today's content.]

01. A Muslim should listen to every argument and then decide what is correct. [T / **F**]

    This is incorrect as debating from opinions or misconceptions can only bring harm. As the Sheikh mentioned from the narration "...*Such that this person aims his arguments at him, and this other person also aims his argument at him. Due to this, it is said the one who makes his religion a target which everyone can aim at with their arguments and controversies will be someone unsteady, who changes positions often.*"

02. True knowledge in Islaam is based upon the foundation of revealed guidance. [**T** / F]

    This is correct. As the Sheikh described those who are misguided and distant away from this foundation, saying "...*they do not stand firm upon the religion, nor adhere closely to the Sunnah.*"

03. The early scholars of Islaam did not see any harm in personal views and opinions. [T / **F**]

    This is incorrect, as this is opposed to following revealed guidance, and the way of the people upon revealed guidance. They held that focusing upon the various personal views and opinions which many different people hold will only make you unsteady in your religion "... *Therefore it is said that the one who makes his religion the target or object of debates and controversies will be unsteady, changing often from one position to another position, such that they do not stand firm upon the religion, nor adhere closely to the Sunnah. As such, this contains a warning against involving yourself in controversies, as they produce misconceptions and innovations within your understanding of Islaam, because the one involved in controversies is unable to stand steadfastly upon the religion and the Sunnah.*"

FILL IN THE BLANK QUESTIONS
[Enter the correct individual words to complete the sentences from today's content.]

04. Some scholars consider 'Umar Ibn 'Abdul-'Azeez, the **fifth** rightly guided **khalifah**.

05. Someone who makes his **understanding** of Islaam the object of **debates** and controversies will be **unsteady**.

06. Controversies produce **misconceptions** and **innovations** within your understanding of **Islaam**.

INTERACTIVE QUESTIONS & EXERCISES

COMPREHENSIVE UNDERSTANDING QUESTIONS
[In a study group or circle of learning with other students, these questions can be answered fully or partially by one student from the lesson, with another student completing the answer to the same question, by giving a comparable but different which is also correct.]

07. Give an example of a misconception related to the correct beliefs about Allaah which people often debate about.
    Answers will vary per student, and should be discussed from any authentic source or sound perspective. An example would be the false belief that Allaah is everywhere, and not as He described Himself in the Qur'aan, as above His Throne in a manner befitting His transcendence over creation.

08. Give an example of a misconception related to women's dress which people often debate about.
    Answers will vary per student, and should be discussed from any authentic source or sound perspective. An example would be the false belief that the hijaab that Muslim women are obligated to wear can be anything they consider modest, and that it does not have specific characteristics described in the Qur'aan and Sunnah.

09. Give an example of a misconception about correcting mistakes which people often debate about.
    Answers will vary per student, and should be discussed from any authentic source or sound perspective. An example would be the misconception that correcting mistakes that people have in fundamental beliefs causes disunity among the Muslims. Rather it is the only true road to our unity.

DAY 23: THE BLESSING OF LEARNING THE SUNNAH WHEN YOUNG

TEST YOUR UNDERSTANDING:

TRUE & FALSE QUESTIONS
[Circle the correct letter for each individual sentence from today's content.]

01. How someone starts out as a Muslim will not affect their practice. [T / **F**]

    This is incorrect. As the Sheikh mentioned "... *in most cases when a young Muslim is raised upon the beliefs of the people of the Sunnah and the Jamaa'ah, then he is someone whom we hope good for, that he continue to remain steadfast upon that. Likewise if a young Muslim is raised among the people of innovation, then generally what is seen is that he continues proceeding upon that innovation he was cultivated within.*"

02. Muslims should strive to gain a foundation of sound knowledge while they are young. [**T** / F]

    This is correct. As the Sheikh mentioned "... *Moreover, it should push us to strive to hold firmly to the beliefs of the people of the Sunnah and the Jamaa'ah. If these leading scholars made such a mistake then you have a significant responsibility to ensure you understand what is correct. Understanding this leads the Muslim youth and the seeker of knowledge to be diligent and gaining understanding of the beliefs of the people of the Sunnah and the Jamaa'ah, holding firmly onto those beliefs with their molar teeth, and praising Allaah for granting you success to be raised upon the correct beliefs of the people of the Sunnah and the Jamaa'ah.*"

03. There have always been books which conveyed the correct beliefs of Islaam since the first three generations of Muslims. [**T** / F]

    This is generally correct. As the Sheikh mentioned a number of examples of scholastic works within the history of the Ummah "... *Additionally, in the area of correct beliefs there is also the work al-Aqeedah at-Tahaweeyah by different scholar, Abu Ja'far Ahmad at-Tahawee, may Allaah have mercy upon him, which generally explains the fundamentals of the religion. It should be noted that Sheikh al-Islaam Ibn Taymeeyah, has many other writings related to the correct belief, which have been collected in Majmou' al-Fataawa as well as separately, as does Ibn al-Qayyim*"

FILL IN THE BLANK QUESTIONS

[Enter the correct individual words to complete the sentences from today's content.]

04. If a Muslim is **raised** upon the **beliefs** of the people of the Sunnah and the Jamaa'ah, he will generally **continue** upon that.

05. The people of the Sunnah understand Allaah's **attributes**, upon the **way** of the first generations of **believers**.

06. Allaah blessed Sheikh **Muhammad** Ibn 'Abdul-Wahaab, to **spread** this revived **Salafee** call.

INTERACTIVE QUESTIONS & EXERCISES

COMPREHENSIVE UNDERSTANDING QUESTIONS

[In a study group or circle of learning with other students, these questions can be answered fully or partially by one student from the lesson, with another student completing the answer to the same question, by giving a comparable but different which is also correct.]

07. Give an example of something we can do to try to ensure that young Muslims today gain a sound understanding of Islaam when they are young.
    Answers will vary per student, and should be discussed from any authentic source or sound perspective. An example would be Muslims in a specific area or community working very hard to establish a small school for their children to learn the correct beliefs and practices of Islaam.

08. What should a Muslim do if he encounters a conflict between the beliefs of a well-known scholar and the beliefs of the Companions?
    Answers will vary per student, and should be discussed from any authentic source or sound perspective. Generally, he should remember that no single scholar is infallible, but the beliefs of the Companions are those of the 'saved sect' and 'the victorious group' which will always be upon the truth in both understanding and practice among the Muslims.

09. Describe one of the books of the beliefs of the people of the Sunnah which you have in your library, and write which scholar authored it.
    Answers will vary per student, and should be discussed from what they actually possess of books. An example would be the excellent translation of the explanation of Thalaatatul-Usul by Sheikh Muhammad al-'Utheimeen, which was published many years ago.

DAY 24: THE IMPORTANCE OF BOTH LOVING & HATING FOR ALLAAH'S SAKE

TEST YOUR UNDERSTANDING:

TRUE & FALSE QUESTIONS
[Circle the correct letter for each individual sentence from today's content.]

01. We should have a strong love for our relatives, even when we see them disobeying Allaah. [T / **F**]

    This is incorrect. As the Sheikh mentioned that the love for the sake of Allaah is conditional "...*Moreover, loving for Allaah and hating for Allaah means: That you love whomever Allaah loves from people and individuals, whatever Allaah loves from actions, rulings, and commands...*" and so this requires hatred for the sake of Allaah "...*Similarly that you hate the one who commits sins and disobeys Allaah, that you hate him even if he is someone close to you. This means even if he is your blood brother from the same father and mother, you have hatred for him for Allaah's sake.*"

02. Our love for individuals does not have any connection to our love for Allaah and His Messenger. [T / **F**]

    This is incorrect. As the Sheikh mentioned "...*It means that you love an individual not because he is someone personally close to you, nor because between the two of you there is cooperation in some worldly endeavor or shared interest in something. Rather that you love him because he is someone steadfast in obeying Allaah, the Most Glorified and the Most Exalted.*"

03. Loving someone for the sake of Allaah is different than loving them for a worldly reason. [**T** / F]

    This is correct. As the Sheikh mentioned "*It means that you love an individual not because he is someone personally close to you, nor because between the two of you there is cooperation in some worldly endeavor or shared interest in something.... This is the belief of the people of the Sunnah and the Jamaa'ah. This is the meaning of loving for the sake of Allaah. For this reason it is said, "you should love for the sake of Allaah the one who obeys Him, even if it is a person who lives far away from you, and opposes you in some matter of your worldly efforts.*"

ANSWER KEY

FILL IN THE BLANK QUESTIONS

[Enter the correct individual words to complete the sentences from today's content.]

04. A Muslim should love someone who **obeys** Allaah, even if they **differ** with him in his **worldly** affairs.

05. You hate the one who commits **sins** and **disobeys** Allaah, even if he is someone **close** to you personally.

06. The scholars have warned us from **listening** to those who generally speak from their own **opinions** and perceptions.

INTERACTIVE QUESTIONS & EXERCISES

COMPREHENSIVE UNDERSTANDING QUESTIONS

[In a study group or circle of learning with other students, these questions can be answered fully or partially by one student from the lesson, with another student completing the answer to the same question, by giving a comparable but different which is also correct.]

07. Give a possible practical example of someone that we hear about but don't know personally, whom we should strive to love for Allaah's sake.
    Answers will vary per student, and should be discussed from any authentic source or sound perspective. An example would be one of the scholars who defends the Sunnah, spreads knowledge of the Sunnah, and calls people to follow the believers way of the first three generations of Islaam.

08. Give a possible practical example of someone that we hear about but don't know personally, whom we should have hatred towards for Allaah's sake.
    Answers will vary per student, and should be discussed from any authentic source or sound perspective. An example would be a caller, in whatever land, who legitimizes the Muslim customary practices involving shirk, by visiting graves and asking the righteous dead to intercede for them.

09. Discuss one possible negative effect of getting in the habit of generally speaking about religious matters from our opinions and perceptions.
    Answers will vary per student, and should be discussed from any authentic source or sound perspective. An example would be that as an individual you will never learn the necessity of turning to the sources of revealed knowledge rather than your own opinion. A second example would be that doing so increases your sins by also misguiding others in Islaam.

DAY 25: A PERSON STANDS UPON THE RELIGION OF HIS CLOSE COMPANION

TEST YOUR UNDERSTANDING:

TRUE & FALSE QUESTIONS

[Circle the correct letter for each individual sentence from today's content.]

01. The people we spend time with do not have any significant effect upon us. [T / **F**]

    This is incorrect. As the Sheikh mentioned "… *If a person has for his close friend and the one he spends time with a person who is upon the Sunnah, then he is considered from the Sunnah. But if his close friend and the one he spends time with is a person upon innovation in the religion, then he is likewise connected to the people of innovation.*"

02. There are no new religious innovations, only those which came about in the past. [T / **F**]

    This is incorrect. As the Sheikh mentioned "…*This means that these different innovations, they are all present. Every form of innovation which existed previously is alive and present today in our age. Moreover, there are in addition to these, other new innovations now, and other new deviated beliefs now, and new affiliations and allegiances upon misguidance, all of which are in addition to what existed previously.*"

03. The previous misguided sects found throughout Muslim history still exist today. [**T** / F]

    This is correct. As the Sheikh mentioned "… *The Jahmeeyah are present generally everywhere, and they are those that say Allaah exists in every place, in the heavens and beneath the earth. We seek refuge in Allaah from this falsehood, which they are saying.*

    The Mu'tazilah are present, the Asha'rees are present, the Raafidhah are present, the Khawaarij are present, the Murji'ah are present, and the Qadareeyah are present. In fact, there are even present those who falsely claim that the Creator and the creation are one! They assert that the Lord is the same as the worshiper, and the worshiper is the same as the Lord. This misguidance is all present, existing today."

FILL IN THE BLANK QUESTIONS

[Enter the correct individual words to complete the sentences from today's content.]

04. Every form of **innovation** which existed previously is alive and **present** today in our age.

05. In addition to old forms of **misguidance**, there are other **new** forms of innovations and deviated beliefs today.

06. Success is being led by Allaah to **obey** Him, and being blessed with **beneficial** knowledge, and to do **righteous** deeds.

INTERACTIVE QUESTIONS & EXERCISES

COMPREHENSIVE UNDERSTANDING QUESTIONS

[In a study group or circle of learning with other students, these questions can be answered fully or partially by one student from the lesson, with another student completing the answer to the same question, by giving a comparable but different which is also correct.]

07. Give a practical example of one way that good companionship may influence a Muslim toward what is good and beneficial to him.

    Answers will vary per student, and should be discussed from any authentic source or sound perspective. An example would be that a good companion would encourage you to attend classes that were available in order to learn the Sunnah, or to attend activities at a good masjid close by.

08. Give a practical example of one way in which bad companionship may influence a Muslim toward what is bad and harmful to him.

    Answers will vary per student, and should be discussed from any authentic source or sound perspective. An example would be that a bad companion might encourage you to be "relaxed" toward your obligations as a Muslim, telling you that it is okay to do whatever you want and not be so strict.

09. Write down two misguided sects or groups which are found in the Muslim world today, and mention a Muslim country where that group or sect can be found.

    Answers will vary per student, and should be discussed from any authentic source or sound perspective. An example would be the sect of the Khawaarij upon a false methodology of jihaad, also knows as Da'eesh or the so called "Islamic State", which is found in Iraq and Syria. They are a group upon misguidance that has many corrupt beliefs and practices which are harming Islaam and the Muslims.

DAY 26: INNOVATION THAT IS DISBELIEF DESTROYS ALL ONE'S GOOD DEEDS

TEST YOUR UNDERSTANDING:

TRUE & FALSE QUESTIONS
[Circle the correct letter for each individual sentence from today's content.]

01. Allaah accepts all of our actions, as long as we are sincere in doing them for Him. [T / **F**]

    This is incorrect, a condition of the acceptance of actions is that someone be a Muslim. As the Sheikh mentioned "... *Because when a person stands upon major disbelief, his good deeds are not accepted by Allaah, due to the presence of that disbelief.*"

02. From the dangers of innovation is the destruction of the rewards of our good deeds. [**T** / F]

    This is correct, and applies to extreme innovation. As the Sheikh mentioned "... *The extreme innovator whose innovation reaches the level of major disbelief, certainly Allaah does not accept from him his deeds, nor his ritual prayers, nor his fasting, nor his obligatory zakaat, until he repents from that matter of major disbelief and significant misguidance that he fell into.*"

03. There are conditions for the acceptance of our deeds by Allaah. [**T** / F]

    This is correct. As the Sheikh mentioned several verses which show this Allaah, the Most High, says ❦*And indeed it has been revealed to you (O Muhammad), as it was to those (Allaah's Messengers) before you: "If you join others in worship with Allaah, then surely all your deeds will be in vain, and you will certainly be among the losers.*❧-(Surah Az-Zumar: 1). And Allaah the Most Perfect said:❦*But if they had joined in worship others with Allaah, all that they used to do would have been of no benefit to them"*❧-(Surah Al-An'am: 88) And Allaah the Most Perfect said: ❦*..And whosoever disbelieves in the Oneness of Allaah and in all the other Articles of Faith, then fruitless is his work, and in the Hereafter he will be among the losers*❧-(Surah Al-Maa'idah: 5)

ANSWER KEY

FILL IN THE BLANK QUESTIONS

[Enter the correct individual words to complete the sentences from today's content.]

04. Both **major** sins and **innovation** in the religion may **lead** a person towards major disbelief.

05. Allaah says that He will make the **deeds** of the **disbelievers** like scattered floating particles of dust.

06. The **extreme** innovator, whose innovation reaches the level of major **disbelief**, is someone who none of their deeds will be **accepted**.

INTERACTIVE QUESTIONS & EXERCISES

COMPREHENSIVE UNDERSTANDING QUESTIONS

[In a study group or circle of learning with other students, these questions can be answered fully or partially by one student from the lesson, with another student completing the answer to the same question, by giving a comparable but different which is also correct.]

07. Give a specific example of any sect or group whose innovation reaches the level of major disbelief, and so have been declared by the people of knowledge to be disbelievers.

    Answers will vary per student, and should be discussed from any authentic source or sound perspective. An example would be the Nusayrees whose innovations in their beliefs are major disbelief in the fundamental evidenced beliefs of Islaam found in the Qur'aan and Sunnah.

08. Give a specific example of any sect or group whose innovation is below the level of major disbelief, and so are Muslims.

    Answers will vary per student, and should be discussed from any authentic source or sound perspective. An example would be the Zaydees of Yemen whom the scholars of the people of the Sunnah say their misguidance in beliefs generally is not at the same level as the Raafidhah.

09. Give a practical example of how someone might associate others with Allaah in their worship, and so have their deeds nullified and rejected.

    Answers will vary per student, and should be discussed from any authentic source or sound perspective. An example would be someone who was an extreme Sufee who believed that only his righteous Sheikh in his grave, can help him. Therefore, he directs all the supplications for his needs to the Sheikh to ask for him, believing that without this they are not answered.

DAY 27: INNOVATIONS IN ISLAAM MAY MISLEAD YOU TO LEAVE ISLAAM

TEST YOUR UNDERSTANDING:

TRUE & FALSE QUESTIONS
[Circle the correct letter for each individual sentence from today's content.]

01. Even though innovations are misguidance, they are not disbelief.   [T / **F**]
    This is incorrect, as it requires a detailed explanation. As the Sheikh mentioned *"... What is correct to say is that some of these innovating matters cause those involved in them to leave the religion, whereas other lesser matters which are innovation do not cause those involved in them to leave the boundaries of Islaam."*

02. A Muslim should free himself from any connection to every form of misguidance.   [**T** / F]
    This is correct. As the Sheikh mentioned *"... Every statement or claim which does not have a basis in the Sharee'ah, you should free yourself from it. Every newly developed opinion or view which does not have a basis within the Sharee'ah, you should free yourself from connection to it. Every followed desire which a person chooses to follow, distance yourself and turn away from it."*

03. Some of the astray sects have beliefs and practices that have taken them outside of Islaam.   [**T** / F]
    This is correct. As the Sheikh mentioned *"... Some innovations cause someone to leave Islaam, such as the beliefs of the Jahmeeyah, and the beliefs of the extreme Qadareeyah. The scholars of Islaam, had stated that such sects have gone outside the boundaries of the seventy-two misguided sects within Islaam."*

FILL IN THE BLANK QUESTIONS

[Enter the correct individual words to complete the sentences from today's content.]

04. A knowledgeable Muslim should free himself from **every** statement of **innovation** around him.

05. **Distance** yourself and turn away from every misguiding **desire** which some people choose to follow.

06. Some matters of **extreme** innovation in the religion, cause an individual to **leave** Islaam.

INTERACTIVE QUESTIONS & EXERCISES

COMPREHENSIVE UNDERSTANDING QUESTIONS

[In a study group or circle of learning with other students, these questions can be answered fully or partially by one student from the lesson, with another student completing the answer to the same question, by giving a comparable but different which is also correct.]

07. Give example of one of the astray sects whose beliefs reach the level of major disbelief in Islaam. Describe that specific belief.

    Answers will vary per student, and should be discussed from any authentic source or sound perspective. An example would be the Raafidhah, some of whom believe that their twelve leaders are absolutely infallible, and that these twelve leaders can control the very atoms of the universe.

08. Give an example of one of the misguided sects or groups who proceeds on innovation, which the scholars do not view as major disbelief. Describe that specific innovation they proceed upon.

    Answers will vary per student, and should be discussed from any authentic source or sound perspective. An example would be the Zaydeeyah who are upon misguidance in relation to issues connected to the first khalifahs.

09. Give a specific example of any newly developed view or opinion some Muslims accept, which was unknown among the Companions of the Messenger of Allaah.

    Answers will vary per student, and should be discussed from any authentic source or sound perspective. An example would be the misguided beliefs of the Ash'arees who misinterpret Allaah's names and attributes in an innovated way, which was completely unknown to the noble Companions.

DAY 28: THE ONE WHO CHANGES ISLAAM IS CURSED BY ALLAAH & CREATION

TEST YOUR UNDERSTANDING:

TRUE & FALSE QUESTIONS
[Circle the correct letter for each individual sentence from today's content.]

01. It is acceptable to accommodate or support an innovator as long as you don't innovate yourself. **[T / F]**

    This is incorrect. As the Sheikh mentioned is found in the authentic hadeeth {*...He who innovates (an act or practice) or gives protection to an innovator, there is a curse of Allaah and that of His angels and that of the whole humanity upon him...*}

02. Innovating something new is blameworthy but not as bad as the many major sins people commit. **[T / F]**

    This is incorrect as innovation in the religion is itself a major sin and considered worse than other major sins. As the Sheikh mentioned "...*So what is meant or intended by this hadeeth narration is both innovation and sinful transgressions, yet innovation is worse and more significant.*"

03. There is no clear way to tell what is considered a major sin by Allaah. **[T / F]**

    This is incorrect. As the Sheikh mentioned "...*As for the meaning of what is considered a major sin, as we've previously discussed, the strongest and most correct regarding its definition is that a major sin is that matter which is mentioned in the source texts of the Sharee'ah as:*

    - *being connected to a judicial punishment which handed out in this world for the person who commits it,*
    - *the person who commits it is threatened with a punishment in the Hereafter,*
    - *when it is mentioned for the person who commits it is cursed,*
    - *or the person who commits it is threatened with being cursed,*
    - *that matter or act is generally connected to the threat of punishment in the Hellfire,*
    - *or that matter or act which is generally connected to earning Allaah's anger.*

    When act is connected to any of these matters in the texts of the Sharee'ah, then it is considered a major sin.

FILL IN THE BLANK QUESTIONS

[Enter the correct individual words to complete the sentences from today's content.]

04. In this discussion what is intended by new **religious** matters is: **innovations**.
05. The one who innovates a **new** matter in Islaam, has committed a major **sin**.
06. The people of **innovation** and **desires** are all those who bring new matters into the religion of Islaam.

INTERACTIVE QUESTIONS & EXERCISES

COMPREHENSIVE UNDERSTANDING QUESTIONS

[In a study group or circle of learning with other students, these questions can be answered fully or partially by one student from the lesson, with another student completing the answer to the same question, by giving a comparable but different which is also correct.]

07. Give a specific example of something new related to giving da'wah that some people have innovated into Islaam.

    Answers will vary per student, and should be discussed from any authentic source or sound perspective. An example would be the misconception that we should focus on calling Muslims to return to good actions and deeds, and not focus on calling to beliefs as this causes separation among us.

08. Give a specific example of the mistake of protecting or accommodating an innovator in Islaam which a Muslim might fall into.

    Answers will vary per student, and should be discussed from any authentic source or sound perspective. An example would be if someone told others to not backbite by talking about the mistakes of a specific caller who calls to innovated practices of group loud dhikr sessions of the Sufees.

09. Explain a specific reason why some people might wrongly believe that making new matters in Islaam is something good.

    Answers will vary per student, and should be discussed from any authentic source or sound perspective. An example would be someone who believes that Islaam evolves and gets better, just as many Christians believe about their religion. They do not understand the meaning of the perfection of Islaam in both its specific beliefs and practices, as well as its principles.

Day 29: The Repentance from Innovation Must Be Clear & Apparent

TEST YOUR UNDERSTANDING:

TRUE & FALSE QUESTIONS
[Circle the correct letter for each individual sentence from today's content.]

01. The sin of innovation must be repented from like other sins and transgressions. [T / F]

    This is correct and what the scholars called for. As the Sheikh mentioned *"…Yet Ibn al-Mubaarak said, "No…" meaning that it will not be accepted by the people of the Sunnah, until you make your repentance as prominent and clearly apparent just as you previously had made your proceeding upon that innovation prominent and clearly apparent."*

02. Repentance from sin and transgression is only something in the heart. [T / F]

    This is incorrect regarding those sins which were outward actions and involved others. True repentance in relation to these has an outward public aspect. As the Sheikh mentioned *"…Meaning make your position upon the Sunnah well-known in those same places and areas in which you previously were well-known to stand upon innovation, such that it be a clear indication of your repentance from that. But as for the mere claim made with the tongue, then this will not be accepted from you."*

03. The Muslims judge other people according to their claims, not their actions. [T / F]

    This is incorrect, in fact the action are also considered. As the Sheikh mentioned *"…It is for this reason that 'Abdullah Ibn al-Mubaarak did not accept from him his claim, or his statement, until he also made readily apparent his repentance by actions. A statement of tongue indicating repentance is not enough until the person also makes apparent in their actions a clear repentance from innovation, just as they previously made clear their position and proceeded upon innovation. Yes."*

FILL IN THE BLANK QUESTIONS

[Enter the correct individual words to complete the sentences from today's content.]

04. Ibn al-Mubaarak abandoned this man mentioned, due to his failure to **openly** make clear his **repentance** from previous misguidance upon the way of the **Jahmeeyah**.

05. The Jahmeeyah wrongly **deny** the meanings and the reality of Allaah's **names** and **attributes**.

06. It is a general obligation upon us to **abandon** the people of innovation, and not to **speak** with them or **sit** with them.

INTERACTIVE QUESTIONS & EXERCISES

COMPREHENSIVE UNDERSTANDING QUESTIONS

[In a study group or circle of learning with other students, these questions can be answered fully or partially by one student from the lesson, with another student completing the answer to the same question, by giving a comparable but different which is also correct.]

07. Give a specific example of one way that a Muslim can make clear his repentance from innovation in our modern age.

    Answers will vary per student, and should be discussed from any authentic source or sound perspective. An example would be for someone who spread misguided ideas of innovation on the Internet, when repenting from that he should clearly state what he did wrong, and that he has abandoned this and is striving to follow the guidance of the Sunnah in what is correct.

08. Name two possible things a Muslim must change, once he repents from some innovation which he previously accepted.

    Answers will vary per student, and should be discussed from any authentic source or sound perspective. An example would be changing his companions and associates, and changing the scholars he listens to.

09. Give a possible example of how the scholars of the Sunnah might clarify the mistakes of the people of innovation in their society. Mention a specific example of when this has occurred.

    Answers will vary per student, and should be discussed from any authentic source or sound perspective. An example would be a scholar writing a refutation clarifying someone's circulated writings which contain misguidance. An example of this would be the refutation of Sheikh Ibn Baaz against Rashid Khalifa, the false prophet, who raised his falsehood in the United States.

DAY 30: WHAT RELIGION WILL YOU DIE UPON?

TEST YOUR UNDERSTANDING:

TRUE & FALSE QUESTIONS
[Circle the correct letter for each individual sentence from today's content.]

01. Maalik Ibn Anas, may Allaah have mercy upon him, was a well-known leading scholar in the city of Mecca. [T / **F**]

    This is incorrect, he was from Medina. As the Sheikh mentioned "...*this was from the statements of Maalik Ibn Anas, may Allaah have mercy upon him, the well-known leading scholar, and leading scholar of Dar al-Hijrah, the city of Medina.*"

02. It is not possible to leave innovation that you fall into. [T / **F**]

    This is incorrect, it is possible for the one Allaah has mercy upon. As the Sheikh mentioned "...*If someone throughout his life is associated and connected strongly to the people of innovation and desires, and attached to the people of innovation, then generally he proceeds upon that, continues his life upon that, and dies upon that- except for the one that Allaah protects from this.*"

03. The people of innovation have leaders who they take their understanding and practice from. [**T** / F]

    This is correct, as shown through the history of the misguided sects in Islaam. As the Sheikh mentioned "...*This is by a man who was present with him when he was close to death, the man who was close to death replied, "Upon the religion of Abu 'Amaarah." This was because he was an innovator. As Abu 'Amaarah was an innovator from amongst the people who have innovated in the religion..*

    ...He replied, "Upon the religion of Abu 'Amaarah." So when he was asked about his religion he replied, "that of Abu 'Amaarah," who was from the people of innovation in his time. This man, who was dying, had this allegiance towards him, and he was connected to him, he supported him and agreed with him in his distorted path of Islaam.."

FILL IN THE BLANK QUESTIONS

[Enter the correct individual words to complete the sentences from today's content.]

04. Abu 'Amaarah, was from the people of **innovation** in his time and a follower of his **desires**.

05. Whatever we are cultivated upon when **young**, then most likely this is what we will **die** upon, except for those whom Allaah, in His mercy, guides.

06. The man who was **dying** had this **allegiance** towards Abu 'Amaarah, rather than being **connected** to the Prophet Muhammad.

INTERACTIVE QUESTIONS & EXERCISES

COMPREHENSIVE UNDERSTANDING QUESTIONS

[In a study group or circle of learning with other students, these questions can be answered fully or partially by one student from the lesson, with another student completing the answer to the same question, by giving a comparable but different which is also correct.]

07. Give an example of something that someone might say that indicated that their love of and connection to their leader is stronger than their love and connection to the Messenger of Allaah.

    Answers will vary per student, and should be discussed from any authentic source or sound perspective. An example would be usually explaining both their beliefs and acts of worship as coming from their specific leader, instead of referring them back to the Sunnah of the Messenger of Allaah

08. Give a possible reason or cause that might make it difficult for people of innovation to realize that they are not actually upon the religion of the Prophet as they claim.

    Answers will vary per student, and should be discussed from any authentic source or sound perspective. An example would be when someone is raised upon innovation and his friends and associates are innovators.

09. Give an example of a sect, group, or movement among the Muslims which people have a biased allegiance towards, which is greater than their attachment and allegiance to the Messenger of Allaah.

    Answers will vary per student, and should be discussed from any authentic source or sound perspective. An example would be the Muslim Brotherhood Organization who generally, much more often, quote their innovating founder Hasan al-Banna, rather than mentioning authentic narrations.

COURSE APPENDIXES

Course Appendix 1:
Leaving The Straight Way Occurs In Two Ways   282

Course Appendix 2:
Concise Descriptions Of Twenty Seven Modern & Historical Sects/Groups/Religions/Ideologies of Misguidance   286

Course Appendix 3:
Warning Away From The One Upon Innovation Even If He Does Good Works   290

Course Appendix 4:
99 Characteristics Of Various Misguided Groups   296

Course Appendix 5:
It Is Not From The Way Of The First Three Generations To…"   316

Course Appendix 6:
The Reality Of Secularism: "We Warn Against This Ideological Colonization…"   324

Course Appendix 1:
Leaving The Straight Way Occurs In Two Ways

All praise is due to Allaah. The author, Ibn Battah, stated, may Allaah the Most High have mercy upon him,

[Know, that leaving the straight way occurs in two ways:

As for the first of them, it is that an individual falls into error and strays from the straight way while he only intends good. Such a person is not followed in his error or mistake, as he is ruined.

Whereas the second of them is the one who willfully differs from the truth and opposes those who came before him who were steadfast upon guidance. Such a person is misguided and leading others to misguidance, a stubborn Shaytaan within this Muslim Ummah.

It is proper that the one who understands this person's state warns the people away from him and explains to them his condition of misguidance to them, otherwise someone else may fall into his innovation and thus also be ruined.]

EXPLANATION OF
SHEIKH 'ABDUL-'AZEEZ AR-RAAJIHEE

[Know] meaning understand with certainty, *[that leaving the straight way occurs in two ways]* meaning that the one who deviates from the straight path and opposes the Sunnah is only one of the following two conditions: The first condition, *[an individual falls into error and strays from the straight way while he only intended good. Such a person is not followed in his error or mistake, as he is ruined.]* This category of person or the one in this condition he is the one that only desired and intended to do good yet even then he is not to be followed in his mistake or error, as indeed this error led him to being ruined.

Meaning that despite not having the intention to turn away from the truth, still he ended up opposing it. This person should not be followed in that matter even if they happen to be from among the Companions of the Prophet, may the praise and salutations of Allaah be upon him, or those who followed the Companions, may

Allaah be pleased with them all.

As for the statement of the author may Allaah have mercy upon him, *[...as he is ruined.]* Then in relation to this there is a more detailed explanation and specified ruling needed.

If this instance of opposing the truth came from one of the scholars with the scholastic ability to form independent Sharee'ah judgments based upon the evidences, and this error was a result or an instance of this scholastic striving to reach the truth, then despite the mistake he is rewarded for his effort to reach the truth, and he is forgiven for his result being an error or mistake. However we do not follow or adhere to them in that mistake. For the scholar who lived before us we continue to ask for mercy for him, since we continue to be aware that he slipped when he opposed a source text. This is what is correct even if the one who made the error was one of the noble Companions of the Prophet....

....Additionally, the authors' statement, may Allaah have mercy upon him, *[....as he is ruined.]*, also requires another detailed explanation. Again, if the one who is mistaken was someone who intended to turn away from the truth, then surely he is ruined. But as for the one who fell into error while striving to reach the correct conclusion, then this individual is not considered ruined.

About the second state, he mentioned:

[Whereas the second of them is the one who willfully differs from the truth and opposes those who came before him who were steadfast upon guidance. Such a person is misguided and leading others to misguidance, a stubborn Shaytaan within this Muslim Ummah.]

If he opposed the truth obstinately and turned away from the truth due to his desires, not simply as the result of a scholastic attempt to reach the truth, but simply due to knowingly choosing to instead follow his desires, then this one is clearly astray and leading others astray. He is considered a rebelling Shaytaan from within this Ummah. Yet this is the case if his errors and opposition to the truth are significant and reach the level of being major. Whereas if his opposition was only in something minor, then he does not reach the level of being given this description of being *[...ruined.]*

Overall, we should see this general description by the author, may Allaah have mercy upon him, as an example or reflection of his strength and vigor, and in light of his severity against the people of innovation in Islaam, the strength of his efforts to defend the truth, and his diligence in warning from the people of innovation. However a further explanation of this mentioned description is required.

There can be situations where an individual opposes what is correct within some of the fiqh issues of the practical implementation of the Sunnah. By this meaning issues such as the number of times that one raises your hands in the ritual prayer or what is correct regarding the short sitting after one's prostrations but done before standing up again in the ritual prayer, and other issues from those matters in which there is clear differing regarding them. The one who differed in these specific types of issues does not merit having this description applied even if he is incorrect. As in some cases someone could oppose what is considered correct from the authentic Sunnah and yet not merit being described with this description of being *[...ruined]*. But if someone opposes the truth in a clear matter in which their opposition in openly practicing it negatively influences others, then this person is misguided and misguiding others, and in this case this description as ruined is clearly valid and applied.

Overall, it is an obligation upon the individual that he warn against innovation in the religion. that he warn against the people of innovation, and the people of misguidance. This is so that the people do not slip or fall into that innovation which would lead them to becoming ruined.

Course Appendix 2:
Concise Descriptions Of Twenty Seven Modern & Historical Sects/Groups/Religions/Ideologies of Misguidance

The following brief descriptions and definitions were mentioned by Sheikh Zayd Ibn Muhammad al-Madkhalee, may Allaah have mercy upon him, as narrated on page 128 the book 'al-Ajweebah al-Athareeyah'

In the name of Allaah, the Most Gracious, the Most Merciful

1. **al-Wathaneeyah:** Pagans whose beliefs and practices manifest themselves in the worship of something other than Allaah, or who worship aspects of His natural creation alongside His worship. This is the association of others with Allaah in worship that Allaah does not forgive.

2. **al-Yahoodeeyah & an-Nasraaneeyah** -Jews and Christians, from among them are people from the Christians, who believe in the Trinity, those regarding whom Allaah said: *Surely, disbelievers are those who said: "Allaah is the third of the three (in a Trinity)....*-(Surah Al-Ma'idah:73)

3. **al-Hulooleeyah:** Those who believe that Allaah is present in every place. Yet Allaah, the High and Mighty is exalted and far above their claim.

4. **al-Itihaadeyyah:** Those who claim that there is an all encompassing unity of all things, meaning there is no difference between the Creator and His creation. Just as one of the misguided, may Allaah destroy him, said:

> *There is not a dog nor a pig*
>   *yet it is one with our Allaah,*
>
> *and there is no Allaah except He*
>   *is one with the Monk in his monastery.*

5. **al-Jahmeeyah:** Those from that sect who deny any that there is any true meaning or reality to Allaah's names and attributes. They deny what is narrated directly within the texts of the Qur'aan and Sunnah.

6. **al-Mashabehah:** Those who attribute characteristics and attributes of the single Creator to the creation, such as the Christians. Those who attribute characteristics of the creation to the creator from those sects that have proceeded upon innovation within the boundaries of Islaam. These sects affirm characteristics which are specific to the creation in its weak and deficient nature for the Creator.

7. **al-Qadareeyah:** Those from that sect who deny Allaah's decree. They say Allaah did not create good and evil, and some of them assert that Allaah created good but He did not create evil.

8. **al-Jabareeyah:** Those from that sect who state that human beings are compelled when they commit evil actions, just as a tree is compelled to bend due to the force of a strong wind against it.

9. **al-Murji'ah:** A sect of which there are of different groupings and levels. From them are those that falsely say when someone has faith or *emaan* then no sins or transgressions harm or reduce that faith, just as they say for the one upon disbelief that he is not benefited by any action of obedience. From them is a group that says *emaan* or faith is only a comprehension or understanding that one holds in his heart. From them are those that say *emaan* or faith is only a statement that you pronounce with your tongue. And from them is a group that removes actions from the boundaries of *emaan* or faith, or considers actions not an essential required part of *emaan* or faith.

10. **al-Mu'tazilah:** Those from that sect who assert that the Qur'aan is a created thing. They also claim that those Muslims who worship Allaah alone yet commit sins and transgressions may remain in Hellfire forever if they have not repented for the transgressions they committed before dying.

11. **al-Khawaarij:** Those from that sect who are upon the methodology of declaring people as disbelievers, outside of the evidenced guidelines of the Sharee'ah. They assert that anyone who commits a major sin or transgression even if they are from those who worship Allaah from the Muslims, then they have committed an act of disbelief in Islaam and that the ruling of such a person is that they will remain in the Hellfire forever if they die without repenting from that.

12. **al-Ashaa'areeyah, al-Kullabeeyah, & al-Maaturedeyyah:** Those from those sects who are people who have opposed the well-known scholars of the Sunnah and the Jamaa'ah in the area of the proper understanding of Allaah's names and attributes, and in the area of faith and what it is comprised of, as well as other areas of Sharee'ah knowledge.

13. **ar-Raafidhah:** Those from that sect who have opposed the guided Muslims in every area of their revealed religion both generally and specifically.

14. **as-Sufeeyah:** Those among whom there are ones who are extreme in their misguidance and innovation and other Sufees who below that in their opposition to what is correct from the Book and the Sunnah. Those that are extreme from amongst them affirm the concept of the unity of the Creator with His creation. Meaning by this that there is no distinction between the Creator and what is created. Such extremists are those who follow the thoughts and concepts of Ibn Arabee, Ibn Saba'een, and other astray individuals.

15. **al-Mufawwidhah:** They are those who state that knowledge of the actual meaning of the attributes of Allaah are delegated to or only known to Allaah. Regarding this group of people Ibn Taymeeyah, may Allaah have mercy upon him said, *"This is the most evil type of atheism."*

16. **al-Waaqafeeyah:** Those who falsely state: We do not say about the Qur'aan that is it created nor do we say that it is not created, we abstain from taking a position.

17. **al-Baataneeyah:** These are people who are from those who are astray disbelievers, as they do not believe in the resurrection or that we will be recompensed for our deeds good or bad (due to their claiming that all revealed texts have a second symbolical true meaning as opposed to the apparent meaning of a verse or hadeeth).

18. **al-Qaraametah:** This is a specific sect is one of the branches al-Baataneeyah

19. **al-'Almaaneeyah:** Secularists, those who believe and advocate that religion should be separated from our lives. They consider religious practice as something which misguides and deludes humanity.

20. **al-Maasooneeyah:** Freemasonry, it is the worst group of those destructive fraternal membership organized associations that are used to serve the interests of the Jewish state and Zionists.

21. **al-Wujoodeeyah-** Existentialism is an philosophical thought which denies the existence of a Lord and Creator, just as it also rejects the sending of infallible messengers and the Resurrection leading to humanity's reckoning and judgement.

22. **al-Babeeyah:** Baabism is a religious movement that disbelieves in everything which the Messenger of Allaah, may the praise and salutations of Allaah be upon him, brought.[1]

23. **al-Qaadeyaneeyah:** This is a religious movement founded by Ghulam Ahmad, a person of disbelief and *zanadeeqah*, meaning from those misguided disbelievers who despite professing Islaam stand upon significant innovation which is at the level of major disbelief in Islaam.

24. **al-Qawmeeyah:** Nationalism an ideology which was found in the period before the coming of Islaam among Arabs. They do not differentiate between those who believe and those who disbelieve in terms of whom they ally with and support.

25. **ar-Raasmaleeyah:** Capitalism: it is an economic ideology that disregards the guidance of the religion of Islaam, and gives no importance to that threat of punishment for one's wrong beliefs and actions that Allaah has informed us of.

26. **al-Ishtiraakeyyah:** Socialism, an economic ideology that rejects the guidance of the Book of Allaah and the Sunnah, and judges and determines what is beneficial and good according to the people desires.

27. **al-Hadaathah:** Modernism is a philosophical movement. The worst of its malignant misguidance is the rejection of the fundamental beliefs of Islaam. They strive to distort the truth of Islaam, deceiving the people so as to convince them to abandon the religion of Islaam.

---

[1] Sheikh Ibn Baaz, may Allaah have mercy upon him, discussing the history of this invented religion of Baabism said *"This sect believes that "The Gate" refers to the ignorant Iranian individual who practiced Sufism named 'Ali Muhammad Rida al-Shiraazi....Their ultimate view was that the "Baab" or Gate was greater and higher in status than all the Messengers, and that what was revealed to him of religion was more complete and more perfect than any previous revelation or religion."* - Majmu' Fataawa as-Sheikh 'Abd al-'Azeez ibn 'Abd-Allaah ibn Baaz, vol. 13- page 169

Course Appendix 3:
Warning Away From The One Upon Innovation Even If He Does Good Works

Sheikh Muhammad Ibn Saaleh al-'Utheimeen, may Allaah have mercy upon, was asked,[1]

Question: There is a man who follows a specific Sufee order from the different paths or orders of the Sufees, he believes Sufism is a valid form of Islaam and engages in some of the innovated practices related to this. However, he is also a person who assists and helps in establishing some beneficial efforts for the general Muslims. So for example, if this man's innovated practices are openly criticized and spoken about and this spreads between the people, he will then stop assisting some of the people engaged in good works and stop helping people involved in some beneficial endeavors. So what is your position about what should be done in this situation?

Answer: Is this person someone who influences others in what he calls people towards?

Questioner: Yes, sheikh, he invites to the innovated practices he is upon.

Sheikh: So in this case which is considered more significant or important, the poverty of the people who are being helped or the danger of the misguidance that he stands upon?

Questioner: That misguidance he is upon.

Sheikh: Yes, the misguidance is more important to consider. As such, if this individual calls to his innovation and is someone who has an influence upon people, it is obligatory to warn the people from him. Even if he stops doing the good he was previously doing, then he is the one choosing to make that good impermissible for himself. But as for the case where he might be left to misguide the people, meaning that his acts of innovation are not exposed, just so that people can keep acquiring a dirham or two from what he possess, then this is not possible to accept at all.

---

[1] Open Door Gatherings: No. 266, Question 7

He was also asked,[2]

Question: Esteemed sheikh, if there is a person regarding whom there have been made a number of evidenced knowledge based observations, whether they are in the area of beliefs or regarding other significant issues, yet in addition to these issues, he possesses significant good. As perhaps he is an eloquent writer, or he has a distinguished position with people, or we see that he has some capabilities in calling to good that no one else has, then what are the guidelines of working with him and benefiting from him in this situation?

Answer: If he is someone who openly shows and engages in some matter of innovation, then it is not proper for someone to work with him nor to show any hesitation and indecision regarding being clear about him. Because even if the first person is not affected and influenced by this criticized person, yet others will still be deceived by him. By this we mean that, due to this first person continuing to work with him the general people would then be fooled into falsely believing that what this innovator stands upon is the truth and is acceptable.

What is necessary is that a person not be someone who wavers and vacillates regarding the people of innovation in the religion, whether this is due to benefiting from them financially or in some matters of knowledge, due to what this wavering inevitably leads to for other people in their being deceived and misled by such individuals.

It Should Be Seen As The Giving Of Advice For The Sake Of Allaah

Question: Regarding speaking about the misguidance of people of innovation, for instance that someone may say, "These people misinterpret both the verses of the Qur'aan and hadeeth narrations." or that people say, "These individuals do such and such of blameworthy actions." are these kinds of statements considered impermissible backbiting if it is discussed between people who were seeking knowledge of Islaam? [3]

Answer: As for statements and discussions regarding the people of innovation and what they have of incorrect concepts, or aspects of their methodology which aren't sound, then this is from the giving of advice and is not to be considered impermissible backbiting. Rather it should be seen as the giving of advice for the sake of Allaah, His Book, His Messenger and to the Muslims.

---

[2] Open Door Gatherings No. 58 Question 10
[3] Open Door Gatherings Number 120. Question 8

Such that if we see someone who is an innovator who is spreading his innovated belief or practice, then it is upon us to clarify and make clear that he is an innovator in the religion of Islaam, so that the people are protected from being harmed by his evil. If we see an individual who has ideas and concepts that contradict what the early generations of Muslims proceeded upon, then it is upon us to explain and clarify these issues. In order that the Muslims generally are not deceived by that.

In addition, if we see an individual who is proceeding on a specific methodology that will lead to harmful consequences for the Muslims, then it is upon us to explain and clarify this. Again, this is done so the people are protected from that individual's evil. This is something undertaken from the direction of offering advice for the sake of Allaah and His Messenger and to the leaders of the Muslims as well as their general people.

Moreover, this should be the case whether those statements regarding the people who have innovated in Islaam are put forth between students or spread in other more general settings. It is not considered impermissible backbiting. As long as it is the case that we continue to fear the spreading of this innovation, or these false concepts, or the possible further spreading of this incorrect methodology which conflicts and opposes the methodology of the first three generations, then it remains an obligation upon us to explain this in order that the people are not deceived by these matters.

FROM THE CORRUPTING EFFECTS OF INNOVATING MATTERS WITHIN ISLAAM

Sheikh Muhammad ibn Saaleh al-Utheimeen, may Allaah have mercy upon him, said, [4]

"Any individual who brings forth innovation in the religion, then we say to him, "certainly you have fallen into transgression and active wrongdoing which the Messenger of Allaah upon him be Allaah's praise and salutations, warned against in his statement *{Be warned against newly invented matters. As every newly invented matter is a religious innovation, and every religious innovation is misguidance.}* [5]

The following are some of the significant aspects of corruption from the corrupting effects of innovation in the religion. Firstly, it is a type of associating others in the worship of Allaah alone. Just as was mentioned by Allaah the Blessed and the Most High, ❮ *Or have they partners with Allaah (false gods), who have instituted for them a religion which Allaah has not allowed.* ❯ –(Surah Ash-Shuraa:21)

---

[4] Open Door Gatherings Number 131, Question 5
[5] As narrated by Imaam Ahmad in his Musnad, Abu Dawood in his Sunan, and which Sheikh al-Albaanee has ruled is authentic.

It is not hidden from anyone that major association of others with Allaah in worship is something which is not forgiven. As Allaah, the Most High, says, ❴*Verily, Allaah forgives not that partners should be set up with him in worship, but He forgives except that (anything else) to whom He pleases...*❵-(Surah An-Nisa':48). What is also outwardly apparent from this noble verse is that associating others with Allaah is not forgiven even if it is minor.

From the corrupting effects of innovation in the religion is that in practicing innovation a barrier or obstacle is put up to your preceding upon the true path of Allaah. This is because an individual becomes occupied with that innovation and turns away from true authentic confirmed forms of worship. Know that no people innovate an innovation in the religion except that they lose what is equivalent to, or similar to it, from practices of the authentic Sunnah, or even a greater amount of what was truly from the Sunnah may be lost due to adopting that innovation.

From the corrupting effects of innovation in the religion, is that it understandably requires subtly maligning the Messenger of Allaah , may Allaah's praise and salutations be upon him. This is undoubtedly the case, as innovating requires believing that the Messenger of Allaah, may the praise and salutations of Allaah be upon him, either did not transmit and teach part of the guidance which he was sent with or that he was in fact ignorant and unaware of something which should be considered from the guidance of Islaam. A clear sign of the falseness of this claim is that regarding any new innovative belief or practice being attributed to Islaam, if we, for example, search for it in the texts of Qur'aan and the Sunnah but we do not find it, then either the Messenger of Allaah upon him be Allaah's praise and salutations, was unaware or ignorant of this matter which they consider part of Islaam, and this itself is speaking against the Messenger and talking badly about him, or it is being asserted that he was actually aware of this new belief or practice but chose not to convey to the people! This is also considered speaking against him and maligning him, because the one who believes this in fact claims that the Prophet did not convey to the humanity some part of Islaam that was revealed to him.

From the corrupting effects of innovation in the religion, is that it undoubtedly requires negating the statement of Allaah , the Most High, where he stated, ❴*..This day, I have perfected your religion for you, completed My Favor upon you, and have chosen for you Islaam as your religion.*❵-(Surah Al-Ma'idah: 3) The belief of one who is innovating a new belief or practice into Islaam necessitates the perspective that the religion of Islaam is not truly complete since we did not find this innovation in the religion of Allaah previously. Therefore, if it is truly part of the religion of Allaah as claimed by the innovator, but it is not found in the sources of the religion, then the religion, as they understand, cannot be something which is complete and perfect. This is a major significant contradiction to the statement of Allaah , the Most High ❴*...This day, I have perfected your religion for you,...*❵-(Surah Al-Ma'idah: 3)

From the corrupting effects of innovation in the religion is that the one who innovates in the religion places himself in a similar position as a messenger who was actually sent by Allaah, as it is not possible for anyone to legislate to the creation what will truly bring them closer to Allaah, the Most High, except the one who Allaah, the Most Glorified and the Most Exalted, Himself has sent with that revealed guidance. Yet there are no prophets sent with such guidance after Muhammad, may Allaah's praise and salutation be upon him and his family.

For this reason the one who innovates in the religion it is as if he is saying that he is bringing something legislated to the people which will bring them closer to Allaah, and this specifically asserts that he is someone who shares with the Messenger of Allaah, may Allaah's praise and salutations be upon him, the actual role of conveying Allaah's guidance, which they did not know before, to humanity!

From the corrupting effects of innovation in the religion, is the speaking about Allaah without true knowledge. Doing so is completely forbidden by the total consensus of all the Muslims throughout the ages. Allaah says the Blessed and the Most High, says, ❞ *Say (Oh Muhammad): "But the things that my Lord has indeed forbidden are great evil sins, every kind of unlawful sexual intercourse, whether committed openly or secretly, sins of all kinds, unrighteous oppression, joining partners in worship with Allaah for which He has given no authority, and saying things about Allaah of which you have no knowledge.*❞-(Surah Al-A'raf:33)

And there are certainly other corrupting effects of innovating in the religion which if someone was to closely examine them he would find that they add to these mentioned harmful effects significantly, but we have held ourselves to what has been mentioned here."

APPENDIX 3

Course Appendix 4:
99 Characteristics Of Various Misguided Groups

The following complete appendix is taken from an appendix to the small work "The Methodology of the People of the Sunnah and Adherence to the Jama'ah in Calling to Allaah." by 'Abdullah Ibn Muhammad Ibn Saaleh al-Ma'taar[1] with an introduction by the esteemed guiding scholar Sheikh Saaleh Ibn Fauzaan al-Fauzaan, may Allaah preserve him.

As is well-known, a matter is not understood except by comprehending that which opposes it. And in light of the fact of what we have presented of some of the characteristics of those who follow the first three generations of Muslims, the Salafees, then it is of some importance that we indicate some of the characteristics of those who oppose them in order to warn against these characteristics. Just as the well-known saying: through their opposites, matters become clear and understood.

Certainly Hudhaifah ibn al-Yamaan, may Allaah be pleased with him, would ask the Messenger of Allaah, may the praise and salutations of Allaah be upon him, about evil situations fearing that he would fall into them. For this reason we present in what follows some of the characteristics of the misguided groups upon which they have developed a methodology of calling and inviting to the religion which opposes the methodology of those who follow the first three generations. Generally they had neglected establishing the correct Islamic beliefs and calling to them and basing one's allegiance to others upon those beliefs. While at the same time these groups and movements have concentrated on issues of ruling and political power, or current societal affairs and situations.

In doing so they have become significant agents working for the spread of innovations and aligning themselves with the people of innovation and placing them in positions of leadership. It has become one of their important priorities to gather and join together significant numbers of people including within those whom they have assembled people who differ significantly, from people of various Sufeeyah paths, people of the sect of the Raafidhah, and those who worship at graves, all together.

So it is clear that among them are those who have become those who love for other than the sake of Allaah, and become those who direct that love towards others despite that they are not the people truly worshiping Allaah alone. From within these groups and movements there are those who attack the scholars who adhere to the way of the Salaf, accusing them of being those who only curry favor from the rulers, and accusing the scholars of being those who only have a ritualistic or simplistic understanding of the religion.

---

[1] Published by Dar Ibn Jawzee, Cairo 1425

They claim these scholars have been deceived regarding the affair of the Muslim rulers, and they accuse them of having a lack of understanding of the current situation of the Muslims, and a failure to properly grasp the overall situations regarding nations and countries. They claim that the scholars are ignorant of the plans of the enemies of Islaam and the secularists. For this reason they do not refer to them, nor take any important rulings related to the Muslim nation from them but only refer to them for rulings regarding matters such as ritual purification, women's menses, by claiming that these Salafee scholars do not understand the larger affairs which are going on around them. And we seek refuge in Allaah from this tremendous slander and false accusation.

At the same time they themselves instigate and provoke the governments against those who call to the way of the Salaf, the first three generations, and chose to engage in economic strikes and political demonstrations, making unlawful actions permissible under the claim of seeking an overall better condition for the Muslims. Yet they chose to remain silent about those wrongdoings found within their own parties and groups as well as those errors found in the statements of their leaders, while accusing the people who call to the worship of Allaah alone as a priority, of being severe and harsh. From those within these groups, parties, and movements are those who criticize the early books of knowledge by labeling them as "weak" and "feeble". Yet they themselves are those who worship their intellects, their invented concepts, and their personal desires.

What follows are summarized characteristics related to one of more of these modern day groups, parties, and movements that call themselves "Islamic":

1. Among these groups are those who alter and change the meaning of the statement "*La ilaah illa Allaah*" from meaning the general comprehensive subservience to Allaah, the Most High, and the required negation and turning away from everything which is worshiped other than Him, to: simply meaning affirming his Lordship as the Creator and Sustainer. Thus they disregard and neglect both "*Tawheed al-Uluheeyah*" or the affirmation that Allaah alone is to be worshiped and obeyed, and "*Tawheed al-Asma'a wa Sifaat*" or the affirmation of understanding Allaah's names and attributes just as Allaah and His Messenger conveyed and explained them.

2. Among these groups are those who give significant importance to the societal and cultural affairs and situations in the Muslim countries, or what they have named "*Fiqh al-Waaqi'a*" "or the "understanding current affairs". They go to extremes and exaggerate the importance of this while lacking insight, not placing it in its appropriate restricted position and status. In their contrived comprehension of this "essential knowledge" they have become arrogant towards the established scholars who stand upon the Sunnah, despite the fact that they themselves are the most ignorant people in relation to comprehensive understanding of the sciences and knowledge of the Sharee'ah, true complete knowledge of the current situation of the Muslims, and current Islamic thought and discourse. They themselves do not give importance to cultivating the correct fundamental beliefs, nor gaining knowledge, nor utilizing specific evidences directly taken from the Book of Allaah, the Sunnah of the Messenger of Allaah, may the praise and salutations of Allaah be upon him, and the established Consensus of the Muslims. They wrongly explain having knowledge of current affairs as merely being aware of news and information related to societal and governmental issues, but fail to properly place and view this information in light of the guidance and evidences of the Sharee'ah.

3. Among these groups are those who occupy themselves within efforts to gain political power, and so expose themselves to harm and injuries without being truly concerned with guiding the people to that sound way to the true methodology of correct beliefs and behavior and seeking understanding of the evidences regarding matters in Islaam.

4. Among these groups are those who claim that their priority is rectifying the corrupt Muslim rulers, and speaking about their errors and transgressions, despite the fact that they do not place the same importance upon rectifying the people who are ruled in those same Muslim lands and cultivating them upon Islaam. They are also those whose misguided position towards the Muslim rulers present today is that they are all disbelievers without any exception, failing to distinguish in a detailed manner between this nation and that nation. They see no difference between the land of Saudi Arabia and other nations but hold in their view that all of these governments are only agents of the West and those who secretly conspire against Islaam. Any government who puts forth any action or endeavor which includes something of giving victory to Islaam then they claim this is only an act of hypocrisy and part of the plotting against the Muslims. The reason for this perspective is because they are students of, and had been raised upon works of, speculative thought and ideas of "Islamic" thinkers.

Their basic position is that of having an evil suspicion of all the rulers generally, while refusing to consider the outward actions of the rulers as valid, despite this being the methodology of the people of the Sunnah. And some of them hold that the only acceptable way is to overthrow the rulers, not to work towards their rectification. This is because as a false fundamental premise they do not believe in the validity of the oath of allegiance given to the Muslim ruler. For they wrongly believe that implementing any man-made laws, even partially to any degree, within a Muslim nation is major disbelief which takes you outside of Islam. This is simply because they have turned away from the established guidelines of the scholars regarding establishing what is disbelief in Islaam.

Similarly they wrongly view that any cooperation with the disbelievers, even in those matters which do not consist of disbelief as held by the people of the Sunnah, is still major disbelief which takes one outside of Islaam. They also hold that revolting against the unjust ruler is permissible even when it is not clearly established that he has committed open clear disbelief- if there is, as they claim, a possible benefit for the Muslims in doing so. As such they have reached a level of severe extremism in this issue. And we ask Allaah for health and well-being.

5. Among these groups are those who preoccupy themselves by requesting solely from the governments in Muslim lands that they implement the Islamic system and Sharee'ah without also seeking that from the members of that society who are individually distant from many aspects of Islaam in belief and practice. This call has instigated the rulers against some of the callers to Islaam and been the cause of their harassment, imprisonment, and even killing. Rather, what they should have done is given priority and importance to the cultivation and education of the individuals and the guidance of society in general, before anything else, along with the giving advice to the rulers with wisdom and sound admonitions.

6. Among these groups are those who openly swear and take an oath within the assemblies of Parliament to protect and preserve the full constitution, which they themselves believe has that within it which opposes the Sharee'ah of Allaah, while refusing to openly indicate and clarify those matters which oppose the guidance of Islaam.

7. Among these groups are those who sit and cooperate in those governmental bodies which legislate matters for the people according to other than that which Allaah revealed, without openly disapproving or speaking out against that opposition.

8. Among these groups are those whose actions have been the cause for many of the sincere Muslims to be thrown into prison and expelled from their homes, due to what those individuals undertook which lacked both insight and wisdom. Certainly there were no beneficial results for the Muslims from what they involved themselves in, only tremendous hardship and difficulty.

9. Among these groups are those who take a very lax and weak position towards innovation in the religion, superstitious practices, and acts of associating others with Allaah due to the claimed need to unite the voices and gather the Muslims in a single rank, or due to some other false pretext and claim. This occurs to such a degree that they have reached the state where they will even intentionally choose someone as their general leader from those people who engage in superstitious practices or perform sinful acts of associating others with Allaah.

10. Among these groups are those who implement the rule or false principle **"We cooperate with each other in that which we agree upon and we excuse each other regarding those matters in which we differ."** Rather what is obligatory in regards to the one who differs with a matter from the Sharee'ah, is that he is advised and then afterwards if he does not accept the evidenced truth then he is boycotted and enmity is shown towards him once the proof is established against him in his clear opposition to any fundamental or principle from the fundamentals and principles of Islaam.

11. Those who align themselves with those rulers who the scholars have established are indeed disbelievers and choose to aid and support them.

12. Among these groups are those who do not attach any importance to the presence of practices of associating others with Allaah, tombs which are revered, dangerous innovations, and graves which are worshiped within their lands. They focus on issues of lesser importance, while their lands drown in such innovated ways of worship, and in false acts of associating others with Allaah through supplicating to the dead, and other misguided acts.

13. Among these groups are those who do not give needed priority in what they write within their books or magazines, nor what they focus upon in conferences they hold, to taking the offensive in combating innovations in the religion and innovators, as well as opposing practices of associating others with Allaah and worship and those who engage in them. Among the individuals in these groups and movements, there is not seen those who establish any foundations for organizations with the essential priority of establishing sound beliefs among the people, meaning the beliefs of the people of the Sunnah and adherence to the Jama'ah. Likewise, within the schools they control and manage, they do not teach from the books of the first generations which establish the correct authentic belief.

14. Among these groups are those who engage in wasting money, excessive talking, exaggeration in speech and what is put out to the media advocating only their methodology and their calling to Allaah. They give greater importance to their outward image than informing people of the truth, and more emphasis on propaganda rather than actual beneficial endeavors. Similarly their general focus is more on conferences, awards, and fundraising drives, and outward demonstrations, than on actually establishing schools, opening masjids, and assisting those who call to the truth.

15. Among these groups are those who form nationalistic political alliances of cooperation with those who are disbelievers in their own countries, and yet they do not rebuke and censure each other for making pacts with those with no connection to Islaam.

16. Among these groups are those who falsely suppose that they have the ability to unite the Muslim people together in some way other than the only true way which is establishing Muslim unity upon the pure correct beliefs of Islaam, and their actions and efforts reflect and stand in accord with this misconception.

17. Among these groups are those who attack the people engaged in political efforts in their lands but do not likewise attack the innovating Sufee groups, nor the people who worship at graves and engage in impermissible superstitious practices. This negligence enables innovations to increase in their lands and firmly take root among the people.

18. Among these groups are those who give little importance to the study of hadeeth sciences and its transmitted knowledge, while focusing upon various intellectual concepts, developed individual views, and philosophical perspectives.

19. Among these groups are those who excessively praise those individuals who are connected to their groups and parties and have extreme support of them, while at the same time defaming and speaking against anyone who criticizes these same leaders and party figureheads. They refuse to recognize their right and position as scholars, that they have due to their acknowledged knowledge and piety. This is especially true if the scholar who criticized one of them is a scholar from those who adhere to the methodology of the Salaf.

20. Among these groups are those who wrongly support the leaders of their groups, organizations, or parties who are known to have beliefs which are clearly deviated from the correct beliefs . Meaning individuals such as those who hold the beliefs of the Ashaarees, the Matureedees, the beliefs of innovators generally, or those who associate others with Allaah in acts of worship and consider it permissible to supplicate to the dead and seek intercession through them.

21. Among these groups are those who discuss the deceptive plots of Shaytaan and warn against them, yet also make the plots and plans of the Eastern and Western nations against the Muslims as something greater than the general deceptive plots of Shaytaan, the accursed the envious.

22. Among these groups are those who incite the impressionable common Muslims by advocating the path of demonstrations, protests, political activities, and other worthless and ineffective "revolutionary" methods that only cause trials. They delude and misguide them without bringing them any result other than individuals being thrown in prison, the people of goodness rounded up together, insulted and treated badly, and the governments oppressing them and others needlessly.

23. Among these groups are those who concentrate within their Friday sermons upon imagined inflammatory issues which incite people, without basing their statements upon sound evidences from the Sharee'ah as found within the Book of Allaah and the authentic Sunnah.

24. Among these groups are those whose methodology is to proceed upon the way of forming party and group based alliances and politically based confederations. They wrongly accept the method of sitting in consultative assemblies with those who are known enemies of the call to purify misconceptions in the Muslims fundamental beliefs and opponents of those focusing on calling Muslims to worship of Allaah alone without partners.

25. Among these groups are those who attack and assault the well known scholars of Islaam and work to defame the leading people of knowledge from amongst the Muslims. They seek to harm the followers of the way of the Salaf, those who adhere to hadeeth narrations, those who give importance to the correct beliefs and to explaining the religion upon evidences.

26. Among these groups are individuals who have a stronger allegiance to the leaders of their groups and organizations than their allegiance to the Messenger of Allaah, may the praise and salutations of Allaah be upon him, and towards the notable scholars of the esteemed first generations.

27. Among these groups are those who innovate matters in their efforts of calling to Allaah, standing upon a methodology which was not known in the time of the Messenger, may the praise and salutations of Allaah be upon him, nor was it known during the time of the rightly guided Khaleefahs who succeeded him.

28. Among these groups are those who wrongly make certain prohibited practices acceptable and permissible either in the name of achieving the greater good or by claiming necessity or by claiming that it is a matter which is subject to independent scholastic reasoning and assessment. Yet in reality these practices do not actually enter into any of these legitimate Sharee'ah causes or justifications.

29. Among these groups are those who refuse to censure and refute the mistakes of those within their organizations and groups even when these mistakes reach the level of opposing the authentic narrations of the Messenger of Allaah, may the praise and salutations of Allaah be upon him, or conflicting with the statements of the people of knowledge from the first three generations.

30. Among these groups are those who always seek and vigorously search for some excuse for an error for those individuals within their organizations and groups, even if their mistake is a significant and considerable one which it is not possible to excuse. But when someone from outside of their organization or group makes the same mistake, they contradictorily strive to raise the entire world and its important people up against him because of it.

31. Among these groups are those who speak and engage themselves with the statements of the leaders of their organizations and groups more than they concern themselves and engage themselves with the statements of the Messenger of Allaah, may praise and salutations of Allaah be upon him, or the statements of the companions of the Messenger, may Allaah be pleased with them all, and the statements of those scholars of this Ummah who adhere to the way of the first generations of believers.

32. Among these groups are those who falsely accuse the people who adhere to the Sunnah with extremism, fanatical adherence, radicalism, and fanaticism, while at the same time they are those who have fallen into haphazardly declaring the Muslims disbelievers and go to actual extremes in matters, yet they do not criticize or blame themselves.

33. Among these groups are those who falsely claim that the established practice of implementing fiqh principles and the statements of the various scholars throughout the ages in these different matters are unnecessarily rigid pronouncements which do not properly take the changing circumstances of the ages and time into consideration. They describe them as books that are weak and shallow, or as books that mostly discuss issues of women's menses and bleeding, or as superficial works not based on valid understanding of the current situations of the Muslims.

34. Among these groups are those who only submit themselves to the guidance of the Sharee'ah in the various matters of religion when what it calls for stands in agreement with their personal desires, their intellectual assessments, and their logical pronouncements.

35. Among these groups are those who incorrectly call the people to take any possible allowance in Sharee'ah matters rather than being resolutely patient and steadfast with a necessary hardship.

36. Among these groups are those who falsely lead the people to believe that the Salafees are incapable of comprehending the different modern societal conditions, and the new evolving situations and circumstances of our modern age.

37. Among these groups are those who invite the people to study Western ideas and foreign philosophies beneath the claim that the people can benefit from this. However at the same time they nearly abandon the statements of the Messenger of Allaah, may the praise and salutations of Allaah be upon him, and the statements of the scholars from the first three righteous generations. From the causes of this is the presence of the large number of those known as callers amongst the Muslims who possess very little knowledge of the transmitted narrations of the Prophet, and the transmitted statements from the early scholars. Yet these same individuals have become proficient and experts regarding the statements of the Westerners and whatever is related to modern politics which are based upon intellectual foundations coming from Jewish scholars as well as those affiliated with the Masons. And they focus on that Western knowledge by claiming to do so because of the need to understand the current affairs.

38. Among these groups are those who generally legitimize impermissible acts such as lying, spying, and other transgressions allegedly for the overall benefit of efforts to call to Allaah. In fact the often employ invented accusations and disgraced fabrications against those who oppose their methodology.

39. Among these groups are those who encourage the efforts of the Shee'ah, support the Shee'ah ideology and the ideals of the Iranian revolution, and advocate revolution whenever possible against the rulers in Muslim lands at any time they believe this is feasible. Similarly, there are those among these groups who promote those efforts to increase the conceptual closeness between the understanding of Islaam held by the Sunnees and the Shee'ah, as well as interfaith conceptual closeness between the Muslims, Jews, and Christians.

40. Among these groups are those who do not stand clearly upon any firm evidenced position. They are easily deceived by the deceptions of the enemies of Allaah and their fabrications and so they fall into accepting them. Yet they do recant from and abandon these positions when the definitive proof is established to them by other Muslims. So they end up changing their "colors" or positions according to the situation and time. This is because their initial understandings were not based upon correct sound knowledge and Sharee'ah evidences or an unbiased objective perspective established for Allaah's sake alone.

Due to this you will see that in one instance or time they show enmity towards the sect of the Shee'ah, yet inconsistently they contradict this position at another time. For this reason, that they are not based upon correct sound knowledge and Sharee'ah evidences, you see that many of their strongly taken positions do not agree with that which is correct according to Sharee'ah evidences.

41. Among these groups are those who restrict themselves to only enjoining what is good while intentionally neglecting to forbid what is evil or wrongdoing while claiming that the forbidding of wrongdoing will cause separation and division, driving away the people who follow them.

42. Among these groups are those who establish their calls upon only specific matters or issues while neglecting other legitimate matters that may be more important and more significant in Islaam than those issues which they have focused upon and adopted.

43. Among these groups are those who chose to rely upon books which undoubtedly include within them false superstitions, innovations in the religion, and matters related to practices of associating others with Allaah in worship.

44. Among these groups are those that affirm the practice of the Sufees to give the oath of allegiance to the head of their Sufee order or group, as is found among the four major Sufee groups: the Naqshabandeeyah, the Qaadereeyah, the Saharoodeeyah, and the Chisteeyah - as well as among others from the Sufees.

45. Among these groups are those who view the danger of Sufism and general innovations in the religion as being less than the danger of other sins and transgressions.

46. Among these groups are those who believe that the acts of shirk related to personal possessions and belongings are more significant than that shirk related to matters of exaggeration towards the individuals considered close associates of Allaah and turning to the righteous people who have died for assistance.

47. Among these groups are those who invite to the way of acknowledging false miracles performed by the people of Sufeeyah, innovated methods of reaching different levels of spiritual consciousness and spiritual realizations, as well as affirming their claims of possessing knowledge of some of the hidden matters.

48. Among these groups are those individuals who offer weak efforts for those issues which are essential to the methodology of the Salafees, while strongly supporting and giving significant attention to all those matters focused upon by those not following the way of the Salafees. The result of this is that you see them at that time when they discuss those issues essential to the Muslims who follow the way of the Salaf, they unenthusiastically tell the people to proceed slowly and carefully. Yet at other times when they discuss positions of their specific party or group then for this they vigorously put forth moving sermons and eloquent poetry which incites the people with false enthusiasm and deceptions.

49. Among these groups are those who proceed upon a blind biased adherence to the specific historical school of jurisprudence. In the rulings they accept, they fail to give proper consideration of the actual evidences found within the Book of Allaah and the Sunnah. Similarly, regarding the fundaments of the religion, then they do not accept and take on any position except when they find it agrees with the desires and dictates of their specific scholars.

50. Among these groups are those who are callers to the religion and enjoin matters upon the people without insight and correct knowledge. They do not consider anyone from the scholars to truly be callers to the religion except for those whom their group judges as truly pious and devout.

51. Among these groups are those who, in their writings and statements, use fabricated hadeeth narrations and unverified superstitious stories, some who rely upon dreams, individual spiritual insights , and the statements of various scholars of Sufeeyah for determining the Sharee'ah validity of actions and rulings, rather than authentic transmitted knowledge.

52. Among these groups are those who do not censure nor speak against the presence of graves in their various well-known centers of religious activities and masjids.

53. Among these groups are those who distribute garments of hijaab that have talismans and mystical numbers sown upon them which they claim has protective power by connection to the old senile sheikhs of their misguided way.

54. Among these groups are those who rely upon the common people and ignorant to give their call and movement support. They neglect the priority of correct beliefs in terms of knowledge as well of their actions and efforts. So they lack any true power or authority over anyone except for some of the common people and people like this.

55. Among these groups are those who wrongly say regarding the respect shown to well known scholars: Certainly some of the people of knowledge have been given such high position, in terms of the people visiting them and going to them, which has not even been given to the sacred Kaa'ba!

56. Among these groups are those who call the people to generally blind follow others in their religion and do not call them to adhere to the evidences found in the source texts of the Qur'aan and Sunnah.

57. Among these groups are those who innovated a new method and way of sending salutations upon the Messenger of Allaah, may Allaah's praise and salutations be upon him, that is not legislated. Such is found in their saying : [Oh Allaah send Your praise upon our Sayideena (leader) Muhammad from Your oceans of light, from the mines of Your secret mysteries, from the tongues of Your evidences and demonstrations, from the throne of Your Majesty, from in front of Your presence, from that exquisiteness of Your dominion, from the treasures of Your mercy, from the path of Your Sharee'ah, the one made zestful and zealous by Your Oneness, the man who was the heart of existence, the reason for all existence, the master of the notable ones from Your creation, the one who proceeded forth from the light of Your illumination. Oh Messenger of Allaah we ask you for your intercession.]

This is found in the book 'Tableeghee Nisaab', in the section of the merits of Hajj. And on another page in the same work there is found the following two blameworthy lines of poetry about the Prophet:

And when we saw in the return of our beloved one
   his exquisite goodness raised within us such love by his closeness to us
that our restless eyes relished our intercession through him
   such that there is no torment or punishment that we fear

58. Among these groups are those who falsely view some forbidden acts of seeking for wealth and material prosperity through other than Allaah to be equal to those false acts of association of others with Allaah directed to false idols.

59. Among these groups are those who wrongly equate the verses of the Qur'aan that mention going forth physically in Jihaad in the way of Allaah with going out for efforts of da'wah and sleeping overnight in the masjids.

60. Among these groups are those who believe in the legitimacy of going to grave sites for the purpose of asking and supplication.

61. Among these groups are those who have wrongly taken an individual who spoke with the concept of the unity of creation with the creator- as a spiritual and ideological leader and guide for them.

62. Among these groups are those who wrongly restrict the meaning of the Shahaadah the testimony of faith in Islaam, saying "*La ilaha ill Allaah*": to mean only one of the following three things:
   1. That what is intended or important by this is that one has certain belief that there is no Creator and Sustainer of the physical universe other than Allaah.
   2. That what is important is that the one who makes this statement before his death will enter into Jannah simply due to its merit.
   3. In terms of a phrase that you can achieve something by through physically pronouncing it: meaning its repetition in an innovated act of ritual remembrance or dhikr of this noble Shahaadah or a shorted form of it by saying, "*Allaah Allaah Allaah*" or "*Huwa Huwa Huwa*" or a similar variation.

63. Among these groups are those who believe that journeying for Allaah's sake does not require anything other than being present in the Masjid, leaning on one of its pillars with your head bowed in ritual dhikr. They see this as the main activity of value of their "journey" and what gives it its true value.

64. Among these groups are those who request that the followers of their Sufee way read Surah Yaseen at night every Thursday, despite that fact that this is an innovation in the religion and that no one, starting with the Companions of the Prophet, from the first three generations ever did it.

65. Those who request that the followers of their Sufee way take a trip to the graveyard once every week, and while there they repeat the phrase: "Allaah is present, Allaah is the beholder", as is known to be done from some of the leaders and their individual followers among those who connect themselves to some of the misguided groups.

66. Among these groups are those who knowingly pray in masjids which are built upon grave sites, and how many there are of these among the Muslims! And some of these people have lessons in these masjids, and then participate in the distribution of pieces of the material from those gravesites which are present in these masjids as blessings, without them criticizing or rejecting this in any way.

67. Among these groups are those who seek the living intercession of the Messenger of Allaah, may the praise and salutations of Allaah be upon him, in this era even though he has died. As indeed Allaah has said, ❦*Say, to Allaah belongs all intercession.*❦-(Surah az-Zumaar: 44) and the remaining intercession is on the Day of Judgement.

68. Among these groups are those who prefer to seek help by supplication to the Messenger of Allaah, may the praise and salutations of Allaah be upon him, rather than supplicating directly to Allaah. And this act is considered a major sin of associating others in worship with Allaah that many who consider themselves Muslim fall into. Yet it is not only many who consider themselves Muslim, who fall into this misguidance, but many who are considered "leaders" of Islamic groups, movements, and organizations!

69. Among these groups are those who believe in the superstitious claims of Ahmad ar-Rafaa'aee the deluded one who claimed that the Messenger of Allaah, may the praise and salutations of Allaah be upon him, pushed his hand out from his grave so that Ahmad ar-Rafaa'aee could kiss it!!

70. Among these groups are those individuals who regularly go to the places of the Sheikhs in order to request "signs" of direction from them for what choices to make in the smallest aspects of their lives, such as marriage or divorce, continuing one's studies or stopping, seeking such and such employment or leaving it. These people enthusiastically visit and travel to them and kiss their hands, due to the belief among them that these "Sheikhs" have knowledge of the hidden affairs and can benefit the people in their affairs.

71. Among these groups are those who give strong consideration to individuals from the people of innovation in the religion, and they follow the directives of these people against the efforts of the people of tawheed.

72. Among these groups are those who actually fight against the people who oppose the people's acts of associating others with Allaah, falsely attempting to use as their proof for this position the statement of Allaah, the Most High, *And insult not those whom they (disbelievers) worship besides Allaah, lest they insult Allaah wrongfully without knowledge...*-(Surah al-Ana'am: 108)

73. Among these groups are those who spend the entire night until morning reciting Qur'aan in a single sitting specifically due to the death of one of the sheikhs of their group or movement.

74. Those who warn the people against authentic transmitted knowledge and the scholars of that knowledge, as they label Sharee'ah-based knowledge as "the knowledge of outward issues" while referring to knowledge of the beliefs and practices of Sufism as "the knowledge of true realities".

75. Among these groups are those who search within the texts of the Book of Allaah and the Sunnah to find that which agrees with their desires and wishes and they attempt to forget or ignore whatever texts and evidences oppose them. They refuse to submit and comply with any authentic evidence if it differs with their positions or the views of their movement or organization and its leaders.

76. Among these groups are those who refuse to submit to the judgment of Allaah and His Messenger in those matters in which they differ with their Muslim brothers. Yet Allaah, the Most High, says, *But no, by your Lord, they can have no Faith, until they make you (Oh Muhammad) judge in all disputes between them, and find in themselves no resistance against your decisions, and accept them with full submission.*-(Surah an-Nisa': 65)

77. Among these groups are those who, in their efforts of calling to Allaah, place great emphasis on the issue of "*Tawheed ar-Rububeeyah*" or acknowledging that Allaah is the Lord of all the worlds. They speak frequently about how tremendous and powerful a Creator and Lord He is, without indicating the need to submit to Him through worshiping Him alone.

But they do not frequently speak about "*Tawheed al-Uluheeyah*" or affirming and acknowledging that Allaah alone must be worshipped without any partners, nor about "*Tawheed Asmaa wa Sifaat*", or believing in Allaah's names and attributes fully without misinterpretation just as they have been conveyed and explained by Allaah Himself and His Messenger.

78. Among these groups are those that say: These Salafees who are focusing on calling first to the worship of Allaah alone cause separation between the Muslims of different groups and movements. Or they claim that the Salafees have an overly strict adherence to the guidelines of Islaam. And if a single individual from among the Salafees makes a mistake, they aggrandize it trying to make it a significant issue and then attempt to connect or attach his incorrect action or behavior to the call of adhering to the way of the Salaf itself.

79. Among these groups are those who make it a priority simply to gather Muslim people superficially together, and then connect them to a party or group through calling for them to give an oath of allegiance to its leader, without actually establishing their unity upon acceptance and submission to the firm principles and foundations of Islaam!

80. Among these groups are those who base their allegiance and disassociation with other Muslims, as something foremost based upon the Muslim's relationship to their organization, their group, or their movement rather than the practice loving and hating any and all individuals for the sake of Allaah and His religion only, and then interacting with the people on that basis.

81. Among these groups are those specific individuals who have chosen to name themselves and their group "*Jama'at al-Muslimeen*". Yet when their specific beliefs and practices are examined, it is seen that they have differed with the Muslims from the people of the Sunnah in matters with clear fundamentals, and in authentic affirmed beliefs.

82. Among these groups are those who falsely label the Salafees, meaning the people of hadeeth- those who call to adherence to the evidence found within the Book of Allaah and the Sunnah and to reject and turn away from anything which differs with the guidance of these two sources- they label them as "*those without any madhhaab*", or "*Wahaabees*", "*those with hatred towards the Prophet's family*", in order to scare and drive the people away from them.

83. Among these groups are those who do not pay attention to any issues of knowledge except when it comes directly from the people of their organization or group. And they actually blame and speak against those who bring forth those issues of knowledge whenever it comes from other than themselves.

84. Among these groups are those who ally themselves politically and become confederates with the enemies of Allaah in a country to stand against other Muslims during the process of national or parliamentary elections as well as the other times, This is due to their fear of the emergence and growing prominence in the land of any Muslims other than the members from their specific group or party.

85. Among these groups are those who work to defame and tarnish the reputations of those individuals striving to spread the correct Salafee methodology amongst the Muslims.

86. Among these groups are those who believe in the false principle that "the ends justify the means."

87. Among these groups are those who show enmity and scheme against anyone who does not work with their organization or group. They defame and slander everyone who opposes them and they falsely legitimize attacking both their honor and reputation.

88. Among these groups are those who give importance to their outward appearance among the people without truly considering actual beneficial results as judged by Islaam, and give importance to having conferences without focusing on the people implementing the advices of the scholars.

89. Among these groups are those who claim to follow the Qur'aan only. These are the individuals who separate between the Qur'aan and the Sunnah, saying we accept and work with that which is found in the Qur'aan but not that which is found in the Sunnah.

90. Among these groups are those who accept the use of authentic singularly transmitted narrations in the area of religious rulings, but reject accepting those same authentic narrations in the area of beliefs, falsely restricting that to that class of authentic narrations with a high number of routes of transmission.

91. Among these groups are those who deny those future matters clearly affirmed in the Book and the Sunnah such as the attributes of Allaah, matters of the unseen, the punishment of Hellfire, the lesser and greater signs of the Day of judgment: such as the decent of 'Isaa, the Beast of the earth, and the sun rising from the direction of the west. Similarly those individuals who deny those hadeeth narrations which are transmitted authentically about Allaah which are understood in a manner that befits His majesty and transcendence, such as the authentic narrations describing Allaah's descending in the last third of the night, or that He stretches out His hand in the night, or that the hearts of the worshippers are between His two fingers, that He laughs, and other authentic narrations which are affirmed and correct, but understood in a manner befitting Allaah's transcendence above creation.

92. Among these groups are those that attribute infallibility to someone other than the Messenger of Allaah, may the praise and salutations of Allaah be upon him, such as their close associates and supporters, ideological guides, or leaders of their way, and in doing so they have made them partners receiving worship other than Allaah.

93. Among these groups are those who instigate and agitate the people against the rulers and the scholars, either through mocking them or speaking against them in general sermons. Also, there are those who attempt to pit one scholar and his statements against another scholar and his statements, dividing up the young to stand upon the foundations of separate and different parties and affiliations. These separations and divisions into groups is a matter whose misguidance is based in the historical period of ignorance before the coming of Islaam. They generally exaggerate the importance of political analysis, and what they have named knowledge of current affairs, and focus on matters that have many claims and outwards calls but few if any real results.

94. Among these groups are those who go beyond the proper bounds of the true Sharee'ah position with the Messenger of Allaah, and show extremism in relation to the Prophet, may the praise and salutations of Allaah be upon him. Yet on one hand they transgress and exaggerate and make him a partner to Allaah, the Most High, while on the other hand they openly reject and turn away from authentic commandments coming from Prophet that are for every Muslim, and do not actually adhere closely to his guidance and his general way.

95. Among these groups are those who bring into the religion of Islam that which is not based in revealed guidance. They seek to become closer to Allaah, as they claim, through these various acts of innovation and superstitious practices which Allaah has not sent down any authority for them doing.

96. Among these groups are those who wrongly turn away from permissible aspects of worldly life found in the Sunnah without a proper Sharee'ah reason, and they encourage the people to love the living of a life of excessive abjectness, unnecessary lowliness, and undue meekness.

97. Among these groups are those who wrongly refuse to use the permissible modern technical means in efforts of calling to Allaah.

98. Among these groups are those individuals who have been tricked and deceived into the misconception that the Salafees hate the Messenger of Allaah, may the praise and salutations of Allaah be upon him. This is despite the fact that the Salafees are those who adhere to and follow him truly and with a true and sincere love of him, and are the ones who follow his Sunnah and way, and the guidance sent to him and his revealed methodology.

The Salafees sacrifice themselves, their wealth, and their time for the sake of supporting the guidance given to the Prophet. They are the ones that hold that loving the Messenger of Allaah comes before loving oneself, one's family, one's wealth, and one's parents. They are the ones who hold that it is a condition for the correctness of one's ritual prayers that the one praying send salutations upon the Prophet may the praise and salutations of Allaah be upon him, and that he was the best of the creation, the noblest of creation, the purest of creation, and the one from creation who had the most fear of Allaah. May the praise and salutations of Allaah be upon him, his household, and all those who follow his guidance until the Day of Judgment.

99. Among these groups are those who gather huge sums of money from Muslims and give them to the people of innovation in the religion and those who are enemies of those Muslims who call to the way of the first three generations. They, at times, knowingly make it impermissible to give to our Muslim brothers from amongst the Salafees around the world. Or, at times, they give wealth to the people of innovation and deviance in the religion, while at the same time giving wealth to the Salafees.

This is done with the excuse of seeking to unite the Muslims or another excuse from the false excuses which they use in those efforts they undertake. This only results in the strengthening of those who oppose the Muslims who proceed upon the path of the Salaf as-Saaleh, the first three generations of Islaam.

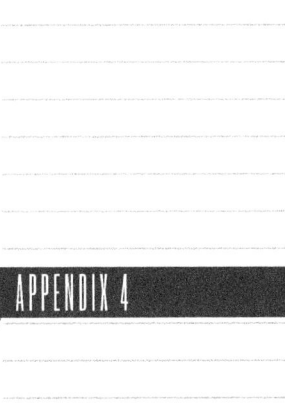

Course Appendix 5:
It Is Not From The Way Of The First Three Generations To..."

The noble Sheikh Muhammad Baazmool, may Allaah preserve him said, [1]

1. It is not from the way of the first three generations of Muslims to simply take knowledge from anyone and everyone until after you have looked at his condition and position in relation to the Sunnah. As it has been rightly said: "This knowledge is your religion, so look carefully as to whom you take knowledge of your religion."

2. It is not from the way of the first three generations of Muslims to neglect or fall short in speaking about the right of Allaah alone to be worshiped, and making this a firm reality in the souls of the people. As this matter, Tawheed, is the very foundation upon which each and every Muslim's Islaam is built upon.

3. It is not from the way of the first three generations of Muslims to engage in acting before having the necessary knowledge. Indeed, they were those who always began with knowledge before actions and deeds. As Allaah, the Most High, has said, ❧ *(So know (O Muhammad) that none has the right to be worshipped but Allaah, and ask forgiveness for your sin, and also for the sin of believing men and believing women* ❧-(Surah Muhammad: 19).

4. It is not from the way of the first three generations of Muslims to leave or turn away from patterning ourselves upon and closely following the Messenger of Allaah, may the praise and salutations of Allaah be upon him.

5. It is not from the way of the first three generations of Muslims to speak against the Companions of the Messenger of Allaah, or even a single one of them.

6. It is not from the way of the first three generations of Muslims to invent and innovate new matters into the religion. From their distinguishing signs is that they followed transmitted knowledge. They did not innovate, finding fully sufficient what had been conveyed to them, so adhere truly to the original state of Islaam and the first believers.

7. It is not from the way of the first three generations of Muslims to give priority to intellectual sciences which are based primarily upon research and investigation; rather their foundations of knowledge were "*Allaah said...*", "*The Messenger said...*", & "*The Companions said...*"

---

[1] The following points were all taken directly from the sheikh's social media pages & website

8. It is not from the way of the first three generations of Muslims to determine or identify the truth by men, such that everything that so-and-so brings must be the truth. Rather one of their distinguishing signs is that they held that a person who understands the truth will then be able to assess and determine those individuals in his time who hold and stand upon the truth , and that through understanding the truth you can become from the people who stand clearly upon it.

9. It is not from the way of the first three generations of Muslims to invent new guidelines and developed principles according to one's opinion. The way of the Salaf was to closely follow the established terminology found in the Qur'aan and Sunnah, such that in their rulings and statements they did not give meanings to verses or hadeeth narrations that were inconsistent and not possibly correct.

10. It is not from the way of the first three generations of Muslims to turn away and abandon adhering to the path of Islaam which the Companions proceeded upon, by conceiving a new understanding outside of what they understood in terms of comprehending the Sharee'ah.

11. It is not from the way of the first three generations of Muslims to derive a ruling or position from every single individual verse or hadeeth narration, until it is shown that is it a verse from the clear unambiguous verses or a hadeeth from those hadeeth narrations containing a definitive meaning which must be adhered to.

12. It is not from the way of the first three generations of Muslims to reject a hadeeth narration which doesn't make sense to our individual minds and intellects, or opposes and contradicts what we understand. Rather their methodology was to follow and affirm every authentic source text. We believe in every aspect of revealed guidance, as its origin is our Lord.

13. It is not from the way of the first three generations of Muslims to enter extensively into speculative discussions and opinion-based debates. Rather they put forth the utmost effort into fundamentally understanding Islaam from the Book of Allaah and the Sunnah, then acting according to these two sources and inviting the people to them.

14. It is not from the way of the first three generations of Muslims to go outside of and beyond what is indicated by the source texts as understood in the fundamentals of the Arabic language alongside the understanding that our righteous predecessors had of those source texts.

15. It is not from the way of the first three generations of Muslims to speak in generalizations and turn away from speaking specifically with detailed explanations.

16. It is not from the way of the first three generations of Muslims to neglect and turn away from actions, deeds, and implementation due to seeking knowledge. It is narrated that they said: *"Knowledge calls out for actions and deeds, such that actions come to stand with it. Otherwise without being accompanied by deeds- knowledge itself eventually leaves and departs."*

17. It is not from the way of the first three generations of Muslims to engage in a great deal of speech and talking. Indeed they used to say, *"The one who speaks frequently makes frequent mistakes and errors."* Some of them were known to remain silent to the degree that people would think that they were unintelligent or feebleminded. Yet this was not the case, their silence was only due to their fear of Allaah regarding their speech.

18. It is not from the way of the first three generations of Muslims to busy and occupy yourself with that which will not benefit you in the next life.

19. It is not from the way of the first three generations of Muslims that every student of knowledge enter into the arena of criticizing and commending individuals. Certainly in every area of Sharee'ah knowledge there are individuals well-known for their proficiency and understanding. So just as we do not generally take knowledge from any and every person, likewise in this area it is not for just anyone to speak in the matters of criticism and commendation of individuals.

20. It is not from the way of the first three generations of Muslims that the student of knowledge become preoccupied with secondary knowledge before focusing upon the study of the Qur'aan and hadeeth narrations. Once he has understood and learned that which is required for him in his religion, then he can seek that desired additional knowledge afterwards.

21. It is not from the way of the first three generations of Muslims to dispute with and oppose the scholars in their guiding statements. Indeed the student should know that he is indeed only a student and in regard to investigating and speaking about some issues, he should leave them to be dealt with by the scholars. It is not for him to enter into the current societal issues and problems among the Muslims nor discuss those significant wide-reaching matters!

22. It is not from the way of the first three generations of Muslims to form parties, secret alliances, and concealed gatherings and efforts separate from others. As it is found in the scholars of the first generations that they said, *"If you see a group of people who gather together in a masjid separating and excluding the general people, then know that they are upon misguidance."*

23. It is not from the way of the first three generations of Muslims to incite and agitate the general Muslims against the ruler and instigate them to oppose him and revolt, or encourage them to engage in demonstrations and the bringing about of a revolution in society. Nor is it from their way to engage in public criticism of the rulers, their government ministers, or those who work for the governments under the rulers.

24. It is not from the way of the first three generations of Muslims to abandon seeking knowledge which is considered obligatory individually, nor that someone be neglectful of seeking knowledge which is generally recommended.

25. It is not from the way of the first three generations of Muslims to start attacking the scholars of the Sunnah and speak negatively about them, dismissing their knowledge and their books, calling for their books to be destroyed and burnt, and saying that the people should stop referring to them simply due to a restricted mistake or error that a known scholar fell into.

26. It is not from the way of the first three generations of Muslims to deal with the mistakes of the people of adherence to the Sunnah in the same way one deals with the mistakes of the people of innovation. As all the sons of Adam make mistakes, so look into the way and methodology of the mistaken individual and deal with that mistake which he has fallen into in a way suitable and in accordance to the general methodology he follows and adheres to.

27. It is not from the way of the first three generations of Muslims to have fanaticism and extremism to a specific derived view or position you hold, considering it above question. As we find those who spoke from the early people of knowledge would say: *"My position is correct with some possibility of it being wrong. And that position which opposes my position is wrong yet has some possibility of it being correct."*

28. It is not from the way of the first three generations of Muslims to declare people as disbelievers in Islaam except upon what is explicitly considered disbelief in the Sharee'ah.

29. It is not from the way of the first three generations of Muslims to make a judgment or declare a specific person as a disbeliever, and outside of the religion, except after having established the proofs against them by fulfilling the conditions and lifting any impediments required to make that declaration of disbelief.

30. It is not from the way of the first three generations of Muslims to make a judgment or declare a specific person as an innovator in the religion except after having established the proofs against them by fulfilling the conditions and lifting any impediments required to make that declaration.

31. It is not from the way of the first three generations of Muslims to fall into extremism regarding the status of the Messenger of the Allaah, may the praise and salutations of Allah be upon him, by placing him in a position or on a level equal with Allaah the Most High.

32. It is not from the way of the first three generations of Muslims to attribute or treat anyone as infallible other than the Messenger of Allaah, may the praise and salutations of Allaah be upon him.

33. It is not from the way of the first three generations of Muslims to make the focus of our call the redistribution of wealth even if done in the name of rectifying economic injustices. Nor is it from their way to make the focus of our call political engagement even if it is done in the name of rectifying wrongs by those governing the Muslims affairs.

34. It is not from the way of the first three generations of Muslims to develop a new practice of giving an oath of allegiance to someone other than that Muslim leader in society who is been entrusted with governing the Muslims and the affairs of their united group.

35. It is not from the way of the first three generations of Muslims to honor or hold in high esteem anyone who proceeds upon innovation in the religion of Islaam.

36. It is not from the way of the first three generations of Muslims to excuse someone due to ignorance unrestrictedly without any limitations or conditions. But we excuse, due to ignorance, the one who fell into error and missed what is right and correct after they put forth sufficient efforts in learning and seeking knowledge and didn't fall short in that. Such that the deficiency from such a person is clearly due to that inadequate knowledge which he received.

37. It is not from the way of the first three generations of Muslims to engage in debating with the people of falsehood. As the Muslim does not expose his sound religion to the danger of desires and doubtful matters.

38. It is not from the way of the first three generations of Muslims to turn away from referring to and returning to the scholars. Rather they were those who called the people to the sittings and lessons of the scholars, and for them to be in their gatherings.

39. It is not from the way of the first three generations of Muslims to act upon only the statement of praise which commends someone when there was also a detailed evidenced criticism against that individual. This is except in those cases when that detailed criticism has been brought to and mentioned to the scholar who originally commended and praised the individual, such that the commending scholar refuted that specific criticism with other specific knowledge and evidences.'

40. It is not from the way of the first three generations of Muslims to act upon a general criticism of an individual whose trustworthiness has been affirmed, except when that general criticism is explained in detail, or was stated by a major or leading scholar which would lead you to be inclined to accept it due to confidence in the leading scholars' understanding and trustworthiness.

41. It is not from the way of the first three generations of Muslims to rely upon the people of innovation from the Muslims nor to unrestrictedly engage and deal with them.

42. It is not from the way of the first three generations of Muslims to turn away, in the matters of Muslim beliefs, from relying upon those authentic hadeeth narrations classified by the scholars of hadeeth as singular, in relation to their routes of transmission.

43. It is not from the way of the first three generations of Muslims to restrict what is considered as definitive knowledge from transmitted texts to only those authentic narrations classified by the scholars of the sciences of hadeeth as having multiple authentic routes of transmission, and reject authentic singular narrations.

44. It is not from the way of the first three generations of Muslims to reject what is transmitted from a reliable individual about someone and to not accept it, rejecting it unless it is heard or read personally by them from the original person.

45. It is not from the way of the first three generations of Muslims to love the people of innovation, nor to have a good opinion of them, nor to be misled by their shouts and cries, nor by their outward declarations. As they affirmed that a person would be with the one whom he loves, as is mentioned in the hadeeth narration.

46. It is not from the way of the first three generations of Muslims to act as if you are superior to the rest of the people. They were those who acted with goodness and gentleness.

47. It is not from the way of the first three generations of Muslims to seek fame and seek to elevate one's status among the people. As certainly love of fame "breaks ones back". So if you slip into this murky condition then it will certainly destroy tremendous amounts of good.

48. It is not from the way of the first three generations of Muslims to rely and focus upon the worldly life while abandoning those actions which benefit us in the Hereafter.

49. It is not from the way of the first three generations of Muslims to always engage in enmity simply because of the occurrence of a dispute that happened between them. Rather they would differentiate in having enmity with others according to the specific situation of the individual involved and the specifics and factors of the issue involved. As differing with the one with a pure intention for the truth upon its path does not ruin good relations in this case.

50. It is not from the way of the first three generations of Muslims to restrict the religion to a single minor issue which if someone agrees with me in that issue then he is considered Salafee and the one who differs with me in that issue then he is not considered Salafee. Rather Salafeeyah is a way and methodology and is not merely a single minor issue.

51. It is not from the way of the first three generations of Muslims to remain silent not offering advice and sincere counsel for the sake of Allaah, His Messenger, His Book, for the leaders of the Muslims and their common people.

52. It is not from the way of the first three generations of Muslims to fall into division, unnecessary differing and mutual hatred among themselves. From the distinguishing signs of the Salaf is that they never fell into hating each other and mutual hostility, rather they were worshipers of Allaah standing together as brothers.

53. It is not from the way of the first three generations of Muslims to involve themselves in trials and troubles, nor to enter and delve into them. Rather they were those who distanced themselves from trials and warned against entering into them.

54. It is not from the way of the first three generations of Muslims to choose blind following of others without following and turning to the evidences. Nor did they have biased attachments and allegiances.

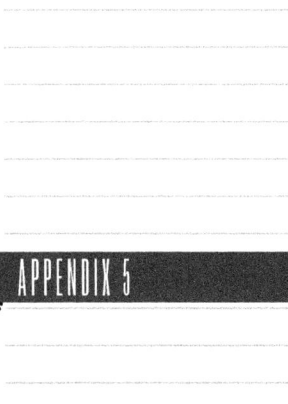

Course Appendix 6:
The Reality Of Secularism: "We Warn Against This Ideological Colonization…"

Sheikh 'Abdul-'Azeez Ibn Baaz, May Allaah Have Mercy Upon Him

Sheikh 'Abdul-'Azeez Ibn Baaz, may Allaah have mercy upon him, said:[1]

"Regarding the socialist Ba'ath Party, the ideology of Communism, as well as the other atheist ideologies which disbelieve in Islaam, such as secularism and others, it is established that all of them oppose Islaam and that those who adhere to these ideologies are in fact more severe in disbelief than the Christians and Jews. Since in relation to the Christians and Jews it is permissible for us to consume the animals they slaughter and eat their food generally and the Muslims are allowed to marry the chaste women from among them. But as for those who are atheists, is neither permissible to eat their food nor to marry their women. Similarly, this is the same case for those who are pagans worshipping aspects of nature, as a class of individuals, their women have not been made permissible to marry nor their food permissible to eat. As such, every individual upon an atheistic ideology and so disbelieving in Islaam is considered more sinful, due to his disbelief, than a Christian or Jew.

These are those from the Ba'ath party and the secularists who reject Islaam and throw it behind their backs desiring something other than the religion of Islaam. This includes those who are known as communists and socialists, meaning every atheistic ideological orientation which does not believe in Allaah, nor believe in the Day of Judgment. Their evil and disbelief is considered more significant and severe than the disbelief from the Jews and Christians.

Similarly, it should be noted that those who worship aspects of nature as pagans, those who worship and venerate graves and the dead within them, and those who worship and venerate trees or stones, they likewise are greater in disbelief than the Christians and Jews. It is for this reason that Allaah has established a distinction in the various distinct rulings of Islaam regarding interaction with them. Certainly, they all stand united upon their general disbelief and are misguided and the final destination for all of them is the Hellfire. Yet they are of different levels in their disbelief and degrees of their misguidance. However it is still the case, that they all stand upon clear disbelief and misguidance, and if they die in this state of misguidance, then their final destination is Hellfire."

[1] Collection of the Rulings of Sheikh Ibn Baaz: volume 6, page 85

Sheikh 'Abdul-'Azeez ar-Raajihee, May Allaah preserve Him

Sheikh 'Abdul-'Azeez ar-Raajihee, may Allaah preserve him, discussing the secularists, explained the following:: [2]

"These individuals, those with an outward profession of Islaam but who are inwardly upon disbelief, when they first appeared they were identified and called hypocrites "*munafiqoon*". Later historically as is found in the time period of Imaam Ahmad and afterwards an individual similar to this was referred to and called by a term which was originally a Farsi language term but later adopted by the Arabs "*Zindeeq*" meaning an astray disbeliever professing Islaam despite having significant innovation at the level of major disbelief.

It has come to pass that in our time, some of those from this type are referred to and called "secularists". The secularists are clearly those who are hypocrites, and they are the "*Zanadeeqah*" or those who profess Islaam but inwardly are disbelievers. The hypocrites in the original time of the Prophet, may Allaah's praise and salutations be upon him, were individuals such as: Abdullah Ibn Ubay who outwardly manifested Islaam yet inwardly within themselves they still disbelieved. And the term "*zindeeq*" is generally applied to mean someone who is a disbelieving atheist.

Today those known as secularists have spread themselves among the Muslims. They attempt to insinuate themselves and place themselves with the Muslims and Islaam, in order to change and so corrupt the Muslims. They intend to alter the societal role of women and so corrupt the Muslim woman by sending her out of her home improperly dressed, habitually exposing her beauty to other women, needlessly driving vehicles and traveling, and unrestrictedly mixing with men outside her family. The result of these things they advocate will be the eventual corruption and degradation of society. Since if the Muslim woman is corrupted then undoubtedly the society itself is corrupted. The secularists have no actual ideological connection or inward adherence to the religion of Islaam, as they are "*zanaadeqah*". Yet they are not able to openly make fully evident what they are truly upon of disbelief and hypocrisy, due to the strength of the Muslims. Because if they unmistakably made apparent their disbelief in the guidance of Islaam they fear that their necks would be struck and their lives lost as the believers and the people of goodness are numerous in Muslim societies. For this reason we find that they equivocate and minimize the reality of their disbelief, while they continually strive to corrupt and insinuate their evil among the Muslims through subtle means and refined methods."

---

[2] From his explanation of the work "The Belief of the First Three Generations and the People of Hadeeth" by as-Saaboonee as found in the fourteenth lecture

Sheikh Saaleh al-Fauzaan, May Allaah preserve Him

Sheikh Saaleh Ibn al-Fauzaan was asked:[3]

Our esteemed sheikh, may Allaah grant you success, is it correct to generalize describing the secularist and the liberals, and even the individual extreme Shee'ah, with the term "hypocrite"?

He replied: "Such people in reality, do not reflect or outwardly show emaan, or faith. What they actually make apparent is their filthy ideologies and what they call for from abandoning Islaam, cursing and speaking against Islaam, as well as cursing the people firmly connected to the religion of Islaam. This is what such people reflect and make apparent. As such, they are not merely from the hypocrites, rather they are worse than them. They are from the "*zanaadeqah*" or astray disbelievers who despite professing Islaam, stand upon significant innovation which is at the level of major disbelief."

He also stated in one of his lectures,[4]

"Knowingly attributing yourself to one of the atheistic ideologies, such as communism, secularism, capitalism, or another disbelieving ideology, is apostasy from the religion of Islaam. If someone from those individuals who connect themselves to, and believe in, these other ideologies also stand forward as being someone who attributes himself to Islaam, then this is major hypocrisy. As the hypocrites are those known to attach themselves to Islaam outwardly, while internally and ideologically they stand with the disbelievers. Just as Allaah mentions regarding them: ❁*And when they meet those who believe, they say: "We believe," but when they are alone with their Shayaateen they say: "Truly, we are with you; verily, we were but mocking*❁-(Surah Al-Baqarah: 14) And Allaah the Most High said: ❁*Those hypocrites who wait and watch about you; if you gain a victory from Allaah, they say: "Were we not with you?" but if the disbelievers gain a success, they say to them: "Did we not gain mastery over you and did we not protect you from the believers?" Allaah will judge between you all on the Day of Resurrection. And never will Allaah grant to the disbelievers a way to triumph over the believers.* ❁-(Surah An-Nisa:141)

Such insincere individuals are deceptive hypocrites, each of them has two distinct faces: One face, which they show and direct towards the believers in Islaam, and another face which they turn to reveal with their associates upon their atheistic beliefs. They have two tongues, one, with superficial statements, which they use when speaking with the Muslims, and a second with which they make clear and expose what they hide of their concealed secret reality. As Allaah says, ❁*And when they meet those who believe, they say: "We believe," but when they are alone with their Shayaateen they say: "Truly, we are with you; verily, we were but mocking.* ❁-(Surah Al-Baqarah:14)

---

[3] From his published work "Aqeedatul-Tawheed, page 82
[4] Transcribed from the lecture "Selections from the Narrated Reports from the Leader of the Sent Messengers- Shawwal 1432

Such individuals upon these ideologies have turned away and rejected the guidance of the Book of Allaah and the Sunnah, while they mock and belittle those who adhere to these fundamental sources of Islaam, holding such believing people in contempt. They are those who refuse to submit and fully comply with the guidance found in the two sources of revelation, the Qur'aan and the Sunnah. Rather they are more satisfied and actually pleased with whatever they possess of contrived worldly knowledge, despite it being something which their increasing themselves in it does not actually benefit them but only increases them in misguidance and arrogant rejection of the truth.

So we see that they look at those who firmly adhere to the revealed sources of guidance as those who should be mocked and ridiculed. Yet in truth- ❬*Allaah mocks at them and gives them increase in their wrong-doings to wander blindly.*❭-(Surah Al-Baqarah: 15). As lastly, it should be known that Allaah has commanded that the Muslims attach themselves clearly to the believers, ❬*O you who believe! Be afraid of Allaah, and be with those who are true (in words and deeds)*❭-(Surah Al-Tawbah: 119)

Sheikh Muhammad 'Alee Ferkous, May Allaah preserve Him

Sheikh Muhammad 'Alee Ferkous stated about secularism, [5] .

"....This is secularism which is currently spread throughout the Muslim world and the Arab lands as a result of colonialism, campaigns from Christian countries, direct evangelical efforts, and the gross heedlessness of those who have been enticed and beguiled from among the people of our own Muslim lands and origins who have elevated its false slogans and calls, those who have executed the conceived plans and goals of the disbelievers. It is supported by those same individuals who have beautified for acceptance by the common people, it's many misconceptions and false claims which stand at the height of misguidance. Some of that which they base their call upon is embodied within the following assertions:

- Their criticism and speaking against the Noble Qur'aan, as well as undermining and causing people to doubt the validity of affirming the belief that Allaah sent prophets with perfect revealed guidance.

- Their assertion that the Sharee'ah is by nature stagnant, and wholly incompatible with modern age and civilization. They state that Europe did not truly start to progress until it wisely turned away from and minimized the influence of religion.

- Their claim that Islaam has failed to embrace evolutionary theories of the development of life, and instead calls to persecute and oppose absolute freedom of philosophical and scientific thought.

- Their claim that the religion of Islaam has already fulfilled its essential aims and original goals, and that nothing really remains of value within it other than a collection of rituals and spiritual practices.

- Their claim that the Arabic language has fallen behind and failed to contribute to modern corpus of knowledge and areas of contemporary advancement, and that the Arabic language is incapable of proceeding and moving forward with those intellectual mechanisms leading to modern progression and development. They assert that regardless of whether or not the Arabic language is the primary or main language in the Arab lands, that it is only marginally used in the majority of western administrative institutions, western universities, and western medical institutions specifically. As such it cannot be considered suitable for our true progress.

[5] Secularism: Its Reality and Danger http://ferkous.com/home/?q=art-mois-13

They call for the French language to take the place of Arabic as the language used for conversation and essential standard for functional communication in the different spheres of life. They also call for the gradual withdrawal and abandonment the Arabic language, according to a calculated and deliberate strategy, due to their knowledge that it is indeed the language of the Qur'aan and that understanding Arabic is the key to understanding the various branches of Sharee'ah knowledge.

- They claim that the Sharee'ah is really only something implemented outwardly or superficially in governance, judicial rulings, and the other areas of societal life anyway. Additionally, as they falsely claim, most Islamic rulings are actually derived from or based on Roman Law in any case.

- They claim that the Sharee'ah is oppressive and harsh in its legislated corporal punishments related to criminal justice, the cutting of limbs, and the practice of stoning. They assert that more appropriate punishments must be adopted. This would be brought about by firstly adopting the religious systems and spiritual orientations from present Western civilizations and emulating them in order that criminal punishments be changed to be more merciful and reflect greater compassion.

These are the general assertions which the people of secularism hold to be true and employ in their efforts to negate the Sharee'ah of Allaah, the Most High. That effort is undertaken through various different methods and means, such as through specific prominent individuals, magazines, newspapers, and other means of promoting their ideas. This is all towards the greater goal of stripping the clear religion of *Hanafeeyah*, the worship of Allaah alone, out of the active life in Muslim societies through their false accusations against it, while also pushing for limitations on implementing of religion and restricting the boundaries, scope, and spheres of interaction in Muslim societies. These people blindly follow the West in what Western societies have adopted and currently practice, towards the objective of removing the bonds and institutions of Islaam, encouraging the discarding of what Islaam advocates and it being actually implemented and established by Muslims, as well as striving to transform Muslim identity. The goal or object intended for the Muslims is the severing of their relationship with Islaam and removing their allegiance towards the religion, as well as their connection and attribution to their Muslim Ummah- by developing and fostering a blind allegiance and love of Western societies and their malicious interests among Muslims.

Since Islaam is both a way of life and a system of governance, it rejects this separation or the establishing of an unpassable barrier in human life between the worlds of our material interests and physical well-being from the world of our spiritual interests and true everlasting existence; with an absolute definitive rejection. Islaam considers knowingly affirming this devised separation as apostasy from Islaam. Likewise Islaam in its purity and soundness, the clarity of its beliefs, and its excellent character cannot accept what has spread of many societal problems and illnesses within Western society which are the results of disbelieving secularism, as well as the spreading of unrestrained sexual licentiousness, unprecedented chaos in people's personalities and characters, personal vices, and filthy disgraceful beliefs and character traits. These matters, along with the dangerous fragmentation of the structure of both the family and society as a whole in western countries are all eventual consequences of the tearing down of the essential belief of Allaah's right to be worshiped alone.

Rather, Islaam commands the Muslim to surrender himself and make every single sphere of his life solely for the sake of Allaah alone. By this, meaning, that his actions and statements, his behavior and conduct, his living and his dying, all become something done for the sake of Allaah the Most Perfect and the Most High, as it is found in the Qur'aan *Say (O Muhammad): "Verily, my Salaat (prayer), my sacrifice, my living, and my dying are for Allaah, the Lord of the 'Alameen (mankind, jinn and all that exists). He has no partner. And of this I have been commanded, and I am the first of the Muslims.*-(Surah Al-An'am: 162-163)

May Allaah's praise and salutation be upon Muhammad and upon his family, and his Companions, and his brothers until the day of reckoning

Sheikh Muhammad Ibn Saaleh al-'Utheimeen, May Allaah Have Mercy Upon Him

Sheikh Muhammad Ibn Saaleh al-'Utheimeen, may Allaah have mercy upon him, was asked, [6]

"What is the ruling on interpreting the meaning of the hadeeth, referring to the hadeeth describing the callers to doors to Hellfire upon the false paths, to mean that those callers are the secularists we find today?"

The sheikh replied: "What I hold to be correct is that what is intended in the narration is general, applying both to the secularist as well as to others upon misguidance, such that the Jahmeeyah, the Mu'tazilah, and others who also fall within this description, are inviters at the doors of Hellfire."

He was also asked[7]: *"Is it permissible for the student of knowledge, who is well grounded in Sharee'ah knowledge, to engage in dialogues with the people who adhere to their personal desires in fundamental beliefs, such as the secularists and others in order to publicly clarify their doubts and misconceptions and refute their false claims and assertions about the religion of Islaam?"*

Sheikh Al-'Utheimeen says: "Are you asking if this is permissible?"

Questioner: Yes.

The Sheikh replied: "I say and hold that it is obligatory, in fact obligatory upon those well-grounded students that they engage in dialogues with these individuals, in conformance with the statement of Allaah the Most High, ❨*Invite (mankind, O Muhammad) to the Way of your Lord (i.e. Islaam) with wisdom (i.e. with the Divine Inspiration and the Qur'aan) and fair preaching, and argue with them in a way that is better.*❩ -(Surah An-Nahl:125) Additionally, if you sufficiently clarify the truth to them, yet these people refuse to recant and repent from their false claims, then it is upon the governmental authority to compel them to abandon those claims, or that the authorities mandate for these secularists discretionary judicial punishments which will deter them from advocating this call to falsehood.

Because it is not in any way acceptable that we leave these misguided people and their Shaytaans free, unrestricted, and unaccountable to say whatever they wish of falsehood within society, while we, all praise is due to Allaah, still possess the ability, the control, and the authority to prevent this. As such, it is required that we restrain these secularists in order that their corruption not spread through the earth. Consider the case of the one whose transgression and harm in society reaches the level of seizing people's wealth. The ruling of the religion in this situation is well

---
[6] Found questions answered during lessons in the sheik's explanation of Saheeh Muslim, Kitab al-Jihaad
[7] Open Door Gatherings No. 235

known, ❧*The recompense of those who wage war against Allaah and His Messenger and do mischief in the land is only that they shall be killed or crucified or their hands and their feet be cut off on the opposite sides, or be exiled from the land. That is their disgrace in this world, and a great torment is theirs in the Hereafter.*❧-(Surah Al-Maa'idah:33). If this is the case of these transgressing people who illegally steal and seize the wealth of people and attack their physical lives, then what of the more severe situation of those who in fact strip away the people's very religion away from them, denying them both success and goodness in this world as well as the next life!?!

For the case of the disbeliever is that he is a loser in relation to both this world as well as the final situation in the hereafter. How is this so? In this world, every day passes never to return, isn't that the case? And what did they, the disbelievers, benefit from it? What did they benefit from that day which permanently passed away? They didn't truly benefit anything of true worth. Even if they reach the highest and most intense of physical pleasures, then that also passes and doesn't really benefit them. That day itself ends and passes, and so does the next, and so forth until a person dies. In this way they are clearly the losers in both.

As in the Hereafter, are they also considered losers or not? Definitely losers! Allaah says, ❧*The losers are those who will lose themselves and their families on the Day of Resurrection. Verily, that will be a manifest loss!*❧-(Surah Az-Zumar:15). So consider that these secularists are people who invite and call people to embrace clear disbelief and atheism which means that what they want from the people to embrace something which actually destroys both their success in this life as well as their success in the next life. So which of these two is the greater form of corruption? These secularists or those criminals who steal and seize people's wealth and violently attack and kill people? Certainly, the secularists are greater and more significant in the harm they lead to since the good of both lives, this world and the next, is lost. Due to this, we clearly warn against this ideological colonization, and this colonization of both the social character and the Islamic way of life which the enemies of the Muslim ummah have planted and spread today through the means such as of satellite channels, the internet, and forms of media that are similar to these.

At present, these enemies are not able to successfully defeat the Muslim Ummah militarily due to our position and circumstances, and all praise is due to Allaah. However they have instead attacked us ideologically, and attacked our Muslim character and the very understanding of the Muslims by spreading doubts and misconceptions among us. As when they find a Muslim state and society weak then they usually seek to dominate it through military means, isn't this the case?

Consider and look at the situation in Chechnya and other Muslim regions. Due to this, it is a requirement upon us, as Muslims, that we think and consider this matter and situation very well, closely, and in great detail. At the very least, we must fortify and strengthen ourselves from the onslaught of the ideological diseases that are directed against us.

Oh Allaah, preserve for us our religion, and make us steadfast upon it until death. Strengthen our national leaders in their opposition to our enemies' efforts. Bless them with a fortification that protects and strengthens them in the face of evil and corruption confronting them.

Our time to speak has ended. And all praise is due to Allaah the Lord of all the Worlds, may Allaah's praise and salutation be upon our Prophet Muhammad and his family, and all his Companions. May Allaah grant us success, and assist us and you in all our affairs."

Course Appendix 7:
The Reality Of Secularism: "We Warn Against This Ideological Colonization…"

Sheikh 'Abdul-'Azeez Ibn Baaz,
May Allaah Have Mercy Upon Him

Sheikh 'Abdul-'Azeez Ibn Baaz, may Allaah have mercy upon him, said:[1]

Regarding the socialist Ba'th Party, the ideology of Communism, as well as the other atheist ideologies which disbelieve in Islaam, such as secularism and others, it is established that all of them oppose Islaam and that those who adhere to these ideologies are in nfact more severe in disbelief than the Christians and Jews. Since in relation to the Christians and Jews it is permissible for us to consume the animals they slaughter and eat their food generally and the Muslims are allowed to marry the chaste women from among them. But as for those who are atheists, is neither permissible to eat their food nor marry their women. Similarly, this is the same case of those who are pagans worshipping aspects of nature, as a class of individuals, their women have not been made permissible to marry nor their food permissible to eat. As such every individual upon an atheistic ideology and so disbelieves in Islaam is considered more sinful, due to his disbelief, that a Christian or Jew.

These are those from the Ba'ath party and the secularists who reject Islaam and throw it behind their backs desiring something other than the religion of Islaam. This includes those who are known as communists, and socialists, meaning every atheistic ideological orientation which does not believe in Allaah, nor believe in the Day of Judgment. Their evil and disbelief is considered more significant and severe than the disbelief from the Jews and Christians.

Similarly, it should be noted that those who worshipping aspects of nature as pagans, those who worship and venerates graves and the dead within them, and those who worship and venerate trees or stones, they likewise are greater in disbelief then the Christians and Jews. It is for this reason that Allaah has established a distinction in the various distinct rulings of Islaam regarding interaction with them. Certainly, they all stand united upon their general disbelief and are misguided and the final destination for all of them is the Hellfire. Yet they are of different levels in their disbelief and degrees of their misguidance. However it is still the case, that they all stand upon clear disbelief and misguidance, and if they die in this state of misguidance, then their final destination is Hellfire,

[]

[1] Collection of the Rulings of Sheikh Ibn Baaz: volume 6, page 85

Sheikh 'Abdul-'Azeez ar-Raajihee, May Allaah preserve Him

Sheikh 'Abdul-'Azeez ar-Raajihee, may Allaah preserve him, discussing the secularists saying: [2]

These individuals, those with an outward profession of Islaam but inwardly upon disbelief, when they first appeared they were identified and called hypocrites "munafiqoon". Later historically as is found in the time period Of Imaam Ahmad and afterwards an individual similar to this was referred to and called by a term which was originally a Farsi language term but later adopted by the Arabs "Zindeeq" meaning an astray disbeliever professing Islaam despite having significant innovation at the level of major disbelief.

It has come to pass that in our time, some of those from this type are referred to and called "secularists". The secularists are clearly those who are hypocrites, and they are the "Zanadeeqah" or those who profess Islaam but inwardly are disbelievers. The hypocrites in the original time of the Prophet, may Allaah's praise and salutations be upon him, were individuals such as: Abdullah Ibn Ubay who outwardly manifested Islaam yet inwardly within themselves they still disbelieved. And the term 'zindeeq' is generally applied to mean someone who is a disbelieving atheist.

Today those known as secularists have spread themselves among the Muslims. They attempt to insinuate themselves and place themselves with the Muslims and Islaam, in order to change and so corrupt the Muslims. They intend to alter the societal role of women and so corrupt Muslim women by sending her out of her home improperly dressed, habitually exposing your beauty to other women, needlessly driving vehicles and traveling, and unrestrictedly mixing with men outside their family. The result of these things they advocate will be the eventual corruption and degradation of society. As if the Muslim woman is corrupted then undoubtedly the society itself is corrupted. The secularists have no actual ideological connection or inward adherence to the religion of Islaam, as they are "zanaadeqah". Yet they are not able to openly make fully evident what they are truly upon of disbelief and hypocrisy, due to the strength of the Muslims. Because if they unmistakably made apparent their disbelief in the guidance of Islaam they fear that their necks would be struck and their lives lost as the believers and the people of goodness are numerous in Muslim societies. For this reason we find that they equivocate and minimize the reality of their disbelief, while they continually strive to corrupt and insinuate their evil among the Muslims through subtle and means and refined methods."

---

[2] From his explanation of the work "The Belief of the First Three Generations and the People of Hadeeth" by as-Saaboonee as found in the fourteenth lecture

Sheikh Saaleh Ibn al-Fauzaan,
May Allaah preserve Him

Sheikh Saaleh Ibn al-Fauzaan was asked:[3]

Our esteemed sheikh, may Allaah grant you success, is it correct to generalize describing the secularist and the liberals, and even the individual extreme Shee'ah, with the term "hypocrite"?

He replied: "Such people in reality, do not reflect or outwardly show emaan, or faith. What they actually make apparent is their filthy ideologies and what they call for from abandoning Islaam, cursing and speaking against Islaam, as well as cursing the people firmly connected to the religion of Islaam. This is what such people reflect and make apparent. As such, they are not merely from the hypocrites, rather they are worse than them. They are from the "zanaadeqah" or astray disbelievers who dispite professing Islaam stand upon significant innovation which is at the level of major disbelief.

He also stated in one of his lectures,[4]

"Knowingly attributing yourself to one of the atheistic ideologies, such as communism, secularism, capitalism, or another disbelieving ideology, is apostasy from the religion of Islaam. If someone from those individuals who connect themselves to and believe in these other ideologies also stand forward as being someone who attributes himself to Islaam, then this is major hypocrisy. As the hypocrites are those known to who attach themselves to Islaam outwardly, while internally and ideologically they stand with the disbelievers. Just as Allaah mentions regarding them: "And when they meet those who believe, they say: "We believe," but when they are alone with their Shayaateen they say: "Truly, we are with you; verily, we were but mocking." (Surah Al-Baqarah: 14) And Allaah the Most High said: "Those hypocrites who wait and watch about you; if you gain a victory from Allaah, they say: "Were we not with you?" but if the disbelievers gain a success, they say to them: "Did we not gain mastery over you and did we not protect you from the believers?" Allaah will judge between you all on the Day of Resurrection. And never will Allaah grant to the disbelievers a way to triumph over the believers. (Surah An-Nisa:141)

Such insincere individuals are deceptive hypocrites, each of them has two distinct faces: One face, which they show and direct towards the believers in Islaam, and another face which they turn to reveal with their associates upon their atheistic beliefs. They have two tongues, one, with superficial statements, which they use when speaking with the Muslims, and a second with which they make clear and expose what they hide of their concealed secret reality. As Allaah says, "And when they meet those who believe, they say: "We believe," but when they are alone with

---

[3] From his published work "Aqeedatul-Tawheed, page 82
[4] Transcribed from the lecture "Selections from the Narrated Reports from the Leader of the Sent Messengers- Shawwal 1432

their Shayaateen they say: "Truly, we are with you; verily, we were but mocking." (Surah Al-Baqarah: 14) Such individuals upon these ideologies have turned away and rejected the guidance of the Book of Allaah and the Sunnah, while they mock and belittle those who adhere to these fundamental sources of Islaam, holding such believing people in contempt. They are those who refuse to submit and fully comply with the guidance found in the two sources of revelation, the Qur'aan and the Sunnah. Rather they are more satisfied and actually pleased with whatever they possess of contrived worldly knowledge, despite it being something which their increasing themselves in it does not actually benefit them but only increases them in misguidance and arrogant rejection of the truth. So we see them look at those who firmly adhere to the revealed sources of guidance as those who should be mocked and ridiculed. Yet in truth- "Allaah mocks at them and gives them increase in their wrong-doings to wander blindly." (Surah Al-Baqarah: 15). As lastly, it should be known that Allaah has commanded that the Muslims attach ourselves clearly to the believers, "O you who believe! Be afraid of Allaah, and be with those who are true (in words and deeds) . (Surah Al-Tawbah: 119) []

Sheikh Muhammad 'Alee Ferkous, May Allaah preserve Him

Sheikh Muhammad 'Alee Ferkous stated about secularism, [5] .

"....This is secularism which is currently spread throughout the Muslim world and the Arab lands as a result of colonialism, campaigns from Christian countries, direct evangelical efforts, and the gross heedlessness of those who have been enticed and beguiled from among the people of our own Muslim lands and origins who have elevated its false slogans and calls, those who have executed the conceived plans and goals of the disbelievers. It is supported by those same individuals who have beautified for acceptance by the common people, it's many misconceptions and false claims which stand at the height of misguidance. Some of that which they base their call upon are embodied within the following assertions:

- Their criticism and speaking against the Noble Qur'aan, as well as undermining and causing people to doubt the validity of affirming the belief that Allaah sent prophets with perfect revealed guidance.

- Their assertion that the Sharee'ah is by nature stagnant, and wholly incompatible with modern age and civilization. They state that Europe did truly start to progress until it wisely turned away and minimized the influence of religion.

- Their claim that Islaam has failed to embrace evolutionary theories of the development of life, instead calls to persecute and oppose absolute freedom of philosophical and scientific thought

- Their claim that the religion of Islaam has already fulfilled its essential aims and

---
[5] Secularism: Its Reality and Danger http://ferkous.com/home/?q=art-mois-13

original goals, and that nothing really remains of value within it other than a collection of rituals and spiritual practices.

- Their claim that the Arabic language has fallen behind and failed to contribute to modern corpus of knowledge and areas of contemporary advancement, and that the Arabic language is incapable of proceeding and moving forward with those intellectual mechanisms leading to modern progression and development. They assert that regardless of whether or not the Arabic language is the primary or main language in the Arab lands, that it is only marginally used in the majority of administrative institutions, universities, and medical institutions in the Western lands specifically. They call for the French language to take the place of Arabic as the language used for conversation and essential standard for functional communication in the different spheres of life. They also call for the gradual withdrawal and abandonment the Arabic language, according to a calculated and deliberate strategy, due to their knowledge that it is indeed the language of the Qur'aan and that understanding Arabic is the key to understanding the various branches of Sharee'ah knowledge.

- They claim that the Sharee'ah is really only something implemented outwardly or superficially in governance, judicial rulings, and the other areas of societal life anyway. Additionally, as they falsely claim, most Islamic rulings are actually derived or based from Roman Law in any case.

- They claim that the Sharee'ah is oppressive and harsh in its legislated corporal punishments related to criminal justice, the cutting of limbs, and the practice of stoning. They assert that more appropriate punishments must be adopted. This would be brought about by firstly adopting the religious systems and spiritual orientations from present western civilizations and emulating them in order that criminal punishments be changed to be more merciful and reflect greater compassion.

These are the general assertions which the people of secularism hold to be true and employ in their efforts to negate the Sharee'ah of Allaah, the Most High. That effort is undertaken through various different methods and means, such as through specific prominent individuals, magazines, newspapers, and other means of promoting their ideas. This is all towards the greater goal of stripping the clear religion of Hanafeeyah, the worship of Allaah alone, out of the active life in Muslim societies through their false accusations against it, while also pushing for limitations on implementing of religion and restricting the boundaries, scope, and spheres of interaction in Muslim societies. These people blindly follow the West in what western societies have adopted and currently practice, towards the objective of removing the bonds and institutions of Islaam, encouraging the discarding of what Islaam advocates and it being actually implemented and established by Muslims, as well is striving to transform Muslim identity. The objected intended for the Muslims is the severing of their relationship to Islaam and removing their allegiance towards the religion, as well as their connection and attribution to their Muslim Ummah- by developing and fostering among Muslims a blind allegiance and love of Western societies and their malicious interests.

APPENDIX 7

Since Islaam is both a way of life and a system of governance. It rejects this separation or the establishing of an unpassable barrier in human life between the worlds of our material interests and physical well-being from the world of our spiritual interests and true everlasting existence, with an absolute definitive rejection. Islaam considers knowingly affirming this devised separation as apostasy from Islaam. Likewise Islaam in its purity and soundness, the clarity of its beliefs, and its excellent character cannot accept what has spread of many societal problems and illnesses within Western society which are the results of disbelieving secularism, as well as the spreading of unrestrained sexual licentiousness, unprecedented chaos in people's personalities and characters, personal vices, filthy disgraceful beliefs and character traits. These matters along with the dangerous fragmentation of the structure of both the family and society as a whole in western countries are all eventual consequences of the tearing down of the essential belief of Allaah's right to be worshiped alone.

Rather Islaam commands the Muslim to surrender himself and make every single sphere of his life solely for the sake of Allaah alone. By this meaning that his actions and statements, his behavior and conduct, his living in his dying, all become something done for the sake of Allaah the Most Perfect and the Most High, as it is found in the Qur'aan "Say (O Muhammad): "Verily, my Salaat (prayer), my sacrifice, my living, and my dying are for Allaah, the Lord of the 'Alameen (mankind, jinn and all that exists). He has no partner. And of this I have been commanded, and I am the first of the Muslims." (Surah Al-An'am: 162-163)

May Allaah's praise and salutation be upon Muhammad and his family, and upon his family, and his Companions, and his brothers until the day of reckoning

Sheikh Muhammad Ibn Saaleh al-'Utheimeen, May Allaah Have Mercy Upon Him

Sheikh Muhammad Ibn Saaleh al-'Utheimeen, may Allaah have mercy upon him, was asked, [6]

"What is the ruling on carrying the meaning of the hadeeth, to mean that those callers are the secularists we find today?

The sheikh replied: "What I hold to be correct is that what is intended in the narration is general, applying both to the secularist as well as to others upon misguidance, such that the Jahmeeyah, the Mu'tazilah, and others who also fall within this description, of inviters at the doors of Hellfire."

He was also asked[7]: "Is it permissible for the student of knowledge who is well grounded in Sharee'ah knowledge to engage in dialogues with the people who adhere to their personal desires in fundamental beliefs, such as the secularists and others in order to publicly clarify their doubts and misconceptions and refute their false claims and assertions about the religion of Islaam.

Sheikh Al-Utheimeen says: "Are you asking if this is permissible?" Questioner: Yes.

The Sheikh replied, "I say and hold that it is obligatory, in fact obligatory upon those well-grounded students that they engage in dialogues with these individuals, in conformance with the statement of Allaah the Most High. "Invite (mankind, O Muhammad) to the Way of your Lord (i.e. Islaam) with wisdom (i.e. with the Divine Inspiration and the Qur'aan) and fair preaching, and argue with them in a way that is better. " (Surah An-Nahl:125) Additionally, if you sufficiently clarify the truth to them, yet these people refuse to recant and repent from their false claims, then it is upon the governmental authority to compel them to abandon those claims. Or that the authorities mandate for these secularists that discretionary judicial punishments which will deter them from advocating to this call to falsehood. Because it is not in any way acceptable that we leave these misguided people and their Shaytaans free, unrestricted, and unaccountable to say whatever they wish of falsehood within society, while we, all praise is due to Allaah, still possess the ability, the control, and the authority to prevent this. As such, it required that we restrain these secularists in order that their corruption not spread through the earth. Consider case of the one whose transgression and harm in society reaches the level of seizing people's wealth, the ruling of the religion in this situation is well known, "The recompense of those who wage war against Allaah and His Messenger and do mischief in the land is only that they shall be killed or crucified or their hands and their feet be cut off on the opposite sides, or be exiled from the land. That is their disgrace in this world, and a great torment is theirs in the Hereafter. (Surah Al-Ma'idah:33). If this is the case of these transgressing

[6] Found questions answered during lessons in the sheik's explanation of Saheeh Muslim, Kitab al-Jihaad
[7] Open Door Gatherings No. 235

people who illegally steal and seize the wealth of people and attack their physical lives, then what is the more severe situation of those who in fact strip away the people's very religion away from them, denying them both success and goodness in this world as well as the next life!?! Since the case of the disbeliever is that he is a loser in relation to both this world as well as the final situation in the hereafter. How is this so? In this world, every day passes never to return, isn't that the case? And what did they, the disbelievers, benefit from it? What did they benefit from that day which permanently passed away? They didn't truly benefit anything of true worth. Even if they reach the highest and most intense of physical pleasures, then that also passes and doesn't really benefit them. That day itself ends and passes, and so does the next, and so forth until a person dies. In this way they are clearly the losers in both.

As in the Hereafter are they also considered losers or not. Rather losers! Allaah says: "The losers are those who will lose themselves and their families on the Day of Resurrection. Verily, that will be a manifest loss!" (Surah Az-Zumar:15). So consider that these secularists are people who invite and call people to embrace clear disbelief and atheism which means that what they want from the people to embrace something which actually destroys both their success in this life as well as their success in the next life. So which of these two is the greater form of corruption? These secularists or those criminals who steal and seize people's wealth and violently attack and kill people? Certainly, the secularists are greater and more significant in the harm they lead to as the good of both lives, this world and the next, is lost. Due to this we clearly warn against this ideological colonization, and this colonization of both the social character and the Islamic way of life which the enemies of the Muslim Ummah have planted and spread today through the means such as of satellite channels, the internet, and forms of media that are similar to these.

At present, these enemies are not able to successfully defeat the Muslim Ummah militarily due to our position and circumstances, and all praise is due to Allaah. However they have instead attacked us ideologically, and attacked our Muslim character and the very understanding of the Muslims by spreading doubts and misconceptions among us. As when they find a Muslim state and society weak then they usually seek to dominate it through military means, isn't this the case?

Consider and look at the situation in Chechnya and other Muslim regions. Due to this, it is a requirement upon us, as Muslims, that we think and consider this matter and situation very well, closely, and in great detail. At the very least, we must fortify and strengthen ourselves from the onslaught of the ideological diseases that are directed against us.

Oh Allaah, preserve for us our religion, and make us steadfast upon it until death. Strengthen our national leaders in their opposition to our enemies' efforts. Bless them with a fortification that protects and strengthens them in the face of evil and corruption confronting them.

Our time to speak has ended. And all praise is due to Allaah the Lord of all the Worlds, may Allaah's praise and salutation be upon our Prophet Muhammad and his family, and all his Companions. May Allaah grant us success, and assist us and you in all our affairs.

APPENDIX 7

APPENDIX 7

APPENDIX 7

APPENDIX 7

APPENDIX 7

APPENDIX 7

APPENDIX 7

THE NAKHLAH EDUCATIONAL SERIES:

MISSION

The Purpose of the 'Nakhlah Educational Series' is to contribute to the present knowledge based efforts which enable Muslim individuals, families, and communities to understand and learn Islaam and then to develop withi,n and truly live, Islaam. Our commitment and goal is to contribute beneficial publications and works that:

Firstly, reflect the priority, message and methodology of all the prophets and messengers sent to humanity, meaning that single revealed message which embodies the very purpose of life, and of human creation. As Allaah the Most High has said,

❲ *We sent a Messenger to every nation ordering them that they should worship Allaah alone, obey Him and make their worship purely for Him, and that they should avoid everything worshipped besides Allaah. So from them there were those whom Allaah guided to His religion, and there were those who were unbelievers for whom misguidance was ordained. So travel through the land and see the destruction that befell those who denied the Messengers and disbelieved.* ❳ –(Surah an-Nahl: 36)

Sheikh Rabee'a ibn Haadee al-Madkhalee in his work entitled, '*The Methodology of the Prophets in Calling to Allaah, That is the Way of Wisdom and Intelligence.*' explains the essential, enduring message of all the prophets:

"So what was the message which these noble, chosen men, may Allaah's praises and salutations of peace be upon them all, brought to their people? Indeed their mission encompassed every matter of good and distanced and restrained every matter of evil. They brought forth to mankind everything needed for their well-being and happiness in this world and the Hereafter. There is nothing good except that they guided the people towards it, and nothing evil except that they warned the people against it. ...

This was the message found with all of the Messengers; that they should guide to every good and warn against every evil. However where did they start, what did they begin with, and what did they concentrate upon? There are a number of essentials, basic principles, and fundamentals which all their calls were founded upon, and which were the starting point for calling the people to Allaah. These fundamental points and principles are: 1. The worship of Allaah alone without any associates 2. The sending of prophets to guide creation 3. The belief in the resurrection and the life of the Hereafter

These three principles are the area of commonality and unity within their calls, and stand as the fundamental principles which they were established upon. These principles are given the greatest importance in the Qur'aan and are fully explained in it. They are also its most important purpose upon which it centers and which it continually mentions. It further quotes intellectual and observable proofs for them in all its chapters as well as within most of its accounts of previous nations and given examples.

This is known to those who have full understanding, and are able to consider carefully and comprehend well. All the Books revealed by Allaah have given great importance to these points and all of the various revealed laws of guidance are agreed upon them. And the most important and sublime of these three principles, and the most fundamental of them all, is directing one's worship only towards Allaah alone, the Blessed and the Most High."

Today one finds that there are indeed many paths, groups, and organizations apparently presenting themselves as representing Islaam, which struggle to put forth an outwardly pleasing appearance to the general Muslims; but when their methods are placed upon the precise scale of conforming to priorities and methodology of the message of the prophets sent by Allaah, they can only be recognized as deficient paths- not simply in practice but in principle- leading not to success, but rather only to inevitable failure.

As Sheikh Saaleh al-Fauzaan, may Allaah preserve him, states in his introduction to the same above-mentioned work on the methodology of all the prophets,

"So whichever call is not built upon these foundations, and whatever methodology is not from the methodology of the Messengers - then it will be frustrated and fail, and it will be effort and toil without any benefit. The clearest proofs of this are those present-day groups and organizations which set out a methodology and program for themselves and their efforts of calling the people to Islaam which is different from the methodology of the Messengers. These groups have neglected the importance of the people having the correct belief and creed - except for a very few of them - and instead call for the correction of side-issues."

There can be no true success in any form for us as individuals, families, or larger communities without making the encompassing worship of Allaah alone, with no partners or associates, the very and only foundation of our lives. It is necessary that each individual knowingly choose to base his life upon that same foundation taught by all the prophets and messengers sent by the Lord of all the worlds, rather than simply delving into the assorted secondary concerns and issues invited to by the various numerous parties, innovated movements, and groups. Indeed Sheikh al-Albaanee, may Allaah have mercy upon him, stated:

"…We unreservedly combat against this way of having various different parties and groups. As this false way- of group or organizational allegiances - conforms to the statement of Allaah the Most High, ❁ **But they have broken their religion among them into sects, each group rejoicing in what is with it as its beliefs. And every party is pleased with whatever they stand with.**❁*–(Surah al-Mu'minoon: 53) And in truth they are no separate groups and parties in Islaam itself. There is only one true party, as is stated in a verse in the Qur'an,* ❁ **Verily, it is the party of Allaah that will be the successful.** ❁*–(Surah al-Mujadilaah: 58). The party of Allaah are those people who stand with the Messenger of Allaah, may Allaah's praise and salutations be upon him, meaning that an individual proceeds upon the methodology of the Companions of the Messenger. Due to this we call for having sound knowledge of the Book and the Sunnah."*

(Knowledge Based Issues & Sharee'ah Rulings: The Rulings of The Guiding Scholar Sheikh Muhammad Naasiruddeen al-Albaanee Made in the City of Medina & In the Emirates – [Emiratee Fatwa no 114. P.30])

Two Essential Foundations

Secondly, building upon the above foundation, our commitment is to contributing publications and works which reflect the inherited message and methodology of the acknowledged scholars of the many various branches of Sharee'ah knowledge, who stood upon the straight path of preserved guidance in every century and time since the time of our Messenger, may Allaah's praise and salutations be upon him. These people of knowledge, who are the inheritors of the Final Messenger, have always adhered closely to the two revealed sources of guidance: the Book of Allaah and the Sunnah of the Messenger of Allaah- may Allaah's praise and salutations be upon him, upon the united consensus, standing with the body of guided Muslims in every century - preserving and transmitting the true religion generation after generation. Indeed the Messenger of Allaah, may Allaah's praise and salutations be upon him, informed us that, *{ A group of people amongst my Ummah will remain obedient to Allaah's orders. They will not be harmed by those who leave them nor by those who oppose them, until Allaah's command for the Last Day comes upon them while they remain on the right path. }* (Authentically narrated in Saheeh al-Bukhaaree).

We live in an age in which the question frequently asked is, "*How do we make Islaam a reality?*" and perhaps the related and more fundamental question is, "*What is Islaam?*", such that innumerable different voices quickly stand to offer countless different conflicting answers through books, lectures, and every available form of modern media. Yet the only true course of properly understanding this question and its answer- for ourselves and our families -is to return to the criterion given to us by our beloved Messenger, may Allaah's praise and salutations be upon him. Indeed the Messenger of Allaah, may Allaah's praise and salutations be upon him, indicated in an authentic narration, clarifying the matter beyond doubt, that the only "Islaam" which enables one to be truly successful and saved in this world and the next is as he said, *{... that which I am upon and my Companions are upon today.}* (authentically narrated in Jaam'ea at-Tirmidhee) referring to that Islaam which stands upon unchanging revealed knowledge. While every other changed and altered form of Islaam, whether through some form of extremism or negligence, or through the addition or removal of something, regardless of whether that came from a good intention or an evil one- is not the religion that Allaah informed us about when He revealed, ❁ *This day, those who disbelieved have given up all hope of your religion; so fear them not, but fear Me. This day, I have perfected your religion for you, completed My Favor upon you, and have chosen for you Islaam as your religion.* ❁ –(Surah al-Maa'idah: 3)

The guiding scholar Sheikh al-Albaanee, may have mercy upon him, said,

"*...And specifically mentioning those among the callers who have taken upon themselves the guiding of the young Muslim generation upon Islaam, working to educate them with its education, and to socialize them with its culture. Yet they themselves have generally not attempted to unify their understanding of those matters about Islaam regarding which the people of Islaam today differ about so severely.*

And the situation is certainly not as is falsely supposed by some individuals from among them who are heedless or negligent - that the differences that exist among them are only in secondary matters without entering into or affecting the fundamental issues or principles of the religion; and the examples to prove that this is not true are numerous and recognized by those who have studied the books of the many differing groups and sects, or by the one who has knowledge of the various differing concepts and beliefs held by the Muslims today."(Mukhtasir al-'Uloo Lil'Alee al-Ghafaar, page 55)

Similarly he, may Allaah have mercy upon him, explained:

"Indeed, Islaam is the only solution, and this statement is something which the various different Islamic groups, organizations, and movements could never disagree about. And this is something which is from the blessings of Allaah upon the Muslims. However there are significant differences between the different Islamic groups, organizations, and movements that are present today regarding that domain which working within will bring about our rectification. What is that area of work to endeavor within, striving to restore a way of life truly reflecting Islaam, renewing that system of living which comes from Islaam, and in order to establish the Islamic government? The groups and movements significantly differ upon this issue or point. Yet we hold that it is required to begin with the matters of tasfeeyah –clarification, and tarbeeyah -education and cultivation, with both of them being undertaken together.

As if we were to start with the issue of governing and politics, then it has been seen that those who occupy themselves with this focus firstly possess beliefs which are clearly corrupted and ruined, and secondly that their personal behavior, from the aspect of conforming to Islaam, is very far from conforming to the actual guidance of the Sharee'ah. While those who first concern themselves with working just to unite the people and gather the masses together under a broad banner of the general term "Islaam," then it is seen that within the minds of those speakers who raise such calls -in reality there is in fact no actual clear understanding of what Islaam is. Moreover, the understanding they have of Islaam has no significant impact in starting to change and reform their own lives. Due to this reason, you find that many such individuals from here and there, who hold this perspective, are unable to truly realize or reflect Islaam, even in areas of their own personal lives in matters which it is in fact easily possible for them to implement. Such an individual holds that no one - regardless of whether it is because of his arrogance or pridefulness - can enter into directing him in an area of his personal life!

Yet at the same time these same individuals are raising their voices saying, "Judgment is only for Allaah!" and "It is required that judgment of affairs be according to what Allaah revealed." And this is indeed a true statement, but the one who does not possess something certainly cannot give or offer it to others. The majority of Muslims today have not established the judgment of Allaah fully upon themselves, yet they still seek from others to establish the judgment of Allaah within their governments...

...And I understand that this issue or subject is not immune from there being those who oppose our methodology of tasfeeyah and tarbeeyah. As there is the one who would say, "But establishing this tasfeeyah and tarbeeyah is a matter which requires many long years!" So, I respond by saying, this is not an important consideration in this matter, what is important is that we carry out what we have been commanded to do within our religion and by our Mighty Lord. What is important is that we begin by properly understanding our religion first and foremost. After this is accomplished then it will not be important whether the road itself is long or short.

And indeed, I direct this statement of mine towards those men who are callers to the religion among the Muslims, and towards the scholars and those who direct our affairs. I call for them to stand upon complete knowledge of true Islaam, and to fight against every form of negligence and heedlessness regarding the religion, and against differing and disputes, as Allaah has said, **...and do not dispute with one another for fear that you lose courage and your strength departs** *–(Surah al-Anfaal: 46). (Quoted from the work, 'The Life of Sheikh al-Albaanee, His Influence in Present Day Fields of Sharee'ah Knowledge, & the Praise of the Scholars for Him.' volume 1 page 380-385)*

The guiding scholar Sheikh Zayd al-Madkhalee, may Allaah protect him, stated in his writing, 'The Well Established Principles of the Way of the First Generations of Muslims: It's Enduring & Excellent Distinct Characteristics' that,

"*From among these principles and characteristics is that the methodology of tasfeeyah -or clarification, and tarbeeyah -or education and cultivation- is clearly affirmed and established as a true way coming from the first three generations of Islaam, and is something well known to the people of true merit from among them, as is concluded by considering all the related evidence. What is intended by tasfeeyah, when referring to it generally, is clarifying that which is the truth from that which is falsehood, what is goodness from that which is harmful and corrupt, and when referring to its specific meanings, it is distinguishing the noble Sunnah of the Prophet and the people of the Sunnah from those innovated matters brought into the religion and the people who are supporters of such innovations.*

As for what is intended by tarbeeyah, it is calling all of the creation to take on the manners and embrace the excellent character invited to by that guidance revealed to them by their Lord through His worshiper and Messenger Muhammad, may Allaah's praise and salutations be upon him; so that they might have good character, manners, and behavior. As without this they cannot have a good life, nor can they put right their present condition or their final destination. And we seek refuge in Allaah from the evil of not being able to achieve that rectification."

Thus the methodology of the people of standing upon the Prophet's Sunnah, and proceeding upon the 'way of the believers' in every century is reflected in a focus and concern with these two essential matters: tasfeeyah- or clarification of what is original, revealed message from the Lord of all the worlds, and tarbeeyah- or education and raising of ourselves, our families, and our communities, and our lands upon what has been distinguished to be that true message and path.

METHODOLOGY:

The Roles of the Scholars & General Muslims In Raising the New Generation

The priority and focus of the 'Nakhlah Educational Series' is reflected within in the following statements of Sheikh al-Albaanee, may Allaah have mercy upon him:

"As for the other obligation, then I intend by this the education of the young generation upon Islaam purified from all of those impurities we have mentioned, giving them a correct Islamic education from their very earliest years, without any influence of a foreign, disbelieving education."
(Silsilat al-Hadeeth ad-Da'eefah, Introduction page 2.)

"...And since the Messenger of Allaah, may Allaah's praise and salutations be upon him, has indicated that the only cure to remove this state of humiliation that we find ourselves entrenched within, is truly returning back to the religion, then it is clearly obligatory upon us - through the people of knowledge- to correctly and properly understand the religion in a way that conforms to the sources of the Book of Allaah and the Sunnah, and that we educate and raise a new virtuous, righteous generation upon this."
(Clarification and Cultivation and the Need of the Muslims for Them)

It is essential, in discussing our perspective upon this obligation of raising the new generation of Muslims, that we highlight and bring attention to a required pillar of these efforts as indicated by Sheikh al-Albaanee, may Allaah have mercy upon him, and others- in the golden words, *"through the people of knowledge."* Something we commonly experience today is that many people have various incorrect understandings of the role that the scholars should have in the life of a Muslim, failing to understand the way in which they fulfill their position as the inheritors of the Messenger of Allaah, may Allaah's praise and salutations be upon him, and stand as those who preserve and enable us to practice the guidance of Islaam. Indeed, the noble Imaam Sheikh as-Sa'dee, may Allaah have mercy upon him, in his work, *"A Definitive and Clear Explanation of the Work 'A Triumph for the Saved Sect'"* pages 237-240, has explained this crucial issue with an extraordinary explanation full of remarkable benefits:

"Section: Explaining the Conditions for These Two Source Texts to Suffice You -or the Finding of Sufficiency in these Two Sources of Revelation.
Overall the conditions needed to achieve this and bring it about return to two matters:
Firstly, the presence of the requirements necessary for achieving this; meaning a complete devotion to the Book and the Sunnah, and the putting forth of efforts both in seeking to understand their intended meanings, as well as in striving to be guided by them. What is required secondly is the pushing away of everything which prevents achieving this finding of sufficiency in them.

This is through having a firm determination to distance yourself from everything which contradicts these two source texts in what comes from the historical schools of jurisprudence, assorted various statements, differing principles and their resulting conclusions which the majority of people proceed upon. These matters which contradict the two sources of revelation include many affairs which, when the worshiper of Allaah repels them from himself and stands against them, the realm of his knowledge, understanding, and deeds then expands greatly. Through a devotion to them and a complete dedication towards these two sources of revelation, proceeding upon every path which assists one's understanding them, and receiving enlightenment from the light of the scholars and being guided by the guidance that they possess- you will achieve that complete sufficiency in them. And surely, in the positions they take towards the leading people of knowledge and the scholars, the people are three types of individuals:

The first of them is the one who goes to extremes in his attachment to the scholars. He makes their statements something which are infallible as if their words held the same position as those of the statements of the Messenger of Allaah, may Allaah's praise and salutations be upon him, as well as giving those scholars' statements precedence and predominance over the Book of Allaah and the Sunnah. This is despite the fact that every leading scholar who has been accepted by this Ummah was one who promoted and encouraged the following of the Book and the Sunnah, commanding the people not to follow their own statements nor their school of thought in anything which stood in opposition to the Book of Allaah and the Sunnah.

The second type is the one who generally rejects and invalidates the statements of the scholars and forbids the referring to the statements of the leading scholars of guidance and those people of knowledge who stand as brilliant lamps in the darkness. This type of person neither relies upon the light of discernment with the scholars, nor utilizes their stores of knowledge. Or even if perhaps they do so, they do not direct thanks towards them for this. And this manner and way prohibits them from tremendous good. Furthermore, that which motivates such individuals to proceed in this way is their falsely supposing that the obligation to follow the Messenger of Allaah, may Allaah's praise and salutations be upon him, and the giving of precedence to his statements over the statements of anyone else, requires that they do so without any reliance upon the statements of the Companions, or those who followed them in goodness, or those leading scholars of guidance within the Ummah. This is a glaring and extraordinary mistake.

Indeed the Companions and the people of knowledge are the means and the agency between the Messenger of Allaah, may Allaah's praise and salutations be upon him, and his Ummah- in the transmission and spreading his Sunnah in regard to both its wording and texts, as well as its meanings and understanding. Therefore the one who follows them in what they convey in this is guided through their understandings, receives knowledge from the light they possess, benefits from the conclusions they have derived from these sources -of beneficial meanings and explanations, as well as in relation to subtle matters which scarcely occur to the minds of some of the other people of knowledge, or barely comes to be discerned by their minds. Consequently, from the blessing of Allaah upon this Ummah is that He has given them these guiding scholars who cultivate and educate them upon two clear types of excellent cultivation.

The first category is education from the direction of one's knowledge and understanding. They educate the Ummah upon the more essential and fundamental matters before the more complex affairs. They convey the meanings of the Book and the Sunnah to the minds and intellects of the people through efforts of teaching which rectifies, and through composing various beneficial books of knowledge which a worshiper doesn't even have the ability to adequately describe what is encompassed within them of aspects of knowledge and benefits. These works reflect the presence of a clear white hand in deriving guidance from the Book of Allaah and the Sunnah, and through the arrangement, detailed clarification, division and explanation, through the gathering together of explanations, comparisons, conditions, pillars, and explanations about that which prevents the fulfillment of matters, as well as distinguishing between differing meanings and categorizing various knowledge based benefits.

The second category is education from the direction of one's conduct and actions. They cultivate the peoples characters encouraging them towards every praiseworthy aspect of good character, through explaining its ruling and high status, and what benefits comes to be realized from it, clarifying the reasons and paths which enable one to attain it, as well as those affairs which prevent, delay, or hinder someone becoming one distinguished and characterized by it. Because they, in reality, are those who bring nourishment to the hearts and the souls; they are the doctors who treat the diseases of the heart and its defects. As such, they educate the people through their statements, and actions, as well as their general guided way. Therefore the scholars have a tremendous right over this Ummah. A portion of love and esteem, respect and honor, and thanks, are due to them because their merits and their various good efforts stand above every other right after establishing the right of Allaah, and the right of His Messenger, may Allaah's praise and salutations be upon him.

Because of this, the third group of individuals in respect to the scholars are those who have been guided to understand their true role and position, and establish their rights, thanking them for their virtues and merits, benefiting by taking from the knowledge they have, while acknowledging their rank and status. They understand that the scholars are not infallible and that their statements must stand in conformance to the statements of the Messenger of Allaah, may Allaah's praise and salutations be upon him, and that each one from among them has that which is from guidance, knowledge, and correctness in his statements taken and benefited from, while turning away from whatever in mistaken within it.

Yet such a scholar is not to be belittled for his mistake, as he stands as one who strove to reach the truth; therefore his mistake will be forgiven, and he should be thanked for his efforts. One clarifies what was stated by of any one of these leaders from among men, when it is recognized that it has some weakness or conflict to an evidence of the Sharee'ah, by explaining its weakness and the level of that weakness, without speaking evilly of the intention of those people of knowledge and religion, nor defaming them due to that error. Rather we say, as it is obligatory to say, "And those who came after them say: ❧ **Our Lord! forgive us and our brethren who have preceded us in faith, and put not in our hearts any hatred against those who have believed. Our Lord! You are indeed full of kindness, Most Merciful.** ❧ *-(Surah al-Hashr: 10).*

Accordingly, individuals of this third type are those who fulfill two different matters. They join together on one hand between giving precedence to the Book and the Sunnah over everything else, and, on the other hand, between comprehending the level and position of the scholars and the leading people of knowledge and guidance, and establishing this even if it is only done in regard to some of their rights upon us. So we ask Allaah to bless us to be from this type, and to make us from among the people of this third type, and to make us from those who love Him and love those who love Him, and those who love every action which brings us closer to everything He loves."

Upon this clarity regarding the proper understanding of our balanced position towards our guided Muslim scholars, consider the following words about the realm of work of the general people of faith, which explains our area of efforts and struggle as Muslim parents, found in the following statement by Sheikh Saaleh Fauzaan al-Fauzaan, may Allaah preserve him.

"Question: Some people mistakenly believe that calling to Allaah is a matter not to be undertaken by anyone else other than the scholars without exception, and that it is not something required for other than the scholars, according to that which they have knowledge of, to undertake any efforts of calling the people to Allaah. So what is your esteemed guidance regarding this?"

The Sheikh responded by saying:

"This is not a misconception, but is in fact a reality. The call to Allaah cannot be established except through those who are scholars, and I state this. Yet, certainly there are clear issues which every person understands. As such, every individual should enjoin the good and forbid wrongdoing according to the level of his understanding, such that he instructs and orders the members of his household to perform the ritual daily prayers and other matters that are clear and well known.

*Undertaking this is something mandatory and required even upon the common people, such that they must command their children to perform their prayers in the masjid. The Messenger of Allaah, may Allaah praise and salutations be upon him, said, { **Command you children to pray at seven, and beat them due to its negligence at ten.**} (Authentic narration found in Sunan Abu Dawood). And the Messenger of Allaah, may Allaah praise and salutations be upon him, said, { **Each one of you is a guardian or a shepherd, and each of you is responsible for those under his guardianship....**} (Authentic narration found in Saheeh al-Bukhaaree). So this is called guardianship, and this is also called enjoining the good and forbidding wrongdoing. The Messenger of Allaah, may Allaah praise and salutations be upon him, said, { **The one from among you who sees a wrong should change it with his hand, and if he is unable to do so, then with his tongue, and if he is not able to do this, then with his heart.** } (Authentic narration found in Saheeh Muslim).*

So in relation to the common person, that which it is required from him to endeavor upon is that he commands the members of his household-as well as others -with the proper performance of the ritual prayers, the obligatory charity, with generally striving to obey Allaah, to stay away from sins and transgressions, that he purify and cleanse his home from disobedience, and that he educate and cultivate his children upon the obedience of Allaah's commands. This is what is required from him, even if he is a general person, as these types of matters are from that which is understood by every single person. This is something which is clear and apparent.

But as for the matters of putting forth rulings and judgments regarding matters in the religion, or entering into clarifying issues of what is permissible and what is forbidden, or explaining what is considered associating others in the worship due to Allaah and what is properly worshiping Him alone without any partner- then indeed these are matters which cannot be established except by the scholars"
(Beneficial Responses to Questions About Modern Methodologies, Question 15, page 22)

Similarly the guiding scholar Sheikh 'Abdul-'Azeez Ibn Baaz, may Allaah have mercy upon him, also emphasized this same overall responsibility:

"...It is also upon a Muslim that he struggles diligently in that which will place his worldly affairs in a good state, just as he must also strive in the correcting of his religious affairs and the affairs of his own family. The people of his household have a significant right over him that he strive diligently in rectifying their affair and guiding them towards goodness, due to the statement of Allaah, the Most Exalted, ❴ **Oh you who believe! Save yourselves and your families Hellfire whose fuel is men and stones** ❵ *-(Surah at-Tahreem: 6)*

So it is upon you to strive to correct the affairs of the members of your family. This includes your wife, your children- both male and female- and such as your own brothers. This concerns all of the people in your family, meaning you should strive to teach them the religion, guiding and directing them, and warning them from those matters Allaah has prohibited for us. Because you are the one who is responsible for them as shown in the statement of the Prophet, may Allaah's praise and salutations be upon him, ❴ **Every one of you is a guardian, and responsible for what is in his custody. The ruler is a guardian of his subjects and responsible for them; a husband is a guardian of his family and is responsible for it; a lady is a guardian of her husband's house and is responsible for it, and a servant is a guardian of his master's property and is responsible for it....**❵ *Then the Messenger of Allaah, may Allaah's praise and salutations be upon him, continued to say,* ❴**...so all of you are guardians and are responsible for those under your authority.**❵ *(Authentically narrated in Saheeh al-Bukhaaree & Muslim)*

It is upon us to strive diligently in correcting the affairs of the members of our families, from the aspect of purifying their sincerity of intention for Allaah's sake alone in all of their deeds, and ensuring that they truthfully believe in and follow the Messenger of Allaah, may Allaah's praise and salutations be upon him, their fulfilling the prayer and the other obligations which Allaah the Most Exalted has commanded for us, as well as from the direction of distancing them from everything which Allaah has prohibited.

It is upon every single man and woman to give advice to their families about the fulfillment of what is obligatory upon them. Certainly, it is upon the woman as well as upon the man to perform this. In this way our homes become corrected and rectified in regard to the most important and essential matters. Allaah said to His Prophet, may Allaah's praise and salutations be upon him, ❴ **And enjoin the ritual prayers on your family...** ❵ *(Surah Taha: 132) Similarly, Allaah the Most Exalted said to His prophet Ismaa'aeel,* ❴ **And mention in the Book, Ismaa'aeel. Verily, he was true to what he promised, and he was a Messenger, and a Prophet. And he used to enjoin on his family and his people the ritual prayers and the obligatory charity, and his Lord was pleased with him.** ❵ *-(Surah Maryam: 54-55)*

As such, it is only proper that we model ourselves after the prophets and the best of people, and be concerned with the state of the members of our households. Do not be neglectful of them, oh

worshipper of Allaah! Regardless of whether it is concerning your wife, your mother, father, grandfather, grandmother, your brothers, or your children; it is upon you to strive diligently in correcting their state and condition..."
(Collection of Various Rulings and Statements- Sheikh 'Abdul-'Azeez Ibn 'Abdullah Ibn Baaz, Vol. 6, page 47)

CONTENT & STRUCTURE:

We hope to contribute works which enable every striving Muslim who acknowledges the proper position of the scholars, to fulfill the recognized duty and obligation which lays upon each one of us to bring the light of Islaam into our own lives as individuals, as well as into our homes and among our families. Towards this goal we are committed to developing educational publications and comprehensive educational curricula -through cooperation with and based upon the works of the scholars of Islaam and the students of knowledge. Works which, with the assistance of Allaah, the Most High, we can utilize to educate and instruct ourselves, our families and our communities upon Islaam in both principle and practice. The publications and works of the Nakhlah Educational Series are divided into the following categories:

Basic / Elementary: Ages 4-11
Secondary: Ages 11-14
High School: Ages 14- Young Adult
General: Young Adult –Adult
Supplementary: All Ages

Publications and works within these stated levels will, with the permission of Allaah, encompass different beneficial areas and subjects, and will be offered in every permissible form of media and medium. Certainly, the guiding scholar Sheikh Saaleh ibn Fauzaan al-Fauzaan, may Allaah preserve him, has stated,

"Beneficial knowledge is itself divided into two categories. Firstly is that knowledge which is tremendous in its benefit, as it benefits in this world and continues to benefit in the Hereafter. This is religious Sharee'ah knowledge. And second, that which is limited and restricted to matters related to the life of this world, such as learning the processes of manufacturing various goods. This is a category of knowledge related specifically to worldly affairs.
...As for the learning of worldly knowledge, such as knowledge of manufacturing, then it is legislated upon us collectively to learn whatever the Muslims have a need for. Yet, if they do not have a need for this knowledge, then learning it is a neutral matter upon the condition that it does not compete with or displace any areas of Sharee'ah knowledge..."
("Explanations of the Mistakes of Some Writers'", Pages 10-12)

So we strive always to remind ourselves and our brothers of this crucial point also indicated by Sheikh Sadeeq Ibn Hasan al-Qanoojee, may Allaah have mercy upon him, in: 'Abjad al-'Uloom', (page 89)

"...What is intended by knowledge in the mentioned hadeeth is knowledge of the religion and the distinctive Sharee'ah, knowledge of the Noble Book and the pure Sunnah, of which there is no third along with them. But what is not meant in this narration are those invented areas of knowledge,

whether they emerged in previous ages or today's world, which the people in these present times have devoted themselves to. They have specifically dedicated themselves to them in a manner which prevents them from looking towards those areas of knowledge related to faith, and in a way which has preoccupied them from occupying themselves from what is actually wanted or desired by Allaah, the Most High, and His Messenger, who is the leader of men and Jinn. Due to this, the knowledge in the Qur'aan has become something abandoned and the sciences of hadeeth have become obscure, while these new areas of knowledge related to manufacturing and production continually emerge from the nations of disbelief and apostasy, and they are called, "sciences", "arts", and "ideal development". This sad state increases every day, indeed from Allaah we came and to Him shall we return....

...Additionally, although the various areas of beneficial knowledge all share some level of value, they all have differing importance and ranks. Among them is that which is to be considered according to its subject, such as medicine, and its subject is the human body. Or such as the sciences of 'tafseer' and its subject is the explanation of the words of Allaah, the Most Exalted and Most High, and the value of these two areas is not in any way unrecognized.

And from among the various areas, there are those areas which are considered according to their objective, such as knowledge of upright character, and its goal is understanding the beneficial merits that an individual can come to possess. And from among them there are those areas which are considered according to the people's need for them, such as 'fiqh' which the need for it is urgent and essential. And from among them there are those areas which are considered according to their apparent strength, such as knowledge of physical sports and exercise, as it is something openly demonstrated.

And from the areas of knowledge are those areas which rise in their position of importance through their combining all these different matters within them, or the majority of them, such as revealed religious knowledge, as its subject is indeed esteemed, its objective one of true merit, and its need is undeniably felt. Likewise one area of knowledge may be considered of superior rank than another in consideration of the results that it brings forth, or the strength of its outward manifestation, or due to the essentialness of its objective. Similarly, the result that an area produces is certainly of higher estimation and significance in appraisal than the outward or apparent significance of some other areas of knowledge.

For that reason, the highest ranking and most valuable area of knowledge is that of knowledge of Allaah the Most Perfect and the Most High, of His angels, and messengers, and all the particulars of these beliefs, as its result is that of eternal and continuing happiness."

We ask Allaah, the most High to bless us with success in contributing to the many efforts of our Muslim brothers and sisters committed to raising themselves as individuals, and the next generation of our children, upon that Islaam which Allaah has perfected and chosen for us, and which He has enabled the guided Muslims to proceed upon in each and every century. We ask him to forgive us, and forgive the Muslim men and the Muslim women, and to guide all the believers to everything He loves and is pleased with. The success is from Allaah, the Most High the Most Exalted, alone and all praise is due to Him.

Abu Sukhailah Khalil Ibn-Abelahyi
Taalib al-Ilm Educational Resources

GENERAL ANNOUNCEMENT:
Taalib al-Ilm Educational Publications is looking for

Distributors:

We are working to make Taalib al-Ilm Education Resources publications available through distributors worldwide. Our present discounts for wholesalers are:

> **50%** discount for any order of **USD $1000** or over retail cost
>
> **60%** discount for any order of **USD $2000** or over retail cost

For further information, please contact the sales department by e-mail: *service@taalib.com*.

Publication Contributors:

Additionally, in an effort to further expand our publication library, we are seeking contributing authors, translators, and compilers with beneficial works of any area of Sharee'ah knowledge for submission of their works for potential publication by us. For details and all submission guidelines please email us at: *service@taalib.com*

> **Referral bonus:** *Individuals who refer a new distributor or publication contributor to us can receive a **$25 PayPal payment** upon:*
>
> 1) *a confirmed contract with a publication contributor or*
> 2) *receipt of a newly referred distributor's initial order at the 50% discount level.*
>
> *Contact us for further information and conditions.*

BOOK PUBLICATION PREVIEW:

30 Days of Guidance [Book 1]:
Learning Fundamental Principles of Islaam

A Short Journey Within the Work al-Ibaanah al-Sughrah With
Sheikh 'Abdul-Azeez Ibn 'Abdullah ar-Raajhee
(may Allaah preserve him)

*The Importance Of Asking To Be Guided In What You Say & Do * The Clear Guidance Of The Final Messenger Is For All Humanity * There Is A Single Straight Path Surrounded By Other False Paths * Every Ummah Divided But Those Upon The Truth Remain * Allaah Is With Those Who Remained Upon Revealed Guidance * Allaah Has Ordered Us To Stand United Upon The Truth & Not Divide * Every Name That Opposes The Guidance Of The Sunnah Is Rejected * The Strangeness Of Islaam Is Something Expected * That One Individual Whose Religion You Should Stand Upon * The Sunnah Is Revealed Knowledge From Allaah * Hold Firmly To The Sunnah As The Rope Of Allaah * Success Is To The Degree You Adhere To The Sunnah * The Incredible Reward For Firmly Holding To The Sunnah * Follow The Prophet's Sunnah & That Of His Guided Successors * Do Not Speak Against The Best Of Generations * Know That Knowledge Is Received And Can Be Lost * The Reality of the People of Misguidance & Their Deceptions * The Believers Are Distinct Upon Revealed Guidance * Advice of The Companions 'Uthman, 'Alee & Ibn 'Abbaas * Those Astray Turned Away From The Guidance Brought To Them * The People Of Misguidance Want You To Turn From Revealed Guidance * Those Who Debate Frequently Change Their Religion * The Blessing of Learning the Sunnah When Young * The Importance Of Both Loving & Hating For Allaah's Sake * A Person Stands Upon The Religion Of His Close Companion * Innovation That Is Disbelief Destroys All Ones' Good Deeds * Innovations In Islaam May Mislead You To Leave Islaam * The One Who Changes Islaam Is Cursed By Allaah & Creation * Repentance from Innovation Must Be Clear & Apparent * What Religion Will You Die Upon?*

Compiled and Translated by:
Abu Sukhailah Khalil Ibn-Abelahyi

[Available: **Now** ¦ price: **(SS) $27.50 (DS) $25
(W) $12** ¦ **(Kindle) $9.99**]

BOOK PUBLICATION PREVIEW:

30 Days of Guidance [Book 2]:
Cultivating The Character & Behavior of Islaam

A Short Journey Within The Work Al-Adab Al-Mufrad With

Sheikh Zayd Ibn Muhammad Ibn Haadee al-Madhkhaalee
(may Allaah have mercy on him)

*Do you understand the nature of Islaam? * What do you have that is equal to this world? * Are you wealthy? * Are you prepared for your reckoning? * Are you always working for good while you can? * Do you remember the benefit in your difficulties? * Which of these two pairs has a greater influence in your life? * Whom do you really love and why? * Who are your close friends? * Do you protect yourself from the harm of others? * Are you a miser or someone who is incapable? * Do you know the best of supplications? * Do you ask Allaah's protection from your own evil? * Do you seek refuge from bad conditions and worship at night? * Do you know which trials contain some betterment for you? * Do you supplicate for your family as both a parent and as a child? * How well do you treat your mother and father? * How do you fulfill your responsibilities towards your household? * Do you know who are the best and worst of Muslim women? * Is your life balanced as was the lives of the Companions? * Do you understand how to give the best of charity? * How do you spend your money? * How many ways of giving charity and doing good do you do * How are you towards your neighbors? * How do you deal with your own faults and those of others? * How do you treat younger Muslims? * How do you interact with other Muslims? * Do you work to change your bad habits? * Do you know the benefits of maintaining family ties? * Do you know what things bring you closer to Jannah?*

Compiled and Translated by:
Abu Sukhailah Khalil Ibn-Abelahyi

[Available: **Now** ¦ price: **(SS) $27.50 (DS) $25 (W) $12** ¦ **(Kindle) $9.99**]

BOOK PUBLICATION PREVIEW:

30 Days of Guidance [Book 4]:
Foundations For The New Muslim & Newly Striving Muslim

A Short Journey Selected Questions & Answers With
Sheikh 'Abdul-'Azeez Ibn 'Abdullah Ibn Baaz
(may Allaah have mercy on him)

*What are the conditions of correct Islaam? * What does it mean that Islaam will be strange?* * Is faith only what is in our hearts? * Who is truly considered a Muslim? * When is it necessary for me to ask a scholar? * Is there both free will and Allaah's decree? * What does it mean to worship others as well as Allaah? * Which innovations in Islaam are good? * How can we know who are from the saved sect? * Who is part of that group of victorious Muslims? * Why are there divisions among the Muslims? * What should my position be towards the schools of fiqh? * What does it mean that the world is cursed? * Which Sufee path is based upon the Sunnah? * Can I study from books without a scholar? * Should we praise the righteous scholars? * What is the guidance of Islaam about our health? * What should I do after falling into sin again and again? * Do I have to make up for my previous negligence? * What is considered impermissible imitation of non-Muslims? * How should I interact with the non-Muslims I know? * As a Muslim man, can I have friends who are women? * What is the ruling about alcohol and about modern drugs? * Are there kinds of music that are permissible in Islaam? * What kinds of media and shows can I watch as a Muslim? * Should we recite the Qur'aan even without understanding? * Is it from the Sharee'ah to make dhikr while working? * What are the rights of both Muslim wives and Muslim husbands? * What is the correct understanding of trusting in Allaah? * As a new Muslim do I need to change my name?*

Compiled and Translated by:
Abu Sukhailah Khalil Ibn-Abelahyi

[Available: **Now** ¦ price: **(SS) $27.50 (DS) $25 (W) $12** ¦ **(Kindle) $9.99**]

BOOK PUBLICATION PREVIEW:

30 Days of Guidance [Book 3]:
Signposts Towards Rectification & Repentance

A Short Journey Through Selected Questions & Answers With
Sheikh 'Muhammad Ibn Saaleh al-'Utheimeen
(may Allaah have mercy upon him)

*How do I work to save myself from Hellfire? * What should I do, as my society has wrongdoing and many sins? * How can I understand what taqwa is, and how can I have it? * How should I call myself to account as a Muslim? What should be in my heart when I intend to do good? * How can I safeguard my intention for Allaah in everything I do? * How can I bring myself peace, and establish love for Allaah's sake? * When I feel that my emaan has gone down what should I do? As a Muslim, how can I make my heart steadfast? * How can I treat the hardness that I sense in my heart? * How should I study and memorize Qur'aan more? How do I keep my mind from being always distracted? * How can I deal with the things that affected my practice of Islaam? * Should I read the fictional writings of disbelievers? * How do I know if I'm spending my time beneficially? How can I stop thinking about the days before I was guided? How can I stop smoking for Allaah's sake? * How to guard my eyesight from what's harmful around me? * How can I change the fact that I'm always thinking about someone? How should I handle still feeling bad for my past mistakes? How can I fight against the whispers that make me doubt things? How do I know if my evil thoughts take me outside Islaam? * How do I know if my bad thoughts mean I am a hypocrite? * How can I wipe away the many wrong things that I did in the past? * Can I use the money I earned when I was sinful and heedless? How can I correct the previous wrongs that I did to other people? * How can I strengthen my practice of Allaah's religion? How do I know which worldly things I should leave for Allaah's sake? * How can I be a sincere worshiper and traveler in this life? * How can I understand the humiliation upon us as Muslims?*

Compiled and Translated by:
Abu Sukhailah Khalil Ibn-Abelahyi

[Available: **Now** ¦ price: **(SS) $27.50 (DS) $25 (W) $12** ¦ **(Kindle) $9.99**]

BOOK PUBLICATION PREVIEW:

Statements of the Guiding Scholars of Our Age

Regarding Books & their Advice to the Beginner Seeker of Knowledge

with Selections from the Following Scholars:

Sheikh 'Abdul-'Azeez ibn 'Abdullah ibn Baaz - Sheikh Muhammad ibn Saaleh al-'Utheimein - Sheikh Muhammad Naasiruddeen al-Albaanee - Sheikh Muqbil ibn Haadee al-Waada'ee - Sheikh 'Abdur-Rahman ibn Naaser as-Sa'adee - Sheikh Muhammad 'Amaan al-Jaamee - Sheikh Muhammad al-Ameen as-Shanqeetee - Sheikh Ahmad ibn Yahya an-Najmee
(May Allaah have mercy upon them)

Sheikh Saaleh al-Fauzaan ibn 'Abdullah al-Fauzaan - Sheikh Saaleh ibn 'Abdul-'Azeez Aal-Sheikh - Sheikh Muhammad ibn 'Abdul-Wahhab al-Wasaabee - Permanent Committee to Scholastic Research & Issuing Of Islamic Rulings
(May Allaah preserve them.)

Book Sections:

1. Guidance and Direction for Every Male and Female Muslim
2. Golden Advice that Benefits the Beginner Regarding Acquiring Knowledge
3. Beneficial Guidance for Female Students of Sharee'ah Knowledge
4 Guidance from the Scholars Regarding Important Books to Acquire for Seeking Knowledge
5. The Warning of the Scholars from the Books of those who have Deviated & the Means and Ways of Going Astray
6. Clear Statements from the Scholars' Advice Regarding Memorizing Knowledge
7. Issues Related to the Verifiers of Books in our Age

Compiled and Translated by:
Abu Sukhailah Khalil Ibn-Abelahyi

[Available: **Now** ¦ price: **(HB) $32.50 (SB) $25** ¦ **(Kindle) $9.99**]

BOOK PUBLICATION PREVIEW:

An Educational Course Based Upon:

Beneficial Answers to Questions On Innovated Methodologies

By the Guiding Scholar
Sheikh Saaleh Ibn Fauzaan al-Fauzaan
(may Allaah preserve him)

This course focuses upon the importance of clarity in the way you understand and practice Islaam, in the midst of today's confusing claims to Islaam.
What is the right way, or methodology, to practice Islaam? Examine evidences and proofs from the source texts of the Qur'aan and Sunnah, along with the statements of many scholars explaining them, which connect you directly to that Islaam which the Messenger of Allaah ﷺ taught his Companions, may Allaah be pleased with them all.

Course Features:
Twenty concise illustrated lessons to facilitate learning & review, with several important textual & course appendices.

Compiled and Translated by:
Abu Sukhailah Khalil Ibn-Abelahyi

[Available: **Now** ¦ price: **(SS) $30 (DS) $27.50 (W) $12** ¦ **(Kindle) $9.99**]

BOOK PUBLICATION PREVIEW:

A Lighthouse of Knowledge
From A Guardian of the Sunnah [Books 1 & 2]

Sheikh 'Rabee'a Ibn Haadee 'Umair al-Madkhalee
(may Allaah preserve him)

Book 1: Unity, Advice, Brotherhood & the Call to Allaah {Section 1 - 5]
Book 2: The Connection with the People of Knowledge, Affairs of Brotherhood & Other Benefits [Section 1 - 8]

Appendices from the statements of some of the well known major scholars of this age

Appendix 1: Clarification From Sheikh Muqbil Ibn Haadee Al-Waadi'ee, May Allaah Have Mercy Upon Him, Regarding The Positions of Two Groups of People In Regard to Warning and Refutations

Appendix 2: Clarification From Sheikh Muhammad Naasiruddeen Al-Albaanee, May Allaah Have Mercy Upon Him, Regarding The Role And Place Of Harshness

Appendix 3: Clarification From Sheikh Saaleh al-Fauzaan Regarding The Final Position Of Sheikh Abdul-'Azeez Ibn Baaz, May Allaah Have Mercy Upon Him, Towards The Group Jama'at At-Tableegh

Appendix 4: Clarification From Sheikh Ahmad An-Najmee, May Allaah Have Mercy Upon Him, That Advising The Muslims Through Refutations Is From The Way Of The First Generations Of Muslims

Appendix 5: Clarification From Sheikh Saaleh al-Fauzaan Regarding The Falsehood of Those Who State That We Should Not Declare the One Who Opposes the Truth as Mistaken Or Wrong

Appendix 6: Clarification From Sheikh Muhammad Ibn Saaleh al-'Utheimeen, May Allaah Have Mercy Upon Him, Regarding Various Concepts and Principles That Conflict With the Way of the Salaf

Appendix 7: Clarification From Sheikh Muqbil Ibn Haadee Al-Waadi'ee, May Allaah Have Mercy Upon Him, Regarding The Matters Obligatory Upon The Muslims in Order to Achieve Unity

Appendix 8: Clarification From Sheikh 'Abdul-'Azeez Ibn 'Abdullah Ibn Baaz, May Allaah Have Mercy Upon Him, Regarding the Responsibility of the Student of Knowledge to Himself and His Society

Compiled and Translated by: Abu Sukhailah Khalil Ibn-Abelahyi

[Available: **Now** ¦ price: **(SB) $25 (HB) $30**
¦ **(Kindle) $9.99**]

BOOK PUBLICATION PREVIEW:

The Cure, The Explanation, The Clear Affair, The Brilliantly Distinct Signpost:

Book 1: Sources of Islaam & The Way of the Companions

Based Upon
'Usul as-Sunnah' of Imaam Ahmad
(may Allaah have mercy upon him)

This initial course book, which is part of a full series, can be vital learning tool, by Allah's persmission, for discussing and learning many of the most important sources of Islaam, how to implement them, and how to avoid common mistakes and misunderstandings.

This full course series is based upon various commentaries of the original text, from the following scholars of our age, may Allaah have mercy upon then or preserve them:

- Sheikh Zayd Ibn Muhammad al-Madkhalee
- Sheikh Saleeh Ibn Sa'd As-Suhaaymee
- Sheikh 'Abdul-'Azeez Ibn 'Abdullah ar-Raajhee
- Sheikh Rabee'a Ibn Haadee al-Madkhalee
- Sheikh Sa'd Ibn Naasir as-Shathree
- Sheikh 'Ubayd Ibn 'Abdullah al-Jaabiree
- Sheikh 'Abdullah al-Bukharee
- Sheikh Hamd al-'Uthmaan
- and other scholars

Each course book lesson has: lesson text, scholastic commentary, evidence summary, lesson benefits, standard & review exercises, as well as the Arabic text & translation of 'Usul as-Sunnah' in Arabic divided for easier memorization.

Compiled and Translated by:
Abu Sukhailah Khalil Ibn-Abelahyi

[Available: **TBA**¦ price: **(SS) $30 (DS) $27.5 (W) $12** ¦ **(Kindle) $9.99**]

CERTIFICATE OF COMPLETION

AWARDED TO:

FOR COMPLETION OF THE COURSE:

30 Days of Guidance:
Learning Fundamental Principles of Islaam

A Short Journey Within the Work Al-Ibaanah as-Sughrah
With Sheikh 'Abdul-'Azeez Ibn 'Abdullah Ar-Raajhee

DATE: _____, 143____

FOUNDATIONS SERIES COURSE (13)
TAALIB.COM

This page is intentionally blank as it is the back side of the certificate of completion..

www.ingramcontent.com/pod-product-compliance
Lightning Source LLC
Chambersburg PA
CBHW060505240426
43661CB00007B/927